David D. Kupp has a Ph.D. in Theology from
the University of Durham and manages World
Vision Canada's programs in East Africa. He has
written, edited and produced numerous print, film
and curriculum resources for Canadian audiences.
He also works as an adult educator and development
facilitator. He travels in Asia, Africa and North
America to research, gather resources and engage
with partner communities.

That Matthew uniquely highlights Jesus as 'Emmanuel' is common knowledge among Gospel commentators. Almost wholly overlooked, however, are the deeper implications of this 'presence' motif for the enterprise of Matthean christology, as well as its centripetal force on readers of the First Gospel.

With an eye to the rhetorical, historical and theological dimensions of the text, David D. Kupp takes a multi-disciplinary approach to the problem. Matthew's presence motif proves much broader and deeper than the three verses commonly cited (1.23; 18.30; 28.20), so they are only the starting-point for the weaving of the Emmanuel Messiah into the story-telling, redaction and christology of the Gospel.

Matthew's Emmanuel employs the lenses of both narrative and historical criticism to produce the first serious monograph in English on the subject of divine presence in Matthew. After giving primacy to a whole-story reading of Matthew's presence motif, David Kupp follows the Emmanuel Messiah to his roots in the familiar social and literary context of Sinai, Jerusalem and the Jewish scriptures. Matthew's development of those sources evolved Jesus' saving presence into a defining christological role in the First Gospel. Matthew is a story that compels, a text with a history and a christological treatise of the Emmanuel Messiah.

SOCIETY FOR NEW TESTAMENT STUDIES

MONOGRAPH SERIES

General editor: Margaret E. Thrall

90

MATTHEW'S EMMANUEL

Matthew's Emmanuel

Divine presence and God's people in
the First Gospel

DAVID D. KUPP

Program Officer, East Africa
World Vision Canada

CAMBRIDGE
UNIVERSITY PRESS

Published by the Press Syndicate of the University of Cambridge
The Pitt Building, Trumpington Street, Cambridge CB2 1RP
40 West 20th Street, New York, NY 10011–4211, USA
10 Stamford Road, Oakleigh, Melbourne 3166, Australia

First published 1996

Printed in Great Britain at the University Press, Cambridge

A catalogue record for this book is available from the British Library

Library of Congress cataloguing in publication data
Kupp, David D.
Matthew's Emmanuel : divine presence and God's people in the
First Gospel / David D. Kupp.
 p. cm. – (Monograph series / Society for New Testament Studies : 90)
Includes bibliographical references and index.
ISBN 0 521 57007 7
1. Bible. N.T. Matthew – Criticism, interpretation, etc.
2. Presence of God – Biblical teaching.
3. People of God – Biblical teaching. I. Title.
II. Series: Monograph series (Society for New Testament Studies) : 90.
BS2575.6P687K87   1996
226.2'06–dc20   96–373   CIP

ISBN 0 521 57007 7 hardback

for Ellen, and

in memory of Claire Rose-Ferguson

CONTENTS

Preface   *page* xiii
List of abbreviations   xvi

1. Introduction   1

    1.1. The question   1
    1.2. The interpreter   4
    1.3. Text and method   5
    1.4. The present state of research   17
    1.5. This study ...   25

2. Matthew's narrative art   28

    2.1. Method and premises   28
    2.2. Narrator and 'point of view'   33
    2.3. Psychological point of view: omniscient   36
    2.4. Spatial point of view: a centripetal Jesus,
           an omnipresent narrator   39
    2.5. Temporal point of view: synchronic and
           retrospective   41
    2.6. Phraseological point of view   44
    2.7. Ideological point of view   46

3. Reading Matthew's story of divine presence   49

    3.1. Matthew 1–2. Narrative introduction: Jesus'
           origins and mission   52
    3.2. Matthew 3.1–4.11. The preparation for Jesus'
           mission   63
    3.3. Matthew 4.12–18.35. The Galilean presence
           of Jesus   66

3.4.   Matthew 19.1–27.50. The Jerusalem presence
of Jesus   88
3.5.   Matthew 27.51–28.20. Narrative close: the
presence of the risen Jesus   100

4.   Paradigms of presence in the Old Testament   109

4.1.   Literature and current discussion   109
4.2.   Divine presence and the patriarchs   113
4.3.   The three encounters: divine presence and
Sinai   116
4.4.   The Davidic/Jerusalem traditions of presence 130
4.5.   Presence without the Temple   134

**5.   'I am with you': the Old Testament tradition
of the saying   138**

5.1.   The Hebrew text (MT)   139
5.2.   The LXX text   141
5.3.   The character of presence in the saying   142
5.4.   The setting   145
5.5.   The historical continuum of God's people   149
5.6.   Implications   150
5.7.   The formula in post-biblical Judaism   151
5.8.   The formula and Matthew   155

6.   Matthew 1: the birth of the 'God-with-us' Messiah   157

6.1.   Tradition and redaction   157
6.2.   Isaiah 7.14   163
6.3.   Matthew's use of Isaiah 7.14   166
6.4.   Redaction and christology   169

**7.   Matthew 18.1–20: the presence of Jesus and his
ἐκκλησία   176**

7.1.   The story thus far ...   176
7.2.   Matthew 18. The community discourse   178
7.3.   Matthew 18.20   180
7.4.   The nature of the 'gathering'   185
7.5.   Parallels of presence: Shekinah and Jesus   192
7.6.   Modes of presence: Jesus and 'the little ones' 196

8.   Matthew 28.16–20: the presence of the risen Jesus 201

   8.1.   The text: language, style and composition 202
   8.2.   The narrative framework: Matthew 28.16–18a 203
   8.3.   Jesus' declaration: Matthew 28.18b 209
   8.4.   Jesus' mandate: Matthew 28.19–20a 212
   8.5.   Jesus' promise: Matthew 28.20b 216

9.   Jesus' presence and Matthew's christology 220

   9.1.   The Temple, worship and Jesus' presence 224
   9.2.   Wisdom and the presence of Jesus 228
   9.3.   Spirit and presence 229
   9.4.   The poor, the little ones and Jesus' presence 230

10. Conclusion 234

   Bibliography 245
   Index of passages 271
   Index of authors 288

PREFACE

When you stand on the edge of the Klondike River in Canada's Yukon, it appears to act as a river should, heading downhill on its eventual trek to the Bering Sea. When you dip your canoe into the water, however, what seemed a steady and regular flow often becomes dancing and swirling, tossing and capsizing.

Today's tumultuous world of biblical studies is much like that river. I remember my initial entry into it. My peers and I blithely embarked on our first NT Introductory course, presuming a serene, methodical trip in pursuit of biblical truth. Competing currents, underwater obstacles and unexpected baptisms by postmodern fire proved more the order of the day once we entered the stream.

I would not trade in those experiences for anything. The past two decades have been a happy collision with the world of ideas, theology and Christian community. Few other generations of students have had the opportunity to confront such an interpretive plethora, from the historical, theological and literary to the more recent rhetorical, liberationist and feminist schools. The evolution is making methodological pluralists of us all, and that is only for the good of interpretation, I believe.

In the midst of such rapid change, another book may seem like an anachronism. The binding of a volume is even posed by some as antithetical to our global electronic information culture: books trap ideas and half-baked visions in static snapshots. But any trepidation we have at surrendering to print ideas that represent only part of our story is mostly false. Apart from the cultural reality that the biblical critical guild continues to live and die by printed hard copy, books are an increasingly necessary antidote to the hundreds of fleeting images we otherwise meet in a day. Books call us back to important things: considered reflection, deeper analysis, core meanings.

In the category of apologies, I offer mine to those readers whose deeper engagement with today's range of interpretive tools makes mine appear like so much fumbling. You may be impatient at my apparent conjugation of historical and reader-oriented criticism. But I am prepared to argue both in favour of a critical pluralism and on behalf of those of us still learning to thread the river currents in our canoes (I like the confessions of Robert Culley, 'Introduction', and Janice Capel Anderson's new foreword to *Over Again*). If I am beginning to understand the reading process, both redaction critic and post-structuralist will gain something from their very different readings here.

This study, like many others, reflects a long and complex journey. It began as a personal investigation of spirituality and community, became an academic investigation, and now comes to print. My debts to many are immense. Footnotes are one way of expressing appreciation for the insights of many which helped propel this study along. But others must be singled out here.

The current text is a revision of my doctoral thesis for the University of Durham in 1992. Particular thanks go to the University of Durham's Theology Department, especially to Jimmy Dunn, prodigious and inexhaustible *Doktorvater*. To him, the faculty and postgraduates at Durham goes much credit for shaping and honing this study, in seminars, papers and countless *ad hoc* sessions. Among the Durham faculty, Walter Moberly and Stephen Barton were often my Moses and Baptist – always sage and surprising. Bruce Longenecker, Margaret Masson, Dennis Stamps and Paul Trebilco would be fine scholars and friends to take on any journey. I must say too that our years in Durham's St John's College, ensconced atop the Prince Bishop's ancient city walls, living and working within that vibrant College community, remain a sturdy and indelible cornerstone of our personal lives and this study.

I want to offer long-overdue public thanks to Roger Mohrlang and Dale Bruner, fine mentors and friends for many years. A better pair of teachers cannot be found, not to mention the prowess each has with the First Gospel. I can only hope to emulate someday the keen skills of these biblical midwives at Whitworth College. My gratitude also to Colin Brown and Donald Hagner. Their dedication to the world of interpretation and hermeneutics went a long way toward refining my own methods.

As examiners, readers and Press editor, the comments of Stephen Barton, Graham Stanton, R. T. France and Margaret Thrall have bettered the final product and prevented numerous mistakes. With more time to continue the dialogue they surely would have prevented many mistakes that remain.

Many colleagues at World Vision Canada have encouraged me to complete this task amidst our heavy daily challenges. These colleagues and our international partners are the stuff of compassion and substance, struggling to match some of the world's inequities with justice and holistic development. They leave little room for interpretation empty of thoughtful, genuine praxis. I have learned much from them.

This study is dedicated to Ellen, with whom I have journeyed through so much life and death, joy and pain in only a few years. Her fearless energy always leaves me humbly thankful for our partnership. And to Emily and the twins, Eric and Daniel: their earthy salt has kept my feet on the ground throughout. About the strength and support from our parents and siblings too little has always been said. But they know. I must mention my grandfather, Emil Bonikowsky, whose life and legends as a pastor in Poland, Siberia, Ukraine and the Saskatchewan prairies sparked in more than one of his fifty grandchildren the desire to serve people, the planet and our Creator.

Finally, together with Chuck and Loretta, Ellen and I want to remember Claire Rose-Ferguson, and all she was becoming.

David D. Kupp
Guelph, Ontario
Easter, 1995

ABBREVIATIONS

AB	Anchor Bible
AnBib	Analecta Biblica
ANE	Ancient Near East
ANET	*Ancient Near Eastern Texts*, ed. Pritchard
ASTI	*Annual of the Swedish Theological Institute*
ATANT	Abhandlungen zur Theologie des Alten und Neuen Testament
ATR	*Anglican Theological Review*
AusBR	*Australian Biblical Review*
BAGD	Bauer, Arndt, Gingrich, Danker: *Lexicon*
BASOR	*Bulletin of the American Schools of Oriental Research*
BDB	Brown–Driver–Briggs, *Lexicon*
BET	Beiträge zur evangelischen Theologie
BETL	Bibliotheca ephemeridum theologicarum lovaniensium
BETS	*Bulletin of the Evangelical Theological Society*
Bib	*Biblica*
BJRL	*Bulletin of the John Rylands Library*
BKAT	Biblischer Kommentar: Altes Testament
BLS	Bible and Literature Series, Almond Press
BN	*Biblische Notizen*
BNTC	Black's New Testament Commentaries
BR	*Biblical Research*
BTB	*Biblical Theology Bulletin*
BU	Biblische Untersuchungen
BVC	*Bible et vie chrétienne*
BWANT	Beiträge zur Wissenschaft vom Alten und Neuen Testament
BZ	*Biblische Zeitschrift*
CBNT	Coniectanea biblica, New Testament
CBQ	*Catholic Biblical Quarterly*
CNT	Commentaire du Nouveau Testament

CTM	*Concordia Theological Monthly*
DBSup	*Dictionnaire de la Bible, Supplément*
EBib	Etudes Bibliques
EKKNT	Evangelisch–Katholischer Kommentar zum Neuen Testament
ET	English translation
ETL	*Ephemerides theologicae lovanienses*
EvQ	*Evangelical Quarterly*
ExpT	*Expository Times*
FB	Forschung zur Bibel
FFNT	Foundations and Facets: New Testament
FRLANT	Forschungen zur Religion und Literatur des Alten und Neuen Testaments
HBT	*Horizons in Biblical Theology*
HKNT	Handkommentar zum Neuen Testament
HTKNT	Herders theologischer Kommentar zum Neuen Testament
HTR	*Harvard Theological Review*
ICC	International Critical Commentary
IDB	*The Interpreter's Dictionary of the Bible*, ed. G. A. Buttrick, et al.
IDBSup	*The Interpreter's Dictionary of the Bible: Supplementary Volume*, ed. K. Crim, et al.
Int	*Interpretation*
ITQ	*Irish Theological Quarterly*
JAAR	*Journal of the American Academy of Religion*
JBL	*Journal of Biblical Literature*
JBR	*Journal of Bible and Religion*
JR	*Journal of Religion*
JSJ	*Journal for the Study of Judaism in the Persian, Hellenistic and Roman Periods*
JSNT	*Journal for the Study of the New Testament*
JSNTSS	JSNT Supplement Series
JSOT	*Journal for the Study of the Old Testament*
JSOTSS	JSOT Supplement Series
JSS	*Journal of Semitic Studies*
JTS	*Journal of Theological Studies*
JTSA	*Journal of Theology: Southern Africa*
KEKNT	Kritisch-exegetischer Kommentar über das Neue Testament
LB	*Linguistica Biblica*

LXX	Septuagint
MT	Masoretic Text
NCB	New Century Bible
NClB	New Clarendon Bible
Neot	*Neotestamentica*
NovT	*Novum Testamentum*
NovTSup	Novum Testamentum Supplements
NRSV	New Revised Standard Version
NRT	*La nouvelle revue théologique* (Tournai)
NT	New Testament
NTAbh	Neutestamentliche Abhandlungen
NTD	Das Neue Testament Deutsch
NTL	New Testament Library
NTS	*New Testament Studies*
NTSR	New Testament for Spiritual Reading
OBO	Orbis biblicus et orientalis
OBS	Oxford Bible Series
OT	Old Testament
OTL	Old Testament Library
OTP	*Old Testament Pseudepigrapha*, ed. J. H. Charlesworth
PTMS	Pittsburgh Theological Monograph Series
RevExp	*Review and Expositor*
RSV	Revised Standard Version
RThPh	*Revue de théologie et de philosophie*
SANT	Studien zum Alten und Neuen Testament
SBEC	Studies in the Bible and Early Christianity
SBL	Society of Biblical Literature
SBLDS	SBL Dissertation Series
SBLSP	SBL Seminar Papers
SBM	Stuttgarter biblische Monographien
SBS	Stuttgarter Bibelstudien
SBT	Studies in Biblical Theology
ScrMin	Scripta minora
SE	*Studia Evangelica* 1, 2, 3 (= TU 73, 87, 88, etc.)
SJ	Studia Judaica
SJT	*Scottish Journal of Theology*
SNTSMS	Society for New Testament Studies Monograph Series
ST	*Studia theologica*
TD	Theologische Dissertationen
TDNT	*Theological Dictionary of the New Testament*
TDOT	*Theological Dictionary of the Old Testament*

TGl	*Theologie und Glaube*
ThD	*Theology Digest*
THKNT	Theologischer Handkommentar zum Neuen Testament
TIM	*Tradition and Interpretation in Matthew*, eds. G. Bornkamm, et al.
TJT	*Toronto Journal of Theology*
TU	Texte und Untersuchungen
TynBul	*Tyndale Bulletin*
TZ	*Theologische Zeitschrift*
WMANT	Wissenschaftliche Monographien zum Alten und Neuen Testament
WUNT	Wissenschaftliche Untersuchungen zum Neuen Testament
ZAW	*Zeitschrift für die alttestamentliche Wissenschaft*
ZNW	*Zeitschrift für die neutestamentliche Wissenschaft*
ZTK	*Zeitschrift für Theologie und Kirche*

1

INTRODUCTION

In all ages of history, men and women have related
memories of moments when they had perceived, with
particular intensity, the presence of their gods. The literature of spirituality, be it Jewish, Christian, or Muslim,
abounds in stories of divine appearances ...
   For more than a thousand years, the religion of Israel
was dominated by the experience, the memory, or the hope
of divine presence.[1]

1.1.   The question

On a personal level, true religion can be defined as *the encounter
between oneself and one's God*, and on the corporate level as *one's
community practising the presence of God*. This study is concerned
with the understanding of God's presence with his people which
appears in the Gospel of Matthew.
   It has long been the endeavour of students of all faiths to
observe, evaluate and codify their religious communities' past
encounters with divine presence, through text, liturgy, theological
dialogue and community life.[2] What sets this study apart from
some recent critical analyses within the Christian tradition is its
subject-matter – an investigation focused on the 'presence motif' in
Matthew – and its approach – a combination of narrative and
historical criticism: the fresh response of a reader to Matthew's
rhetorical design, and the practised assessments of the redaction
critic.
   Some scholars have made the claim that the Judeo-Christian
biblical record as a whole is more accurately characterized as an

---

[1]   Samuel Terrien, *The Elusive Presence*, pp. 63, 404.
[2]   Cf. W. H. G. Holmes, *The Presence of God*; W. J. Phythian-Adams, *The People
and the Presence*.

account of the presence of God, acting in the midst and on behalf of the people of God, rather than the oft-cited theme of covenant.[3] This is not the place to argue that case, but certainly 'divine presence' manifests itself unarguably as a dominant concern in every strand of Hebraic theology as developed by the ancient authors from their complex of cultus and faith. These understandings of divine presence, though continuous in essence, were in focus radically transformed by first-generation Christian experiences of Jesus and his resurrection. No longer was divine presence mediated through the cult and Temple of Jerusalem, but through the person and community of the Messiah.

For most NT authors, divine presence is indeed an issue. The early Christian spiritualization of the Temple is already at work in Stephen's quotation of Isaiah in Acts 7.49–50. In a number of places, Paul pursues in cultic language a concern for divine presence: the church and the believer as the holy Temple of God, indwelt by the Spirit (1 Cor. 3.16; 6.19; 2 Cor. 6.16); access to God's grace through Jesus (Rom. 5.1f.); as well as the believer as inseparable from God (Rom. 8.38f), as a holy sacrifice before God (Rom. 12.1), and, in various places, being σὺν Χριστῷ (12x), which frequently captures that note of eternal eschatological fellowship with Christ.[4]

Among the gospel narratives, Jesus' expression of divine presence, pre- and post-resurrection, is understood and interpreted in very different ways. Mark is variously explained as proclaiming the risen Jesus absent until the parousia,[5] as seeing Jesus divinely present with and active in his church even now,[6] and as being ambiguous on the point.[7] Luke's annunciation story uses the symbol and language of the cloud of presence (Luke 1.35; cf. Exod. 40.35).[8] There is no question for Luke that Jesus himself leaves his followers (Luke 24.51; Acts 1.2, 9–11) and remains functional through his name and Spirit. Many disciples in Acts and 1 Corinthians choose to live radical lives, in expectation of Jesus' imminent return (Acts 2.42ff.; 1 Cor. 7.26, 36). The fourth evange-

---

[3]   Especially Terrien, *Presence*; cf. Ronald E. Clements, *God and Temple.*
[4]   See also David Renwick's concern for divine presence in a less obvious passage, 2 Cor. 2.14–3.18, in *Paul, the Temple, and the Presence of God*, pp. 47–156.
[5]   So T. J. Weeden, *Mark: Traditions in Conflict*; D. Crossan, 'A Form for Absence', pp. 41–55.
[6]   Ernest Best, *Following Jesus*, especially chapter 31.
[7]   J. A. Ziesler, 'Matthew and the Presence of Jesus', p. 55.
[8]   Cf. Terrien, *Presence*, pp. 415–16.

list's use of Wisdom and Word personifications in his prologue also evidences some fundamental continuity with Hebraic presence theology. John carefully develops a picture of the risen Christ as the exalted and absent Jesus who remains present and active through his Spirit.[9]

Within Hebrews, through Jesus' blood, access to God's holy Temple became the operative messianic role (10.19–22).[10] In Revelation Jesus and God's presence are eschatologically anticipated to replace the Temple and dwell among people (Rev. 21.2f., 22). A number of other texts in Hebrews, 1 Peter and Revelation employ temple and priest language when describing believers' new access to God (Rev. 1.5–6; 1 Pet. 2.9ff.; Heb. 4.14–16; 6.19–20; 9.24).

Matthew has a different picture. The author of the First Gospel was one of Christianity's earliest and most distinctive students of divine presence. Matthew exhibits a deliberate interest in this question, particularly as captured by the evangelist's unique christological use of Isaiah's Emmanuel prophecy and pointed emphasis on the special character of the presence of Jesus. Jesus comes as the Emmanuel Messiah – 'God with us' (1.23); his presence is the focus of his people's gatherings (18.20); he dies, reappears and commissions them to a powerful, authoritative mission undergirded by his presence (28.16ff.). He never leaves, but in fact promises to stay with his followers 'to the end of the age' (28.20). He breathes no spirit on them, does not ascend and promises no παράκλητος.

This particular predilection within the First Gospel I have chosen to call Matthew's *presence motif*. The purpose of this study is to examine the story of Matthew and this motif within it, in order to understand better the particular nexus there between God and his people, especially as embodied in Jesus' role as Emmanuel Messiah.

Certainly the major 'presence' texts – 1.23, 18.20 and 28.20 – have been the focus of attention before. But what weight do these passages carry within the whole story of Matthew? Are there other elements that support this motif? Rarely has an interpreter assessed Matthew's presence motif as an element within the full narrative and redactional fabric of the Gospel.

---

[9] See Clements, *God*, pp. 138–40; Ziesler, 'Matthew'; Terrien, *Presence*, pp. 410–20, for discussions and references. Cf. Norman Perrin, *The Resurrection Narratives*, pp. 5ff.

[10] Cf. further William Barclay, *The Letter to the Hebrews*, p. xiii.

1.2.   The interpreter

> Every encounter with tradition that takes place within
> historical consciousness involves the experience of the
> tensions between the text and the present. The hermeneutic
> task consists of not covering up this tension by attempting
> a naive assimilation but consciously bringing it out.[11]

A number of assumptions and criteria have guided this investigation. Every interpreter brings a particular *Weltanschauung* to the
text. Thomas Kuhn's and others' work on paradigms has rendered
somewhat vacuous the presumption that interpretation is neutral,
that the text can be divorced from the interpreter's paradigm, and
that correct interpretive tools assure objectivity. Critical objectivity
remains an important goal, but must be tempered by a clear
understanding of the weight and nature of one's presumptions and
interpretive goals, so as to make publicly accountable our biblical
and theological discourse.[12]

Concerning my own stance, then, I write as an urban Canadian
and as a member of a pluralistic Christian community. We assume
that the biblical texts to a significant degree function normatively in
our wrestlings with contemporary existence as the people of God.
Scripture is seen to have application to issues both local and global,
spiritual, social and physical in nature. In this setting my assumption is that rigorous investigation of the biblical text, however
'academic', will be theological from the start, or at minimum will
spring from an ideological and social context, even if it claims to be
'theologically disinterested'. This stems directly from my presumption that the gospel texts are stories which are written to engage
readers in a process of transformation and elicit acts of Christian
faith. In his indictment of the historical-critical paradigm, Walter
Wink insists that the uninvolved objectivity of the interpreter
stands in direct antithesis to the very nature of the Bible's subject-
matter, rendering its ancient mandate for personal and social
transformation impotent in the present.[13]

[11] Hans-Georg Gadamer, *Truth and Method*, p. 273; see Anthony Thiselton, *The Two Horizons*, especially pp. 307–10; Michael Crosby, *House of Disciples*, p. 6.

[12] See Robert Morgan, *Biblical Interpretation*, pp. 186–200; cf. Francis Watson's review in *Theology* 92, pp. 298–9.

[13] *The Bible in Human Transformation*, pp. 2–15. See a similar conflict among some literary critical practitioners: Robert Polzin, 'Literary and Historical Criticism of the Bible', pp. 106–11; Robert Fowler, 'Who is "The Reader" of Mark's Gospel?', pp. 5–10.

Methodology must also reflect an attempt to bring the text into dialogue with the immediate world, i.e., I am interested in a 'fusion of horizons'.[14] Wink's assertion that biblical criticism is often no longer part of a dynamic community, actively involved in the concretization of its critical results in modern life, indicates to some degree the results of overspecialization and entrenchment of the discipline within academic institutions.[15] My own presumption, however, is that by means of a healthy methodological eclecticism, Matthew's narrative and the interpreter, as both reader and critic, can engage in an act of co-creation. Acting as the implied reader, he or she fulfils what is already implicit in the structure and rhetoric of Matthew, and, acting as the critic, he or she contextualizes historically these responses, and is compelled to struggle with the issues of Christian discipleship.

The present methodological ferment in gospel studies prods the critic to be increasingly 'self-aware' – the attempt to read the text today often simultaneously involves meta-critical reflection on the assumptions implicit in that reading. These comments in no way certify that the reader of this study will find it to be a model of holistic integration. At the end of writing I can merely claim to have been increasingly conscious of such a need, and of the tension which exists between the parameters set by the biblical critics' guild for such an exercise as this and some of the assumptions already noted above.[16]

1.3. Text and method

What is a Gospel? The sea of ink given to this question by even the present generation of NT scholars has been anything but tranquil. In terms of Matthew's Gospel, of the array of introductory issues it is pertinent to note here a few; others will emerge later.[17]

Without prejudging the identity of the historical author, this study refers to the first evangelist by means of the masculine pronoun, and to the author and text of the First Gospel as

[14] 'Horizonverschmelzung', see Gadamer, *Truth*, pp. 270, 273.
[15] See also Morgan, *Interpretation*, pp. 133–5, 204–5, 271ff.
[16] See Stephen Moore, 'Doing Gospel Criticism As/With a Reader', for a tongue-in-cheek, albeit penetrating, critique.
[17] Recent surveys are available in the introductions of Ulrich Luz, *Das Evangelium nach Matthäus. Mt 1–7*; W. D. Davies and Dale C. Allison, *Matthew 1–7*. Graham N. Stanton, 'The Origin and Purpose of Matthew's Gospel', covers well the period 1945–80, some of which is updated in *A Gospel for a New People*.

'Matthew', for the sake of simplicity. No connection is implied with the apostle of that name mentioned in the Gospel. The old consensus is dissolving around Antioch as the First Gospel's provenance, a hypothesis which tended to strain the limitations of *Gospel* anyway by assuming a close relationship between the evangelist and a single community. I second Stanton's more recent swing in 'Revisiting Matthew's Communities' towards a wider geographical region including a string of affiliated Christian groups to which Matthew's author has links.

Matthew's relationship with Mark is most likely based on Mark's priority. Students of the Gospels are not unanimous on this issue, but it appears to be the best working hypothesis. Matthew and Luke also appear to share about two hundred and thirty verses of non-Markan material in common, but the traditional acceptance of a hypothetical Q document used by both authors has not figured largely in this study.[18] The First Gospel in its entirety, not merely those points at which it diverges from its sources, is taken to manifest a consistent redactional and rhetorical perspective. Comparisons are made on the assumption that they can reveal Matthew's distinctiveness even where direct literary dependence or judgements of priority cannot be certain.

The question of Matthew's sources is more complex than the two-source hypothesis allows, and the extent of pre-synoptic oral and written sources is underestimated in some discussions. Matthew's and the other Gospels' relationships to these sources are probably less linear and more interdependent than is implied by neat delineations like 'the document Q' or 'Matthew used Mark'.[19]

Structure

Numerous scholars have tried to unlock the design of Matthew's Gospel by means of a single, comprehensive model of its structure. B. W. Bacon's pentateuchal analysis has proven more durable than most, and has produced numerous offspring, but it omits too many

---

[18] On this issue see E. E. Ellis, 'Gospel Criticism', pp. 36–8; cf. Luz's review and statement in favour of a Q source which circulated in various recensions, *Matthäus 1–7*, pp. 18–31; also Allison and Davies' extensive restatement in favour of the traditional two-source stance, *Matthew 1–7*, pp. 97–114.

[19] For more complex synoptic–source relations see M.-E. Boismard, *Synopse des quatre évangiles* II, p. 17; cf. E. P. Sanders and Margaret Davies, *Studying the Synoptic Gospels*, pp. 93–111; J. A. T. Robinson, *Redating the New Testament*, pp. 93–117; R. T. France, *The Gospel According to Matthew*, pp. 34–8.

elements of the text from its scheme.[20] Other analyses, such as Jack
Kingsbury's threefold model,[21] the chiasmus model[22] and so-called
'triadic structures',[23] are also unable to account well for the
variables of the text, or are not convincing enough to have
warranted significant acceptance.[24] Certain portions of the Gospel
are carefully structured by means of various literary devices and
markers which signal breaks and narrative movement, but these are
internal structures which are subsumed under the rhetorical design
of the narrative story. In this sense it is the plot *per se* which
provides the Gospel with its structure. The formulas and chiasms,
repetitions and numeric patterns, geographic and temporal signposts, the narrative-discourse patterns, the inclusio, the summaries
– all of these individual narrative techniques *together* create the
powerful drama of the story's plot. Structure thus is found in the
principle of progressive narrative development.[25]

Method and reading

The Gospels can and have been read and used in a wide variety of
ways: as canonical validation (or as prophetic denunciation) of
ecclesiastical, social and political practices; as sources of historical
information about the events of Jesus' life or about the author, his
ideas and his community; as sources for theological propositions
and ethical paradigms; as texts for devotional reading; as liturgical
resources for church worship.[26]

[20] 'The "Five Books" of Moses Against the Jews', pp. 56–66.

[21] See, e.g., *Matthew: Structure, Christology, Kingdom*, pp. 1–37; followed by David
Bauer, *The Structure of Matthew's Gospel*.

[22] E.g., H. B. Green, 'The Structure of St Matthew's Gospel', pp. 47–59; A. Di
Marco, 'Der Chiasmus in der Bibel', pp. 37–58; H. J. B. Combrink, 'The
Macrostructure of the Gospel of Matthew', pp. 1–20.

[23] Dale C. Allison, 'The Structure of the Sermon on the Mount', pp. 423–5; Davies
and Allison, *Matthew 1–7*, pp. 58–72.

[24] See my criticisms below, pp. 50–2 and pp. 73–4. Frans Neirynck, 'ΑΠΟ ΤΟΤΕ
ʹΗΡΞΑΤΟ and the Structure of Matthew', pp. 21–59, for a thorough review and
critique of the three-part model; P. Bonnard, *L'évangile selon saint Matthieu*,
p. 7; D. P. Senior, *The Passion Narrative According to Matthew*, pp. 26f.;
Stanton, 'Origin', p. 1905; Robert H. Gundry, *Matthew: A Commentary on His
Literary and Theological Art*, p. 11. Davies and Allison, *Matthew 1–7*, p. 72,
despite their assertion that triadic structures permeate the Gospel, in the end
follow Gundry's assessment that Matthew is 'structurally mixed'.

[25] Whether a total structural pattern can thereby be found is doubtful. See Frank J.
Matera, 'The Plot of Matthew's Gospel'; R. T. France, *Matthew: Evangelist and
Teacher*, pp. 153–4.

[26] See Christopher Tuckett, *Reading the New Testament*, p. 1; cf. Anthony

Certainly in being recontextualized in different modern settings
the gospel stories perform a variety of actions on readers which
supersede the confines of any particular ancient form.

> A narrative, for example, seldom merely narrates. It may
> also inform, direct, nourish a sense of community soli-
> darity on the basis of corporate memory, produce grief or
> joy, or constitute an act of celebration.[27]

Most scholars would today agree that Matthew was not deliberately penned primarily as a new Mosaic law and pentateuchal
code,[28] an ecclesiastical treatise,[29] a community rule of discipline,[30]
or a liturgical formulary.[31] The jury is still out on the question of
gospel as an ancient genre and whether it is more unlike than like
anything else in first-century literature. The Gospels must have
been narratives comprehensible to their original addressees and
hence not totally *sui generis*, but dependent on existing generic
antecedents for their coding.[32] Seymour Chatman's comment is in
order:

> No individual work is a perfect specimen of a genre – novel
> or comic epic or whatever. All works are more or less
> mixed in generic character.[33]

Thiselton, 'Reader-Response Hermeneutics, Action Models, and the Parables of
Jesus', p. 112; David Howell, *Matthew's Inclusive Story*, p. 12.

[27] Thiselton, 'Reader-Response', p. 108.
[28] See G. D. Kilpatrick's adoption of Bacon's paradigm, *The Origins of the Gospel According to St Matthew*, pp. 107ff., and W. D. Davies' caution, *The Setting of the Sermon on the Mount*, p. 93; cf. Kingsbury's rejection, *Structure*, pp. 5–6.
[29] Cf. the varied adoptions in Hubert Frankemölle, *Jahwebund und Kirche Christi*; Günther Bornkamm, 'The Authority to "Bind" and "Loose" in the Church in Matthew's Gospel'.
[30] Contra Krister Stendahl, *The School of St Matthew*.
[31] Contra Michael Goulder's development (*Midrash and Lection in Matthew*) of Kilpatrick's suggestion (*Origins*) that Matthew was composed for regular litur-gical readings. See Leon Morris, 'The Gospels and the Jewish Lectionaries', pp. 129–56, for a critique of lectionary hypotheses.
[32] See Norman Petersen, *Literary Criticism for New Testament Critics*, pp. 44–5; H. J. B. Combrink, 'The Structure of the Gospel of Matthew as Narrative', pp. 65–6. For reviews and discussion of the gospel genre, cf. Graham Stanton, 'The Gospel Traditions and Early Christological Reflection', pp. 191–204; Robert Gundry, 'Recent Investigations into the Literary Genre "Gospel"', pp. 97–114; Aune, 'The Problem of the Genre of the Gospels', pp. 9–60; Robert Guelich, 'The Gospel Genre', pp. 183–219; F. G. Downing, 'Contemporary Analogies to the Gospels and Acts', pp. 51–66; Werner Georg Kümmel, *Intro-duction to the New Testament*, p. 37.
[33] *Story and Discourse*, p. 18. This is certainly the case with Matthew, given its strong dependence on Jewish scriptures and concern for the 'life of Jesus'. It is

It is worth noting the current shift in consensus about gospel genre towards ancient Graeco-Roman *bioi* as working models for the evangelists. I remain yet to be completely persuaded that Matthew fits easily as a subset of ancient *bioi* but am happy to see that current genre theory rejects rigid classification in favour of more dynamic genre family resemblances. In that light viewing the First Gospel alongside *bioi* has potential for understanding Matthew's characterization of Jesus in relationship to other lives, e.g. Moses.[34]

Whatever Matthew's genre, in form it is a narrative text, a story. That Matthew is a narrative, a story, is hardly a revolutionary thought, but important methodologically. My exercise of 'narrative criticism' (apparently a coinage of gospel scholars) follows the parameters currently canonized by narrative critics of the Gospels. Although it owes a great debt to New Criticism, the roots of gospel narrative criticism in the tradition of biblical scholarship make it an enterprise distinct from the much broader and more contentious arena of secular literary criticism, despite similar preoccupations (plot, character, point of view etc.).

On the question of analysing Matthew in terms of the literary categories and genre of modern narrative fiction, it is most relevant to note that the First Gospel, although an ancient text, does meet the criteria for a modern narrative and can be assessed inductively as such; it has a story and story-teller, and is a narrative with an artistically arranged plot. Obviously Matthew did not consciously develop his text using our terms of story, discourse, plot, narrator, implied reader and characterization, but these modern categories are universal features which the author, deliberately or unknowingly, employed in the ancient text.[35]

---

doubtful that 'Gospel' *per se* can be labelled a literary genre; see Davies and Allison, *Matthew 1–7*, pp. 4–5, n.8.

[34] See recent work on the issue by Perry Kea, 'Writing a *bios*'; Stanton, 'Revisiting Matthew's communities' and 'Matthew: ΒΙΒΛΟΣ, ΕΥΑΓΓΕΛΙΟΝ or ΒΙΟΣ?', David Aune, *The New Testament in Its Literary Environment* and 'The Problem of the Genre of the Gospels'. Cf. also Charles Talbert, *What is a Gospel?*; Philip L. Shuler, *A Genre for the Gospels*; G. Strecker, *Der Weg der Gerechtigkeit*; Rolf Walker, *Die Heilsgeschichte im ersten Evangelium*.

[35] See Moore, *Criticism*, for extensive discussion of the applicability of these methods to the Gospels. Cf. Combrink, 'Structure', pp. 65–6; R. A. Culpepper, *Anatomy of the Fourth Gospel*, pp. 8–11; Lynn Poland, *Literary Criticism and Biblical Hermeneutics*, pp. 65–105; Mark Powell, *What is Narrative Criticism?*, pp. 23–34.

A narrative whole

The Gospel is to be read first as a story with integrity and unity, and second as an ancient canonical text requiring social, literary and historical contextualization for interpretation. As Northrop Frye wrote:

> The primary understanding of any work of literature has to be based on an assumption of its unity. However mistaken such an assumption may eventually prove to be, nothing can be done unless we start with it as a heuristic principle. Further, every effort should be directed toward understanding the whole of what we read.[36]

Such an emphasis upon Matthew's narrative unity is not merely the claim of the self-declared gospel literary critics;[37] it has also been recognized as the essential starting-point by more traditional critics.[38]

The primary assumption that Matthew is an integral story requires us to read Matthew as a whole text, without dependence upon any particular source theory, without dissection or prioritization of the narrative's elements in terms of tradition and redaction.

A traditional gospel commentary like the new Matthew addition to the ICC series illustrates the problem. Through a formidable collection of data, secondary references and technical expertise, the authors have built a voluminous study directed by and large at penetrating *behind* the text of the First Gospel to reconstruction of its sources, historical development and socio-literary referentiality.

One frequently looks in vain amidst this wealth of detail for a discussion which engages the gospel story *in* the text as meaningful and rhetorically whole. This is not to decry the value of the details, but in this case the leaves, branches, roots, origins and orientation of individual trees have largely overwhelmed a sense of the forest.[39]

That Matthew is an integral story means that the Gospel projects

---

[36] 'Literary Criticism', p. 63; also in R. W. L. Moberly, *At the Mountain of God*, p. 19.

[37] See, e.g., A. G. Van Aarde, 'God Met Ons', p. 29; Janice Capel Anderson, 'Double and Triple Stories, the Implied Reader, and Redundancy in Matthew'; Combrink, 'Structure', p. 10; Bauer, *Structure*, pp. 11–13; J. D. Kingsbury, *Matthew as Story*, pp. 1–2; Howell, *Story*, pp. 12, 33; cf. R. A. Edwards, *Matthew's Story of Jesus*, p. 9.

[38] See, e.g., Luz, *Matthäus 1–7*, pp. 24–7; Guelich, 'Genre', p. 219.

[39] For more discussion on what a commentary should be, see René Kieffer, 'Was heißt das, einen Text zu kommentieren?', pp. 212–16.

a narrative world into which the story's events fit, peopled by its
characters and defined by a certain set of values. The reader is
invited by the narrator to become part of this world through the act
of reading. This also means the narrative world Matthew projects is
self-defining and closed; 'that is, it is conceptualized as a complex
structured entity in which partial meanings are dependent upon
their relationship to the whole'.[40]

Interpretation: structural, historical and theological

Some debates along the methodological spectrum in gospel studies
are concerned with the historical referentiality of the text and the
relevance and availability of authorial intent.[41]

To what degree, however, is the historical–literary debate a
question of one method of interpretation being 'right', and the
others 'wrong'? The gospel texts themselves are not so easily
categorized in accordance with strict adherence to a single theory of
reading. Biblical texts exhibit at least three dimensions – the
structural, historical and theological – which are to a great extent
inseparable and interdependent.[42] Matthew certainly has a *structural dimension* as exhibited in its narrative form, literary wholeness, rhetorical devices and semantic tendencies, and in its basic
functionality as a story. The *historical dimension* of Matthew is
found in its reference to past events concerning Jesus, in its
historically contextualized language, in its veiled inclusiveness of
the author's temporal setting and community links, and in its
participation in the transmission of traditions. And as a story
concerned with divine messianic intervention among humankind,
the gospel text encounters the reader with its *theological dimension*,
in statements about God, his people and their salvation through his
Messiah.

If, then, a text like Matthew consists of these three closely related
dimensions, and if for understanding to occur the hermeneutic task

---

[40] Howell, *Story*, p. 33.
[41] Schuyler Brown: 'Biblical scholars seem strangely unconcerned about the
problem of "the intentional fallacy"' ('Reader Response', p. 236 n.4). For the
original term see William Wimsatt and Monroe Beardsley, *The Verbal Icon*,
pp. 3–18. Cf. also E. D. Hirsch, *Validity in Interpretation*, pp. 209–44. See Polzin,
'Criticism', pp. 101–3, for several attempts to repudiate structuralists and New
Critics in defence of biblical historical criticism.
[42] See Bernard Lategan, 'Current Issues in the Hermeneutical Debate', p. 5; cf.
Howell, *Story*, p. 19.

requires some sort of fusion of author's and reader's horizons, then our interpretive approach cannot be unidimensional. Schuyler Brown has noted the 'diametrically opposed conclusions' historical critics frequently come to, and more recently he wants to relocate meaning as that 'generated by a reader reading a text'.[43]

In Terry Eagleton's scheme, modern literary theory can be categorized roughly in three stages: (1) 'a preoccupation with the author [Romanticism and the nineteenth century]'; (2) 'an exclusive concern with the text [New Criticism]'; and (3) 'a marked shift of attention to the reader over recent years'.[44] In such a scenario, the traditional historical-critical paradigm fits most closely into the first stage. Hence John Barton's observation that the literary concerns of traditional biblical criticism were generally the same as those of secular literary criticism prior to the rise of the New Critical movement, which

> was unequivocally committed to the quest for the original author's meaning and intention; to studying texts in their historical context; and to approaching them as vehicles through which ideas were conveyed, rather than as art-objects in their own right.

In terms of literary criticism, then, the biblical scholar has not been so much 'out of *touch*' as 'out of *date*', according to Barton.[45] Ulrich Luz finds that historical-critical exegesis, so dominant for decades in German and Swiss NT studies, has slid into 'theological and existential insignificance'.[46]

A number of gospel critics now constitute what is amounting to a complete 'literary swerve'. They have moved their focus from history and theology to story and rhetoric, in a rather dramatic paradigm shift. Especially relevant here are the developments of numerous SBL seminar groups, and numerous editions of *Semeia*. Krieger's images of the text as 'window' and 'mirror' have been used more than once to illustrate this shift.[47] According to these

---

[43] 'Biblical Philology, Linguistics and the Problem of Method', p. 297, and 'Reader Response', p. 232. See also Thiselton's comments, 'Reader-Response', pp. 82–3.

[44] *Literary Theory: An Introduction*, p. 74.

[45] Barton, *Reading the Old Testament*, p. 155.

[46] *Matthew in History*, p. 11.

[47] See Murray Krieger, *A Window to Criticism*, pp. 3–4; and cf. Petersen, *Criticism*, p. 19; Bernard Lategan, 'Reference: Reception, Redescription, and Reality', p. 92; James Barr, 'Reading the Bible as Literature'; J. Barton, *Reading*, pp. 163ff.; Van Aarde, 'God Met Ons', p. 32; Howell, *Story*, p. 24.

gospel critics' employment of Krieger's imagery, within the historical-critical school the text of Matthew functions as a 'window' through which the interpreter can catch glimpses of the Gospel's composition process, bits of the historical Jesus, the historical circumstances of 'the Matthean community', and the theological concerns of the first evangelist. To mix metaphors: on this model the Gospel becomes a 'tell', with layers of development to be subjected to stratification, sifting and differentiation on the basis of apparent tensions, breaks and seams in the text. To dig the tell is to uncover meaning; the presumption is that meaning, though asserted as being in the text, is drawn from the far side of the 'window', out of the antecedent causes of earlier traditions, texts, practices and cultures.

Having been converted to story, however, the new gospel narrative critic asserts that the meaning of the text lies on this side of it, between the text of Matthew and its reader. Krieger's image here is of the text as a 'mirror'. Meaning is the product of the reader's experience of the text as a whole, as he or she responds to the narrator's call to suspend disbelief, take on the role of the implied reader, and enter into the narrative world with its values, norms, conflicts and events. Meaning arises essentially from the connection of these two worlds through confrontation in the story's mirror, which ultimately alters the reader's beliefs and perceptions of his or her own real world in light of the 'better' beliefs and perceptions in the world of the story.

Within Krieger's analogy, then (or at least in some employments of it), old and new gospel critics stand poles apart in their understandings of the 'meaning' of the text. One is a disinterested historian, the other is a participative reader. One interpreter pursues the ghost of authorial intent and 'original meaning' in vertical, genetic relationships of words, expressions and pericopes; the other interpreter pursues the organic production of meaning in the face-to-face engagement of the reader with the plot, characters and rhetoric of the story.

But the perceptions of a methodological chasm, and the polarization of gospel scholars by such an employment of Krieger's window and mirror, seem at places to be the result of misperception and caricature. For example, many redaction critics continue to refine their practice, using history not for speculative reconstruction but to clarify the social context and historical filters which have shaped a Gospel's rhetoric. On the other hand, very little gospel narrative criticism actually involves purely 'a-historical' interpretation of a text removed from its context.[48]

What is at stake here is the question of what it really means *to read* the Gospels. Neither the historical nor narrative-critical school seems capable of incorporating the experiences of an *actual* reader or listener, either historic or modern; both remain essentially cerebral.[49]

But reader-response exegesis of the Gospels has become increasingly congenial of late, not only because *the reader* has been so ascendant, but because some gospel critics have 'rediscovered' through it the freshness of the text as apprehended by a hypothetical *virginal reader*.[50] For Stephen Moore, the irony is clear: reader-oriented exegetes, in moving away from traditional historical criticism, have by means of a different road moved a significant step closer to the original hermeneutic horizon of the Gospels. In other words, with its concern for the act of reception, reader-response has gone back to the primary *event* of the gospel hearing – its *aural* appropriation in an *oral* reading. Thereby the critic's 'reader' is used to uncover the rhetorical force of the narrative, its left-to-right reception of the verbal string, as a *temporal* experience bound to the text's flow of words, requiring the reader's active involvement, exploration and anticipation.

Moore claims that the historical-critical school, with its predominantly visual, private, silent appropriation of the text, has failed to apprehend the importance of this experience of reading, and encouraged the rigorous objectification of the text as a static, spatial form over against its temporal eventness in reader-reception theory. This is a practice magnified by the guild's print culture: the biblical text with its artificial scientific stratification by means of chapters, verses, synopses, concordances and lexica.[51]

But neither approach is without its problems in terms of describing the reception of the text. The rigorous comparative

[48] See 'Revolt' in Petersen, *Criticism*, pp. 25–8. Polzin, 'Criticism', pp. 99–114, juxtaposes the statements of Edgar Krentz, *The Historical-Critical Method*, p. 72, with those of Daniel Patte, *What is Structural Exegesis?*, p. 10. Cf. H. J. B. Combrink, 'The Changing Scene of Biblical Interpretation', pp. 9–10.

[49] For extended discussion of the following see Moore, 'Doing'; and Morgan, *Interpretation*, Chapter 7.

[50] See Moore's description of the 'jaded' redaction critic versus the fresh 'virginal' reader's response, 'Doing', pp. 85–6; Gadamer, *Truth*, p. 238: 'A hermeneutically trained mind must be, from the start, sensitive to the text's quality of newness'; in Thiselton, *Horizons*, p. 305.

[51] See also Jeffrey Staley, *The Print's First Kiss*, pp. 1–5.

method of redaction critics functions by means of complete famil-
iarity with and objectification of the text. Yet the presupposition by
some literary critics of a first-time hearer, unfamiliar with the
unfolding story and wholly dependent upon a sequential reading,
denies the traditional nature of our Gospels and their original,
mainly Christian, audiences who surely knew something of the
story.[52]

In essence, though, this new breed of critic has begun to reorient
the traditional priorities of the scholarly guild.

> The narrative world of a gospel is not an exact reflection of
> either the world of Jesus or that of the evangelist. Un-
> doubtedly the narrative worlds of the gospels are related in
> various ways we have not yet fully understood to both the
> world of Jesus and the social world of the evangelist.
> Primarily, though, the narrative world of a gospel is a
> literary world created by the author.[53]

Redressing the balance

The need to balance our reading methods therefore does not allow
for this study a singular approach – to assess the presence motif in
Matthew purely as a rhetorical phenomenon. I would assert that
gospel criticism remains incompatible with an a-historical structur-
alism which severs the text from any sense of context and absolutizes meaning into the reading experience alone. It thereby
succumbs to what some have called the 'affective fallacy' (reducing
the text to the reader's apprehension of it). Given that the structural, historical and theological dimensions of the Matthean narrative are interrelated, the literary-critical paradigm employed to
investigate Matthew's structural dimension does not invalidate the
historical and theological questions which must also be asked of the
narrative.

I have no wish to fulfil Eagleton's prognosis, that the attempt to
combine critical approaches

---

[52] Moore has highlighted another irony: narrative criticism of the Gospels has
maintained a strong, implicit connection with the authorial intention of traditional criticism, now replaced by literary intention. See *Criticism*, pp. 12, 35–8,
54.

[53] R. Alan Culpepper, 'Story and History in the Gospels', p. 472. Cf. Petersen,
Criticism, p. 40; and J. D. Kingsbury, 'Reflections on "The Reader" of
Matthew's Gospel', pp. 458–9.

is more likely to lead to a nervous breakdown than to a brilliant literary career.[54]

But I follow along with Petersen who has called for a 'bifocal' approach which neither absolutizes the texts merely as windows to their contexts, nor absolutizes the texts as mirrors which reflect the reading event.[55] The narrative world of the gospel text is both autonomous (story-wise) and historically derivative from first-century Palestine, and the latter connection allows for shared codes and shared experiences which form the basis for communication.[56] Given the cultural and linguistic gap that exists between us and the first-century context, 'holistic' reading first distances and then reasserts the connection between text and interpreter, while checking an over-easy domestication of the message.[57]

In this study my desire is do two things: a narrative assessment of divine presence in Matthew, and a socio-historical assessment of divine presence in the world of the First Gospel, without violating the premises of either method, and not without due recognition of their differing synchronic and diachronic fields of reference.

> Methods are inherently complementary because a text is both an event in time (thus eliciting inquiry into genetic relationship – diachronic or historical-critical study) and an internally coherent work with a life of its own (thus eliciting inquiry into internal relationships – synchronic, structuralist or literary study).[58]

A distinction must be drawn between the historical-critical exercise in which texts merely become tools for the historian's reconstruction of events and ideas and the one in which historical data are employed to inform our reading of the text.[59] It is the latter employment which should prove most fruitful for delineating the significance of the presence motif within Matthew's story. The

[54] *Theory*, p. 198.

[55] Criticism, pp. 24f.; also Howell, *Story*, pp. 28f. Krieger denies any false dichotomy between the approaches and wants to see 'the mirrors as windows too', *Window*, pp. 3–70; see also Polzin, 'Criticism', pp. 104f., with further references.

[56] See W. S. Vorster, 'Meaning and Reference', p. 57; and Lategan, 'Reference', p. 74.

[57] See Walter Wink, *The Bible in Human Transformation*, pp. 19–31; W. S. Vorster, 'The Historical Paradigm'; cf. Anthony Thiselton, 'The New Hermeneutic', pp. 315–17; Howell, *Story*, p. 29.

[58] Leander Keck, 'Will the Historical-Critical Method Survive?', p. 123.

[59] So Culpepper, *Anatomy*, p. 5; Thiselton, 'Reader-Response', p. 100.

priority given to narrative in this circular relationship of methods is temporal; literary and historical analysis are equal servants in the task of interpretation.

1.4. The present state of research

Most recent attempts to assess the importance of the question of divine presence in Matthew are the by-products of larger analyses of the First Gospel. A few scholars have focused specifically on the presence motif, and one or two have approached the question from a literary-rhetorical perspective. A *de facto* consensus exists: current students of Matthew generally agree that the Emmanuel prophecy and Jesus' promises of presence form a redactional and christological theme of secondary significance in Matthew. Few have attempted more than a perfunctory analysis.

A growing consensus

The past few decades have seen a gradual rise in interest in our subject-matter. Early this century, for example, in such commentaries as those by Allen, Holtzmann, Klostermann, McNeile, Plummer and T. H. Robinson, apart from a few technical and historical comments, the Emmanuel prophecy and Jesus' promises of presence are passed over without mention, and their introductions assess no significance to the motif for the Gospel's theology and christology.

In subsequent studies gospel scholars sought to understand and define more carefully the individual creativity within each evangelist's tapestry. Bacon, Bultmann, Schlatter and colleagues appreciated the evangelists as more than skilful editors, and their anticipation of redaction criticism within the evolution in interpretive methods undergirded the subsequent increased focus on Matthew's Emmanuel theme. Questions began to appear concerning the prominence of the presence motif within the First Gospel's theology, its origins in the OT and Judaism, and its relation to the post-resurrection experiences of the Matthean community.

In an article often cited for its examination of the biblical 'God with us' language, W. C. Van Unnik in 1959 offered his characterization of the Emmanuel theme in Matthew, including the important recognition of inclusio between 1.23 and 28.20:

The promise to the disciples in Matt. 28:20 gets its full force in this perspective: after having set that enormous task (v.19), Jesus who has now all authority comforts his weak followers (cf. 26:56) and assures them of His powerful assistance ... That is the surprising declaration at the moment of departure. Matthew returns at the end to the beginning: Jesus was (1:23) and is 'Immanuel' (28:20).[60]

Several pages later, Van Unnik summarizes his assessment of NT references to divine presence by incorporating the Emmanuel motif into a continuous OT–NT *heilsgeschichtlich* paradigm:

Jesus, the Messiah = Christ = Anointed One with the Spirit, the mediator of the new Covenant, is the IMMA-NUEL and does His work of salvation; His followers, anointed with the Spirit, form the new Israel and stand in the line of the prophets, heroes and kings of the old Israel, obedient to God's will and assured by His blessing.[61]

Kilpatrick's *Origins of the Gospel According to St Matthew* (1946), Bornkamm's 'The Stilling of the Storm in Matthew' (1948) and Michel's 'The Conclusion of Matthew's Gospel' (1950) heralded a new focus on the distinctive features of Matthew. Michel's seminal statement, that 'Matt. 28:18–20 is the key to the understanding of the whole book', brought part of that focus to bear on Jesus' unique promise to be with his followers (p. 35). This concern for specific sources and traditions behind Matthew's presence language broadened in the work of Klostermann, Lohmeyer and others to include analysis of conceptual links and theological trajectories.[62] The connection between the presence christology in Matthew and the theology of presence in the OT and Judaism

[60] *'Dominus Vobiscum*: The Background of a Liturgical Formula', p. 287; also Günther Bornkamm, 'The Risen Lord and the Earthly Jesus', *TIM*, p. 326, originally published in 1963. On literary inclusion in Matthew cf. Léon-Dufour, 'The Synoptic Gospels', pp. 164–8; and Fenton, 'Inclusio and Chiasmus in Matthew'. See David Bauer, *Structure*, pp. 124–7, and Howell, *Story*, pp. 226–8, for the rhetorical significance of inclusio in Matthew's structure.
[61] Van Unnik's emphasis, *'Dominus'*, p. 293.
[62] E. Klostermann, *Das Matthäusevangelium*; E. Lohmeyer, 'Mir ist gegeben alle Gewalt', pp. 22–49; W. Trilling, *Das wahre Israel*, pp. 49–51; Gerhard Barth, 'Matthew's Understanding of the Law', *TIM*, pp. 135–7, 142; Bornkamm, 'Lord', *TIM*, pp. 301–27, esp. 326. Cf. Stanton's overview, 'Origin', pp. 1891–5.

evoked the observation that Matthew's emphatic dependence upon the OT includes a deliberate adoption of OT presence themes.[63]

One result has been the widespread recognition that the Emmanuel motif and Jesus' promises of presence are particularly the province of Matthew among the Gospels. Ulrich Luz comments on Matthew 1.23:

> Anspielungen auf das Mit-uns-Sein Gottes durchziehen das ganze Evangelium (17,17; 18,20; 26,29). Vor allem aber hat Matthäus durch den letzten Vers seines Evangeliums (... 28,20) eine Inklusion geschaffen, die ein Grundthema markiert: Die Gegenwart des erhöhten Herrn bei seiner Gemeinde erweist ihn als Immanuel, Gott mit uns.[64]

> (Allusions to God's Being-with-us are drawn throughout the whole gospel (17,17; 18,20; 26,29). Above all, however, Matthew has created an inclusio through the last verse of his Gospel (... 28,20), which marks a fundamental theme: The presence of the exalted Lord with his community proves him to be Immanuel, God with us.)

And R. T. France:

> This highest level of Matthew's Christology is effectively summed up in two verses (1:23; 28:20) which are often regarded as a 'framework' around the Gospel.[65]

But the agreement that Matthew's presence motif provides a *Grundthema* for the Gospel has not necessarily inspired consensus around the character and significance of that motif for his story as a whole. C. H. Dodd saw in Matthew's references merely a proclamation of Christ's perpetual abiding presence, as figurative.[66] J. A. T. Robinson refers to Jesus' promise in Matthew 28.20 as fully inaugurated eschatology, while Barth, Schweizer and Marxsen want to define Jesus' presence in terms of the ongoing legacy of his commandments and preaching of the law.[67] For Ziesler, on the

---

[63] See, e.g., Terrien, *Presence*, pp. 411–34; Frankemölle, *Jahwebund*, pp. 8–10.

[64] *Matthäus 1–7*, p. 105.

[65] *Matthew*, p. 48; cf. pp. 79–80, 276, 416; Davies and Allison, *Matthew 1–7*, p. 217.

[66] *New Testament Studies*, pp. 60–2. See Van Unnik's criticism of Dodd and others for making Jesus' presence merely static, '*Dominus*', pp. 273–4.

[67] J. A. T. Robinson, *Jesus and His Coming*, p. 66; G. Barth, *TIM*, pp. 135–6; Eduard Schweizer, 'Observance of the Law and Charismatic Activity in Matthew', p. 218; and *The Good News According to Matthew*, p. 534;

other hand, the message of 18.20 and 28.20 stems from a delicate balance of Matthew's very high christology, his understanding of the monarchy of God and a general caution about Spirit language.[68]

G. M. Styler, in assessing the development of Matthean christology over Markan, detects among other things the beginnings of an interest in ontology in the First Gospel, based in part on the material special to Matthew where the presence of Christ with his followers is stressed.[69] This prompted a rebuttal from David Hill who asserts that this material highlighted Christ's divine *function* among his people, not his ontology, as evident from Matthew's tripartite view of NT time.[70] In his commentary on Matthew, however, Robert Gundry finds too much deity in Matthew's presence motif.

More recently J. D. Kingsbury has again taken up this question. In several places he attempts to link the presence motif with his reading of the fundamental message of Matthew's story.

> The key passages 1:23 and 28:20, which stand in a reciprocal relationship to each other, highlight this message ... Strategically located at the beginning and the end of Matthew's story, these two passages 'enclose' it. In combination, they reveal the message of Matthew's story: *In the person of Jesus Messiah, his Son, God has drawn near to abide to the end of time with his people, the church, thus inaugurating the eschatological age of salvation.*[71]

Kingsbury goes on to find support for his 'Son-of-God' christology in this reading of Matthew's presence motif and sees defined in it the disciples' relationship with Jesus, as well as the community's social parameters and authority.[72]

One of his students, David Bauer, has adopted Kingsbury's tripartite structure for the First Gospel and the feature of inclusio. Bauer asserts that all the references to the presence of Jesus with his

W. Marxsen, *The Resurrection of Jesus of Nazareth*, p. 165. Note that H. J. Held ascribes less significance to the theme; 'Matthew as Interpreter of the Miracle Stories', *TIM*, p. 299.

[68] 'Presence'.
[69] G. M. Styler, 'Stages in Christology in the Synoptic Gospels', pp. 404–6.
[70] David Hill, *The Gospel of Matthew*, pp. 64–6.
[71] *Story*, pp. 41–2 (Kingsbury's emphasis); cf. *The Parables of Jesus in Matthew 13*, pp. 28–9, 78–81.
[72] *Story*, pp. 53–5, 131–2, 154–8.

community, in their deliverance, prayer, discipline, suffering and endurance (1.23; 18.20; 26.29), are part of a deliberate structural movement to the climactic declaration of 28.20. The 'with you/us' theme recurs throughout the Gospel and reaches a point of climax at 28.20.[73]

Hubert Frankemölle and A. G. Van Aarde

Two scholars have pursued Matthew's 'with us' language as a primary element of their research. From disparate geographical hemispheres, each has sought to elaborate afresh the purpose and place of the Emmanuel Messiah in Matthew's Gospel.

Hubert Frankemölle devotes the major portion of *Jahwebund und Kirche Christi* to the question of the christological and theological basis for the community in Matthew. Frankemölle's study of Matthean ecclesiology is redaction-critical in method, an attempt at reconstruction of the specific make-up of the community behind the text of Matthew, especially as revealed through the editorial use of μεθ' ὑμῶν language in 1.23, 18.20 and 28.20.[74]

Frankemölle begins by reiterating previous scholarly observations on the importance and interrelationship of these verses, but expands the μεθ' ἡμῶν/ὑμῶν language into a *Leitidee* for the First Gospel, founded in OT covenant theology. Behind the text of Matthew, Frankemölle identifies a gentile church and presumes a crisis over the Jewish rejection of Jesus and the destruction of the Temple: is God faithful to his promises and to his people?

For Frankemölle, Matthew asserts that the covenant people of God have carried on in the community of Jesus' followers, who have replaced Israel, and this is evident by YHWH's renewal of his covenant through his divine presence with the church. Frankemölle's careful examination of the sources and employment of Matthew's μεθ' ἡμῶν/ὑμῶν language reveals the first evangelist's composition of 'covenant theology' (*Bundestheologie*), built in the fashion of the Chronicler and Deuteronomist to explain YHWH's sovereignty and judgement of his people in history.[75] The central point is that YHWH has renewed his covenant by coming to dwell with his people, the church, through the supreme agency of his Emmanuel Messiah, Jesus.[76] This divine presence and the renewal

---

[73] Cf. David Bauer, *Structure*, especially pp. 124–7. [74] *Jahwebund*, pp. 7–83.
[75] See *Jahwebund*, pp. 335–42.
[76] See *Jahwebund*, pp. 7–80, 321–5.

of the covenant bring with them the inherent responsibility of obedience to YHWH's will, as expressed through his Messiah, by the new covenant people.[77]

Frankemölle's presentation is not without problems, in part owing to his schema of salvation history. No one would protest the observation that the distinct horizons of the earthly and exalted Jesus (or the temporal points of view of the plot and narrator) do at points coalesce in Matthew's story, but Frankemölle has completely removed any distinctions.[78] This thorough dehistoricization of the past does not serve the rhetorical, redactional or theological nuances of the Gospel's horizons.

Ultimately, the service to which Frankemölle puts his examination of Matthew's μεθ᾽ ἡμῶν/ὑμῶν language, namely his assertion of a community in need of assurance regarding God's faithfulness, is not borne out by the story. As Kingsbury points out, based on his use of the OT, Matthew already assumes to be certain what Frankemölle contends the author is setting out to prove to his community – the faithfulness of God and the ongoing validity of his covenantal promises.[79]

Frankemölle's work has significant value for this study, however. He has helped to highlight Matthew's indebtedness to OT presence, even if he has overdrawn the parallels with the Deuteronomist and Chronicler. Unanswered questions remain from his work, especially concerning the nature of the fundamental continuity between YHWH's OT and NT people. Similarly, Frankemölle's insistent characterization of Matthew as 'covenant theology' remains unconvincing. More importantly, Frankemölle has left parts of the presence motif within the story essentially unexplored, as will be discussed below.

The second major study of relevance here is the less accessible Afrikaans doctoral dissertation of A. G. Van Aarde, 'God Met Ons: Dié Teologiese Perspektief van die Matteusevangelie'.[80] He purports from the beginning to have embarked on both a 'teologiese' and 'metodologiese eksperiment' which has discovered that

---

[77] See *Jahwebund*, pp. 273–307.

[78] See Stanton's criticisms, 'Origin', p. 1940; and David Bauer, *Structure*, pp. 51–2 – but Bauer falls victim to this same criticism on occasion, when he seems to blur the distinction between Jesus' teaching and the disciples' (who are commissioned, but never teach in plotted time), and when he dehistoricizes the discourses in order to explain their orientation; see pp. 58, 133–4.

[79] Kingsbury, *Structure*, p. 38.

[80] DD, University of Pretoria, 1983.

the basic theological idea which Matthew imparts to his readers, is the message that *God* is *with us* by means of the mission of the 'Son of God' (Jesus) and the mission of the 'sons of God' (the disciples).[81]

As Van Aarde's entire thesis is thereafter given over to his own particular investigation of 'God met ons' as 'die dominante teologiese perspektief in die vertelling', it does provide the lengthiest among recent analyses of Matthew's Emmanuel motif.

As far as his 'metodologiese eksperiment' goes, Van Aarde gathers from among several approaches to the Gospels as narrative texts, in order to allow the proper synthesis of '*idee* en *tegniek*' in the First Gospel to be drawn out (cf. pp. 7, 30).

(1) Van Aarde presumes that 'meaning' is necessarily genrebound. The identification of literary genre (both ancient and modern), in terms of the 'holistiese konteks' of Matthew, is critical for unlocking the 'idee' of the text.[82] He gives preference to the modern 'poëtiek' of the Gospel.

(2) The theology of Matthew must be determined text-immanently within the bounds of the genre 'narrative', and not via the presumptions of a historical 'Sitz im Leben Ecclesiae' (p. 30).

(3) Matthew is the literary product of a 'redactor-narrator'. The content ('inhoud') of Matthew is a combination of redactional activity (based on Matthew's sources, especially Mark) and new narrative activity. Identifying Matthew's 'idee' requires diachronic and synchronic methods of the investigation.

(4) 'The result of our investigation brings us to the apprehension that Matthew has created an analogy between pre-Easter and post-Easter "events" and that he grounds this "analogy" in the presence of Jesus as *God with us* in both "time-periods".'[83]

Thus Van Aarde's 'metodologiese eksperiment' analyses 'narrative point of view' ('vertellersperspektief') in the First Gospel to uncover the theology of Matthew, while trying not to confuse the

[81] 'En onses insiens is die basiese teologiese idee wat Matteus sy lesers meedeel, die boodskap dat *God met ons* is deur middel van die sending van die "Seun van God" (Jesus) en die sending van die "seuns van God" (die dissipels)' (p. 6, Van Aarde's emphasis).

[82] 'Die "idee" (inhoud) van 'n teks word met behulp van genre-ontleding ontsluit' (p. 29).

[83] 'Die resultat van ons ondersoek sal ons bring by die verskynsel dat Matteus 'n analogie geskep het tussen die voor-pase en die na-pase "gebeure" en dat hy hierdie "analogie" grond in die teenwoordigheid van Jesus as *God met ons* op beide "tydsvlakke"' (p. 31, Van Aarde's emphasis).

'narrated world' ('vertelde wêreld') and the 'real world' ('werklike wêreld'). Van Aarde attempts simultaneously to maintain a historical-critical foot in Matthew's socio-religious context and a redaction-critical foot in the world of Matthew's editorial intentions (see pp. 29–37).

Such an 'eksperiment' is no small challenge, and I am grateful for the precedent it provides for this study. Van Aarde attempts to balance the structural and historical dimensions of the text, while remembering the different horizons of text and interpreter. Where I think his 'metodologiese eksperiment' runs into some difficulty, however, is at the very point of its strength. He does sometimes confuse that which he wants to avoid confusing – the narrated and real worlds – by attempting to press text and history simultaneously. In the process Van Aarde produces a number of anomalies. It is difficult, for example, to find justification, methodologically or otherwise, for his statement that 'Matthew has not, however, created a separate narrator in his narrative; he himself is the narrator.'[84] Such an unwillingness to recognize functional distinctions within the narrative personages of the First Gospel contradicts Van Aarde's methodological stance. Instead of employing narrative and redactional criticism in a dialogical and complementary fashion, Van Aarde has sought a synthesis which obscures on the one hand their fundamental differences and on the other hand their particular contributions to the task of exegesis.

Van Aarde's 'teologiese eksperiment' also shows some mixed results. For example, on the positive side he has rightly highlighted several unhappy tendencies in traditional investigations of christological titles (pp. 63–5). But does Van Aarde ultimately achieve his oft-expressed thesis?

> Our purpose is to show that the organizing principle which connects the analogous pre-Easter Jesus-mission with the post-Easter disciple-mission in the 'plotted time' of Matthew's Gospel is the *God with us*-theme. In short: the *God with us*-theme is the kernel of the Matthean narrator's *ideological* perspective out of which he has constituted his total narrative ('plot') – *phraseologically, psychologically, temporally* and *spatially*.[85]

---

[84] 'Matteus het egter nie in sy vertelling 'n aparte verteller geskep nie; hy is self die verteller' (p. 35, cf. p. 56).

[85] Van Aarde's emphasis, p. 119. See similar statements on pp. 6, 31, 87, 125, 139, 142, 176.

Two problems arise: (1) Despite these repeated statements, Van
Aarde never undertakes a thorough examination of the 'God with
us' theme as a narrative motif encountered by the reader in the
story, or as an expression of the author's own editorial interests. Its
dominance as a theological motif is frequently asserted by Van
Aarde, but not actually drawn from either a linear reading or a
redaction-critical examination.[86] (2) The 'God with us' theme is
presented as a constituent element of a pre-and post-Easter mission
analogy; Van Aarde's thesis is dependent upon whether he can
legitimate his proposed analogy.

But in the end it is Van Aarde's 'analogie' which is not entirely
convincing. The parallels and correspondences he evinces between
the pre- and post-Easter sequences do not add up to the full
compositional portrait he desires. The format of this analogy, once
imposed upon the story, begins to constrict interpretation of
various narrative elements, rather than to explain them for the
reader. There is no question that a powerful relationship of
continuity exists between the earthly Jesus' mission and the post-
Easter community in Matthew's story, but this relationship is also
defined by various fundamental elements of *discontinuity* and
transformation, including the changes in perception of Jesus' presence, and the Jewish–Gentile shift in mission focus.

Van Aarde's 'analogie' begins to appear as another version of the
redactional 'transparency' between Gospel and community employed by other scholars, rather than materializing out of a fresh
reading of the text.

1.5. This study ...

Frankemölle, Van Aarde and other commentators thus provide us
with helpful foundations, but they leave several important questions unanswered. The dominant concerns of students looking at
Matthew's presence motif to date have been external to the story.
Most have assumed that the first evangelist is 'historicizing' post-
Easter experiences or being 'transparent' to his community,[87] and
their assessments of his presence motif have presumed the same.

---

[86] In one of the few places he directly addresses the appropriate texts he depends on
Frankemölle: 'The expression μεθ' ὑμῶν is the *theologische Leitidee* of Matthew's
Gospel' (p. 122).

[87] See especially Ulrich Luz, 'The Disciples in the Gospel According to Matthew',
for this discussion. See Strecker, *Weg*, pp. 45–7, 184–6, for the term 'historicizing'; 'transparency' is derived from R. Hummel, *Die Auseinandersetzung*

Most have also adopted a particular theological construct of
Heilsgeschichte as their interpretive paradigm for Matthew and
they have incorporated their reading of these passages on the
presence of God and Jesus into their paradigm.[88] And even in the
cases of Frankemölle (a-historical *Bundestheologie*), Kingsbury
(Son-of-God christology), Van Aarde (pre-/post-Easter 'analogie')
and David Bauer (Kingsbury's tripartite structure elaborated), a
strong, pre-existing agenda has too often manipulated their comments on presence in Matthew.

What is missing in existing commentary on Matthew's presence
motif is a comprehensive analysis which begins and builds from its
employment rhetorically within the entirety of the first evangelist's
story, and then compares its narrative significance to appropriate
historical and literary concerns. This study intends to fill that gap,
at least to the extent that it builds its foundation first and foremost
on the integrity of Matthew's narrative, presupposing the gospel
story to have an inherently dramatic structure in which the presence
motif plays a part. But since we are concerned with the worlds of
both readers and author, we will then pursue the historical and
theological dimensions of the presence motif.

Has the assignment become thereby unbearably complex? Not in
the sense that this study claims to perform a new synthesis of
formalist literary technique with traditional biblical criticism. In
borrowing from selected aspects of narrative theory and redaction
criticism I take to heart, rather, the words of John Barton, when he
argues that 'literary competence' is the goal of criticism. An
interpreter is literarily competent who knows 'what sort of questions it makes sense to ask' of a particular work.[89]

Our initial concerns are therefore rhetorical. Narrative criticism
will be discussed more carefully and relevant terms defined in
Chapter 2. In Chapter 3 the presence motif will be traced through
Matthew's story with a view to the implied reader's interaction with
the text. Characters, rhetorical devices and points of view will be
discussed, to help us understand the motif's development.

Our concerns subsequently are referential – the social, literary
and historical issues surrounding Matthew's presence motif. The

   zwischen Kirche und Judentum im Matthäusevangelium. Cf. J. D. Kingsbury, *Jesus
   Christ in Matthew, Mark and Luke*, p. 87, and *Structure*, pp. 31–7.
88 See Howell's overview and critique of *Heilsgeschichte* as the major category of
   interpretation for recent Matthean scholarship, *Story*, pp. 55–92.
89 J. Barton, *Reading*, pp. 16–17; cf. 198–207.

thrust of Chapter 4 is to examine divine presence as a dominant motif within Matthew's most important literary context: the Jewish scriptures. In Chapter 5 we will examine the 'I am with you' saying and its μεθ᾽ ἡμῶν/ὑμῶν language in the same scriptures. Chapters 6–8 will take a closer redactional look at several critical presence passages in Matthew, guided by the narrative investigation of Chapter 3, and the background provided in Chapters 4 and 5.

Whether these results allow us to talk about an Emmanuel christology for Matthew will be pursued in Chapter 9.

2

MATTHEW'S NARRATIVE ART

> A text has no life of its own. It 'lives' only as an electric
> wire is alive. Its power originates elsewhere: in a human
> author. There is another point of comparison: however
> powerful the author's act of creation, the text lies impotent
> until it also comes into contact with a human reader.
>
> ... those at the receiving end are in control. It is they
> who decide what to do with the powerful resource they
> possess – whether and how to use it. They have all the
> power in their hands.[1]

The aim of this chapter is to assess briefly the role of narrative
criticism, in order to ask how the motif of presence is expressed
through Matthew's rhetoric. Such an exercise involves swapping a
traditional focus on the evangelist's *theology* for a new focus on
story, and the elements thereof.

2.1. Method and premises

As Stephen Moore has recently explained, narrative criticism,
especially as conceived of and increasingly practised by gospel
critics, is above all preoccupied with the evangelist's story, particularly in terms of plot and character. Plot has long been defined as a
set of events connected by both temporal succession and causality:
'The king died and then the queen died of grief' is a plot; 'The king
died and then the queen died' is not.[2] Our acts of reading are driven
by a powerfully innate desire to supply causal links even where they
are not explicit (e.g., in the case of 'The king died and then the
queen died' the reader naturally tends to assume that the queen's

---

[1] Morgan, *Interpretation*, p. 269.
[2] This is E. M. Forster's well-known example from *Aspects of the Novel*, p. 93; also
cited in Moore, *Criticism*, p. 14.

death had something to do with the king's).[3] As Moore notes, this natural desire to impose maximum plot coherence on the events of a narrative is quite evident in gospel studies: witness scholars' enduring puzzlement over enigmas such as Mark's naked young man (Mark 14.51–2), and the abrupt ending in Mark 16.8.

Within the reading experience, character is inextricably tied to plot: each is produced and defined by the other. Characters especially find their definition through interaction with other characters in the story, while in the Gospels the narrator plays an essential role in supplying information about characters.

The narrative critic's pre-eminent concern with a Gospel's story also entails careful attention to questions of discourse. As a means of explaining in tandem both the 'what' (story) and the 'how' (discourse, or rhetoric) of narrative, Seymour Chatman's two-storey model of narrative communication has proven helpful for numerous gospel critics. Coming out of structuralist studies in the late 1960s and early 1970s, his synthesis in *Story and Discourse* of various Continental and Anglo-American textual concerns has provided for critics a means of mapping intelligibly the interrelationships of the Gospels' various narrative elements.[4]

It was in the SBL Markan Seminar in the 1970s that narrative criticism initially established itself within gospel studies in the North American scene, and in academic pockets such as Sheffield University.[5] Rhoads and Michie's *Mark as Story* and Culpepper's *Anatomy of the Fourth Gospel* have become touchstones within the area, not only in their employment of Chatman's paradigm, but in the parameters which they established for the field of gospel narrative criticism.[6]

---

[3] So Chatman, *Story*, pp. 45–6; cf. Moore, *Criticism*, pp. 14–15.

[4] See Raman Selden, *A Reader's Guide to Contemporary Literary Theory* for an overview of the literary critical field. See Terry Eagleton's *Literary Theory: An Introduction* for a colourful condensation and critique of the roots and development of modern literary theory; cf. also Robert Detweiler, 'After the New Criticism'. See Moore's contextualization of Chatman in *Criticism*, pp. 43ff.

[5] So speculates Moore, *Criticism*, pp. 7–8. See David Rhoads, 'Narrative Criticism and the Gospel of Mark', for a survey of the resultant spate of literary work on Mark in the 1970s. Cf. Norman Petersen, 'Point of View in Mark's Narrative'; Robert Tannehill, 'The Disciples in Mark'; and 'Gospel of Mark and Narrative Christology'; Frank Kermode, *The Genesis of Secrecy*.

[6] See also Paul Achtemeier, *Mark*; Tannehill, *The Narrative Unity of Luke–Acts* I; Kingsbury, *Story*; Staley, *Kiss*; Howell, *Story*. R. M. Frye, 'A Literary Perspective for the Criticism of the Gospels', and Norman Perrin, 'The Evangelist as Author', also proved influential.

Narrative structure: rhetoric and story

Within Chatman's model, narrative is a two-storey structure, divided between 'story' and 'discourse' (or 'rhetoric', as renamed by Rhoads and Michie, and used here). 'Story' is the *content*, or the *what* of narrative; 'rhetoric' is the *expression*, or the *way* of narrative. 'Story' consists in the content or chain of *events* (actions, happenings) and *existents* (characters, settings), hence the 'plot' as discussed above. 'Rhetoric' is the means or medium (*manifestation*) whereby the content is communicated, as well as the autonomous discourse elements (*structure*) which narratives share in any medium.[7]

What Chatman provides, then, is a model which integrates the form (rhetoric) and content (story) of a narrative into functionally interrelated parts of a whole.

Theorists of narrative communication commonly presume a teller (or sending party), a story and an audience (or receiving party).[8] Three personages are normally distinguished within the sending party: the *real author*, *implied author* and *narrator*, and three in the receiving party: the *real reader*, *implied reader* and *narratee* (see fig. 2.1).[9] Critics have long found it helpful to distinguish, for example, between the author and narrator in a text. These further delineations are essential for highlighting distinctive roles within narrative communication. In narrative the real author and reader only communicate with each other through their implied counterparts:

> only implied authors and audiences are immanent to the work, constructs of the narrative-transaction-as-text.[10]

In the process of text creation, authors generate a rhetorical version of themselves within the narrative. Through a series of decisions about plot, characterization, rhetorical devices, the role of the narrator and so on, the author creates a complex 'second self' which corresponds to the sum of his or her choices in constructing the narrative. The reader infers this image of the author in the process of reading and responding to the rhetoric of the text.

[7] See Chatman's full explanation; *Story*, pp. 20–6.
[8] See Robert Scholes and Robert Kellogg, *The Nature of Narrative*, p. 240.
[9] These have been extensively treated elsewhere, and will only be briefly outlined here; see the discussion and references in Wayne Booth, *The Rhetoric of Fiction*, pp. 70–6; Chatman, *Story*, pp. 28, 147–51; cf. Rhoads, 'Criticism', pp. 420–2.
[10] Chatman, *Story*, p. 31.

Narrative text

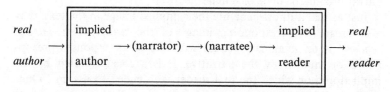

Figure 2.1. Rhetoric: a diagram of narrative's discourse[11]

In terms of the First Gospel, the author incorporated traditions, story elements and rhetorical nuances which probably do not fully represent or agree with his actual person, as a result of any number of secondary and external influences. He, as the *real author*, in this way added to the sum of rhetorical decisions which equals the *implied author*. The implied author or 'second self' of the evangelist, then, is discerned in Matthew by the reader as 'a selecting, structuring, and presiding intelligence'[12] which communicates not directly, but as the creating person who is implied by the totality of a given work when it is offered to the world.[13]

In most cases, and certainly in the gospel texts, the implied author invents a *narrator* who acts as the voice of the story. There is possible an entire hierarchy of 'degrees of narratorhood',[14] and, even though the narrator in Matthew is not a character in the narrative ('undramatized') and shares the implied author's point of view, it is important to distinguish between the two.[15] In the case of Matthew we relate as readers to the narrator, our guide, as a person, hence this study employs a personal pronoun. That the

[11] Adapted from Chatman, *Story*, p. 151. Moore, *Criticism*, p. 46: this 'diagram has subtly yet considerably shaped the way New Testament literary critics today conceive of the gospel text'.

[12] Moore, *Criticism*, p. 46. 'The author's generation of this textual second self is a profoundly rhetorical act (e.g., Luke 1:1–4).'

[13] Wayne Booth, *Critical Understanding*, p. 269. See Booth's fivefold typology of authors, pp. 268–70, and cf. *Fiction*, pp. 70–6, 151. Different narrative texts by the same author may have different implied authors, e.g., with Luke–Acts (see Tannehill, *Luke–Acts* II), the Johannine literature (see Staley, *Kiss*), or even the letters of Paul (see Norman Petersen, *Rediscovering Paul*).

[14] See the full discussion and further references in Chatman, *Story*, chap. 5.

[15] For more on the distinction between implied author and narrator, see Mieke Bal, 'The Laughing Mice, or: On Focalization'; and Staley, *Kiss*, pp. 27–30.

masculine is used here is only for convenience; the Matthean narrator could be male or female.[16]

Just as real authors generate their implied image in the text, they also create a corresponding image of the reader. This *implied reader*[17] is an imaginary reader with the ideal responses presupposed or implied by the narrative; it is a role projected by the implied author which the real reader is intended to assume. Once the real reader enters into this 'fictional contract', thereby becoming the implied reader, she or he appropriately interprets, anticipates and doubts, becomes amazed and angry, experiences suspense and sympathizes with characters in accordance with the ideal of this role.

Understanding what the real reader must do to read a text, and the degree to which the implied reader is textually immanent or transcendent, has been a major preoccupation within reader-response criticism. 'The reader's' rapid growth in popularity has managed to collect for him/her a plethora of labels, including Intended, Implied, Encoded, Composite, Informed, Authorial, Hypothetical, Historical, Model, Mock, Ideal and Flesh-and-Blood.[18] Chatman and Booth work with an implied reader who remains essentially internal to the text, a creation of the author.[19] Iser's reader, however, has one foot inside and the other outside the text, neither wholly ideal (wholly manipulated by the text) nor wholly actual (wholly free to interpret individually), but part creation of the text and part real individual with a viewpoint from outside the narrative world.[20]

Narrative-critical gospel studies have chosen, by and large, the 'reader-in-the-text', or intratextual reader, of Chatman.[21] It is important, however, not to absolutize either implied author or

---

[16] Cf. Janice Capel Anderson, 'Over and Over and Over Again', pp. 43–4; Culpepper, *Anatomy*, p. 17.

[17] See the term as first coined by Wolfgang Iser, *The Implied Reader*.

[18] Cf. Booth, *Fiction*, pp. 122–3, 274, 284, 302–4; Chatman, *Story*, pp. 27, 28, 41–2, 149–51. For overviews of reader-response criticism see Steven Mailloux, *Interpretive Conventions*, pp. 19–65; Susan Suleiman, 'Varieties of Audience-Oriented Criticism'; Jane Tompkins, 'Introduction to Reader-Response Criticism'. For its applications in NT criticism, see Fowler, 'Who'; Culpepper, *Anatomy*, pp. 205–27; E. V. McKnight, *The Bible and the Reader*; and *Postmodern Use of the Bible*; Moore, *Criticism*, pp. 71–107.

[19] See, e.g., Booth, *Fiction*, p. 138; *Understanding*, pp. 100–6; Chatman, *Story*, pp. 149–51.

[20] Wolfgang Iser, *Reader*, p. 284; *The Act of Reading*, pp. 27–38.

[21] See Moore's bibliography; *Criticism*, p. 72 n.3. Cf. Anderson, 'Over Again', pp. 34–6.

implied reader as completely encoded inhabitants of the text. The 'reading' process (aural, oral and visual) is much more dynamic, with implied personages to some degree both a textual structure and partly created by the structured act of reading. Bernard Lategan captures the balance:

> Author and reader stand in a 'chiastic' relationship to one another: the implied reader is a construct of the real author, and the implied author is a construct of the real reader. The first is necessary to prepare the expected response to the text, the latter is a textguided image in order to get a grip on this intended response.[22]

The third personage of the receiving party, the *narratee*, when present in the text is the narrator's counterpart as the one to whom he addresses his remarks.[23] In Luke–Acts, for example, the narrator's immediate addressee is identified as Theophilus. In Matthew, however, a clear distinction between narratee and implied reader is not essential.[24]

2.2. Narrator and 'point of view'

The narrator is one of the most important rhetorical elements in the discourse of the First Gospel, serving not just as the voice of the implied author, but as the story-teller, a powerful guiding presence for the reader of the text, filtering, selecting and evaluating every element of the narrative world, its characters and events.

> At one moment the narrator may speak in his or her own voice (e.g., Matthew 1.22; Mark 13.14; Luke 1.1–4; John 2.21) to shape the reader's interpretation of the story; at another he or she may cede these explanatory functions to a reliable speaker within the story: an angel, Jesus, a heavenly voice, or even a Gentile soldier (Matthew 27.54 = Mark 15.34) or a demon (e.g., Mark 1.24; 3.11; 5.7). Or again he or she may nuance his or her phrasing so as to covertly stamp his or her own view of what is being told

---

[22] 'Reference', p. 73; contra Anderson's wholly encoded implied author. Cf. the comments of Howell, *Story*, pp. 163–4.
[23] See Chatman, *Story*, pp. 151–2, 253–62.
[24] See Kingsbury, *Story*, p. 38; Edwards, *Story*, p. 10; Anderson, 'Over Again', pp. 37–8; cf. Culpepper, *Anatomy*, pp. 205–27.

upon the telling (e.g., when the gospel narrator refers to Jesus as 'the Lord').[25]

'Point of view' for literary critics designates the fluid, variable relationship between tale, teller and audience, in the telling and receiving of the tale.

From the range of possible levels of narration and types of narrators Matthew evinces a narrator who is not a character in the story ('undramatized').[26] He speaks in the third person, as if an observer; is not temporally or spatially limited in telling the story ('omnipresent'), but is apparently present as an invisible observer at every scene. He is able to discuss the thoughts and feelings of the characters, and to offer explanatory asides and interpretations to the reader ('omniscient'). He displays a consistent ideological point of view, in agreement with the implied author, when narrating the story ('reliable').[27]

Despite the narrator's critical function, only recently have students of the First Gospel given the topic much space.[28] Although the categories provided by Booth, Uspensky, Chatman and Lanser are widely referred to by gospel critics, their application to Matthew's narrator receives extended commentary only in Anderson, Kingsbury, Weaver and Howell, and briefer reference by others.

Similar comments can be made about 'point of view', that rhetorical activity where an author attempts from within a social system of assumptions, beliefs and values to impose a story world upon a reader (or listener) by means of narration. Within Matthean interpretation Anderson's, Weaver's and Howell's analyses are the most comprehensive to date.[29] Chatman is careful to point out

---

25 Moore, *Criticism*, p. 26.

26 See fuller discussions of these options in Booth, *Fiction*, pp. 149–63; Chatman, *Story*, pp. 146–62; Boris Uspensky, *A Poetics of Composition*, pp. 8–100; Lanser, *The Narrative Act*, pp. 85–225; cf. also Culpepper, *Anatomy*, pp. 18–20; Moore, *Criticism*, pp. 25–6. Cf. the applications to Matthew by Dorothy Weaver, *Matthew's Missionary Discourse*, pp. 31–57; Howell, *Story*, pp. 161–203.

27 For Booth's term 'unreliable narrator' see Chatman, *Story*, pp. 148–9. For its relevance to Matthew, see Weaver, *Discourse*, pp. 31–41. Culpepper, *Anatomy*, p. 32, notes that 'reliability' here is a question of literary analysis, whereas the 'truth' and 'historical accuracy' of the narrative are the province of believers and historians, respectively.

28 For example, Davies and Allison (*Matthew 1–7*, pp. 72–96) include in twenty-five pages of detailed examination of 'Literary Characteristics' only one brief reference to the implied author. The narrator's role is not addressed. So too with David Bauer, *Structure*, even though he uses literary-critical categories.

29 Some of the best-known discussions of point of view include Booth, *Fiction*; Gerard Genette, *Narrative Discourse*, chaps. 4–5; Lanser, *Act*; Uspensky, *Poetics*.

both the importance of 'point of view' and the difficulty of defining and distinguishing it from the concept of narrator's voice.[30] In narrative texts the implied author, narrator and characters can have one or more kinds of point of view, with a literal, figurative or transferred sense.

In the case of Matthew these complications give rise to conflict when the narrator has a clearly different ideological point of view from, e.g., the Jewish leaders. An alignment of the points of view of the narrator and a character, e.g., Jesus, produces a sympathetic characterization. Matthew is no different from most other narratives: it is the narrator's intention that the reader assume his point of view. For Uspensky the most common failure to achieve this purpose is where the reader and author are culturally distant from one another, a highly relevant observation for modern readers of the biblical texts.[31]

There are five basic characters or character groups in Matthew: Jesus, the disciples, the crowds, an assortment of Gentiles and the Jewish leaders.[32] As an element of narrative characterization, corporate personality is utilized in Matthew to a notable degree – this in contrast to many other narrative forms.

Few individuals other than the protagonist are developed as characters with significance for the plot, and they more often function as representatives of a character group, e.g., Peter as the prototypical disciple; the Roman centurion (8.5–13) and Canaanite woman (15.21–8) as adding to the prototype of faith.[33] The narrator guides the implied reader's understanding through his own

For other adaptations within gospel studies see Petersen, 'Point of View'; Culpepper, *Anatomy*, pp. 13–50; Rhoads and Michie, *Mark as Story*, pp. 35–44; Moore, *Criticism*, pp. 25–40. Cf. A. G. Van Aarde, 'Plot as Mediated Through Point of View: Mt 22.1–14'.

[30] *Story*, pp. 151–8.   [31] *Poetics*, p. 125.

[32] Anderson ('Over Again', p. 93) and J. D. Kingsbury ('The Title "Son of David" in Matthew's Gospel', pp. 599–600) identify 'the supplicants' as another major character group, but the narrator treats them as either individual minor characters or another element of the needy crowds (cf., e.g., Matt. 8.1–2; 4.23; 9.2, 12, 20–1, 32–3, 35–6); so too Paul Minear, 'The Disciples and the Crowds in the Gospel of Matthew'. Minear is wrong, however, to include the Gentiles in the crowds; cf. also Stanton's similar tendency in his discussion of 4.25 ('Revisiting', pp. 14–16). For the narrator the identity of the Gentiles as a distinct character group is important for the crisis over who constitutes the people of God; cf. Anderson, p. 93 n.1.

[33] See Anderson, 'Over Again', pp. 97–8. See E. M. Forster's seminal discussion of the distinctions between 'round' and 'flat', and 'dynamic' and 'static' characters (*Aspects*, pp. 108–18) and between story and plot, and fable and *sujet* (p. 130); cf. Scholes and Kellogg, *Narrative*, pp. 204–6.

position in relation to these characters and by arranging and contrasting episodes of interaction of the four character groups with the protagonist, thus revealing the nature and ideological disposition of each. The position of the Matthean narrator *vis-à-vis* the characters becomes more visible when one delineates the different categories of point of view using the five 'planes' denominated by Boris Uspensky: the psychological, phraseological, spatial, temporal and ideological point of view.[34]

2.3. Psychological point of view: omniscient

The psychological plane is a rather complex aspect of point of view, encompassing just what sort of distance from or affinity to each event and character is maintained by the narrator.[35] Matthew's narrator shows the ability to penetrate the surface of his characters; in this respect he proceeds on the psychological plane as 'omniscient'.[36] He interprets, explains and reconstructs events after the fact; he narrates the emotions, motivations and sensory experiences of his characters; he provides glimpses inside their minds and thoughts.

All of these insights are critical to Matthew's presence motif. On the psychological plane the narrator is able to provide vital insight into the meaning of Jesus' presence and person, and to interpret interaction of the story's characters with the person and presence of Jesus. As an example of this ability, the Matthean narrator knows from 1.1 (cf. 1.17, 18) that Jesus is ὁ χριστός, even though in the story Joseph first learns of Jesus' messianic role at 1.21-3, and no character actually applies the title to Jesus until 16.16. And

---

[34] See Uspensky, *Poetics*; cf. Chatman, *Story*, pp. 215-20; Lanser, *Act*. Uspensky would protest any overly rigid application of his categories, given his insistence that their delimitation is somewhat arbitrary (see pp. 6-7). He discusses at length possible interrelations and combinations of various points of view in a text (pp. 101ff.).

See Anderson's application of these categories to Matthew ('Over Again', pp. 53-89), and Kingsbury's discussion (*Story*, pp. 33-7). Cf. Weaver, *Discourse*, pp. 41-57, and especially Howell's recent elaborations in *Story*, pp. 166-203. Cf. also Uspensky's categories in Petersen, 'Point of View'; Rhoads and Michie, *Mark*, pp. 35-44; Culpepper, *Anatomy*, pp. 20-34; also Petersen, *Paul*, esp. pp. 10-14.

[35] See a complete explanation in Uspensky, *Poetics*, pp. 81-97. Cf. Lanser, *Act*, pp. 202-14.

[36] See Anderson, 'Over Again', pp. 79-87; Howell, *Story*, p. 175. Kingsbury appears to confuse the theological and narratological use of the terms 'omniscience' and 'omnipresence', *Story*, p. 32; also Weaver, *Discourse*, pp. 34-5.

because of his psychological point of view, in 1.22–3 the narrator is able to summarize Jesus' messianic role with his identification as Emmanuel.

By making the implied reader privy to a character's inward thought or feeling the narrator is able to bring the implied reader quickly into his confidence and establish a positive 'personal' relationship – a mutually shared, privileged viewpoint which shapes the implied reader's response to and assessment of the characters.

Regarding the protagonist, Jesus, the narrator's psychological point of view is frequently aligned with his, evident in both 'simple' and 'complex' inside views of Jesus, and in the fact that his portrayal of Jesus is far more detailed than any other character or group. The narrator often provides the implied reader with a privileged inside view of Jesus' emotions and perceptions:

8.10	he marvelled [at the centurion's faith]
14.14	he saw a great throng; and he had compassion on them
26.37–44	he began to be sorrowful and troubled ... he prayed ...

(see also 3.16; 4.2; 9.36; 20.34; 21.18)

But the narrator also provides *complex* inside views of Jesus; in other words, *the narrator* shares *his* omniscient ability with Jesus. Jesus displays inside views of other characters in the story, he knows (γινώσκω, οἶδα, ὁράω) their thoughts or activities. Within Matthew only the narrator and Jesus display this ability.[37] For example:

9.4	Jesus, knowing [the scribes'] thoughts
12.15	Jesus, aware of [the Pharisees' plans], withdrew
16.8	But Jesus, knowing [the disciples' discussion] ...

(see also 9.2; 9.22; 12.25; 22.18; 26.10)

The disciples provide a major character group which the narrator most often treats as a single entity, so that his inside views apply to them as a whole. Most of their feelings are responses to Jesus himself.

14.26	the disciples ... were terrified
17.13	then the disciples understood

[37] One exception might be Pilate's inside perception of the Jewish leaders' envy in 27.18. Cf. also Matt. 3.13; 4.1; 14.31; 16.17; 17.25 for several implied cases of simple and complex insight. See further discussion in Anderson, 'Over Again', pp. 79–87; Kingsbury, *Story*, pp. 36–7; Van Aarde, 'God Met Ons', pp. 57–60.

17.23   and they were greatly distressed
28.17   but they doubted
            (see also 8.27; 12.1; 16.12; 19.25; 20.24; 21.20;
            26.8, 22; but cf. 12.1; 20.24; 26.8)

Peter in particular functions as the representative of the character
group of the disciples.

14.30   he was afraid, and beginning to sink ...
            (see also 17.6; 26.75)

The Jewish leaders are also treated *en masse* as regards their
paradigm of character traits. Seldom does the narrator worry about
precise religious and political differentiation between chief priests,
scribes, Pharisees and Sadducees, being concerned centrally with
their role as antagonists conjoined in hostility to Jesus.[38] Thus the
narrator's inside and surface views of them consistently reveal that
hostility.

2.3–4   [Herod] was troubled, and all Jerusalem ... the
               chief priests and scribes
16.1   And the Pharisees and Sadducees came ... to
               test him
21.46   they feared the multitudes
26.59–60   Now the chief priests and the whole council
               sought false testimony against Jesus, that they
               might put him to death
               (see also 7.29; 9.3; 12.10; 19.3; 21.15, 45;
               22.22, 34–5, 46)

Similarly, Jesus' and the Baptist's assessments of the Jewish leaders
are consistent and reinforce for the implied reader their alignment
with the narrator (e.g., 3.7–10; 12.39; 15.3, 14; 19.8; 23.2–36). In
terms of their acceptance or rejection on the narrator's evaluative
scale, the Jewish leaders and Jesus end up as polar opposites: the
former fail to do God's will; Jesus is fully obedient.

The narrator's inside observations of the third major character
group, οἱ ὄχλοι, reveal them as consistently more amenable to
persuasion, and impressed by Jesus' authority.

---

[38] Numerous commentators have noted the historical discontinuity here; see Sjef
van Tilborg, *The Jewish Leaders in Matthew*, pp. 1–7; Walker, *Heilsgeschichte*,
pp. 11–33. But this is a good example of the suspension of disbelief required of
readers entering their implied role in the Gospel. See Anderson, 'Over Again',
pp. 119–77, for an analysis of verbal repetition around the religious leaders'
characterization.

7.28–9   crowds were astonished at his teaching, for he taught them as one who had authority, and not as their scribes

12.23   And all the people were amazed, and said, 'Can this be the Son of David?'

21.46   they held him to be a prophet

       (see also 9.8, 33; 13.54, 57; 15.30–2; 22.33)

A number of the minor characters in the story are also subjected to the omniscient psychological point of view of the narrator. Each in some way contributes to the negative or positive set of characterization traits compiled progressively throughout the story for the implied reader. They include Joseph (1.19–20; 2.13–14, 22), Herod the Great (2.3, 16), Herod the tetrarch (14.5–6, 9), the magi (2.10, 12), the woman with the haemorrhage (9.20–1), the young man (19.22), Pilate (27.14, 18, 24), the centurion and others (27.54), the two Marys (28.8) and Jerusalem's people (2.3; 21.10).

The consequences are not surprising. The implied reader's attitudes to Jesus and the religious leaders are led in completely opposite directions through the narrator's inside views. On the psychological plane, then, the implied reader has an overwhelming advantage over characters in the story, e.g., knowing from Matthew 1 that Jesus is ὁ χριστός, Ἐμμανουήλ.

2.4. Spatial point of view: a centripetal Jesus, an omnipresent narrator

The *spatial* point of view is regarded in Uspensky's scheme as a different 'plane' of expression.[39] The narrator's spatial position in relation to the characters and events in Matthew is again most closely aligned with Jesus. This also has particular significance for the reader's understanding of Jesus' role as Emmanuel.

The narrator accompanies Jesus like a movie camera, hovering over almost every episode from the time of his baptism to his death, even when no other characters are present or aware of the episode (e.g., 4.1–11; 14.23; 26.39, 42, 44). That the narrator and Jesus do not remain aligned spatially in the infancy narratives and after Jesus' death provides a critical indicator of the literary frame of the narrative.[40] This spatial alignment with Jesus is broken at nu-

---

[39] *Poetics*, pp. 58–65.

[40] So Anderson, 'Over Again', pp. 77–9; cf. Uspensky, *Poetics*, pp. 137–51, for the creation of a text's frame through the shift between internal and external authorial positions.

merous minor points in the narrative,[41] and on three significant occasions (14.1–12; 26.69–75; 27.3–10). Each of these departures by the narrator, whether to observe another conversation or to narrate a sub-plot removed from the action of Jesus, serves to support his protagonist role.

This close spatial alignment, and the reactions of the story's characters to Jesus' presence, highlight the power of his person as Emmanuel:

> all movement in the story flows towards Jesus, as if there were a great centripetal force at work drawing all the other characters into his presence.[42]

The narrator's particular use of προσ- compounds and other verbs, including προσέρχομαι,[43] προσκυνέω,[44] προσφέρω[45] and ἀκολουθέω,[46] to highlight Jesus as the constant spatial focus is ample demonstration of this centripetal force of his persona in the narrative world. That Jesus is so dominantly at centre stage repeatedly highlights his Emmanuel nature.

The narrator's 'omnipresence' allows him to move easily between the independent activities of Joseph, the travelling magi and Herod.[47] At Jesus' baptism the narrator proves privy to the apparently private vision (εἶδεν) of the opened heavens and the descending dove (3.16–17). He is also present with Jesus in his solitary fasting, testing and dialogue with the Tempter, accompa-

---

[41]   Cf. 2.1–10, 12, 13, 16–18; 3.1–12; 8.33; 9.26, 31; 11.2; 12.14; 14.1–12; 21.6–7, 10–11, 25–6; 22.15; 26.3–5, 14–16, 58, 69–75; 27.3–10, 51–3, 57–8, 62–5; 28.1–8, 11–15; cf. 8.13b; 15.28b.

[42]   Weaver, *Discourse*, p. 46.

[43]   Of fifty-two occurrences, thirty-six portray movement towards Jesus (4.3, 11; 5.1; 8.2, 5, 19, 25; 9.14, 18, 20, 28; 13.10, 36; 14.15; 15.1, 12, 23, 30; 16.1; 17.14, 19; 18.1, 21; 19.3, 16; 20.20; 21.14, 23; 22.23; 24.1, 3; 26.7, 17, 49, 50; 28.9). Only twice is Jesus the subject of προσέρχομαι (17.6–7; 28.18). The word has cultic overtones in the LXX; is often used by Josephus of those approaching kings. Johannes Schneider, 'προσέρχομαι', *TDNT* II, p. 683: 'The circle of powers, men, groups and classes which came to Jesus with differing concerns is brought out with astonishing clarity.'

[44]   In 2.2, 8, 11; 8.2; 9.18; 14.33; 15.25; 20.20; 28.9 and 17, Jesus is the object of προσκυνέω.

[45]   Cf. 2.11; 4.24; 8.16; 9.2, 32; 12.22; 14.35; 19.13; 22.19.

[46]   Disciples following Jesus: 4.20, 22; 8.19, 22, 23; 9.9; 10.38; 16.24; 19.21, 27, 28; 26.58; 27.55. Crowds and supplicants following Jesus: 4.25; 8.1, 10; 9.27; 12.15; 14.13; 19.2; 20.29, 34; 21.9; cf. 9.19. Cf. J. D. Kingsbury, 'The Verb *akolouthein* ("to follow") as an Index to Matthew's View of His Community', for its theological significance within the Gospel.

[47]   See the term in Chatman, *Story*, pp. 212–13.

nying them from wilderness, to Temple top, to mountain peak (4.1–11).

For the sake of the narrative's progression the narrator is not only present when Jesus prays alone in the hills (14.23) and in Gethsemane (26.39–44); he is also with the disciples in the boat (14.24), and with Jesus before Caiaphas while observing Peter in the courtyard (26.57–75). He frequently observes the private plottings of the Jewish leaders against Jesus;[48] he is with Judas the betrayer in his private dealings;[49] he is often present where another character would be impossible or inappropriate.[50]

A close relationship between the psychological and spatial planes of point of view, then, becomes quite apparent, but the distinction must also be noted. Whereas the narrator's omniscience is measured, plausible and maintains the narrative's verisimilitude, the narrator's omnipresence stretches these bounds and does minimize the narrative's verisimilitude. But it also increases correspondingly the reader's reliance upon the narrator's authoritative, almost 'god-like' role, his supratextual nature as an immediate, non-stationary (though ideologically aligned) observer of Jesus.[51]

From a spatial point of view, Jesus remains the focus; the story's events move consistently towards him. Even as the narrator's spotlight follows him across the stage Jesus' Emmanuel nature is the centripetal force for the character groups throughout who move in and out of the reader's eyesight.

2.5. Temporal point of view: synchronic and retrospective

The narrator in Matthew tells the story from two temporal perspectives: (1) temporal contemporaneity with Jesus, i.e., he controls the pace of the narrative NOW of the story, and (2) retrospective past-tense narrative, i.e., he speaks consciously from the narrative NOW of his time, fully aware of the relationship between the time the narrating takes place and the time at which

---

[48] 12.14; 21.25; 22.15; 26.3; 27.1–2, 20, 63–6; 28.11–15.
[49] 26.14; 26.48; 27.3–5.
[50] 8.13; 11.2; 14.1, 28; 17.1–8; 19.3; 27.27–31.
[51] So Culpepper, *Anatomy*, pp. 26–7, regarding John's Gospel. John's narrator, however, occasionally slips into the first person plural (John 1.14, 16; 21.24; cf. 3.11). Employment of a 'god-like' omniscient narrator in scripture is less a threat to verisimilitude than in modern fiction; contra Meir Sternberg, *Expositional Modes and Temporal Ordering in Fiction*, p. 295.

the story events take place.[52] Again, this has significance for Matthew's Emmanuel motif, for the narrator uses synchronic and retrospective time to emphasize different aspects of Jesus' presence.

Within the story NOW the narrator proceeds in essentially chronological fashion, using the activities of Jesus to count time at a pace which varies from 'summary' (e.g., 1.1–17; 4.23) to 'real-time' dialogue (e.g., the five major discourses), coupled with narration of concrete detail (e.g., 3.4). Apart from temporal gaps (e.g., between 2.23 and 3.1), frequent brief narrative explanations, interpretive comments and OT citations, the narrator more explicitly disrupts the chronological sequence of the story at 14.3–12 and in 27.52–3. The narrator sometimes deliberately anticipates events for the implied reader prior to their happening (anterior narration), and at other times he narrates events as they occur (simultaneous narration). Most often the narrator's temporal stance is to recount events from the past (subsequent narration).

Temporal retrospectivity in Matthew is narration at story time which is informed by the evaluative perspective of post-story time. Here one of the narrator's first significant observations comes in his citation of the Emmanuel prophecy. In Matthew this second horizon, the temporal perspective of the implied author, particularly reveals itself in narrative and discourse statements directed to the implied reader:

24.15   'let the reader understand'
27.8   that field has been called the Field of Blood *to this day*
27.53   coming out of the tombs after his resurrection
28.15   this story has been spread among the Jews *to this day*

Here the narrator knows what the characters cannot know and connects the implied reader explicitly to his own time, looking back from a post-resurrection time future to that of the story world.

Where memory and OT scripture intertwine to provoke retrospective interpretation we have an important indicator of the implied author's approach to history. He is not interested in a

---

[52] See Chatman, *Story*, p. 63, for categories. Uspensky combines the spatial and temporal planes under a single heading on space and time, *Poetics*, pp. 57–80; on time see pp. 65ff. Luz and Lampe, 'Diskussionsüberblick', p. 424, and Luz, *Matthäus 1–7*, p. 58, discuss these two temporal horizons as an 'inclusive story'; Howell has adapted the term as the focus of *Matthew's Inclusive Story*.

merely descriptive chronicle of Jesus, for the real significance of Jesus comes through the vantage point of retrospective interpretation. OT scripture, particularly in the Matthean narrator's own formula citations, has a critical role in providing a properly interpreted story of Jesus through carefully chosen guideposts for the reader: 'All this took place to fulfil what the Lord had spoken by the prophet ... '[53] This temporally retrospective point of view thus provides for synthesis of Jesus' traditions, interpretation by means of scripture, a post-Easter awareness of his presence, and a general post-Easter appreciation of the glory of the risen Jesus which reflects back through the whole narrative, all the while maintaining the verisimilitude of the story's own temporality. Temporal coalescence also allows Jesus' exalted Emmanuel status to be made evident to the implied reader from Matthew 1. The double temporal perspective of the narrative is conducted from both Jesus' point of view and the narrator's.[54] In the statements above (Matt. 24.15; 27.8, 53; 28.15) the narrator is fully aware of the distinction between his time and the narrative time (although Matt. 10's dual horizons remain troublesome).[55]

However, temporal *synchronicity* is as important as retrospectivity for the narrator. At least eighty times the narrator's past tense shifts to the historical present[56] and briefly and vividly aligns the temporal positions of the narrator, characters and implied reader (λέγει, 46x, has Jesus as subject 43x; λέγουσιν, 14x, has subject speaking to Jesus 13x).[57] Over and again the implied reader

---

53 Cf. 1.22–3a; 2.5b-6, 15, 17–18, 23b; 3.3; 4.14–16; 8.17; 12.17–21; 13.14–15, 35; 21.4–5; 26.56; 27.9–10.

54 See Uspensky, *Poetics*, pp. 66–70, for multiple temporal positions.

55 The dual temporal perspectives in Matthew have often been explained historically and theologically; cf., e.g., the discussion in Bornkamm, *TIM*, p. 34; Ziesler, 'Presence (1)', pp. 59–60; Donald Carson, 'Christological Ambiguities in Matthew'. Eugene Lemcio, *The Past of Jesus in the Gospels*, pp. 49–73, builds his case too narrowly on terminological grounds.

   Frankemölle, *Jahwebund*, insists that linear time is collapsed in Matthew into the present of his own community. His historical focus is defined 'mit dem Schema atl Verheißung – ntl Erfüllung' (p. 377). Jesus has turned history into the verb πληροῦν: 'Dieses Wort bezeichnet in kürzester und prägnantester Weise die theologische Grundidee des Mt' (p. 388).

56 See J. C. Hawkins, *Horae Synopticae*, pp. 144–9; cf. Anderson's revision of Hawkins' list, 'Over Again', pp. 65, 71–3. Cf. Wolfgang Schenk, 'Das Präsens Historicum als makrosyntaktischen Gliederrungssignal im Matthäusevangelium', pp. 464–75.

57 Anderson ('Over Again', pp. 65–6) notes that Jesus and the narrator are the only ones in the Gospel to use the historical present, probably because only Jesus and the narrator ever narrate. She adds the possible exception of the Sadducees

is invited in this temporal shift to listen to and observe Jesus directly by aligning temporally with the characters in the story. Similarly the implied reader finds him-/herself situated contemporaneously with Jesus for the duration of his main discourses, where there are no narrative interruptions to reintroduce a past-tense perspective. When Jesus uses ἐγὼ δὲ λέγω ὑμῖν this contemporaneity is further augmented for the story audience.[58]

Finally, by means of direct speech and temporal references in the commissioning of 28.16–20, the story closes with the temporal and spatial convergence of the narrator, implied reader, Jesus and the eleven disciples: 'and look, I am with you always, to the end of the age'. Here the implied author seeks, by aligning all four parties on the planes of time and space, a final alignment on the ideological plane, so that the commission and promise of Jesus' presence ultimately translate into an intersection of the story world and the post-resurrection world of the implied reader.

The two temporal levels of Matthew's story become important then for the reader's understanding and experience of Jesus as Emmanuel. They allow for narrative reflection on the experience of Jesus' presence in both temporal positions – of Jesus in the story NOW and of Jesus in the present of the narrator and implied reader.

2.6.   Phraseological point of view

Points of view in a story are sifted and categorized by the explicit speech patterns of the narrator and characters. Such is the case with the narrator and Jesus in Matthew: the former by commentary, framing, phraseology and terminology, titles and interpretive quotations, and the latter by assessing and subordinating other characters' points of view within his own speech.

Matthean scholars have already made numerous helpful observations on christological titles. They have noted, for example, the consistency with which Judas, opponents and strangers use Διδάσκαλε and Ῥαββὶ when addressing Jesus, over against the consistent use of Κύριε by disciples and followers.[59] Much work remains to

---

narrating their story in 22.23–8; I would add the Baptist in 3.7–12. Cf. Howell, *Story*, pp. 169–75.

[58] See Matt. 5.18, 20, 22, 26, 28, 32, 34, 39, 44; 6.2, 5, 16, 25, 29; 8.10, 11 etc. See Weaver, *Discourse*, pp. 48–9.

[59] See Bornkamm, 'End-Expectation and Church in Matthew', pp. 41–2, for the initial observations; see Lemcio, *Past*, pp. 60–2, for some recent (though unconvincing) criticism.

be done, however, on the relation of speech patterns to ideological points of view in Matthew.[60]

The relative speech patterns of the narrator and characters give the most obvious and tangible evidence of their particular ideological alignment. Via these patterns Janice Capel Anderson sets out in 'Over Again' to demonstrate through an analysis of verbal repetition in Matthew the convergence of the phraseological and ideological.

In the case of the Matthean narrator, his frequent dependence upon formulaic phrases supports his ideological stance. The narrative is punctuated by his retrospective fulfilment formulas and citations, closing formulas for the five speeches,[61] summaries of Jesus' ministry,[62] and formulas signifying temporal breaks – 'from that time on' (4.17; 16.21; 22.46); 'from that day' (26.16); 'from that moment' (26.64); cf. 'then he began' (11.20). Added to these features, the narrator's patterns of OT interpretation also reveal his full alignment with the evaluative perspective of Jewish scripture – as the Word of God itself. This assumption is integral to his OT prophecy/NT fulfilment scheme as the paradigm for understanding the history of divine presence and salvation culminating in Jesus, and adds immensely to the reliability of the narrator's speech acts.[63]

One of the more obvious phraseological devices of the narrator, parallelism – verbal, syntactical and material – also undergirds most strongly his skilfulness as a story-teller.[64] Similarly, the narrator's ideological control of the text is apparent in his positive and negative characterizations. The vocabulary applied to Jesus' activity, for example, includes ἀφίημι + ἁμαρτία,[65] διδάσκω,[66] ἐλεέω,[67] ἐξουσία,[68] θεραπεύω,[69] ἰάομαι,[70] καθαρίζω,[71] κηρύσσω,[72] πληρόω,[73] σώζω,[74] whereas Jesus' opponents' activ-

---

[60] See Bruce Malina and Jerome Neyrey, *Calling Jesus Names*, pp. 35–8, for the force of positive and negative labelling.

[61] 7.28; 11.1; 13.53; 19.1; 26.1.   [62] 4.23; 9.35; cf. 11.1.

[63] Cf. L. Hartman, 'Scriptural Exegesis in the Gospel of St. Matthew and the Problem of Communication', p. 134; Kingsbury, *Story*, p. 35; Howell, *Story*, pp. 168–9.

[64] See the list in Weaver, *Discourse*, pp. 37–8; cf. Luz, *Matthew 1–7*, pp. 37–41; Davies and Allison, *Matthew 1–7*, pp. 88–96.

[65] 9.2, 5, 6.   [66] 4.23; 5.2; 7.29; 9.35; 11.1; 13.54; 21.23; 22.16; 26.55.

[67] 9.27; 15.22; 17.15; 20.30, 31.   [68] 7.29; 9.6, 8; 21.23–7; 28.18.

[69] 4.23, 24; 8.7, 16; 9.35; 12.15, 22; 14.14; 15.30; 17.18; 19.1; 21.14.

[70] 8.8, 13; 13.15; 15.28.   [71] 8.2, 3; cf. 11.5.   [72] 4.17, 23; 9.35; 11.1.

[73] 1.22; 2.15, 17, 23; 3.15; 4.14; 5.17; 8.17; 12.17; 13.35; 21.4; 26.54, 56.

[74] 1.21; 8.25; 9.21–2; 14.30; 18.11; 27.40, 42.

ities include ἀναιρέω,[75] ἀπόλλυμι,[76] ἐνθυμέομαι + πονηρός,[77] ζητέω,[78] θυμόομαι + λίαν,[79] πειράζω[80] and ταράσσω,[81] in each case directed against Jesus.

This phraseological control is also maintained throughout with OT formula citations, summaries and speech-closing formulas. Also included are the narrator's numerous translations, cultural notes, and personal and etymological labels (e.g., 1.1, 21, 23a; 3.3; 4.18; 10.2–4; 13.34, 58; 16.12; 17.13; 22.23; 24.15; 26.25, 48; 27.3, 8, 15–16, 33, 46; 28.15).[82] At some points the narrator's explanations seem to presume that the implied reader is not competent in the cultural and linguistic codes used (e.g., 1.21, 23; 22.23; 27.15, 33, 46), but in other places no explanation is given (e.g., 5.22; 6.24; 10.25; 27.6). A higher, rather than lower, degree of shared codes is probably assumed; especially if the explanations are seen instead as part of Matthew's rhetorical strategy of repetition and redundancy. At minimum, his dependence on the OT to persuade presupposes that the implied reader shares Matthew's profound respect for the texts as scripture.

2.7. Ideological point of view

Ideological point of view is most fundamental to text. Assessment of the psychological, spatial, temporal and phraseological expressions of the narrator's point of view points consistently to an underlying system of values and ideology by which he operates. If the surface compositional structure is readily traceable in these first four aspects of point of view, analysis of the ideological relies to a certain degree on 'intuitive understanding'.[83] Within any story, at the level of deep compositional structure we find a view of the world by which the implied author has shaped the composition. This may mean a single dominating point of view or multiple evaluative views. The implied author, the narrator and each of the characters are possible vehicles of an ideological point of view.

---

[75] 2.16.   [76] 2.13; 12.14; 27.20.   [77] 9.4.

[78] Cf. 2.20; 21.46; 26.16; 26.59.   [79] 2.16.

[80] 4.1, 3; 16.1; 19.3; 22.18, 35.   [81] 2.3.

[82] See Anderson, 'Over Again', pp. 45–7. See the various forms of commentary listed by Booth, *Fiction*, chap. 7; Chatman, *Story*, p. 228.

[83] Uspensky, *Poetics*, p. 8; see pp. 8–16. For the connection between text and ideology, see, e.g., Terry Eagleton, *Criticism and Ideology*, and *Theory*. For another perspective on whether ideology rests in the text or reader, see Adam, 'Matthew's Readers, Ideology, and Power'.

In Matthew the narrator's evaluation of the ideological conformity of his characters fits into three categories: (1) acceptance of
Jesus' mission and message (ideologically aligned), (2) rejection of
Jesus (ideologically opposed), and (3) wavering obedience to Jesus
(in ideological transition). In other words, he has only one standard
of judgement: full conformity and obedience to the will of God as
defined by alignment with (ἀκολουθέω) Jesus; 'doing the will of the
Father', 'thinking the things of God'.[84]

The narrator's assessments of all the characters according to his
dominant point of view thus have direct implications for their
social affiliations within the narrative world: those aligned ideologically with the narrator are 'inside' Jesus' select inner circle; those
seeking him a second circle; those opposed are 'outside'. Those who
prove to be ideologically aligned with the narrator are those who
experience the salvation of Jesus, are drawn to his Emmanuel
presence and will gather in his name with his empowerment among
them. Those who prove to be ideologically opposite to the narrator
are excoriated and judged by Jesus, e.g., in Matthew 23.

Within his ideological alignment with his protagonist, the narrator portrays Jesus as the authoritative and reliable representative
of God's presence and salvation.[85] Each of the character groups in
Matthew – Jewish leaders, disciples, crowds and Gentiles – is
assessed through its interaction with and response to Jesus. The
character group of the Jewish leaders stands implacably opposed to
Jesus as the antagonists in an ever-tightening spiral of conflict with
him. The disciples function as Jesus' inner circle of adherents whose
primary alignment is to him, but who vacillate along a variable
learning curve. The crowds are assessed positively for the most
part, but follow Jesus without full apprehension of him; the
narrator depicts them as subject to the authority of Jesus and
impressed by his teaching, but also malleable in the hands of the
Jewish leaders. The momentary evaluation of other characters, e.g.,
notable Gentiles, on the other hand, is often singularly positive.

---

[84] Cf. e.g. 3.8; 4.10; 5.17–20; 5.48; 6.24, 33; 7.21; 12.50; 15.3–9; 16.23; 26.39–44;
28.20. Kingsbury's (*Story*, p. 34) and Weaver's (*Discourse*, p. 87) stance does not
seem to allow for the occasional ambivalence so clearly part of the crowds,
disciples and Peter. Cf. Culpepper, *Anatomy*, p. 33.

[85] Cf. Petersen, 'Point of View', pp. 107–8; Anderson, 'Over Again', pp. 57–68;
Howell, *Story*, pp. 190–202. Anderson elaborates the various ways – character
reliability, favourable inside views, joint verbal repetition – in which Jesus'
viewpoint becomes identified with that of the narrator.

These different character groups in Matthew are juxtaposed by the narrator's contrasting arrangement of episodes, so that the implied reader can evaluate and compare various ideological viewpoints through their interaction with Jesus, and Jesus' with them.

3

READING MATTHEW'S STORY OF DIVINE PRESENCE

The adoption of the narrative-critical paradigm requires a change in reading strategy. For narrative critics, the centre of authority shifts from the author or text towards the reader, in recognition that the reader participates with the story-teller and tale in producing meaning from the narrative world. The following reading adheres to the sequential flow of Matthew's narrative, and focuses on plot elements like anticipation–fulfilment and acceptance–rejection. The limitations of this study have precluded the luxury of a sustained, moment-by-moment story of reading which incorporates the many details of the narrative. The agenda here is to highlight those significant features which illuminate Matthew's presence motif.

This study is concerned less with a reader-response analysis than with story and rhetoric. In so far as the reader's experience is integral to the construction of the story world and meaning, reference will be made to the implied reader's participation and responses. I am assuming that, in Iser's words, the implied reader

> incorporates both the prestructuring of the potential meaning by the text, and the reader's actualization of this potential through the reading process.[1]

Or, as Howell words it, the implied reader is 'both textual structure to be realized and structured act of realization'.[2] In other words, the implied reader as *textual structure* already inhabits the narrative text as the audience which 'embodies all the predispositions necessary for the literary work to exercise its effect'.[3] In this sense the implied reader hears the entire Gospel from first to last word, receives every textual strategy and rhetorical device and plays fully the role that Matthew first sought when he wrote the Gospel and thought of an audience. As realized textual structure, then, the

---

[1] *Reader*, p. xii.   [2] *Story*, p. 210.   [3] Iser, *Act*, pp. 33–4.

implied reader would appear definable and even somewhat 'ideal', but as *structured act* the implied reader does not simply perform the score automatically as encoded.

> The implied reader is also the stance readers take when they read, and the actions they perform in processing the textual structures.[4]

The narrative-critical gospel exercise undertaken here amounts in many ways to a second story of reading superimposed on the first story of Matthew's Gospel, or 'narrative commentary', according to Moore.[5] The focus has shifted from a traditional verse-by-verse analysis of propositional content, to an explication of the reader's journey through the primary narrative, by means of a commentator's second plotted narrative – almost a form of targumic rewriting. In fact, the implied reader here (as in most narrative-critical studies, I suspect) is not neutral – she/he inevitably includes me, the gospel critic wielding the pen, in a very real socio-historical setting. I intend to complicate further this targumic rewriting through additional dialogue with others in the footnotes.

The importance of the narrative framework

Before we engage Matthew's story *per se* it is worth reassessing the boundaries of Matthew's prologue from a narrative perspective. 'Few things are more essential to appreciating a story than understanding the manner in which the narrator begins.'[6] Matthew 1–2 sets the tone, priorities and orientation for the whole of the First Gospel. From the perspective of the implied reader entering the story, these important first perceptions provide an indelible education as to correct interpretive techniques and expectations of reading competence.

Not infrequently these opening chapters of the Gospel have been discussed in terms of their formal, traditional and historical discontinuity with the 'Markan' core of Matthew.[7] But Matthew 1–2 is indispensable for a proper reading of the gospel plot; the whole

---

[4]   Howell, *Story*, p. 211.   [5]   *Criticism*, p. 23.

[6]   Frank Matera, 'The Prologue as the Interpretive Key to Mark's Gospel', p. 3. See Sternberg, *Modes*, pp. 93–4, on this 'primacy-recency' effect. Cf. the remarks of J. M. Gibbs, 'Mark 1.1–15, Matthew 1.1–4.16, Luke 1.1–4.30, John 1.1–51: The Gospel Prologues and their Function'; O. J. F. Seitz, 'Gospel Prologues: A Common Pattern?'.

[7]   Cf. e.g. R. Brown, *The Birth of the Messiah*, pp. 26–30; Schweizer, *Matthew*,

cannot be understood apart from this opening story of Jesus' beginnings.

The boundaries of the prologue are a major element in the wider disagreement about the structure of Matthew. The arguments in favour of the sort of tripartite division of Matthew asserted by Kingsbury (1.1–4.16; 4.17–16.20; 16.21–28.20) have found recent support in the extended defence provided by one of his students, David Bauer. According to this theory the infancy, baptism and temptation episodes comprise a unified whole demarcated by the ἀπὸ τότε ἤρξατο of 4.17.[8]

Kingsbury builds on Krentz's 'The Extent of Matthew's Prologue' and has been adopted by others.[9] Against Kingsbury, et al., the thematic and literary unity of Matthew 1–2 *per se* must be asserted, especially the striking manner in which the narrator's shift in spatial, temporal and phraseological point of view demarcates Matthew 1–2 and 27.51–28.20 as a distinctive narrative frame for the story.

In the story Matthew 3.1–4.11 functions as the preparation for Jesus' public ministry,[10] so a more plausible view of the opening structure of Matthew treats Matthew 1–2 and 3.1–4.11 as two discrete, though interrelated, sections which lead into the compositional and literary unity of the Sermon in Matthew 5–7, introduced by the narrator's first summary notes on the Galilean mission in 4.12–25. Matthew 4.17 does signal a transition, but the narrative as a whole does not *suddenly pivot* here the way Kingsbury and Bauer claim. Matthew 4.12–22 altogether functions as the *transitional narrative* which places Jesus in Capernaum and initiates his Galilean mission, with the ἀπὸ τότε of 4.17 referring to the temporal events of 4.12: after Jesus heard of John's arrest he withdrew to Capernaum and there began to proclaim his message.[11]

Ultimately this aspect of Bauer's extended defence of his mentor's thesis fails to convince. Recently Luz has decided that Matthew 1.1–4.22 is the proper 'Präludium' to the Gospel, while

---

pp. 22–4; Luz, *Matthäus 1–7*, pp. 94–6; Davies and Allison, *Matthew 1–7*, pp. 149–283.

[8] See Kingsbury, *Structure*, pp. 1–39; David Bauer, *Structure*, pp. 73–84.

[9] See the list in David Bauer, *Structure*, p. 153 n. 37; cf. E. Lohmeyer, *Das Evangelium Matthäus*, pp. 1, 64, 264.

[10] So too R. Edwards, *Story*, pp. 15–18.

[11] Cf. Matera, 'Plot'; Frans Neirynck, "ΑΠΟ ΤΟΤΕ ᾽ΗΡΞΑΤΟ and the Structure of Matthew'; who argue similarly for 4.12–22 as the beginning of Jesus' public ministry.

Davies and Allison find 'Kingsbury's tripartite outline too precariously based' and want to emphasize the division between 2.23 and 3.1.[12] The tripartite Kingsbury scheme has yet to counter properly a number of serious criticisms.[13] Particularly vulnerable is the tripartite scheme's inability to incorporate acceptably the fivefold speech and formula pattern of the First Gospel, a weakness which Bauer admits.[14]

A number of features support Matthew 1–2 as the Gospel's opening narrative frame. The narration is from a viewpoint external to Jesus, without spatial alignment between Jesus and the narrator. Jesus never speaks. No character is introduced into the birth story until Jesus has been situated temporally and ideologically in 1.1–17. Prior to John's appearance and Jesus' baptism the narrator views Jesus from the external perspective of each subordinate character, establishing ideological alignments and antagonists. Thereafter the narrator shifts to an internal viewpoint aligned spatially with Jesus, which is maintained until his death, whereupon the narrator's viewpoint again becomes external (27.51). Matthew 1–2 and 27.51–28.20 thus form the Gospel's narrative frame, on the basis of the narrator's external–internal shift in viewpoint. The shift between Matthew 2 and 3 constitutes a shift from telling to showing; a shift from the narrator's own characterization of Jesus by means of a series of subordinate characters and episodes in Matthew 1–2 to Jesus' own self-characterization in his words and activities in Matthew 3ff.

3.1.   Matthew 1–2. Narrative introduction: Jesus' origins and mission

The narrator's first concern is to identify Jesus – 'Christ, son of David, son of Abraham' (1.1) – as connected with a people; Jesus both culminates and disrupts the long line of God's people Israel.

---

[12]   Luz, *Matthäus 1–7*, pp. 25, 85, 168–70; Davies and Allison, *Matthew 1–7*, pp. 61, 287. Cf. B. M. Nolan who treats Matthew 1–2 as a unity, but then refers to 1.1–4.17a as a unit; *The Royal Son of God*, pp. 98–103.

[13]   Neirynck, 'Le rédaction mathéenne et la structure du premier évangile', pp. 56–8; J. P. Meier, *The Vision of Matthew*, p. 56 n. 21; M. Meye Thompson, 'The Structure of Matthew', pp. 195–238; David Hill, 'The Figure of Jesus in Matthew's Gospel', pp. 42–4; and Davies and Allison, *Matthew 1–7*, pp. 61–2, 287, 386–7.

[14]   *Structure*, pp. 44–5, cf. pp. 129–34. See Dan O. Via's attempt to deal with the tripartite and fivefold patterns simultaneously, 'Structure, Christology and Ethics in Matthew'.

His genealogy is a 'perfect' and 'perfective' rhetorical score, almost a rhythmic anthem, which demonstrates for the implied reader that God has been active within the history of his people since its founding members. This line of God's people has been 'telic' in design, finding its end in ὁ Χριστός.

The narrator sweeps the implied reader from the foundations of God's people in their first patriarch Abraham to the Messiah's early childhood 3x14 generations later; he incorporates all of Israel's history. His choice of settings is no less expansive, covering much of ancient Israel's known world, including 'the East', Canaan, Egypt, Judea and Galilee. And he exhibits a consistent mythology within the standard two-level cosmology: God, who is no other than the transcendent YHWH of Israel (see ἄγγελος κυρίου, cf. 1.20, 24; 2.13, 19; 28.2), is continually active in that world on behalf of his people. They have a special relationship to this present and intrusive God who demonstrates an immanent, saving will on their behalf within their history.

God's past presence with his people

The significance of this identification of Jesus is not fully explained to the implied reader within the genealogy. Two other features, however, alert the implied reader to view the patriarchal listing as representing more than merely a male enterprise within ethnic Israel: (1) The genealogy's patrilineal pattern is interrupted by the inclusion of four female names,[15] an appropriate foreshadowing of the important role women will play in Jesus' inner circle. (2) The ἐγέννησεν sequence is broken at the end when Joseph is called τὸν ἄνδρα Μαρίας instead of Jesus' father, and the phrase Μαρίας, ἐξ ἧς ἐγεννήθη Ἰησοῦς introduces a tension with the narrator's sonship labels in 1.1. But the implied reader finds no explanation in the genealogy and can only anticipate it in what follows.

The narrator, however, has already made clear that the genealogy is not merely a means of tracing and legitimizing his protagonist's ancestry. The carefully ordered listing of the generations of Israel, the emphasis on David and Abraham, and the

---

[15] Commentators have pointed to these inclusions as having (1) soteriological, (2) ethnic or (3) paradoxical theological significance, foreshadowing Mary's role. See M. D. Johnson, *The Purpose of the Biblical Genealogies*; R. Brown, *Birth*, pp. 72–4, and Jane Schaberg, *The Illegitimacy of Jesus*, pp. 20–34, for discussion. See Janice Capel Anderson, 'Matthew: Gender and Reading', pp. 9–10, on the gender bias of Matt. 1–2.

specific references to the Babylonian exile (1.11, 12, 17) also constitute the narrator's assessment that YHWH has been actively present in every period of Israel's history; the divine blueprint even incorporated the era of the μετοικεσία. In language (βίβλος γενέσεως, 1.1) and style the genealogy can even evoke for the reader a parallel with the story of creation, and align God's presence in the beginning of heaven and earth with his presence in the new beginning with Jesus.[16] But while the genealogy contextualizes the Messiah Jesus within the continuum of YHWH's past involvement with his people, its broken pattern warns of a shift in the traditional order of divine presence in Israel.

God's immediate presence with his people

The narrator moves to the contemporary stage of his narrative world and introduces the characters within the events of Jesus' birth and infancy in Matthew 1.18–2.23. It is notable that *every character and event* of these episodes is in some way subject to the extraordinary presence of YHWH, including the minor characters: Mary, Joseph, the magi, Herod, the people of Jerusalem, and the chief priests and scribes. Divine presence has a direct and perceptible impact, through the media of the Holy Spirit, angelic voices, dreams, celestial messages and the voice of God through the prophets. The narrator resolves the tensions of the disrupted genealogy in 1.1–17 by means of a chain of divine interventions in 1.18–2.23 on behalf of the one who is called Χριστός: Jesus is mysteriously conceived through the Spirit; Joseph drops his plans for divorce and takes up paternal responsibility for Mary's child; the magi are guided to the site of the child and ultimately outwit Herod's schemes; and Joseph undertakes a series of divinely guided journeys whereby the infant Messiah's life is miraculously spared.

These heightened phenomena of God's presence in the now of the story are presented to the implied reader as a new era of divine immanence. This emphasis comes through the narrator's OT fulfilment citations, five of which are concentrated in Matthew 1–2 (1.22–3; 2.5–6, 15, 17–18, 23). With Jesus the age of prophecy has become the age of fulfilment. These citations repeatedly enhance for the implied reader the reliability of the narrator, for with each citation an explicit element of continuity and fulfilment between the

---

[16] See Crosby, *House*, pp. 82–5.

OT and Jesus is highlighted, the plan and presence of God is emphasized, and the word of God itself endorses the narrator's direct commentary. Through the sheer consistency of his verbal repetition the narrator's observations to the implied reader gain repeated confirmation.

The opening frame of the story, then, presents Jesus to the implied reader as YHWH's Messiah of both continuity and transformation, and the narrator introduces his person and mission against the backdrop of YHWH's active presence with his people past and present.

God's presence in the event of Jesus' birth

Through the emphatic use of Spirit language (ἐν γαστρὶ ἔχουσα ἐκ πνεύματος ἁγίου, 1.18; γεννηθὲν ἐκ πνεύματός ἐστιν ἁγίου, 1.20) the narrator represents the conception of Jesus as an important moment of divine immanence on behalf of YHWH's people. The narrator is little concerned with the details of conception and birth *per se*; for the narrator the origin of the Messiah Jesus is nothing less than a creative act of YHWH's Spirit.[17] For the implied reader Jesus' continuity with and disruption of his lineage find unexpected explanation: Joseph's obedience (1.24–5) assures Jesus' descent from Israel's great leaders and confirmed the narrator's sonship titles (1.1);[18] the extraordinary involvement of the Spirit confirmed the narrator's use of the messianic title (ὁ Χριστός, 1.1, 16, 17, 18) and explains the genealogical hitch.

YHWH's active presence thus surrounds and permeates the narrator's description of Jesus' origins and explains Mary's place in Jesus' genealogy, the culmination of Israel's past. The narrator's primary interest has been theocentric – the unequivocal establishment of YHWH as 'first cause' – from the beginning the God of Israel is active and sovereign in the life of his chosen Messiah.[19] Thus the narration of 1.18–25 is another full and immediate

---

[17] Commentators generally find no hint of the Spirit acting as Mary's male sexual partner; e.g., see Herman Waetjen, 'The Genealogy as the Key to the Gospel According to Matthew', pp. 220–5; R. Brown, *Birth*, pp. 124–5, 137; Anderson, 'Gender', p. 10.

[18] Cf. Krister Stendahl, 'Quis et Unde?', pp. 60–1; A. Schlatter, *Der Evangelist Matthäus*, p. 25; R. Brown, *Birth*, pp. 133–5.

[19] Regarding Schaberg's illegitimacy hypothesis, it is noteworthy that only when Jesus' illegitimacy is a problem in the reader's actual world does Matthew's story become a means of addressing the issue.

exercise of the narrator's omniscient point of view on the implied reader's behalf, and this inside information, confirmation of some of the narrator's previous claims, enhances his reliability for the implied reader.

God's presence in the person and mission of Jesus

The first OT fulfilment quotation in Matthew 1.22–3 interrupts the story as an obvious interjection by the narrator. He uses the prophecy to interpret for the implied reader the presence and purpose of YHWH in these events, not only through the prediction of Mary's virginal conception of the Messiah, but to presage Jesus' future recognition as Ἐμμανουήλ.[20] The birth of Jesus is presented as conspicuously continuous with the OT and with divine design, but more emphatically as an unprecedented instance of YHWH's agency for and among his people: fulfilment is now. Jesus is the turning-point of history in Matthew's story.[21] Within the sequence of events in Matthew 1–2 divine presence past and present is explained not as direct but as mediated encounters with the God of Israel. The narrator thus assumes a basic dialectic between divine immanence and transcendence; the constant counterpoint to this sequence of God's immediate, yet mediated, activities is the assumption of his otherness – nowhere does the implied reader find God directly accessible as a character in the plot. But the narrative build-up of Matthew 1.1–23 now asserts that something dramatic, undefined and portentous is happening with God's presence in the event of Jesus' birth.

For the implied reader the question of Jesus' origins in Matthew 1 remains more functional and relational than ontological in significance.[22] This the narrator asserts authoritatively through the voices of YHWH's angel (1.21) and prophetic voice (1.22–3). These parallel explanations of his name and mission are thus divinely given. As 'Jesus', 'he will save his people from their sins', and as 'Emmanuel', he will be seen as 'God with us'. *These are the narrator's programmatic statements* for Jesus; he is the new divinely

[20] Cf. R. Edwards, *Story*, p. 13.
[21] Whether that means a two- or three-stage *heilsgeschichtlich* scheme for Matthew is unclear at this point; see Howell's overview, *Story*, pp. 55–92.
[22] Some commentators are quick to employ later terminology here such as 'incarnation' and 'pre-existence'; cf. e.g. D. A. Carson, 'Christological Ambiguities in Matthew'; Gundry, *Matthew*, pp. 24–5. Note F. Dale Bruner's correlation of the present text and later issues of Christian interpretation, *Matthew* I, pp. 20–35.

ordained mediate agent between τὸν λαὸν αὐτοῦ and their God.
Hence the narrator asserts nothing less than that divine salvation
and presence are the focal point and *raison d'être* for Jesus' own
existence, and he puts his own reliability on the line by predicting
that in Jesus' person and role as rescuer and reconciler, the presence
of God will be evident with them.

But this means that Matthew's rhetorical strategy was never
simply to conceive of 'Jesus' as only a proper name, his favourite
term for his protagonist; it functions as *a christological identifier* in
each one of its 150 possible occurrences.[23] Each time it occurs, it
impels the reader to look for Jesus' key christological significance.
Each time 'Jesus' occurs, it therefore draws the reader back to the
link between Jesus and Emmanuel. Their respective explanations in
1.21–3 provide the reference points for the reader's content of
'Jesus'.

How is the implied reader to view the double naming and
explanation of the Messiah as Ἰησοῦς and Ἐμμανουήλ? Does
Matthew 1.21–3 go beyond claiming that Jesus represents *the hope
and sign* that YHWH is present with his people,[24] to *the identification* of Jesus as 'God with us' himself?[25] Again the answer: *in
relation to the implied reader*, at this point in his narrative the
narrator leaves that question open, in order to allow the characterization of 'Jesus' throughout the story to supply the answer.
Nothing less than the entire gospel story will be required to fill the
content of Jesus as saviour and Emmanuel as God with us.

The juxtaposition of the two names 'Jesus' and 'Emmanuel'
provides a close parallel:

1.21 τέξεται δὲ υἱὸν, καὶ καλέσεις   τὸ ὄνομα αὐτοῦ Ἰησοῦν
1.23 τέξεται   υἱὸν, καὶ καλέσουσιν τὸ ὄνομα αὐτοῦ Ἐμμανουήλ
1.25   καὶ ἐκάλεσεν   τὸ ὄνομα αὐτοῦ Ἰησοῦν

Both names are reliably uttered (by the angel and by scripture) and
both will be applied to the Messiah child in the future. In meaning
and significance they are thus presented as inextricably interdependent. The conflict in the bestowal of two different names is clarified
by the angel's καλέσεις of v.21 and the narrator's καλέσουσιν of
v.23. With the former verb YHWH's angel instructs Joseph to

[23] So Fred Burnett, 'The Undecidability of the Proper Name "Jesus" in Matthew'.
[24] See, e.g., Bonnard, *Matthieu*.
[25] See J. C. Fenton, 'Matthew and the Divinity of Jesus', p. 81; Carson, 'Matthew',
pp. 80–1.

name the child 'Jesus' in an act asserting his paternity and Jesus'
legitimate place in his genealogy; with the latter verb the narrator
announces that in fulfilment of the prophet's words a people will in
the future call Jesus 'Emmanuel', recognizing in his salvation that
'God is with us'.

In 1.24–5 the narrator indicates that Joseph carries out the
angel's instructions. 'Jesus' becomes the child's personal name and
role identification, and already the anticipated καλέσεις of v.21 is
fulfilled. The narrator's characterization of Joseph as δίκαιος (1.19)
is confirmed and extended in the first employment of the plot device
of acceptance–rejection. Joseph was on the brink of rejecting Mary
and the Messiah child; Joseph's acceptance thus provides the first
contribution to the implied author's paradigm of the true follower,
polar opposite to the Jerusalem rejection of Matthew 2. Elsewhere
in Matthew only Jesus is called δίκαιος (27.19).[26]

'Emmanuel' remains unbestowed, an attribution which the narrator asserts will in the future be applied publicly to Jesus. In
looking about for the subject of καλέσουσιν the implied reader
logically assumes τὸν λαὸν αὐτοῦ of 1.21, i.e., those whom Jesus
saves from their sins will perceive in him and with them the
presence of God, and ascribe to him the sense of '*Emmanuel* – God
with us'.[27] In this sense, then, Jesus *embodies* the divine mission to
save his people: 'For he *himself* will save his people from their sins'
(αὐτὸς γὰρ σώσει τὸν λαὸν αὐτοῦ ἀπὸ τῶν ἁμαρτιῶν αὐτῶν) –
Jesus himself, as the ultimately personal mode of YHWH's presence, is the means of his people's rescue.

We must be clear, then, that Matthew's narrator draws his
readers quickly to the heart of the matter. Matthew 1.21–3 is no
less than the christological pivot of the Gospel. In the presentation
and explanation of Jesus-saviour, Emmanuel – God with us, the
reader is given both the presiding image for interpreting the story
and the fundamental, unanswered question of his characterization
– how is this double naming to be fulfilled? Does Emmanuel signify
only God's active presence? Or is Jesus the same as God? Here is
Matthew's reading lens, his ideological cipher for the narrative.[28]

---

[26] Cf. Howell, *Story*, pp. 116–17.

[27] Frankemölle draws a further connection between the subject of καλέσουσιν and
πάντα τὰ ἔθνη in 28.19 (see *Jahwebund*, pp. 16–19) but for the implied reader this
is a connection which may arise even earlier in the story.

[28] This carefully encoded ambiguity, with the symmetry between 'Jesus', 'Emmanuel' and their explanations, allows Burnett to ascribe to the proper name Jesus
'a metatextual character' which 'will continue to be a stable point for the reader

The crises of sin, divine absence and the identity of God's people

The opening narrative frame of the story is made complete, however, only by the narrator's explanation of the world of crisis and conflict into which the implied reader plunges in Matthew 1–2. In the genealogy's broken patterns, the narrator has already alluded to the inadequacy of the normal royal blood line for the purposes of God. Following from the personal crisis of pregnancy which challenged Mary and Joseph in 1.18–25, the narrator introduces a crisis of much more fundamental proportions, a crisis of sin and divine absence among God's people, broached initially in the characterizations of the Messiah's mission and persona as 'Jesus' and 'Emmanuel' in 1.21 and 23. On the one hand, ὁ λαὸς αὐτοῦ are described in terms of αἱ ἁμαρτίαι αὐτῶν and thus their need for someone σώζειν them. Furthermore, the narrator's anticipation of their future recognition of this Ἐμμανουήλ Messiah as μεθ' ἡμῶν ὁ θεός implies the current lack of any such perception on their part; the crisis of sin has invoked a crisis of blindness to divine presence. Hence the implied reader is introduced in the opening narrative frame to a correspondence between salvation and divine presence on the one hand, and sin and divine absence on the other. This presence/absence correspondence will prove programmatic for the story.

The apprehension of this crisis among 'his people', and its incumbent correlation between sin and the departure of divine presence, is part of a strategic plot arrangement, in that it precedes the episodes of fierce conflict in Matthew 2 involving Herod, Jerusalem and the magi, the flight to Egypt and the massacre of the infants, and the return from Egypt. Here the narrator establishes two essential patterns which prove normative for the story: the pattern of proper response to Jesus (acceptance, worship and obedience to God, already initiated by Joseph, and now modelled by the magi), and the pattern of rejection, as characterized by Jesus' opponents. The magi are paradigmatic of acceptance of Jesus: they are responsive to the divine sign and YHWH's call, are reliable witnesses to the person of Jesus (2.2), and share the point of view of the narrator and of the angel (hence of God); they

(the primacy effect) so that *in each occurrence* of the name this semantic determination will impel the reader to determine its meaning'; 'Undecidability', p. 128.

persistently seek Jesus (2.1–2, 9); they rejoice when they find him (2.10), worship him (2.2, 11), and offer him their costly gifts (2.11).

Herod, the chief priests and scribes, and 'all of Jerusalem', however, are paradigmatic of rejection, and the reader is given the sense of collusion (πᾶσα Ἱεροσόλυμα μετ᾽ αὐτοῦ, 2.3), so that Herod's character functions representatively for all of them. Herod misinterprets Jesus' mission as king, and he feels threatened and deeply troubled (2.3); he deceives the magi and seeks to entrap Jesus (2.7–8) and ultimately to kill him (2.16). Equally powerful is the contrast between the magi as gentile outsiders, and Jerusalem and Herod, who represent for the narrator the core of Israel; this insider–outsider model the narrator stands on its head.[29] All three episodes in Matthew 2 thus initiate and exemplify the central conflict of the Gospel. Herod, the chief priests, scribes and all of Jerusalem run full face into the messianic fulfilment of prophecy which strikes at their very existence and inspires their anxious collaboration and Herod's tragic slaughter of the infants.[30]

In this way too, the die is cast in 2.3–18 in terms of the protagonist–antagonist characterization fundamental to the story. Jesus is contrasted to Herod and the Jewish leaders of Jerusalem in terms of his fulfilment of God's will: he is YHWH's chosen, divinely born Emmanuel Messiah, but they refuse him. They are the antitypes of the leaders God wants for his people. Their rejection only further highlights Jesus as the archetypal divine son Israel; he alone is worthy of the description ὁ υἱός μου (2.15), which is applied to him in direct contrast to the leaders in Jerusalem who so far prove completely unworthy to be sons of David and Abraham and the leaders of YHWH's people. The magi provoke a contrast between themselves and Herod and the Jewish leaders in terms of their response to the presence of God: the magi are exemplary seekers of the Emmanuel Messiah; the leaders reject YHWH's agent of presence and salvation.

But the narrator also introduces a further element of crisis (and profound irony) to the story. The anticipated condition of 'his

---

[29] Cf. D. Bauer, *Structure*, pp. 66, 82–3. Bauer attributes Herod's misunderstanding at least in part to his inability to appreciate Jesus' kingship in terms of his self-sacrifice and the cross. But this is not a legitimate expectation for a sequential reading; the implied reader is not told of any sacrificial element of Jesus' kingship until 20.28; 26.28; 27.37.

[30] Contra Shuler, *Genre*, p. 105, who sees no direct conflict in Matt. 1–9. On Herod's attempt to kill Jesus as an example of rejection cf., e.g., J. C. Fenton, *Saint Matthew*, p. 44; H. B. Green, *The Gospel According to Matthew*, pp. 56–7.

people' needing Jesus' Emmanuel agency for salvation from their sins (1.21–3) is certainly fulfilled in Matthew 2. But the thorough rejection by Herod, Jerusalem and its leaders in Matthew 2 provokes a more foundational question: if Jerusalem has already rejected Jesus, what then is his relationship to τὸν λαὸν αὐτοῦ of 1.21? Who are they? To this point in the narrative the implied reader has been led to assume that 'the people' of Jesus are the natural descendants of those listed in 1.1–17. Jesus, son of David and Abraham, has come to save his fellow descendants, the people of Israel, the children of Abraham and David, from their sins. Herod's response in Matthew 2, however, along with πᾶσα Ἰεροσό-λυμα and πάντες οἱ ἀρχιερεῖς καὶ γραμματεῖς τοῦ λαοῦ, casts some confusion on the issue. As Jesus' fellow descendants, the rulers and inhabitants of Jerusalem should have exemplified the people of God, Jesus' people. Their rejection of Jesus, and the magi's acceptance, already anticipates some sort of redefinition of τὸν λαὸν αὐτοῦ.

Many commentators attempt to establish in Matthew 1.21 a socio-historical reference for ὁ λαός which is static throughout the Gospel, referring either to ethnic Israel,[31] or to Matthew's new ἐκκλησία of Jews and Gentiles.[32] The fundamental narrative tension over this very question is thereby often missed. By the end of Matthew 2 the identity of ὁ λαός has become an open question needing a full reading of the story for its resolution. The answer is not provided until the key references at the end of the story (cf. 27.25; 28.16–20) and any retrojection of this answer dissolves prematurely one of the Gospel's central crises.[33]

Matthew 1–2 thus provides for the implied reader the dialectic by which the story is to be read. In Matthew 1 the implied reader meets the people of YHWH, past and present, and the Messiah whom God has chosen to resolve their crisis of sin. In Matthew 2 the implied reader meets the first respondents to Jesus. Those who lead 'his people', the ethnic insiders, reject him, and the outsiders seek and worship him. This first dialectic of presentation–response, with the contrast between acceptance and rejection, foreshadows the struggle within the story as a whole, the crisis of identity: *Who*

---

[31] E.g., Luz, *Matthäus 1–7*, p. 105.

[32] So most commentators, e.g., Davies and Allison, *Matthew 1–7*, p. 210.

[33] Similarly with the *heilsgeschichtlich* transformation of the term in Frankemölle's reading, *Jahwebund*, pp. 193, 218; also Trilling, *Israel*, p. 61, who sees Matt. 1.21 as the one exception to the rule that ὁ λαός nowhere in the NT relates to the Christian community.

*will constitute the people of God? Who will be saved and come to call
Jesus 'Emmanuel'?*[34] *How will the deadly antipathy between Jesus
and his Jerusalem opponents be resolved?*

These added crises contain bittersweet elements of irony. Those
whom the implied reader first believes Jesus has come to save
immediately deny their Messiah. Paradoxically, in order to find ὁ
τεχθεὶς βασιλεὺς τῶν Ἰουδαίων, the magi require help from the
scholars of scripture gathered by Herod, but these Jewish leaders,
in correctly reading the texts and guiding the magi to the Messiah-
king in Bethlehem, cannot understand them and refuse themselves
to worship the one to whom they point, the one who fulfils their
own scriptures.

The magi apparently perceive Jesus' kingship in relation to
Jerusalem, but Jerusalem's reaction ironically casts even their
perception into doubt, and Jesus' ultimate entry into the holy city
as the humble king (21.1–10) and final withdrawal (24.1) bear out
this irony. Furthermore, in Matthew 2 Jerusalem, the holy city of
David, its leaders and king provide the story's initial paradigm of
rejection, spurning the Son of David whom YHWH has provided
for their own salvation. Those who are guardians of the holy city
have barred from it and from 'his people' the one whom they
should be calling 'God with us'.

Only the reader has been told of the Messiah child's future
identification as Emmanuel; for the implied reader, then, it is the
true Israelite, the divinely chosen 'God-with-us' Messiah who is
driven from Jerusalem, the home of the Jewish leaders and the
keepers of the sacred traditions, and from Judah, to Egypt. Upon
his return from protective exile (2.19–23)[35] he is once again rejected
there and can only find a home in Galilee. Each step of the way he
requires YHWH's miraculous protection and intervention against
the very ones who should have sought his salvation and recognized
in him the divine agency of messianic presence. How much of this
initial conflict foreshadows and anticipates for the implied reader
Jesus' subsequent relativizing of Jerusalem's assumptions of divine
presence and sacred space? The parameters of the community in
Matthew 1.21–3 – a people in sin and without divine presence who
come to find salvation in YHWH's Emmanuel Messiah – already
exclude the leaders and king of the city of Jerusalem, the mountain

---

[34] R. Edwards, *Story*, p. 15, appears to overlook this wider role for Matt. 1–2.
[35] 2.19–21 may be an implicit citation of Exod. 4.19–20; for different perspectives
see Dale Allison, *The New Moses*, pp. 142–4; Luz, *Matthew* I, p. 144 n. 13.

of God's presence. These explanations of Jesus' person and mission, and his initial conflicts with Jerusalem, are provided as Gospel-wide characterizations and plot devices for the implied reader.

3.2. Matthew 3.1–4.11. The preparation for Jesus' mission

Matthew 1–2 and 3.1–4.11 are two discrete sections; the first constitutes the narrator's introductory frame to the Gospel, and the second concerns Jesus' adult preparation for active mission.[36] John the Baptist is an integral part of Jesus' preparation for mission, and he is also introduced as the fulfilment of prophetic anticipation (3.3). John's proclamation, his encounter with the Pharisees and Sadducees and his baptism of Jesus reinforce and develop further three central themes already introduced in Matthew 1–2.

(1) John reiterates in his proclamation the narrator's theme of a special advent of God's presence and Kingdom. For John, in 'the coming One' Israel will confront the final eschatological era. John explains his own call for repentance as the necessary preparation of the community for the coming rule and judgement of God (3.2, 10–12), which he associates with ὁ ἐρχόμενος, who ἰσχυρότερός μού ἐστιν (3.11). Here the plot device of anticipation (of 'the coming One') is answered already in 3.15: an internal prolepsis.[37] The extent to which John recognizes Jesus as the Emmanuel Messiah is not made clear to the implied reader, but John's reaction to him (3.14) is consistent with his words about him (3.11–12). The narrator also substantiates John's proclamation with a citation from Isaiah 40.3, so that the implied reader quickly observes an ideological alignment of John with the narrator, and with Jesus and ἡ ὁδός κυρίου (3.3):

> the character of John is introduced in order to *establish the identity and character of Jesus* and to foreshadow the fate of Jesus (and secondarily of the disciples). Although important distinctions are made between John and Jesus (3:11, 14; 11:10–11, etc.), the overwhelming impression created is that of a parallel between John and Jesus.[38]

---

[36] Contra Kingsbury, *Structure*, p. 13, δὲ in 3.1 is disjunctive, not connective; the temporal ellipsis and thematic shift in the narrative is too significant a break. See Hill, 'Figure', p. 43; cf. Howell, *Story*, p. 120.

[37] See Howell, *Story*, p. 123.

[38] Anderson, 'Over Again', p. 103 (Anderson's emphasis); see pp. 237–42 for the Johannine sub-plot of Matthew.

(2) The confrontation between John and the Jewish leaders in 3.7–10 exhibits the same programmatic acceptance/rejection contrast already demonstrated in the responses of the magi and Jerusalem to Jesus. The initial negative characterization of Israel's political and religious leaders in Matthew 2 is now amplified in the case of the Pharisees and Sadducees: γεννήματα ἐχιδνῶν is John's indictment (3.7).[39] John scorns their attempt at repentance as lacking 'worthy' or 'good fruit' (3.8–10),[40] and denounces their dependence upon their status as Abraham's progeny (3.9).[41] John's scathing denunciation and the narrator's specific notation of his proximity to Jerusalem strengthen the undifferentiated ideological alignment of the representatives of the religio-political establishment in both Matthew 2 and 3, without regard for the various cultic, political and religious factions. With strong images of eschatological harvestry (3.12) the Baptist reinforces the acceptance–rejection theme and adds to the growing crisis of the identity of God's people. A clear distinction is introduced, however, between the religious leaders and the crowds, refining somewhat the 'all Jerusalem' of Matthew 2.3. John's success with the crowds in his ministry anticipates Jesus' and contributes to their parallel characterization.

(3) The theocentric focus elaborated so frequently by the narrator in Matthew 1–2 moves explicitly into the story world in the baptism of Jesus, both in the divine rationale which Jesus himself emphasizes (πληρῶσαι πᾶσαν δικαιοσύνην, 3.15) and in the heavenly utterance which provides the first open ratification within the story world of the narrator's citation (ἐκάλεσα τὸν υἱόν μου) in 2.15. Apart from the narrator the characters within the literary frame of Matthew 1–2 have made only limited additions to this theo-/christological portrait. That the Baptist supplies the story's first major assessment of Jesus from a (human) character also points to the shift from the literary frame of the text to its body proper.

The voice from heaven is a significant intrusion into the story (3.17).[42] In this divine utterance the narrator's portrait of his main character is given the heavenly seal of approval. In seeing the Spirit-dove alighting on himself, Jesus privately (εἶδεν, v.16), and

---

[39] Note Jesus' repetition of the epithet in 12.34 and 23.33, the latter with a question.
[40] A recurrent theme in the story, cf. 7.16–20; 12.33–5.   [41] Cf. 8.10–12.
[42] One of only two such instances where YHWH is given such direct representation; cf. Jesus' transfiguration, 17.5.

the implied reader narratively, also receive visual verification of the narrator's earlier Emmanuel–God-with-us citation.[43]

The temptation story of 4.1–11 brings to focus another dimension of the conflict central to the plot of Matthew, this time through a clash between the Tempter, ὁ διάβολος, and Jesus. The confrontation concerns Jesus' sonship as divinely declared at the baptism, cast through several Deuteronomic citations as a representative repetition of Israel's experience in the wilderness. The implied author appears to assume at least this degree of shared cultural codes on the part of the implied reader.[44] Jesus is both tested by God (again the action is part of the divine plan, 4.1) and tempted by the devil.[45] The encounter, with both parties quoting scripture, consists of the challenges of hunger, submissive obedience and idolatry, moving spatially from desert to Temple pinnacle to mountain-top. The narrator has already in 2.13–15 identified Jesus in Exodus language as God's true son Israel, and here the connection is reiterated and broadened, although without explicit parallels.[46]

This threefold testing and temptation, then, with its cosmic proportions, functions to confirm YHWH's public proclamation of 3.17, and corroborates the narrator's own assessment in 2.15: the

---

[43] The degree to which the incidents in 3.16–17 are evident to the crowds of 3.5–7, or to anyone else, is not clear. At this point the implied author seems more interested retrospectively in the christological significance of the event than the finer details of audience. This is important for *his* audiences: καὶ ἰδού! (vv. 16, 17). Contra Kingsbury, *Structure*, pp. 13–14, the narrator gives no clear indication that the temporal shift (τότε, v. 13) removes the crowds. While the singular form of εἶδεν (v. 16) implies Jesus alone as the recipient of the vision, the third-person form of the proclamation (οὗτός ἐστιν ὁ υἱός μου, v. 17) assumes an audience.

Opinions are thus divided on who sees and hears what; cf. France, *Matthew*, p. 95; Kingsbury, *Structure*, p. 14; Davies and Allison, *Matthew 1–7*, p. 330; W. C. Allen, *Matthew*, p. 29; Klostermann, *Matthäusevangelium*, p. 25; M.-J. Lagrange, *Evangile selon saint Matthieu*, pp. 55–6; W. F. Albright and C. S. Mann, *Matthew*, pp. 30–1; Hill, *Matthew*, pp. 96–7; Schweizer, *Matthew*, p. 56; H. C. Kee, 'Messiah and the People of God', p. 349; Luz, *Matthäus 1–7*, p. 156; Daniel Patte, *The Gospel According to Matthew*, p. 51.

[44] Cf. Tertullian, *De bapt.* 20; T. L. Donaldson, *Jesus on the Mountain*, p. 92; Kingsbury, *Story*, pp. 55–7; Davies and Allison, *Matthew 1–7*, pp. 352–3.

[45] Gundry, *Matthew*, p. 55; Davies and Allison, *Matthew 1–7*, p. 366.

[46] However, Luz, *Matthäus 1–7*, pp. 162–4, expresses some caution about the story's wider paraenetic interpretation. Gerhardsson, *The Testing of God's Son*, speculates that, based on rabbinic interpretation in *m.Ber.* 9.5 and *Sipre. Deut.* on 6.5, we have in Matt. 4.1–11 a haggadic exposition of the *Shema'* by a converted rabbi, with correspondences between 'your whole heart, soul and strength' and the three temptations. Cf. Eduard Schweizer, *Matthäus und seine Gemeinde*, p. 19.

adult Jesus, now by virtue of his conscious subordination to the
word (3.4), the will (3.7) and the worship and service (3.10) of
YHWH, is worthy of recognition as YHWH's true son Israel,
called out of Egypt.

3.3.   Matthew 4.12–18.35. The Galilean presence of Jesus

When John is arrested Jesus withdraws and takes up residence in
Capernaum (4.13). The narrator's fulfilment citation (vv. 14–16),
with its reference to Γαλιλαία τῶν ἐθνῶν as ὁ λαὸς in darkness on
whom a great light has dawned, once again highlights Jesus'
mission to save. It also re-emphasizes the question of the identity of
ὁ λαὸς αὐτοῦ (1.21), as well as the significance of Galilee as a
narrative setting. Through the information supplied by the narrator
in 2.22–3; 3.13 and 4.12–16, the implied reader is aware (1) that
Galilee has become Jesus' home in fulfilment of divine revelation in
dream and scripture; (2) that Galilee represents for Jesus a place of
safety from opponents; (3) that Galilee provides the current focus
for Jesus' presence and mission – there he represents a 'light' to
those in darkness; and (4) that Galilee has a special connection to
the Gentiles.

It is also narratively significant that almost every geographical
move of Jesus to this point in the story has resulted from conflict
with his opponents in Jerusalem. In this manner Galilee, as a focus
for Jesus' ministry, is the antithesis of Jerusalem, the focus of
opposition to the Messiah. The Emmanuel Messiah, even prior to
public ministry, was not welcome in Jerusalem or Judea, but only
in Egypt; and now he finds his abode in Γαλιλαία τῶν ἐθνῶν,
continuing the theme that the Messiah of God's presence has no
home in God's holy city.[47]

That 4.17 does not begin the second section of a tripartite
division of Matthew has been argued earlier; here it is sufficient to
note that 4.17 comes in the middle of and reiterates the story's
temporal (ἀπὸ τότε) and thematic transition to Jesus' Galilean
mission, and thus a transition from confusion about, towards
redefinition of, God's people.

The narrator's summary of Jesus' proclamation in 4.17 is iden-

[47] This *narrative* emphasis on and antithesis between Jerusalem and Galilee is
overlooked or underrated by W. D. Davies, *The Gospel and the Land*,
pp. 211–43; Sean Freyne, *Galilee, Jesus and the Gospels*, pp. 360–4; Davies and
Allison, *Matthew 1–7*, pp. 379–80.

tical to his summary of the Baptist's proclamation in 3.2: Μετα-
νοεῖτε, ἤγγικεν γὰρ ἡ βασιλεία τῶν οὐρανῶν.[48] The identical
proclamations re-emphasize the Jesus–John parallel,[49] and point to
the eschatological significance of Jesus' role as Emmanuel Messiah,
within the rhetorical theme of acceptance and rejection.[50] In a
further summary (4.23) the narrator characterizes Jesus' Galilean
ministry as a mission of teaching (διδάσκω), proclamation
(κηρύσσω) and healing (θεραπεύω).

From the beginning of his Galilean mission the definition of 'his
people' is top priority for Jesus. His presence and proclamation,
according to the narrator, have immediate and powerful effect. He
begins by calling four disciples (4.18–22), and with their swift
obedience the narrator characterizes them very positively. Building
on the initial follower prototypes provided by Joseph and the magi,
this continues also the clarification of 'his people', as those who
respond to Jesus' presence and answer the call to follow him. In
4.18–22 and 23–5 the narrator juxtaposes two distinct kinds of
adherents: observers (οἱ ὄχλοι) who follow after Jesus as a charismatic figure, and followers (οἱ μαθηταί), those who are on their
way to recognizing Jesus as the 'God-with-us' Messiah, and, in
renouncing everything, meet the narrator's and Jesus' criteria for
discipleship.[51] These constitute an outer and inner group around
Jesus. It is to the inner group that the Kingdom is explained in the
Sermon of Matthew 5–7.

There is nothing overtly retrospective about the characterization
of the crowds and disciples; the implied reader is not directed by the
narrative discourse to identify them with particular character
groups outside the narrative world.[52] The crowds (οἱ ὄχλοι) are

---

[48] These illustrative summaries are important expositional guideposts for the read-
er's understanding of the plot direction; so Howell, *Story*, pp. 130–1; cf.
Sternberg's discussion, *Modes*, pp. 24–30; Lohmeyer, *Matthäus*, p. 65; Gerd
Theissen, *Miracle Stories of the Early Christian Tradition*, p. 205.

[49] A high proportion of John's words in 3.1–12 are repeated later by Jesus: 3.2 =
4.17 (cf. 10.17); 3.7 = 12.34 = 23.33; 3.8, 10 = 7.16–20 = 12.33–5; 3.10b =
7.19; 3.10 = 13.42a, 50; 3.12 = 13.30. See Anderson's discussion of verbal
repetition in the rhetorical parallels between Jesus and John, 'Over Again',
pp. 98–108; also J. P. Meier's analysis, 'John the Baptist in Matthew's Gospel'.

[50] 'Wo das Evangelium Jesu vom Himmelreich verkündet wird (4,17), werden
menschen in radikalen Gehorsam gerufen' (Luz, *Matthäus 1–7*, p. 176).

[51] See the recurring call of Jesus to leave home, family and possessions: Matt. 8.21;
9.9; 10.35–9; 19.27. Contra Gundry (*Matthew*, p. 66), Matthew does not use
'"the crowds" and "his disciples" interchangeably'.

[52] Scholars have often made this equation with groups outside the narrative world,
e.g., the disciples are the evangelist's audience and the Jewish leaders of the story

68   *Matthew's Emmanuel*

presented in a basically positive, if ambivalent, light; their dilemma
is not their own doing. Matthew's crowds are essentially the Jewish
masses, as is clear from their location (Jerusalem), language ('Son
of David') or juxtaposition with the Jewish leaders and 'their'
synagogues.[53] According to the narrator's repeated inside view,
when Jesus

> saw the crowds, he had compassion (ἐσπλαγχνίσθη) for
> them, because they were harassed (ἐσκυλμένοι) and help-
> less (ἐρριμένοι), like sheep without a shepherd.
> (9.36; cf. 10.5–6; 14.14; 15.24, 32)

It is notable that when Jesus restricts both his mission and the
disciples' to Israel he characterizes the nation specifically as τὰ
πρόβατα τὰ ἀπολωλότα οἴκου Ἰσραήλ (10.6; 15.24). The phrase
both implicates the Jewish leaders as failed guides, in line with
Jesus' specific accusations of the same elsewhere (23.2–7, 13–15, 16,
24, 26), and again highlights a crisis undergirding the story – the
crowds are the Jewish masses in search of redefinition. The crowds
function then as the territory over which the conflict between Jesus
and the Jewish leaders rages. If they heed Jesus' call and proclamation, they can join the inner circle of disciples and thus constitute
the saved community of 'his people'. The Jewish leaders are
condemned as implacably opposed to Jesus' proclamation and
presence, but the crowds are open and receptive, often amazed at

are his contemporary Jewish rivals. See, e.g., Paul Minear's variation on this
theme, *Matthew: The Teacher's Gospel*, pp. 10–12, cf. 'Disciples', pp. 28–44.
   But Howell has rightly cautioned against moving 'too easily or directly from
text to life-setting in the evangelist's community'. The Gospels are not 'allegories'
or 'cryptograms' directed to the evangelist's contemporaries (*Story*, p. 206). So
also Elizabeth Struthers Malbon, 'Disciples/Crowds/Whoever', p. 123, on Mark;
L. T. Johnson, 'On Finding the Lukan Community', p. 93, on Luke. J. A.
Baird's audience categories are not well supported in Matthew (*Audience
Criticism and the Historical Jesus*, pp. 32–53).
53 See, e.g., 7.29 where the reaction of οἱ ὄχλοι to Jesus' teaching refers to οἱ
γραμματεῖς αὐτῶν; cf. 9.33–6; 12.23; 14.5; 19.2; 20:29–31; 21.8–11; 22.33; 23.1;
26.47, 55. This does not mean that 'the crowds' in Matthew are exclusively
Jewish, but essentially so. Stanton ('Revisiting', pp. 14–16) builds too large a case
in favour of Matthew's crowds including Gentiles, against Anthony
Saldarini's sharper distinction between the Jewish leaders and the crowds who
represent the Jewish communities of Matthew's day (*Matthew's Christian-Jewish
Community*, pp. 38–40). Granted that Matthew's crowds play a slightly more
ambivalent role in the story, and that Saldarini's historical equivalence to these
two groups over-simplifies, Stanton borders on short-changing the important
narrative tension between the (Jewish) crowds and religious leaders in Matthew.
The crowds in 4.25 are not paradigmatic.

Jesus (e.g. 9.8; 12.23; 15.31; 22.23), and persistently following him and treating him as a charismatic leader (e.g. 4.25; 8.1, 18; 11.7; 12.46; 15.30; 17.14; 19.2). They are not antithetic to, but essentially distinct from the disciples of Jesus, for they are subject to the persuasions of the Jewish leaders (26.47; 27.20) and their perceptions of Jesus are less complete (13.10–17; 14.5; 16.14; 21.11, 26, 46). A key to their narrative characterization is Jesus' own attitude: he has great compassion for the crowds while he denounces their leaders.[54]

The relationship of the Emmanuel Messiah to the two character groups of disciples and crowds is displayed in the narrator's treatment of them in 5.1–2 as two distinct concentric circles around Jesus. Having called his first four disciples, Jesus has established the nucleus of his new eschatological community. In 5.1 Jesus reacts to the ὄχλοι πολλοί generated by his teaching, proclamation and healing throughout Galilee by ascending the mountain for an ostensibly private session with his inner circle. The Sermon constitutes his messianic interpretation of the Torah, delivered as his guide to the radical character and requirements of membership in this inner gathering. The text of 5.1–2 is unambiguous: it is *his disciples* who come to him (προσῆλθαν) after he sat upon the mountain, and it is to them (ἐδίδασκεν αὐτούς) that he directs his teaching. The implied reader is left in no doubt that the principal addressee group of the Sermon is the inner circle, the disciples, even though the crowds appear ubiquitously present at the end, as potential members of the inner circle (cf. 7.28–9).[55]

The impact of the Sermon as a whole on the implied reader is at least sixfold. (1) It reinforces Jesus' theocentric origins and orientation – he has an extramundane perspective on the world, interpreting life and applying the Torah with firsthand divine authority. (2) It reinforces Jesus' fundamental alignment with 'the law and the prophets' and enhances the rhetorical anticipation–fulfilment motif.[56] (3) It presents a portrait of the praxis of δικαιοσύνη, one

---

[54] See further van Tilborg, *Jewish Leaders*, pp. 142–65; Donaldson, *Mountain*, pp. 114–15; Davies and Allison, *Matthew 1–7*, pp. 419–20.

[55] See R. Edwards, *Story*, p. 19. The reference in 7.28 to the crowds' amazement also facilitates the narrator's contrast of Jesus' supra-Mosaic authority with the lack among 'their scribes' (7.29). Luz, *Matthäus 1–7*, p. 197: 'Die Bergpredigt hat also zwei gleichsam konzentrische Hörerkreise, Jünger und Volk.'

[56] Cf. Donaldson, *Mountain*, p. 114: 'Matthew presents the Sermon not just as a teaching collection but as part of an event of eschatological fulfilment.' Cf. Robert Guelich, *The Sermon on the Mount*, pp. 27–33.

which exceeds that of the Pharisees and Sadducees (5.20) and is a vital code for this new eschatological community. The emphasis on 'doing' maintains the importance of the acceptance–rejection motif even in the Sermon.[57] (4) It stands in continuity with Jesus' primary message in 4.17 and with the basic thrust of John's message in 3.7–12, and builds further the implied reader's reception of Jesus' teaching and character as authoritative and reliable. (5) Within the Sermon, and in each of his discourses, Jesus shares with the narrator the critical role of mouthpiece for the implied author's point of view. (6) Furthermore, the mode of discourse aligns Jesus and narrator, and makes contemporaneous narrator, characters and implied reader, so that Jesus addresses the implied reader directly.

Scholarship has been and remains divided as to what degree the Sermon evokes an image of Jesus as the new Moses. In this respect the Sermon provides an excellent example of a polyvalent text – one which can evoke a multiplicity of valid responses by actual readers, given the individual contextual circumstances of each narrative transmission.[58] Dale Allison's *New Moses* is a richly interwoven tapestry drawn from the full wealth of all available Moses–Jesus typology. But some caution is required. There may even have been some among Matthew's communities who could see a similar level of Moses–Jesus interpenetration. But Allison's reading is just that – one reading along the possible spectrum. It is not just a question of Allison's fecund literary-historical imagination. His Jesus–Moses typologies represent reading within a certain culture, into which only some readers fit, ancient or modern. Strictly for the implied reader, then, Jesus' mode and content of discourse does not require Allison's portrayal of him as the new Moses.

Parallels between the Sermon and Sinai are certainly available, however, to readers informed by and familiar with the Jewish traditions. These parallels include Jesus as (the new) Moses, their sitting posture,[59] and the similar topography. The special preparations of the participants for the mountain-top encounter are notable, e.g., in Exodus the people are made ready through purification (MT: *qdš*; LXX: ἁγνίζω), washing (MT: *kbs*; LXX:

---

[57]   Cf. H. D. Betz, 'The Sermon on the Mount'.

[58]   See Susan Wittig, 'A Theory of Polyvalent Reading'.

[59]   The usual posture for studying and teaching the Torah; cf. Matt. 23.2, see Donaldson, *Mountain*, p. 112 n. 33.

πλύνω) and warnings against proximity to the mountain (Exod. 19.10–15), while in Matthew the disciples arrive at the mountain having repented (μετανοέω, 4.17), obeyed a summons to follow (4.19) and left behind their livelihoods (εὐθέως ἀφέντες, 4.20, 22).

Both Sinai and the Sermon are interested in defining God's people by means of authoritative, normative utterances from their divinely appointed leaders. The reader of Matthew is left with no doubt that Jesus' words must be heard and acted upon by his followers (7.24–7). Unlike Sinai, however, where divine presence is encountered in theophany and reflected in Moses, the new community in Matthew encounters a different agency of divine presence in God's chosen Son, the God-with-us Messiah who teaches with astounding personal, not the delegated or reflected, authority of Moses (7.28). In his most extensive references to ὁ νόμος Jesus deliberately transcends and subsumes within his character any possible Mosaic categories (cf. 5.17–20, 21–2, 27–8, 31–2, 33–4, 38–9, 43–4).

Having come down from the mountain (8.1), Jesus continues his Galilean mission with the performance of a series of mighty works and continued calls to obedience in Matthew 8–9,[60] so that the identical summaries in 4.23 and 9.35 (teaching, proclamation and healing) form an inclusio, or bracket around the chapters (5–9) which narrate these activities.[61] Those ministered to are often the socially marginalized in the Jewish world – lepers, demoniacs, Gentiles, women. He also calls a tax-collector to follow him, and the picture of 'his people' gains further definition, for in his amazement at the gentile centurion's faith he tells his followers:

> 'Truly I tell you, with no one in Israel have I found such faith. I tell you, many will come from east and west and sit at table with Abraham, Isaac, and Jacob in the kingdom of heaven, while the sons of the kingdom will be thrown into the outer darkness.'
>
> (8.10b–12a)

---

[60] For these miracle stories as enhanced personal encounters between Jesus and others see J. D. Kingsbury, 'Observations on the "Miracle Chapters" of Matthew 8–9', pp. 570–3. Cf. Held, *TIM*, p. 241, for these stories as formulaic accounts within a single basic structure.

[61] On this bracket cf. J. Schniewind, *Das Evangelium nach Matthäus*, p. 125; Schweizer, *Matthew*, p. 233; F. W. Beare, *The Gospel According to Matthew*, p. 237. Weaver, 'Discourse', p. 120, wants 9.35 to function as an introduction to 9.35–11.1 as well.

Matthew 8.23–7: divine presence in the storm

Jesus' Emmanuel authority and the character trait of 'little faith' among his followers come to the fore here. The narrator employs much of his normal language within the episode. The disciples 'follow' (ἀκολουθέω) Jesus into the boat, 'come' (προσέρχομαι) to him, and call him Κύριε. The narrator signals something special (καὶ ἰδού) and Jesus labels his disciples ὀλιγόπιστοι. But the event has paradigmatic overtones for the reader's perceptions of Jesus and the disciples in the story world, as well as in his/her own.[62] The disciples' cry for salvation (σῶσον, cf. 1.21) reaches to the heart of Jesus' primary role as his people's Messiah. The reader sees the power of Jesus' divine presence bring peace to chaos, almost in parallel to the Genesis creation. Yet Jesus is not entirely happy with the need for his intervention. His ὀλιγόπιστοι implies an inadequate perception of the storm and his presence by the disciples. This is reinforced by the narrator's reduction of them to ἄνθρωποι in 8.27. There their enquiry is explicitly christological: 'What sort of man is this?'[63]

In 9.35–11.1 Jesus takes another step towards the formation of 'his people' by formally calling the Twelve and sending them out on a mission modelled on his own proclamation and healing (but not teaching). The narrator's identification of Judas Iscariot as 'the one who betrayed him' (10.4) is a note to the implied reader about Jesus' coming rejection. As he begins his second discourse, Jesus' instructions in 10.5–42 prepare the disciples for acceptance and rejection of their own mission, building on his reference to persecution in 5.10–12. The objects of their ministry are 'the lost sheep of the house of Israel' (10.6) – again the marginalized come to the fore as candidates for 'his people'. Hence the focus of the disciples' mission is found in their foreshadowed solidarity with Jesus both in ministry and suffering.[64]

At 11.1 the implied reader is left with a tension between the disciples having been 'sent out' under Jesus' elaborate instructions and no narrative indication that they have gone. Another tension exists within Jesus' instructions, between their restriction of mission to Israel (10.5–6) and their anticipated mission to the Gentiles

---

[62]   Even apart from Bornkamm's seminal redactional reading over three decades ago, the story carries rich narrative symbolism for the fresh reader.

[63]   See the discussion of Matt. 14.22–33 below, pp. 77–8.

[64]   See Schuyler Brown, 'The Mission to Israel in Matthew's Central Section', p. 77.

(10.18–20). Either the narrator's story at this point lacks coherence, or the fulfilment of the sending-out lies in the future – the narrator's dominant use of anticipation supports the latter conclusion on the part of the implied reader. Given that their ministry is to parallel Jesus', it may be that the disciples require a more complete understanding of his model and its implications.[65]

> Whether or not the author intends for his reader to think that the journey took place immediately, took place later in Jesus' ministry, or could only occur after the resurrection and commission (Matthew 28.18–20) the expectation and visualization of a missionary tour has been created in the mind of the reader apart from any narration of it.[66]

Jesus has ostensibly met only with remarkable success to this point in his ministry. From a spatial point of view he has been established as the centripetal focus of the story, drawing all other characters 'towards' him. But the motif of conflict and rejection which the narrator introduced in the infancy stories and the ministry of the Baptist, and which was alluded to in the Sermon; in preliminary skirmishes in Matthew 9 over forgiveness of sins, table fellowship and authority; in Judas' description and in the mission discourse; now in Matthew 11–12 swells to direct confrontation concerning interpretation of the Torah, and open repudiation of Jesus' persona and mission.[67] Having just warned the disciples of persecution (10.16–23), Jesus himself now meets the first opposition to his adult mission. In 11.16–19 he accuses 'this generation' of petulant childishness in its reactions to the Baptist and himself. Signalling a new phase in his own proclamation, in 11.20–4 he 'began to denounce' the cities where his ministry met with no repentance.

Like ἀπὸ τότε ἤρξατο in 4.17; 16.21, τότε ἤρξατο in 11.20 is also pregnant with meaning. In Matthew 11 the motif of rejection arises in earnest and in 11.20 Jesus, for the first time, takes on the role of judge and refiner, the one who baptizes ἐν πνεύματι ἁγίῳ καὶ πυρί (3.11). John the Baptist's expectations are first met here in the very context in which his doubts are expressed (11.2–6). Jesus has completed his first Galilean tour, called the Twelve and established

---

[65] Weaver, *Discourse*, pp. 127–8; see her overview of approaches to Matt. 10 on pp. 13–24.

[66] J. L. Magness, *Sense and Absence*, p. 67; cf. in Weaver, *Discourse*, p. 213.

[67] See Kingsbury, *Story*, pp. 118–22.

the core identity of his people, and now begins the public separation of his new people.[68]

The Sabbath controversies and the demand for a sign in Matthew 12 evoke open and public opposition from the Jewish leaders, while the apparent alienation of even his family members (ἔξω ἐστήκασιν, 12.47; cf. 10.21) from his true mission brings Jesus to a declaration about true kin. This requires the implied reader, in light of 10.21 and the knowledge of Jesus' relationship to God as Father, to redefine the identity of even parents and siblings in light of 'his people'.[69]

Matthew 11–12 is thus a watershed in the Galilean mission, and in the First Gospel.[70] The central conflict of the Gospel, between Jesus and the Jewish leaders, has finally blown into full and public antagonism within the narrative world itself.[71] In 11.20 Jesus begins openly to acknowledge and decry this opposition. The corollary of declared political or religious opposition, of course, is more carefully defined political and religious boundaries, and by means of Jesus' declarations the narrator has further reinforced the contrast between the disciples and the opponents of Jesus. Matthew 1.21–3 again comes to mind. The Emmanuel Messiah has undertaken his commission 'to save his people from their sins', and his proclamation and presence have initiated a process of polarization within

---

[68] See Robert Tannehill, *The Sword of His Mouth*, pp. 122–8, for the rhetorical provocation of the reader's imagination with this saying.

Kingsbury, Bauer, et al., claim that Matt. 4.17 and 16.21 provide Matthew's tripartite structure with its critical pivots. But the verbal similarities between 11.20 and the two 'formulas' of 4.17 and 16.21 are worth noting.

4.17   ἀπὸ   τότε ἤρξατο   ὁ Ἰησοῦς   κηρύσσειν καὶ λέγειν
11.20   τότε ἤρξατο   ...   ὀνειδίζειν τὰς πόλεις
16.21   ἀπὸ   τότε ἤρξατο   ὁ Ἰησοῦς   δεικνύειν τοῖς μαθηταῖς

If 4.17 and 16.21 are 'remarkable' because they are asyndetic (Bauer, *Structure*, p. 85), the same must be said of 11.20; it too is asyndetic, as are 78 other occurrences of τότε in Matthew. Although the construction ἀπὸ τότε is rare (Matt. 4.17; 16.21; 26.16; Luke 16.16), and τότε is extremely common in Matthew (89x; Mark: 6x; Luke: 14x; John: 10x; NT: 159x), τότε does more than designate new pericopes in Matthew; it is a strong plot device signalling both temporal and causal connectivity (contra Frankemölle, *Jahwebund*, p. 352. See Theissen, *Stories*, pp. 198–201; A. H. McNeile, 'Tote in St Matthew', pp. 127–8; Howell, *Story*, p. 112).

I am not asserting a structural significance for 11.20 on par with 4.17 and 16.21, but it is a turning-point in the story, and the bluntness of the tripartite structural thesis does need modification.

[69] See R. Edwards, *Story*, p. 46.

[70] Cf. Luz, *Matthäus 1–7*, pp. 19, 25, who identifies Matt. 11 as marking a structural transition for the Gospel.

[71] Cf. Bernard Lategan, 'Structural Relations in Matthew 11–12', pp. 115–29.

Israel between those who abandon everything to gather and follow
him, and those who reject his Kingdom proclamation, unable to
perceive his divine authority and calling.

Hence in 11.25–30 the implied reader meets a statement of
startling clarity, concerning the Father, the Son and the followers
of Jesus. In vv. 25–6 the implied reader overhears Jesus' direct
praise (ἐξομολογοῦμαι) of the Father (πάτερ, κύριε τοῦ οὐρανοῦ
καὶ τῆς γῆς), in v. 27 listens to a declaration of Jesus' self-
perception, and in vv. 28–30 hears his invitation: μάθετε ἀπ' ἐμοῦ.
'His people' are now given the further identifying mark of νήπιοι
(v. 25) and of οἱ κοπιῶντες καὶ πεφορτισμένοι who respond to his
offer of ἀνάπαυσις (v. 28). Jesus declares himself to be the sole
arbiter in this process of the gathering of God's people, and to be
alone in his complete interdependence with his Father (v. 27).

These self-claims are theocentric in nature – everything takes
place in accord with the will of the Father (11.25–6; cf. 12.50). But
the Son himself chooses who stand in this inner circle (11.27), and
thus who constitute the people of God; the σοφοί and συνετοί
(religious leaders) have already been excluded. The narration has
built to this point in the story. The conflict and dual crisis presented
by the narrator in 1.21–3 and 2.1–23 have now grown in Matthew
11–12 to dominate the life and mission of the adult Jesus: in his
activity as the Emmanuel Messiah come to save his people, he has
been forced by rejection and opposition to define the insiders and
outsiders on new terms. Yet these new grounds are not without
continuity with the old; Jesus' theocentricity is a primary means by
which the narrator maintains the link between Israel and 'his
people'. The selection process for membership among God's people
is under divine control.[72] But 'his people' are now gaining significant christocentric definition as well (11.28–30). Thus Matthew
11.25–30, in a context of newly evoked open enmity, stands as both
a reaffirmation of YHWH's presence and as a further revelation of
Jesus' exclusive expression of his presence.

Matthew 12.6: a presence greater than the temple

In this context of Jesus' striking self-revelations, and the public
antagonism of the Jewish leaders, the reader cannot escape the
politico-religious dimensions of Jesus' further authoritative asser-

[72] R. Edwards, *Story*, p. 47.

tion in 12.6: 'I say to you, something greater than the Temple is here.'[73] In light of his declarations in 11:25–30, and his further claim as 'Lord of the Sabbath' in 12.8, and his direct personal comparisons in 12.41–2, the 'something greater' in 12.6 can be nothing less than Jesus himself.

Along with 11.25–30 this 12.6 amounts to one of Jesus' boldest christological self-declarations in Matthew thus far. In the midst of his opening skirmishes with the religious establishment, Jesus declares that his Emmanuel presence is greater than that of the Temple. The subsequent decision of the Pharisees in 12.14 to destroy Jesus implies their repudiation of his claim to divine presence, and makes their conflict with him irreversible. Jesus' declaration and their response carry overtones of deep significance for the entire Jerusalem and Temple establishment.[74]

Jesus' differentiation between those on the outside and those in the inner circle of his presence is subsequently drawn in continuously sharper terms by the narrator.[75] In the two halves of his third major discourse in Matthew 13, Jesus turns away from the crowds by means of incomprehensible parabolic address (13.1–33), while reserving his explanations for the inner circle of disciples (13.36–52), who *do* understand (v. 51).[76] The inner circle's privileged sight and hearing is emphasized even further in Jesus' beatitude of 13.16–17, where they exceed even what the prophets and righteous were allowed to know.

Somewhere within the story's temporal sequence between 11.2 and 14.1–2 John the Baptist has been beheaded by Herod the tetrarch. The narrator has reserved the story for this momentary flashback in order to explain Jesus' withdrawal (ἀναχωρέω, 14.13; cf. his identical reaction to John's arrest in 4.12)[77] from possible political confrontation. The implied reader is reminded of the alignment of Jesus and John, and is notified of the extension of political opposition from King Herod of the infancy narratives to

---

[73] Stanton, *Gospel*, p. 130, and others are probably right to see 12.6 as modelled on the Q logia in 12.41–2.

[74] Stanton's claim that 'There is no anti-temple polemic here' puzzles me (*Gospel*, p. 83). In the context of escalating public tension with the religious leaders, 12.6 must at least sound like a challenge to the Temple's current status, especially given the growing understanding inside and outside the narrative of Jesus as Emmanuel.

[75] See below, pp. 86–8, for discussion of 12.30.

[76] See Howell further for the careful merging of Jesus' and the narrator's points of view here through intermingled discourse and commentary and rapid shifts in audience; *Story*, pp. 193–8.

[77] Cf. also 14.5; 17.12; 21.26, 46. See Anderson, 'Over Again', pp. 106–7.

his successor in Galilee: the rejection from every level of Jewish leadership continues. The many parallels established between Jesus and John must be seen by the implied reader as foreshadowing a similar fate for Jesus. Ironically, Herod's mistaken identification of Jesus as John *redivivus* correctly anticipates Jesus' own resurrection.

Matthew 14.22–33: more divine presence in the storm

In the second storm account, with Jesus walking on the water (14.22–33), a number of features have paradigmatic significance in the narrator's retelling. Some of them evoke for the reader the similar passage in 8.23–7 (see above, p. 72). This repetition of that story setting not only indicates its importance but paves the way for the narrator's deeper development of the christological theme of Jesus' absence from and presence with the disciples. The narrator specifically notes the departure of the disciples even before Jesus dismisses the crowd. The narrator then links the report of Jesus' ascent alone onto the mountain to pray with the report of the disciples' struggles out on the lake. Hence a correlation between Jesus' separation and the disciples' inability to reach the other side – Jesus' physical absence precipitates a crisis amongst his innermost group of followers. The corollary, of course, is the notable correlation between Jesus' restored presence and the calming of the sea, the disciples' reaction of worship (προσκυνέω) and confession – Ἀληθῶς θεοῦ υἱὸς εἶ (14.33) – and the successful crossing to the other side (14.34).

Peter's own attempt to walk on the water has a similar impact on the implied reader. It is coupled with the inability of the disciples to recognize Jesus as he comes to them on the water. The narrator is continuing to build his composite picture of the disciples for the implied reader, now using terminological links between this story and the stilling of the storm in 8.23–7. The disciples' cry earlier – Κύριε, σῶσον (8.25) – is now echoed by Peter: Κύριε, σῶσόν με (14.30). Jesus described the disciples then as ὀλιγόπιστοι (8.26; cf. 6.30); he now addresses Peter: Ὀλιγόπιστε, εἰς τί ἐδίστασας; (14.31).

From this low point of fear and doubt the disciples move to a high point with their confession of Jesus as 'Son of God'. Jesus has thus far only been referred to five times in this way: by the narrator in his formula citation in 2.15 (τὸν υἱόν μου), by the heavenly voice at Jesus' baptism (ὁ υἱός μου, 3.17), twice by the devil in his

temptations (Εἰ υἱὸς εἶ τοῦ θεοῦ, 4.3, 6), and by the two Gadarene
demoniacs (υἱὲ τοῦ θεοῦ, 8.29). Jesus has referred to himself as 'the
Son' when speaking of his interdependence with the Father in
11.27, but here in 14.33 the confession 'Son of God' is for the first
time that of his followers. The disciples have answered their own
earlier question ('What sort of man is this?', 8.27) with their full
declaration. Thus the implied reader, who has been aware of this
identity since the accounts of Jesus' origins in Matthew 1–2 and the
baptismal voice in 3.17, has seen the absence, presence and
salvation of Jesus in the incident on the lake produce this advanced
recognition in the disciples, whose understanding of Jesus, if
flawed, continues to progress. It is not evident, however, that the
disciples are ready to take up their commission of Matthew 10.
They have yet to comprehend fully the nature of his mission and
presence, and their delegated authority from him.

The overwhelming response of the crowds in 14.35–6 is juxtaposed with the resumption of the Pharisees' and scribes' opposition
in 15.1–9. The narrator makes the pointed notation that these
Jewish leaders are ἀπὸ Ἱεροσολύμων (15.1) and picks up the
original motif of Jerusalem's rejection of the Emmanuel Messiah
first introduced in Matthew 2.

The disciples express apparent concern that the Jerusalem Pharisees have been offended by Jesus' words (15.12), the implication
being that they hold these Jewish leaders in some esteem. Jesus
replies with two parabolic images. The first refers to his weeds
parable in 13.24–30 – what the Father has not planted will be
uprooted – and indicates that these Jerusalem leaders stand outside
YHWH's plan. The second portrays the chaos of the blind leading
the blind, with the first of several harsh critiques of their ability as
guides of Israel (cf. 23.2–7, 13–15, 16, 24, 26). Between these two
images Jesus instructs the disciples: ἄφετε αὐτούς (15.14). The
effect of such direct admonition and images only drives further the
wedge between these increasingly disparate groups in Matthew.

The narrator carefully notes in 15.21 that Jesus 'went away from
there and withdrew' into the non-Jewish territory of Tyre and
Sidon. This movement is again in geographical opposition to
Jerusalem and has the appearance of a retreat from the Pharisees
and scribes who came from the holy city to the south. In this
context Jesus rebuffs the needs and then praises the faith of the
Canaanite woman, telling his disciples that he has been sent only to
'the lost sheep of the house of Israel', as in his restriction on their

mission in 10.5–6 (cf. 10.23). Jesus may be reminding the disciples that his retreat to gentile territory is only for strategic avoidance of a conflict, not part of his mission agenda.[78]

But something fundamental is also increasingly communicated to the implied reader, who has been reminded by the narrator since the first signs of crisis over the identity of 'his people' in Matthew 1–2, and at several points subsequently (especially with the centurion in 8.5–13), that Israelite ethnicity is less and less a sufficient criterion for the community of God's people; Jesus himself may be anticipating and justifying the extension of his mission to the Gentiles.[79] A tension thus exists with 10.5–6 and 15.24 where Jesus has given notice that he is still defining 'his people', despite all opposition and rejection, in the terms of the genealogy of Matthew 1, as the children of Abraham and David. His words of judgement and anger are directed at the *leaders* of his people; 'the lost sheep of the house of Israel', i.e., leaderless Israel, remain his mission focus.

Matthew 14.13–21/15.32–9: presence and empowerment

One possible answer to this tension is that in the two feeding stories (14.13–21; 15.32–9) the disciples remain unready to take up their Matthew 10 commission. This is evident in their attitude to the crowds ('Send them away!', 14.15; 15.23) in contrast to Jesus' compassion (14.14, 16; 15.32; cf. 9.36). More too is revealed of their continued dependence on his immediate physical presence for any sense of ability and authority. Their incredulity in each case at the task of feeding (14.17; 15.33) is only overcome by Jesus. Only when he blesses and breaks their meagre rations (14.17–19; 15.34–6) are they enabled to pass out the food to everyone's satisfaction (14.19–20; 15.36–7). Their empowerment to distribute the food parallels Jesus' (he gave the loaves to the disciples, and they gave to the crowds) and depends fully on their proximity to Jesus' presence and on his direct agency, as with Peter in the intervening water-walking story. Thus far the disciples have acted only in the context of Jesus' ministry; they never address the crowds, only Jesus.

Matthew 16.5–12 is a positive step in the narrator's characterization of the disciples' development. The theme once again is the disciples' lack of comprehension, this time regarding Jesus' warning about the leaven of the Pharisees and Sadducees. Jesus again

[78] Cf. R. Edwards, *Story*, p. 56.
[79] See Anderson, 'Stories', p. 78; Donaldson, *Mountain*, pp. 132–5.

addresses them as ὀλιγόπιστοι (16.8) and by a series of questions returns to his warning about the religious leaders. The incident ends with the narrator's note to the implied reader: τότε συνῆκαν (16.12), a conclusion about the disciples which functions in three ways to advance substantially the implied reader's image of this inner group: (1) According to the narrator the disciples have progressed in their understanding and development. This is supported terminologically: 16.8 is the fourth and last time the disciples are addressed as ὀλιγόπιστοι (cf. 6.30; 8.26; 14.31). The disciples will suffer another setback in 17.14–21 and Jesus will attribute ὀλιγοπιστία to them (17.20), but he no longer characterizes them personally as οἱ ὀλιγόπιστοι). (2) The implied reader shares a deeper wariness of the Jewish leaders, convinced of their increasing perversity. (3) The implied reader and disciples are drawn through Jesus' questions inside the parabolic nature of his teaching and encouraged to look for its deeper meaning.

It is important that the question of the Son of man's identity which Jesus then poses to the disciples is thus raised in the context of their growing understanding. Having reported the various responses of those outside the inner circle, Peter speaks for the disciples: Σὺ εἶ ὁ χριστὸς ὁ υἱὸς τοῦ θεοῦ τοῦ ζῶντος (16.16). Twice now, in close conjunction, the disciples have recognized Jesus as Son of God (cf. 14.33), and in each case Peter seems to function as the character group's key spokesperson (cf. 14.26–8; 15.12–15; 16.13–16, 21–2; 18.21; 19.25–7). To this point, however, not one character in the narrative world of Matthew has recognized Jesus by the title ὁ χριστός; the title has only appeared in the narrator's own ascriptions in Matthew 1–2 and in the single narrative reference in 11.2, and occurs now for the first time in the mouth of a character.[80] This identification of both Jesus' messianic persona and his divine origins within the story world reinforces what the implied reader has known since 1.1, and underscores again the retrospective point of view employed by the narrator on the implied reader's behalf. As a new element in the disciples' confession it emphasizes for the implied reader a momentous step in their improving perception.

---

[80] 16.21 remains the only positive confession of Jesus as ὁ χριστός by a character within the story. It anticipates ironically the anti-confession of the high priest's question in 26.63. Otherwise it occurs as an anarthrous vocative – Χριστέ – on the lips of his mocking persecutors, and he is referred to by Pilate as τὸν λεγόμενον χριστόν (27.17, 22).

This confession invokes a closer alignment between the disciples in Matthew 16 and 'his people' in 1.21, the ones Jesus has come to save, who will call him 'Emmanuel'. Jesus' theocentric response to Peter's words (16.17–20) highlights this alignment when he blesses Peter (Μακάριος εἶ, 16.17; cf. 5.3–12; 11.6; 13.16) as the 'Rock'. The narrator already appends this label in 4.18, leaving it unexplained (and contra-indicated in 14.28–31) until 16.18. Jesus credits Peter's confession to a prophetic insight revealed by 'my Father who is in heaven', language directly expressive of the heavenly Father's revelation to babes so highly praised by Jesus in 11.25–6. In 16.18–19 the implied author uses Jesus as a mouthpiece to project a series of incidents beyond the temporal boundaries of the story: Jesus declares ταύτῃ ἡ πέτρα to be the foundation upon which he will build his ἐκκλησία, describing its construction in the cosmic language of the eschatological conflict into which his life and ministry have been thrust (cf. 4.1–11). He also promises to Peter the rabbinical authority and responsibility of binding and loosing, forbidding and permitting. He speaks with divine authority, reminiscent of his blessings and ἐγὼ δὲ λέγω declarations in the Sermon of Matthew 5–7, and evoking the Father–Son intimacy asserted in 11.25–30.

The images of 'building my ἐκκλησία', the 'keys', and 'binding and loosing' are new. It is no accident that they coincide with new exhibitions of growing cohesion and comprehension on the part of the disciples, and with Peter's confession of Jesus as ὁ χριστός, Son of God. The disciples are no longer called ὀλιγόπιστοι and the ἀσύνετοι, but because of Peter's confession are anticipated as the foundation of Jesus' own saved and confessing ἐκκλησία, with new authority and responsibilities in the forefront of the cosmic battle for the formation of this new community.

Peter's confession reinforces the dual 'Jesus–Emmanuel' designations of 1.21–3 and highlights the implied author's deliberate rhetorical redundancy in using this initial presentation to organize the implied reader's understanding of the story and protagonist. In confessing Jesus as ὁ χριστός and ὁ υἱὸς τοῦ θεοῦ, Peter is beginning to comprehend these key explanations of Jesus' messianic mission ('he will save his people from their sins') and persona ('God with us'). Peter is closer to seeing Jesus as the active and saving presence of God. This Christ/Son-of-God confession is so powerful and unprecedented that Jesus forbids them to tell anyone (16.20). A threshold has been crossed with this confession whereby Jesus now anticipates building τὸν λαόν αὐτοῦ (1.21) into μου ἡ ἐκκλησία (16.17). The disciples will at some point be transformed from his inner circle of followers into the nucleus of this community of Jesus. Crossing this threshold includes the recognition that current structures (i.e., the Jewish leaders and their synagogues) cannot contain his people – they need a new form of gathering, Jesus' ἐκκλησία.

That these events of 16.13–20 do form a critical juncture in the plot is further confirmed by the narrator's carefully composed transition phrase in 16.21. Its parallel, in 4.17 (cf. 11.20), stands within the transitional sequence of 4.12–22 which moved the implied reader from Jesus' preparation to his mission proper in Galilee. Here the narrator signals a shift in Jesus' training of his disciples, a new preparatory stage for the 'building' (οἰκοδομέω) of his 'community' (ἐκκλησία). The implied reader has known previously that Jesus' opponents are plotting his death (12.14), but there is some question as to whether the disciples have really understood (or been present at) Jesus' repeated reference to and explanation of the sign of Jonah (12.40; 16.4). The narrator now explains that 'from that time', i.e., after Peter's climactic confession and Jesus' announcement of his coming community in 16.13–20, Jesus began to describe explicitly to the disciples his coming suffering and death in Jerusalem at the hands of the Jewish leaders, and his resurrection.

This is the first in a series of passion–resurrection predictions (16.21; 17.22–3a; 20.18–19;[81] cf. 10.38; 12.40; 20.28) and passion predictions (17.12; 26.2; 26.45) which are delivered to the disciples in private, and are therefore known only by them, the narrator and the implied reader. These predictions heighten the ongoing 'suspense of anticipation' which compels the implied reader through the story, as each prediction repeats the previous and gradually reveals more details. The predictions are ideologically aligned with the narrator and often provide the occasion to teach the disciples the true path of humility and suffering. 'The disciples model the wrong responses and Jesus authoritatively indicates the proper ones.'[82]

---

[81] See the formal pattern identified between these three by W. G. Thompson, *Matthew's Advice to a Divided Community*, pp. 94–5. Cf. Anderson's criticisms, 'Over Again', pp. 227–9.

[82] Anderson, 'Over Again', p. 227. For a fuller commentary see pp. 215–37. Through repeated misunderstanding of the predictions by the disciples, the

Peter's rebuke (16.22) evidences the still limited perception of his confession in v. 16 (cf. 14.28), for he finds it impossible that the living God's own Messiah could be subjected to such maltreatment. Jesus' startling response (16.23) is not so much an indictment of Peter's character, as a further harsh notice of the cosmic arena in which the members of the ἐκκλησία will soon operate. Jesus' direct rebuke of Satan recalls his earlier resistance to testing (cf. 4.10) and begs the question of Peter's own inspiration: he spoke prophetically in 16.16, but here his utterance is anti-prophetic.

Similarly, on the mountain of transfiguration, Peter responds to the fearful, Mosaic transformation of Jesus' appearance by offering to build three booths. The narrator's report of God's voice leaves the implied reader in no doubt that Peter has again spoken presumptuously. God's own declaration of his Son here parallels his utterance at Jesus' baptism, but this time he adds the sharp rebuke: 'Listen to him!' (17.5), i.e., Peter does not listen.[83]

The significance of the transfiguration becomes clear during the descent from the mountain (17.9–13). In v. 9 Jesus 'commands' (ἐντέλλομαι)[84] them not to tell anyone about 'the vision' (τὸ ὅραμα) until the Son of man has been raised from the dead. This vision comes, significantly, *after* the confession of 16.16 and after Jesus has identified his ἐκκλησία as those who will perceive by divine revelation God's salvation and divine presence in him, and be obedient to his mission. The transfiguration thus functions to reinforce, once again by heavenly vision and voice (cf. 3.16–17), for the disciples and the implied reader Jesus' stature as God's Emmanuel Messiah and Son, while Jesus' order in v. 9 makes clear that his transfiguration will make sense only in the post-resurrection context. It is important that Peter does not protest Jesus' reference to his death again; rather a discussion ensues about Elijah, which concludes with the narrator's comment: 'Then the disciples understood ...' (συνῆκαν, 17.13; cf. 16.12). Thus the characterization of the disciples continues to improve. That Jesus does not differentiate here between the political establishment (*Herod* actually killed John, 14.1–12) and the religious establishment (17.12) affirms the

---

implied reader is prepared for their ultimate abandonment of Jesus, Peter's betrayal and their restoration in Galilee.

[83] See further links between this event and the baptism; Benno Przybylski, 'The Role of Mt 3:13–4:11 in the Structure and Theology of the Gospel of Matthew', pp. 227–35; Donaldson, *Mountain*, p. 152.

[84] Matthew: 5x; elsewhere only for divine commands (4.6; 15.4; 19.7), and in the final commission for the commands of Jesus (28.20).

narrator's first blanket characterization of Jesus' opposition as both political and religious in Matthew 2.1–12.

Matthew 17.17: Jesus' frustrated presence

Jesus' frustration at the inability of the other nine disciples left on their own to heal the epileptic boy (17.14–21) points out another presence–absence dilemma similar to that in the feeding stories and with Peter's water-walking. Once again the implied reader is shown a notable correlation between the physical absence of Jesus and the incapacity of the disciples, and a correlation between his restored presence and the success of their efforts. Jesus' exasperation is with the very assumption of that correlation, and its misapprehension of the Emmanuel aspect of his messianic mission: 'How much longer must I be with you? [μεθ' ὑμῶν, cf. 1.23; 28.20] How much longer must I put up with you?' (17.17). That the disciples still depend on Jesus' *physical* intervention on their behalf inspires Jesus' character-ization of them as γενεὰ ἄπιστος καὶ διεστραμμένη (17.17),[85] and points out their ὀλιγοπιστία (17.20). Jesus again uses the mustard-seed phenomenon (cf. 13.31–2) to assert that with a little faith nothing will be impossible for the disciples, independent of Jesus' physical proximity and empowered by his Emmanuel presence.

This attempt by the disciples to heal the epileptic boy constitutes their first independent step of ministry, in line with their Matthew 10 commissioning. Their failure again points out their inability yet to undertake the larger mission task. Jesus' exasperated 'How much longer must I be with you?' underlines his dilemma as their leader and teacher: when would they learn the correlation between his mission, Emmanuel persona and their faith? When would they understand that his being μεθ' ὑμῶν with divine, messianic power is more truly empowering than their requirement for his physical intervention? Only when their faith grew to encompass this deeper sense of his messianic 'withness' would they be ready to carry out their mission, detached from Jesus' immediate physical activity. This episode of ὀλιγοπιστία seems only reinforced by their intense

---

[85] Previously Jesus condemned 'this generation', his contemporaries in general (11.16–19), and elsewhere the Jewish leaders seeking a sign ('perverse and evil generation': 12.38–45; 16.4; also 23.29–36; cf. 24.34). But here it is the disciples who are faithless, and Jesus is frustrated with how typical they are of their unbelieving contemporaries. Cf. France, *Matthew*, pp. 212–13, 266; contra Kingsbury, *Story*, p. 131.

distress at Jesus' repeated prediction of suffering, death and resurrection in 17.22–3; they cannot yet see its messianic significance.

Matthew 18: Jesus' presence with the gathered ἐκκλησία

The discourse on the community in 18.1–35 is introduced by the
disciples' question about their relative status in the 'Kingdom of
heaven', a key element in John's, Jesus' and the disciples' (future)
proclamations (cf. 3.2; 4.17; 10.7), and the phrase which recalls
Jesus' teaching in the Sermon, his parables of Matthew 13, and
most recently his statement about the keys in 16.19. In 18.2–4 he
rejects the apparent over-confidence of the disciples: their humble
social status, equal to that of a child, is required even for *entrance*
into the Kingdom of heaven. In 18.5–20 the emphasis turns to 'the
little ones' (οἱ μικροί, cf. 10.42; 18.6, 10, 14), those who have
already become childlike, humble disciples, and to the question of
their reception by others. The μικροί have a special status in the
world; to receive one of them is to receive Jesus himself.

Here the implied author uses Jesus' words to establish for the
implied reader a critical principle in understanding Jesus' presence
among his people. There is a special identification between the
μικροί and Jesus; to welcome them is to welcome Jesus, and this
intimate equivalence is based on nothing less than the Father's
constant favour and vigilance for them (18.10, 14). The woes of
18.7–9 are a condemnation for those who would trip up and
persecute these followers. The setting is expanded with cosmic,
eschatological terminology, and illustrated by the parable of the
lost sheep in 18.12–13. To treat the μικροί contemptuously is to
treat Jesus contemptuously, and God, who is in control, is vitally
interested in every one of the μικροί.

The issue raised in 18.15–20 is initially more pragmatic: how to
deal with an offence among the brothers. One must begin with
humility and settle the issue quietly. If the offender's refusals are
adamant the authority of the ἐκκλησία is invoked, first through the
witness of a few, then in excommunication by the whole ἐκκλησία.
The agreement of two or three in the community substantiates the
Father's will; this agreement validates the exercise of binding and
loosing, first promised to Peter in Matthew 16, and now the
authority and responsibility of the community. The emphasis on
the unity of heaven and earth, and the intimacy of Father and Son,
recalls the statements in 11.25–7, here with the μικροί being drawn

into the relationship. The narrator began with a child ἐν μέσῳ
αὐτῶν (18.2); now Jesus himself declares that he is ἐν μέσῳ αὐτῶν
whenever they gather in his name (18.20).

Jesus outlines in 18.20 a more advanced understanding of what it
means for him to be 'with' his disciples, advocating a presence
which moves beyond the limitations of physical proximity, and
thus beginning to answer their dilemma of impotence, fear and
little faith, raised previously in situations of his physical absence
(14.22–33; 17.14–21). This presence will require the physical proximity of only two or three of the μικροί, who have gathered in Jesus'
name. Such a gathering is not part of the plotted story, but is
anticipated as a regular occurrence outside of story time.

Συνάγω has already been frequently employed by the narrator
for the assembly or gathering of people, with the purposes of these
assemblies often strongly polarized in line with the narrator's point
of view (see 2.4; 3.12; 12.30; 13.2, 30; and see further in the story:
22.10, 34, 41; 25.32, 35, 38, 43; 26.3, 57; 27.17, 27, 62; 28.12).
Whenever the various elements of the Jewish leadership 'gather
together' (συνάγω) in Matthew, the assembly (called by Herod, to
test Jesus, to plot against him) is sinister and opposes the will of
God and his Messiah (cf. 2.4; 22.34, 41; 26.3; 26.57; 27.17, 62;
28.12).

Added to this negative characterization by the narrator of their
acts of assembly is the negative characterization by both the
narrator and Jesus of their regular *place* of assembly, the συναγωγή. The συναγωγή in Matthew has already been identified for
the implied reader as a key (if contentious) arena for Jesus' teaching
and healing (4.23; 9.35; 12.9–14; 13.54), as a place of opposition
(12.9–14), as a stage for the religious exercises of the hypocrites
(6.2, 5; 23.6), and as a future arena for floggings (10.17; 23.34). The
implied reader never perceives the συναγωγή *per se* as merely a
neutral venue for assembly; six times συναγωγή is characterized in
third-party terms as the συναγωγὴ/αἱ αὐτῶν, i.e. as *someone else's*
gathering place (by the narrator: 4.23; 9.35; 12.9; 13.54; by Jesus:
10.17; 23.34 – ταῖς συναγωγαῖς ὑμῶν, in Jesus' direct attack). And
every other occurrence of συναγωγή depicts it as the locus of the
Jewish leadership's hypocrisy. In the end the implied reader, finding
the narrator reliable in every other area, begins to view *their/your
synagogues* with some suspicion, as belonging within the realm of
Jesus' opponents, and providing no venue or support for the
gathering of 'his people'. This becomes especially clear in Jesus'

words in 23.34 where the antecedent for συναγωγαῖς ὑμῶν is the
scribes and Pharisees, whom Jesus is fiercely challenging. 'Gathering', *per se*, is not the issue. The rhetorical distinction made is
between *their/your* gatherings or synagogues, and *our* gatherings
(which becomes known in Matthew as Jesus' ἐκκλησία).

Therefore, whenever Jesus or his disciples gather (συνάγω) it is in
favour of the Kingdom and aligns with the narrator's point of view
and the divine will (3.12; 12.30; 18.20; cf. 13.2; 25.35, 38, 43). This
marked polarity between the acts and places of assembly of Jesus
and the acts and places of assembly of the Jewish leaders is further
enhanced in a number of cases by use of συνάγω in the language of
eschatological judgement; here 'gathering' refers metaphorically to
the separation of the disciples and opponents (wheat and chaff,
wheat and weeds, good and bad fish) for eternal blessing or fire (cf.
3.12; 13.30, 47; 22.10; 25.32). Uttered in a context of hot polemical
debate with the religious establishment, after a conflict in the
synagogue with the Pharisees where the implied reader has learned
of their plot to destroy him (12.9–14), Jesus' saying in 12.30 is
paradigmatic in its expression of this polarity associated with the
activity of συνάγω in Matthew:

> ὁ μὴ ὢν μετ' ἐμοῦ κατ' ἐμοῦ ἐστιν, καὶ
> ὁ μὴ συνάγων μετ' ἐμοῦ σκορπίζει

In context this saying incorporates not just the antithesis of
'gathering for the Kingdom' versus 'scattering against it', but
includes a dual contrast between:

> gathering/being with (in the presence of) Jesus, and
> scattering/being with (in the presence of) Beelzebul

In 12.30 Jesus' restricted inner circle of followers gains careful
definition again by means of the critical principle of being 'with'
him (μετ' ἐμοῦ). The privilege of being 'with' Jesus continues to
gather significance. It means far more than being those most privy
to his physical person. The fact that his messianic mission and
persona as God's presence have been combined so clearly since
1.21–3 has evolved into a 'witness' for the disciples which requires
obedience to and solidarity with Jesus' mission to perform God's
will in suffering and death. Being 'with' him increasingly calls for
complete alignment with him, spatially and ideologically.

But this critical principle of 'withness' has gained its explicit
antithesis in 12.30, and has application to 18.20. 'To gather in

Jesus' name', for his sake, in 18.20 provokes for the implied reader not only a picture of a small assembly of disciples evoking the authoritative, God-with-us presence of Jesus, but it also raises the spectre of its antithesis – the Jewish religious establishment assembled *against* the authoritative presence of Jesus, namely a polarity of communities in Matthew's narrative world between μου ἡ ἐκκλησία[86] and αἱ συναγωγαὶ αὐτῶν. That the gathering in 18.20 is εἰς τὸ ἐμὸν ὄνομα[87] drives the wedge only further. The purpose, orientation and authority of this community are found in the name of Jesus; his persona of divine presence delimits and defines the parameters of its every act of assembly, and excludes those who would gather for a contrary purpose and under another authority.

Much within Matthew 18 is applicable within both the story and narrative NOW. The implied author is providing information at both levels, with the implied reader as the obvious recipient of the references to the extratextual ἐκκλησία. Its experiences and events remain unplotted and do not fit the picture painted of Jesus' ministry in Matthew's story world. Thus Jesus' promise in 18.19–20 is in historical terms anachronistic and the question of discipline in Matthew 18 presupposes a community life with parameters and shared experiences more defined than any within the story. This anticipated form of Jesus' presence – his post-resurrection proximity to the community – and this new orientation – in his name – will relativize the spatial and temporal restrictions on the assembly of 'his people' in his presence. Where is Jesus? – he will be 'there' (ἐκεῖ), wherever and whenever the μικροί gather in his name. That Jesus' presence in their midst will be no less efficacious than has been his physical proximity and intervention on behalf of the disciples is apparent from their authority via community agreement to bind and loose with heavenly sanction. With this declaration the implied reader can anticipate the means and possibility of personally experiencing and participating in this community marked by the presence of Jesus.

3.4.   Matthew 19.1–27.50. The Jerusalem presence of Jesus

In Matthew 19.1 the narrator closes the speech of Matthew 18 using his typical formula for marking the end of Jesus' major discourses. He also gives notice of Jesus' departure from Galilee

---

[86] Note the emphatic word order in 16.18.
[87] Note the emphasis provided by ἐμόν.

into Judea, a move first anticipated in 16.21 and now part of a persistent series of geographical signposts which mark the way to Jerusalem with mounting tension (16.21; 17.22, 24; 19.1; 20.17, 29; 21.1, 10, 12, 17, 18, 23; 24.1, 3). This move is not merely a change of location; Jesus is deliberately reversing his lifelong flight and returning to the land of his birth, to the scene of Herod's original bloody campaign against him, and to the source of his constant opposition from the Jewish leaders. He now enters the final phase of his story, the anticipated conflict which the implied reader knows will test utterly Jesus' and the narrator's claims about his mission and person as divinely ordained, and will prove or discredit entirely Jesus' vision for discipleship and for the ἐκκλησία gathered in his authoritative presence.

On the final approach to Jerusalem Jesus anticipates with greater specificity again, and for the final time, his suffering ahead (20.17–19) and finds another opportunity to emphasize the 'first last, last first' theme in answer to the request for privileged places in the Kingdom from the mother of James and John. This, and the ensuing indignation from the other ten, reveal the disciples' ongoing mixed characterization, and their incomplete comprehension regarding what is to come: the 'cup' which he will drink (20.22–3) and the service – 'to give his life as a ransom for many' (20.28) – which he will render, and its implications for their own mission and suffering. Outside Jericho the repeated cries of the blind men – 'Son of David!' (20.30–1) – and Jesus' reaction not only recall the narrator's initial ascription in 1.1 and the other healing situations when the title has been used (9.27; 12.23; 15.22) and when Jesus has been stirred by deep compassion (9.36; 14.14; 15.32; 20.34), but also remind the implied reader that Jesus is on his way to the holy city of David. The perception in the blind men's response stands in ironic contrast to the 'blindness' of the Jewish leaders.[88]

Jesus' arrival in Jerusalem on the back of an ass and a colt (21.1–22) is a sequence of deliberately staged symbolic actions. His is the approach of a 'humble king' (βασιλεύς ... πραΰς, 21.5) to Zion. His humble stature here recalls his earlier beatitude (5.5) and his self-description (11.29), and his humbly royal entry into this 'city of the great King' (5.35) now models for the disciples his stated requirement that they too attain the social status of children,

---

[88] The crowd's rebuke of the blind men (20.31) may be a subtle intimation of a shift toward their rejection of Jesus at his trial; so Howell, *Story*, p. 149.

or μικροί, to enter the Kingdom of heaven (18.1–14). Whether or not the donkey procurement (21.2–6) evidences Jesus' foreknowledge of the event or a natural occurrence,[89] the narrator uses it to reconfirm Jesus' alignment throughout the story with the divine plan in scripture. Jesus, son of 'David the king' (1.6), and labelled 'King of the Jews' by the magi (2.2), is clearly juxtaposed here with the only other two characters in the story called 'king': Herod (Matthew 2.1, 3, 9), and Herod the tetrarch who beheaded the Baptist (14.9).[90] The crowds' acclamation and the narrator's citation corroborate for the first time the assertion of the magi. This triumphant entry into Jerusalem reverses his fearful flight to Egypt years ago, as an infant who was perceived as the usurper-king, away from the very city towards which he now rides as humble king. It also foreshadows Jerusalem's coming misperceptions of Jesus' political kingship in his trial and crucifixion, a style of kingship never claimed by Jesus (Matt. 27).

At his birth the whole city was 'troubled' (2.3). Now Jesus' presence shakes 'the whole city' (πᾶσα ἡ πόλις, 21.10; cf. 2.3). People identify him as 'the prophet Jesus from Nazareth of Galilee' (21.11). This apparent contradiction with the earlier 'Son of David' acclamation finds explanation in Jesus' prophetic activity and words in clearing out the Temple precincts. Both his introduction – γέγραπται – and citation from Jeremiah emphasize his subjection to the Father (21.12–13). The implied reader and all characters concerned are suddenly and violently aware of the importance to Jesus of the Temple's sanctity as the holy place of presence. Ὁ οἶκός μου οἶκος προσευχῆς κληθήσεται, he quotes. The symbolism of Jesus' 'cleansing' the Temple reaches as far back as Matthew 1, for if it was as Son of David, humble king, that he rightfully entered the royal city, it is as the 'God-with-us' Messiah that he now symbolically destroys the entire sacrificial worship system of the Temple (driving out sellers *and* buyers) and foreshadows his predictions of its demise and replacement (see 23.38; 24.2).[91] The Temple proper is no longer relevant in the coming

---

[89] See France, *Matthew*, pp. 297–8.
[90] Cf. βασιλεύς elsewhere in 2.2; 5.35; 10.18; 11.8; 17.25; 22.7, 11, 13; 25.34, 40; 27.11, 29, 37, 42.
[91] E. P. Sanders (*Jesus and Judaism*, p. 69), B. F. Meyer (*The Aims of Jesus*, pp. 170, 197), Lloyd Gaston (*No Stone on Another*, p. 86), France (*Matthew*, pp. 300–1) and others are correct to see Jesus' demonstration as charged with symbolism. What precisely Jesus' action symbolized is widely debated (see the prevalent views in Sanders, *Jesus*, pp. 61–76). A narrative approach to the text

eschatological Zion, whose adherents will now gather around him. Jesus visually stakes the claim he made earlier about Jerusalem's holy place: 'I tell you, something greater than the Temple is here' (12.6). His claim is both a prophetic challenge to Israel's cultic *status quo*, and an unmistakable provocation of the religious authorities to recognize his personal supersession of their authority and system.

Jesus responds to his opponents' challenges with a series of parables which highlight the Jewish leaders' history of rejection, both within and outside the temporal bounds of the plotted story, and his conclusions are emphatic: the tax-collectors and prostitutes, who *did* believe John the Baptist and repent, will get into the Kingdom before the religious leaders (21.31–2), from whom the Kingdom will be taken away and given to a nation producing its fruits (21.43). The implied reader is drawn back to the picture of the withered fig-tree (21.18–22); Jesus has now notified his antagonists that their fruitless condition spells not only their personal judgement, but the transfer of the Kingdom of God to another people (ἀρθήσεται ἀφ' ὑμῶν ἡ βασιλεία τοῦ θεοῦ καὶ δοθήσεται ἔθνει ...). The redefinition of 'his people'[92] – the building of his ἐκκλησία – excludes the Jewish leaders.

As the conflict deepens, Jesus confronts the 'chief priests and Pharisees' with the parable of the marriage feast (22.1–14) in which he addresses both the story and narrative NOW. The implied reader is bound to look outside the plotted story for correspondences to Jesus' difficult and powerful pictures of the murdered servants and son (21.35–9) and the burned city (22.7). This reiterated motif of replacement and judgement is not lost on the Pharisees, who angrily conspire to entangle Jesus (22.15).

Several more confrontations conclude with the narrator's summary in Matthew 22.46. Jesus has the final word, and his opponents are left speechless, their public humiliation heavily implicit in the narrator's statement that 'no one dared ask him anything anymore from that day' (ἀπ' ἐκείνης τῆς ἡμέρας). With this summary, then, the story reaches another transition, from the period of attempts by members of the religio-political establishment

helps to clarify that Jesus' action symbolizes a change of eras in Jerusalem worship, foreshadowing the Temple's demise, and the regathering of God's people in Jesus' presence.

[92] Here spoken of in terms of ἔθνος; cf. Graham Stanton, 'The Gospel of Matthew and Judaism', pp. 269–70; Trilling, *Israel*, p. 65; Howell, *Story*, p. 151; for various interpretations.

to challenge and defeat Jesus in the public forum, to the behind-the-scenes exercise of political power against him to destroy him.

Jesus launches a final attack against the scribes and Pharisees in the woes of Matthew 23, addressed to the disciples and crowds, still in the Temple, with no mention of his enemies in the audience.[93] The damning portrait builds from his commentary on their leadership style (vv. 2–12) through to a series of woes which employ the cry Οὐαὶ ὑμῖν, labelling the scribes and Pharisees ὑποκριταί[94] with various forms of blindness (τυφλός).[95] These are interspersed with illustrations. The scribes and Pharisees are duplicitous; preaching and practice, word and deed, advice and fruit do not align in their lives. The language of condemnation in Matthew 23 recalls the Baptist's demand for fruit worthy of repentance (3.8) and the characteristics vilified by Jesus in the Sermon (5.20; 6.1–18); their arrogance also contradicts his teachings on the ἐκκλησία (18.5–9) and his own humble approach to the holy city (20.26–8).

The rhetorical effect of this long, uninterrupted speech on the implied reader is to substantiate the reliability of Jesus' previous condemnations of hypocrisy in the religio-political establishment of Israel, and to reinforce further the narrator's contrast between the activities of hypocrisy observable in the συναγωγαί of Jesus' opponents and the humility and service required in the messianic mission and ἐκκλησία of Jesus. The opponents of Jesus have become the antitypes of the true followers of Jesus.[96]

The final woe includes a reference to Jesus sending προφήτας καὶ σοφοὺς καὶ γραμματεῖς to the scribes and Pharisees, whom they will persecute and kill (23.34).[97] The tension between ἀποστέλλω here and ἀπέστειλεν in 10.5 reinforces the implied reader's anticipation of the unfulfilled Matthew 10 mission as a future event outside the plotted story's temporal parameters. The Matthew 23.34–5 description corresponds to the disciples' commission in Matthew 10 and Jesus' warnings of persecution there; the implied reader identifies these two sendings by Jesus and their similar fates, but also reads of the opponents' sentence to hell (γέεννα, 23.33).

But Jerusalem also comes in for condemnation in 23.37–9; as already noted in Matthew 2, 15 and 19, the city is paradigmatic of

---

[93] But note the shift to second-person address in 23.13.
[94] 23.13, 14, 15, 23, 25, 27, 29.   [95] 23.16, 17, 19, 24, 26.
[96] Cf. R. Edwards, *Story*, p. 79.
[97] See D. E. Garland, *The Intention of Matthew 23*, pp. 173–5, for the disciples as the object of ἀποστέλλω here.

the opposition which met God's Emmanuel Messiah from the first news of his birth. Now Jesus cries out in first-person address to Zion, with the same intensity, compassion, authority and Father–Son intimacy of 11.25–30. But Jerusalem has sealed its own fate by rejecting the envoys, and now the Messiah, of God. In turn it is now rejected by God's Emmanuel Messiah, and here again Jesus is the voice for the implied author's point of view. His words regarding Jerusalem operate on two levels, within the story and within the narrative space shared by narrator and implied reader, where they are perfectly intelligible. Jerusalem will not see him again until it takes up the same cry/confession voiced by his followers in Matthew 21.9: 'Blessed is he who comes in the name of the Lord!' (23.39). This phrase ἀπ' ἄρτι delivers with it a temporal reference of apparent eschatological significance, as will become clear to the implied reader when it also appears in 26.29, 64. The implied reader is left wondering whether Jerusalem's utterance points to its future recognition of Jesus only as final judge, or welcoming him as its Messiah king.[98]

Matthew 24: the withdrawal of presence

Jesus' extended discourse in 24.4–25.46 is significant for its setting and narrative preface, elaborating the movement of Jesus from the Jerusalem Temple. Jesus, following his lament over Jerusalem's rejection, swears his absence from the holy city of divine presence (λέγω γὰρ ὑμῖν, οὐ μή με ἴδετε, 23.39). The narrator follows with the report of Jesus' physical departure from the Temple and his prediction of its total destruction. For the implied reader this departure culminates a sequence of story elements concerning Jerusalem, beginning as early as the episodes of Matthew 2 and the Baptist's rejection of the repentance of the Jerusalem leaders in Matthew 3, and combining with Jesus' own assertion: λέγω δὲ ὑμῖν ὅτι τοῦ ἱεροῦ μεῖζόν ἐστιν ὧδε (12.6), the burning of the city in the wedding-feast parable (22.7), the desolation of the 'house' of Jerusalem (23.38), and the repeated indictment of the city for the murders of those sent. With Jesus' withdrawal the picture of the religious establishment's repudiation of the saviour, and its rejection by YHWH, is complete – the Emmanuel Messiah leaves emphatically and the holy city awaits destruction. The story has

---

[98] Cf. P. Benoit, *L'évangile selon saint Matthieu*, p. 144; Bonnard, *Matthieu*, p. 344; Hill, *Matthew*, p. 316.

come full circle back to Jerusalem's arrogant repudiation of the 'God-with-us' Messiah in Matthew 2, a repudiation which has brought divine judgement upon itself and fulfilled Jesus' prediction of destruction in 23.38. For the implied reader Jesus' departure from the Temple represents Jerusalem's and Israel's loss of his agency of the divine presence and, given the narrator's and Jesus' alignment in 1.23 and 18.20, the loss of the presence of God.[99]

According to the narrator the disciples do realize something of the eschatological significance of Jesus' departure from the Temple, and his prediction of its destruction.[100] This and the connection they make between 'the sign of your coming' and 'the close of the age' (24.3) mark a milestone in their own perception, here regarding the relation of Jesus' ministry to Jerusalem. Matthew 24–5 also signals the end of Jesus' public ministry. In his last great discourse Jesus speaks privately of the end only to those within his inner circle. From a spatial point of view the story's focus on the centripetal power of Jesus' presence remains the same, but the audience scope, once broadened successively to all characters and character groups (cf. 4.18–22; 4.23–4, 25–6; 9.3–18), now has successively shrunk as the story climaxes (cf. 22.46; 23.1; 24.3).[101]

Following various signs preceding the end – false messiahs and sufferings (24.4–14) – the details of the close of this age are narrated (24.15–31), including the desolating sacrilege (with a direct and possibly polyvalent comment by the narrator: 'Let the reader understand', 24.15),[102] tribulations and cosmic signs. The remainder of Jesus' speech about the end is composed primarily of parables and parabolic sayings which supply admonitions and warnings, anticipating and predicting events beyond the plotted story.

---

[99]   So too Garland, *Matthew 23*, pp. 26, 200; Fred Burnett, *The Testament of Jesus-Sophia*, pp. 130, 164, from a redactional perspective. Burnett, p. 122, also argues that the relation of ἱερόν in 24.1 to οἶκος in 23.38 makes Jesus' act of leaving the Temple equivalent to his departure from the whole nation. Cf. also D. R. A. Hare, *The Theme of the Jewish Persecution of Christians in the Gospel According to St Matthew*, pp. 148–9.

[100]   See Bornkamm, 'End-Expectation', pp. 15–51, for a seminal assessment of the paraenetic value of Matthew's eschatology within his community.

[101]   Cf. Kingsbury, *Story*, p. 84.

[102]   Petersen on Mark 13.14 is relevant here: 'At least one of the functions (metalinguistic) of the parenthetical "let the reader understand" (13.14) is to call attention to the coded reference to the Temple. But another function may well be to call attention to *events* of which the reader (addressee) is aware, thereby linking the time of Mark's writer to these events!' (*Criticism*, p. 72).

Matthew 25.31–46: Jesus' presence – eschatologically crucial

Much of the parabolic imagery, especially in Jesus' final apocalyptic discourse, 25.31–46, concerns the eschatological division of 'all the nations' (πάντα τὰ ἔθνη) into the sheep – inheritors of the Kingdom – and goats – consigned to eternal punishment. Matthew 25.31–46 comes to the reader as Jesus' last words in his final discourse. The passage poses several sharp questions for the reader and interpreter, however, including: Who are 'all the nations' (πάντα τὰ ἔθνη) gathered for this judgement? Who are 'the least, my brothers'? Who are the hungry, naked, ill, imprisoned and strangers?

τὰ ἔθνη has normally referred to the Gentiles in Matthew's story, i.e., the whole world, everyone outside of Jesus' inner circle, the crowds and religious leaders.[103] But does adding πάντα here keep the term exclusively gentile? In Matthew 24.9, 14; 25.32; 28.19 (cf. 24.30) πάντα τὰ ἔθνη could be larger; it could include the Jewish crowds and gentile adherents and masses. Jesus' growing antipathy to the Jewish leaders has never spelled outright rejection of the Jewish crowds, the people of Israel. Even in 21.43 the target audience is explicitly the leaders, not the people. As well, other judgement scenes in Matthew seem to include both Jews and Gentiles (8.12; 11.20–4; 12.41–2; 13.36–43). The latter passage, 13.36–43, is a helpful reminder that for Matthew the final tally of insiders and outsiders will only come at the end. Within the judgement scene of Matthew 25, then, Matthew may not have nailed down the categories as tightly as a reader might expect.

To this point the story's portrayal of ἐλάχιστος (5.19), μικροί (10.42, 11.11; 18.6, 10, 14) and relevant uses of ἀδελφός (for members of Jesus' inner circle, 5.22–4, 47; 7.3–5; 12.49–50; 18.15, 21, 35; 23.8; 28.10) has included the disciples, close followers, members of Jesus' ἐκκλησία. They are essentially synonymous terms. So 'the least' here is not a subset of 'my brothers', but refers to all of them: 'these brothers of mine, the least' is probably a more accurate translation.[104] In the wider world, set against their larger and more powerful Jewish and gentile counterparts, those in Jesus' inner circle are 'little ones', 'the least'. Applied within the story in this apocalyptic vision of judgement, 'the least, the brothers, the

103 So Wolfgang Schenk, *Die Sprache des Matthäus*, p. 217.
104 So Schuyler Brown, 'Faith, the Poor and the Gentiles', p. 173.

little ones' are all the members of the future community of Jesus, his inner circle at the end of time.

Whatever the ambiguity of τὰ ἔθνη in 25.32, what is clear to the reader, then, is that this final judgement is on the basis of how Jesus' followers, his inner circle, have been treated by the world (everyone else). So many of the themes of the Gospel, therefore, rush together here. Most striking for the reader is the powerful boost this apocalyptic vision provides to Matthew's Emmanuel motif. The important news of 25.31–46 is again Jesus' intimate, powerful identification with his own μικροί. The presence of the King, the Son of man, is with 'his people', his ἐκκλησία, entirely consistent with the presence motif right from Matthew 1.

The rest of the world at the judgement (the outsiders) is surprised by both the manner and object of Jesus' presence. They were unaware of Jesus' presence in 'the least'; he was incognito. Therefore the reader has a core insight into Matthew's characterization of Jesus as Emmanuel, in what will prove to be an important elucidation of 28.20. If 'all the nations' expected God's Emmanuel presence anywhere, it was not among the hungry, naked, ill, imprisoned and foreigners of Jesus' followers. Jesus' fierce Emmanuel protection of his community's members has thus come to the fore: the readers see *themselves* as 'the least' and 'the brothers'. The discourse is about what *others* are to do for *them*, the 'little people' within the post-resurrection ἐκκλησία. The story functions as an encouraging, proleptic vindication of the hardship, torture, persecution and death which Jesus has said his followers will suffer in their mission. Their treatment by others will prove to have eternal implications.

Matthew 26: Jesus' 'withness' in sacrament

Following Jesus' last major discourse the narrative's movement towards the final conflict quickens notably and Jesus anticipates the decisive event imminently. In the Passover celebration the elements of bread and wine, in the context of eating together, are given powerful symbolic significance. Participation in a common cup points towards his covenant of blood 'which is poured out for many for the forgiveness of sins' (26.28), an elaboration of the angel's first explanation of 'Jesus' in 1.21: 'He will save his people from their sins.' Here the implied reader sees in part the material shape to one of the fundamental questions of the opening narrative frame: *how* will Jesus bring salvation to his people?

But the language of both Jesus and the narrator heightens the symbolism of the meal and subsequent events for the presence motif as well. Nine times in Matthew 26 Jesus' exclusive association with his inner circle of disciples is emphasized by means of μετά + genitive.[105] That Jesus plans for a Passover 'with' his disciples, that he celebrates it 'with' them, that he anticipates a future celebration 'with' them in his Father's Kingdom, that he shares his Gethsemane experiences 'with' them and seeks their support, that they are 'with' him at his arrest, and that Peter is accused of being 'with' him – these words of Jesus and the narrator point beyond mere accompaniment at the story level. In the Supper celebration Jesus' 'withness' gains further definition beyond his earthly person and physical presence. These tangible symbols will provide the ἐκκλησία with a critical means of experiencing his post-resurrection presence with them. And the implied reader is drawn into a critical sequence of story events where being 'with' Jesus, being in his presence, means personal companionship, obedience, and full participation and acceptance of his mission – in other words, full ideological alignment with his person, teaching and suffering.

And herein lies the story tension – even as the implied author is defining these criteria for 'withness', the disciples continue to miss the mark and appear unfit for their ministry. They accompany Jesus but abandon him; they obey him but fall away; they worship him but have doubts. Jesus' request in 26.38, μείνατε ... μετ' ἐμοῦ, contrasts directly with their *en masse* departure in 26.56; they have misunderstood the nature of his mission and person. The measure of true discipleship here is to remain in Jesus' presence; even Peter's attempt ends in humiliation, although his repentance anticipates renewed discipleship in Jesus' presence. It is the implied reader who remains the beneficiary of all the commentary, OT fulfilment citations, the words of Jesus, the faltering examples of the disciples. Only the implied reader has been privy to every plotted event in the story. The disciples have missed the narrator's opening exposition,

[105] 26.18, 20, 29, 36, 38, 40, 51, 69, 71. Debates continue over how transparent these references might be to the experiences of the post-Easter church; see, e.g., Kingsbury's assertions in *Structure*, pp. 30–2; *Story*, pp. 105–6. Cf. Howell's (*Story*, pp. 230–2) disagreements with Kingsbury's focus on μετά in Matthew. Some of Howell's criticism is justified, but he has missed the larger picture of Matthew's presence motif.

numerous events, and Jesus' own struggles in baptism, temptation and Gethsemane. The implied author, then, is not seeking a simplistic identification between implied reader and disciples; from his or her privileged position the implied reader has been more 'with' Jesus than any of his followers. Only the implied reader understands, is able to evaluate all characters according to the implied author's criteria, and goes 'with' Jesus (narratively and ideologically) to the end.

For the implied reader, the disciples' thrice-repeated inability to remain 'with' Jesus contrasts sharply with his stamina in staying with his Father's will, a final threefold 'testing' of the theocentricity of the Son which culminates in his announcement that 'the hour' and 'the betrayer' are 'at hand' (26.45–6).

> ἰδοὺ ἤγγικεν ἡ ὥρα ...
> ἰδοὺ ἤγγικεν ὁ παραδιδούς με

The verb ἤγγικεν has already occurred in the three summary pronouncements of the Kingdom's proclamation by John the Baptist, Jesus and the disciples (3.2; 4.17; 10.7):

> ἤγγικεν (γὰρ) ἡ βασιλεία τῶν οὐρανῶν

and has been used to report Jesus' approach to Jerusalem (21.1) and the coming of the harvest time in the parable of the vineyard and the tenants (21.34). Each use of the verb, then, is interconnected with the anticipation of the Kingdom, and points the implied reader to Jesus' final conflict as central to its arrival.

From 26.57 till his risen appearance, Jesus moves from the role of 'actor' to become silent object of the action, experiencing the suffering foreshadowed by the narrator (10.4; cf. 4.12; 11.2; 14.1–13), which he himself had been predicting (10.38–9; 16.21; 17.9, 12, 21–2; 20.18–19; 26.2, 20–5), and which he had warned his disciples to expect.[106]

Jesus' circumlocutory affirmation in 26.64, his only words before the high priest's council, of the high priest's 'Are you the Christ, the Son of God?' parallels the confessions in 14.33 and 16.16, and God's own declarations in 3.17 and 17.5. The difference in response, however, reflects the central contrast of the story: earlier the realization evoked worship from his followers and heavenly voices expressing divine paternal pleasure; now among his oppo-

---

[106] See Weaver, *Discourse*, pp. 145–7, on Jesus' role reversal.

nents it inspires condemnation for blasphemy, physical abuse and mockery.

The narrator loads the response of the council with heavy irony, for they mock their own religious traditions and scriptures by taunting Jesus to prophesy (26.68), even as the implied reader knows of his accurate predictions. Ironically, the accusation that Jesus claimed to destroy and rebuild the Temple (26.61–2) is framed as an unwitting assertion of Jesus' transfer of God-with-us presence to his ἐκκλησία, even as he has chosen to remain powerless for the sake of scripture's fulfilment (26.52–4). For the post-70 CE reader there is the added irony of the allusions to the Temple's fate, while Jesus' powerless death itself fulfils the anticipated destruction and false accusation (cf. 22.6–7; 27.40). Irony, so strong in the infancy narrative, is dominant in the passion story, forming thematic inclusio between the two passages in several places. In Matthew 2 the Jewish leaders in Jerusalem, despite knowing the scriptural connections with the baby Messiah, cannot respond with worship and acceptance, a rejection which clearly anticipates the Jewish leaders' rejection in Matthew 26–8. Judas, integral to the plot, seeks an opportunity (εὐκαιρίαν, 26.16) to destroy Jesus, even as the implied reader hears Jesus seeking the same καιρός (26.18); Judas is caught unawares in the fulfilment of God's will, as with characters throughout Jesus' infancy. In Matthew 2 Herod tried to kill Jesus and in Matthew 27 Jerusalem succeeds. Similar inclusio occurs between 'all Jerusalem' in 2.3 and the language of those gathered in 27.1, 25.[107]

Irony is for insiders, in this case for implied readers, and it strengthens the bond between implied reader and author.[108] As a weapon, irony has victims, in this case the Jewish leaders. In the process the implied reader rejects the surface meaning of the texts to discern more deeply the implied author's meaning, all the while rejecting the value system of the Jewish leaders, who do not recognize the deeper meaning of their own words and actions.

Behind the trial scene before Pilate stands the concerted pressure of the Jewish leaders to have Jesus condemned, for Pilate remains, in the narrator's omniscient depiction, a victim of circumstances: he

[107] See more elaboration of the irony and inclusio here in C. H. Lohr, 'Oral Techniques in the Gospel of Matthew', pp. 410–12, 427–9; Senior, *Passion*, pp. 18–23; Nolan, *Son*, pp. 104–5; R. Brown, *Birth*, p. 183; Kingsbury, *Story*, pp. 48–9; Patte, *Matthew*, pp. 353–5.

[108] See Paul Duke, *Irony in the Fourth Gospel*, especially pp. 29–42, for a discussion of irony's functions; cf. Culpepper, *Anatomy*, p. 180.

marvels greatly at Jesus (27.14); he offers Jesus or Barabbas for release (27.17); he perceives the base motivation of the Jewish leaders (27.18); and he receives his wife's dream revelation[109] of Jesus as a 'righteous man' (27.19). This, juxtaposed with the narrator's note that the people had been persuaded by the chief priests and elders to call for Jesus' destruction (27.20), and Pilate washing his hands as an assertion of innocence (27.24), reinforces the implied reader's favourable view of Pilate and suspicion of the Jewish leaders.

Matthew 27.25 represents a critical moment when Jesus loses the loyalty of οἱ ὄχλοι (27.15, 20, 24) and they and their children take responsibility for his blood. Even this final abandonment, however, is blunted by the culpability of the Jewish leaders who have persuaded οἱ ὄχλοι to destroy Jesus (27.10), and who stand unable to answer Pilate's final question: 'What evil has he done?' (27.23). The narrator may also preserve a favourable disposition towards the crowds with the implication of openness on the part of the people (λαός) to the news of the resurrection in 27.64.

Throughout the crucifixion and the subsequent mockeries and taunts of the soldiers, passers-by, Jewish leaders and robbers, the implied reader stands with the narrator and the silent Jesus in full awareness of his true status, and fully cognizant of the tragic irony of his indictment as 'king' and of the ironic derision of his role as Son of God and Emmanuel Messiah, even as that role is being fulfilled in dying (cf. 16.24–5; 26.28).

3.5.   Matthew 27.51–28.20. Narrative close: the presence of the risen Jesus

Several arguments were advanced above for seeing 27.51–28.20 as the closing narrative frame of the story. The death of a protagonist forms a natural termination in itself. At the same point in our story the narrator's spatial alignment makes a significant shift away from Jesus, to an external point of view. The narrator's concern becomes the impact of Jesus' death on the cosmic level through various signs and miraculous events (27.51–4), which on the human level effect the soldiers' confession. For a significant portion of the closing frame (27.55–6, 61; 28.1–11a) the narrator aligns himself spatially

---

[109] Κατ' ὄναρ; cf. 1.20; 2.12, 13, 19. For the force of this verbal repetition see Anderson, 'Over Again', pp. 209–15; Lohr, 'Techniques', p. 413. Cf. the redactional analysis of R. Brown, *Birth*, pp. 105–19.

with the faithful women followers who did not abandon Jesus, and with the Jewish leaders, to observe their final machinations (27.62–6; 28.11–15). Only in 28.9–10 and 28.17–20 are the narrator and implied reader spatially reunited with Jesus.

This conclusion to the story (27.51–28.20) is a careful summary and thorough evocation of its beginnings (Matt. 1–2). Numerous correspondences reinforce these opening and closing passages as the story's narrative frame:[110]

1.23	μεθ᾽ ὑμῶν ὁ θεός	28.20	ἐγὼ μεθ᾽ ὑμῶν εἰμι
1.1–2	the four women, the magi	28.19	πάντα τὰ ἔθνη
1.5–20	special role of women	27.55–28.10	special role of women
1.18–2.23	God commands, directs	28.16–20	Jesus directs, commands
1.24–2.23	faithful obedience	27.55–28.16	faithful obedience
2.2, 8, 11	ὁράω + προσκυνέω	28.17	ὁράω + προσκυνέω
1.20–2.20	ἄγγελος κυρίου	28.2–7	ἄγγελος κυρίου
2.22	εἰς Γαλιλαίαν	27.55; 28.7, 10, 16	εἰς Γαλιλαίαν
2.3–23	Jerusalem rejection	27.62–6; 28.11–15	Jerusalem rejection
1.20, 23; 2.1, 9, 13, 19	ἰδού	27.51; 28.2, 7, 7, 9, 11, 20	ἰδού
1.18–25	Lord, Holy Spirit, Son	27.54; 28:19	Father, Son, Holy Spirit
2.10	χαρὰ μεγάλη	28.8	χαρὰ μεγάλη

The exceptional faithfulness of Jesus' closest women followers, the two Marys, has been emphasized in their presence at the crucifixion, and at his burial, and is now reiterated in their return to the tomb. In contrast to the disciples' mass abdication, their steadfastness now recollects the narrator's careful delineation of the four women of the genealogy and Mary in Matthew 1, and the implied reader is encouraged to ponder the special role of these women disciples in Jesus' ἐκκλησία. It is these faithful members of the community who first receive the angel's announcement, are shown the empty tomb, and are commissioned to take the resurrection message to the other disciples, along with the instructions to meet with Jesus in Galilee. 'Joy' (χαρά) is a somewhat rare commodity amidst the often bitter conflicts of this story,[111] but here, in great measure and mixed with φόβος, it describes the

---

[110] These parallels are often used to support chiastic approaches to Matthew's structure; cf. Lohr, 'Techniques'; Combrink, 'Structure'; Fenton, 'Inclusio'; P. Gaechter, *Die literarische Kunst im Matthäusevangelium*; H. Schieber, 'Konzentrik im Matthäusschluss'. But see Meye Thompson's criticism, 'Structure'. Cf. the lists in Frankemölle, *Jahwebund*, pp. 321–5; Davies and Allison, *Matthew 1–7*, p. 60.

[111] Twice in the plotted story, in an inclusio of Jesus' birth (2.10) and resurrection

women as they raced from the empty tomb with the news. The women are also the first followers to see the risen Jesus; neither he nor the resurrection *per se* is described, but their immediate reaction is prostrate worship. The disciples have been mentioned twice, by the angel and Jesus, and are kept deliberately in the implied reader's foreground by the narrator, whose movement of the events points at every turn to the directing hand of the Father.[112]

The narrator interrupts this sequence of resurrection encounters in order to provide one final look at Jesus' opponents (28.11–15). Their characterization and repudiation of the Emmanuel Messiah remain consistent to the end. The reaction of the chief priests and elders to the guards' report of the events at the tomb (and the narrator implies that they receive a full account, ἅπαντα τὰ γενόμενα, 28.11) is deception and bribery. Significantly, the narrator portrays them as on the defensive, needing to concoct a story to *deny* the resurrection – symbolizing a defeat in and of itself.

The narrator's final statement on the religious establishment is directed to the implied reader: 'this story is still told among the Jews to this day' (28.15). Ἰουδαῖος is a term used within a narrowly defined context in the story, occurring otherwise only in the phrase βασιλεὺς τῶν Ἰουδαίων as applied to Jesus by the magi (2.2), Pilate (27.11) and the Roman soldiers (27.29, 37), in each case used by Gentiles to describe the Jews. In other words Ἰουδαῖος thus far has been a term of discrimination, used by one distinct group – the Gentiles – to designate another distinct ethnic group. Furthermore, every time the term arises it does so at the heart of an extreme conflict between Jesus and his opponents, implying specifically the Jerusalem religious and political establishment. But in 28.15 the narrator himself takes up the term, as a final reinforcement of the story's great polarization between the protagonist and his antagonists, and between their respective communities. Of equal importance, however, with μέχρι τῆς σήμερον [ἡμέρας] the narrator projects the two-community distinction outside of story time, to emphasize that the polarity of communities exists in perpetuity. The implied reader is given the narrator's interpretive key (point of view) by which to look at the post-story world and explain the contemporary division between the ἐκκλησία of Jesus and the group represented by Ἰουδαῖοι.

(28.8), characters react with χαρὰ μεγάλη. Every other occurrence is in parables; cf. 13.20, 44; 25.21, 23.
[112] Edwards, *Story*, p. 93.

The story of the disciples ends where it began, on a mountain, in Galilee, where Jesus first introduced a nucleus of them to the precepts of the Kingdom. The implied reader has thus confronted six significant mountains in Matthew (4.8; 5.1 and 8.1; 15.29; 17.1 and 9; 24.3; 28.16), in a pattern which reveals a linked chain of rhetorically significant peaks. In each case ὄρος is the setting for a momentous event in Jesus' ministry, and each of the first five ὄρος settings has anticipated in some fashion the final ὄρος, the mountain of commissioning in 28.16–20.[113] As already noted, the humble, obedient Son on the mountain of temptation (4.8) forms an inclusio with the vindicated, risen Son of the final mountain. The mountain in Matthew 5–7 also corresponds fundamentally with the final mountain, for, on the former, Jesus gathers his disciples for the first time and explains to them the Kingdom values of the community which he is calling into being. On the latter mountain he commissions them, among other things, to make this teaching the basis of their mission (28.20).

But, as important as this narrative topography is, the narrator also uses geography to stress the obedience of the disciples (28.16). For all their ups and downs, progress, set-backs and ultimate abandonment of Jesus, the narrator reports that ἐπορεύθησαν εἰς τὴν Γαλιλαίαν εἰς τὸ ὄρος οὗ ἐτάξατο αὐτοῖς ὁ Ἰησοῦς.

This obedience, then, is the antepenultimate step in their restoration as his inner circle, as 'his people'. The implied reader has been prepared for this moment by a series of anticipatory comments directing the disciples back to Galilee for reunion with the risen Jesus (26.31–2; 28.5–7, 10).[114] Jesus' instructions to the women are to be given τοῖς ἀδελφοῖς μου (28.10), which already assumes their restoration (cf. 12.46–50; 18.15–17, 20, 21, 35; 23.8; 25.40). For the implied reader this rising expectation highlights the significance of the story's final spatial alignment of disciples and Jesus in 28.16–20. Galilee signifies the renewal of their discipleship, and Jesus' post-resurrection ability to summon their obedience anticipates more than a reunion there: 'Go quickly' (28.7) points ahead to urgent business.

The penultimate step in restoration comes when the Eleven first

---

[113] Donaldson, *Mountain*, reaches this conclusion primarily on the basis of his analysis of ὄρος as a theological-historical symbol in Matthew, but the same conclusion is true of ὄρος as a rhetorical device, supported by verbal repetition (contra Donaldson, p. 195; cf. Anderson, 'Over Again').

[114] See Petersen, *Criticism*, pp. 76–7.

see Jesus. Their reaction to his risen person is like the women's in 28.9 – προσεκύνησαν (28.17) – and recalls their response to Jesus in the boat in 14.33. Astonishingly, however, the narrator notes the admixture of doubt with their worship, also recalling Peter's doubt when sinking in the water (14.31). Even in this final act of worship, the disciples, or some of them, are uncertain, so that the narrator's mixed characterization of their faith persists to the end, despite the fact that they are confronted by the risen Jesus. In effect it provides a fully human portrait of the Eleven and of discipleship for the implied reader.

Jesus' final words (28.18b–20) are prefaced by the narrator's note 'and Jesus approached them' (προσέρχομαι, 28.18a) – a move rarely made by the protagonist, and here one of reassurance for the benefit of the disciples, in their doubtful worship. In only one other place (Matt. 17.7) did Jesus approach (προσέρχομαι) his disciples, there prostrate at his transfiguration, and in need of reassurance. To begin with, (1) Jesus asserts that he has been given universal authority, and (2) he reasserts the source of this authority as the Father – ἐδόθη. Both themes connect with his declaration in 11.25–30, but point to the resurrection as the complete, theocentric vindication of his sonship and messiahship.

Jesus then focuses on the disciples, commanding them with 'all' authority to make disciples of 'all' nations, a commission to be carried out through the activities of baptizing and teaching. Here comes to full fruition the story's implicit and increasingly anticipated inclusion of the Gentiles in Jesus' mission, a motif which now proves a solid strand of the story since Jesus' origins, encompassing the magi and a steady stream of encounters by Jesus with the faithful from outside Israel.[115] Since baptism has not been mentioned since Matthew 3 and the triadic ὄνομα formula has no precedent within the story, the implied reader is encouraged to seek their significance based on whatever information his or her contemporary community can supply.[116]

---

[115] Cf. Matt. 2.1–2; 3.9; 4.15–16; 8.11; 10.18; 12.18, 21; 21.43; 24.14; 25.32. Many commentators see in 'son of Abraham' (1.1) an anticipation of the Gospel's final universalism. But Matthew does not explicitly support a correspondence between Abraham and the Gentiles. That the reader already shares these cultural codes can be argued historically, but whenever Abraham is mentioned within Matthew he is the original patriarch of Israel; the Pharisees and Sadducees feel secure in their lineage from him; cf. 1.1, 2, 17; 3.9 (2x); 8.11; 22.32. Cf. M. D. Johnson, *Genealogies*, p. 225, who sees 'son of Abraham' supporting Davidic messiahship.

[116] Edwards, *Story*, p. 94.

Πάντα ὅσα ἐνετειλάμην gathers together Jesus' entire teaching within the story and places it before the disciples and implied reader, with the final challenge to accept and obey in the story. Jesus' own obedience as Son is recalled and vindicated. Teaching is for the first time made a responsibility of the disciples, but it clearly derives from Jesus' own teaching, so that the Eleven are called to pass on what Jesus taught them.

Jesus' final declaration is in the first-person voice of YHWH's Emmanuel: 'Look, I am with you always, right to the end of the age.' The implied reader is presented with Jesus' personal assertion of the narrator's third-person citation of Isaiah 7.14 in Matthew 1.23, and his translation of Emmanuel as 'God with us'. That the risen Jesus can undertake such a powerful first-person statement of divine presence finds its basis in the divine bestowal of universal authority in 28.18. He does not *give* this authority to the disciples; he himself incarnates that divine authority in their midst. Their mission therefore depends fully on his ongoing presence for its fulfilment. Hence the lessons of the water-walking, the feeding of the crowds and the attempted healing remain valid: they cannot always depend on the physical intervention of the pre-resurrection Messiah to pull them from the water, break the bread or complete their failed healing attempts. But theirs will be a derived commission; the disciples will always draw their authority and empowerment from Jesus' own universal, post-resurrection authority among their gathering.

That he designates the Eleven, and the new community drawn from πάντα τὰ ἔθνη, as the locus of his presence, in full alignment with his declaration of presence in 18.20, also finalizes the redefinition of 'his people'. And that the risen Jesus is able to utter his own promise – ἐγὼ μεθ' ὑμῶν εἰμι – of divine presence answers fully the question as to how his covenant of blood, crucifixion, death and resurrection is able to bring salvation to 'his people': resurrection is not merely demonstrative of God's authority and a vindication of his Messiah, but empowers Jesus to promise unreservedly his perpetual, efficacious presence with his disciples in their long-unfulfilled commission of Matthew 10, now become universal. In the resurrection the mission and person of the Emmanuel Messiah have become the powerful presence of the risen Jesus promised to the people of his ἐκκλησία.

The crisis of the identification of 'his people', initiated by Jerusalem's repudiation of the Emmanuel infant in Matthew 2, and exacerbated by the opponents of Jesus throughout the story, has dramatically escalated, through various statements by Jesus disassociating 'his people' from the leaders of ethnic Israel, to its culmination here in the community of disciples to be drawn from all nations. The implied reader finds that the Galilean commission of Matthew 10 issued by the earthly Jesus, unfulfilled, is now overtaken by the universal commission issued by the risen Jesus. This shift away from an Israel-only focus creates something of a conundrum for the reader. The utter opposition of Israel's leaders, and the basic complicity of the crowds at his crucifixion, make some sense of the shift, but do not remove the tension completely.[117]

That Jesus takes on the language of divine presence in a promise directly to his disciples – ἰδοὺ ἐγὼ μεθ' ὑμῶν εἰμι – is not only the ultimate step in their restoration as his inner circle, but also a statement of the community's boundaries and exclusivity. When Jesus notified the Pharisees that 'something greater than the Temple is here' (12.6), symbolically cleansed and destroyed the Temple, his Father's house, then declared the 'house' of Jerusalem 'desolate', withdrew from the Temple and predicted its total destruction (23.38–24.2), he relativized any possibility of Israel's religious establishment claiming divine presence as a function *ex officio* of the holy city. For the implied reader his departure from the Temple is his departure as the personal expression of God's true presence, the persona identified as 'Emmanuel'. Already in 18.20 the implied reader saw that the ἐκκλησία's activity of gathering in Jesus' name provided sufficient locus for divine authority and his presence, without reference to Jerusalem, its religious authority or sacred space, and independent of Jesus' physical proximity; now in 28.20 Jesus unequivocally himself declares his presence to be the presence of God. For the implied reader, who has seen the polarity of communities growing ever more intense within the story, the corollary of such a declaration is obvious: the presence of Jesus

---

[117] Weaver, *Discourse*, p. 151, finds in 28.18–20 the complete resolution of the unfulfilled Matt. 10 commissioning, but she dissolves too easily the narrative tension between the commanded exclusivity of Matt. 10.5–6 and the universality of Matt. 28.19. The latter does not simply subsume the former, especially since Weaver even claims that the earlier commission in Matt. 10 now becomes part of the whole body of Jesus' teaching which must be passed on. Here the temporal and eschatological assumptions implicit in passages like 10.23, and the continuing mixed characterization of the disciples, cannot be ignored. They are rather part of a larger narrative tension concerning the definition of 'his people'. In the end the implied reader is left with something of a puzzle, one on which critics have yet to find agreement.

with his people spells the absence of God among those who have
repudiated his presence. The shift of 'his people' from Israel's
leadership is a shift in God's presence, both in terms of its new
definition in the risen Jesus, and in terms of its new recipients – his
ἐκκλησία from πάντα τὰ ἔθνη.

Finally, that Jesus declares his presence in perpetuity both brings
an eschatological perspective to his promise and deals decisively
with any problem of his physical absence from the community. For
the implied reader this is critical. In 18.20 the narrator provided the
means by which the implied reader could engage contemporaneously with the community gathering in Jesus' name and presence,
and here he reinforces that means by relativizing the temporal
bounds on Jesus' presence, now to be with them πάσας τὰς ἡμέρας
ἕως τῆς συντελείας τοῦ αἰῶνος. Thus in 28.16–20 the implied
reader is brought into unique temporal, psychological and ideological alignment with the narrator, Jesus and the Eleven.[118] The
implied reader shares the same temporal location as the disciples
receiving the commission – between the resurrection and the
parousia. For the implied reader then, Matthew's final commissioning is a beginning as well as an ending, and Jesus' promise of
presence is just as fully applicable to the implied reader as to the
disciples. Similarly, Jesus' commissioning of the disciples becomes a
command to the implied reader to accept his mission and mandate
as the risen Emmanuel Messiah.

The story ends at this dramatic juncture, with the implied reader
drawn into the commission and ἐκκλησία of Jesus, and called to
obey his ongoing, powerful presence. But does the story really end
with all conflict between characters and points of view synthesized,
cancelled or harmonized? I think not – three major characters and
character groups remain intact at the end: Jesus, the Jewish leaders
and the disciples, while the crowds and Gentiles combine to become
the new universal field for the commission. In terms of Jesus'
overriding purpose as first defined in Matthew 1.21–3, his opponents remain effective and belligerent (28.11–15), the disciples
remain complex in character and commitment (28.17), and Jesus
has been elevated as Son, more completely than ever, to YHWH's
agent of salvation and divine presence (28.18–20). The fundamental
conflicts and characterizations carry over into the post-narrative
world. Jesus' post-resurrection authority and presence thus does

[118] Cf. Anderson, 'Over Again', pp. 70, 155.

not overwhelm others – it remains an invitation to obedience, empowerment, community and a promise. It depends on the story's deepest ironies: the nature of God's presence, the means of God's salvation (crucified Messiah), the first–last inversion (μικροί are the greatest in the Kingdom), the reign of the humble king, the role of women. These promise to remain ironies and tensions in the reader's post-narrative world.

Even though Jesus' God-with-us presence has found its deepest expression at the end of the story, it is not a resolved reality, able to be grasped by the readers. In fact, the future promise of 1.23 becomes the future promise of 28.20. The loop is open and unending, an invitation to readers to keep reading and rereading beyond the end of the story. The readers are to find the content of Emmanuel – God with us through radical obedience by joining the story of the ἐκκλησία of Jesus carrying out his universal commission between the resurrection and the parousia.

The sense with which Matthew concludes – open-ended dialogue, rather than external narrative closure; forward references to the unnarrated future (Jesus' promised presence), rather than his narrated departure; universal, temporally unbounded and un-plotted commission, awaiting fulfilment – connects actual readers to their own present. There the texts' structures, story, point of view and unresolved tensions guide their completion of the story within their own experiences.[119]

---

[119] Cf. Howell, *Story*, pp. 225–9; Weaver, *Discourse*, pp. 152–3. Contra Matera's focus on worship and confidence, 'Plot', p. 242; and contra Magness' missing ending of Matthew, *Sense*, pp. 81–2.

4

PARADIGMS OF PRESENCE IN THE OLD TESTAMENT

We have looked at some rhetorical features of Matthew's presence motif through the prism of narrative criticism. The same motif can be investigated referentially, i.e., via its literary, historical and social correspondences in Matthew's first-century CE world. For Matthew the Jewish scriptures are his most obvious touchstone. An investigation of OT divine presence will help to clarify the key social and religious context from which Matthew's presence motif was drawn. The discussion of divine presence in the OT and in recent commentary is potentially vast. It is important to outline some parameters for the relatively brief engagement of the issue here.

(1) In reflection of their importance in OT narrative, I am engaging with three basic models of divine presence provided by the patriarchal, Sinaitic and Davidic streams of theology. This chapter will outline some of the essential distinctives and convergences of divine presence in these traditions.

(2) I am not elaborating these models in strict dependence on an existing source theory. Although many critics hold that the basic insights of pentateuchal criticism remain intact in the midst of recent criticism, more important is the question of how the OT models of presence may have appeared to a first-century CE Matthew.

4.1. Literature and current discussion

Talking about 'OT presence theology' touches on two larger, related discussions: the centre of OT theology, often ascribed to covenant, and the nature and relationship of the Mosaic/Sinaitic tradition and the Davidic/Zionistic tradition of Jerusalem.

On the first account it is important to acknowledge that some debate exists as to whether the great stress placed on covenant as

the major ideological category and form of socio-religious organization for early Israel is warranted.[1] Samuel Terrien, for example,
finds little evidence that 'covenant consciousness constituted the
determinative trait of Israel's religion', or that 'the covenant motif
provides an adequate principle for the organic presentation of
Israel's faith and cultus ... The motif of presence is primary, and
that of covenant is secondary.'[2]

On the second account, contemporary scholarship has commonly juxtaposed the Mosaic and Davidic covenant traditions.
The Mosaic tradition is often portrayed as historical and particu-
laristic in nature, with a God who intervenes decisively on behalf
of his people, above all in the Exodus; the Davidic as cosmic in
orientation and built upon Zion mythology. The Mosaic covenant is conditional on obedience; the Davidic sees covenant as
unconditional promise – Israel's election is inviolable and bound
up with the Davidic dynasty established on Jerusalem's secure
mountain. For the Mosaic circle God is one who manifests
himself periodically and retreats, while for the Davidic circle
God's presence in the Temple is constant; thus the personal,
historical divine presence of Sinai versus the cultic, royal, divine
presence of Zion.

Such an identification of these streams of tradition is a clear
benefit to the OT reader; whether the streams are best interpreted
in terms of this 'conflict model' is less clear. The Sinai–Zion
relationship is complex; each theological stream exhibits accommodation to the various socio-political realities of its day, i.e., 'the
Mosaic tradition tends to be a movement of protest ... the Davidic
tradition tends to be a movement of consolidation'.[3]

This debate has been seen as excessively polarized. Among
others, J. D. Levenson and B. C. Ollenburger have criticized such
delineation of the Mosaic and Jerusalem streams as an artificial

---

[1]   E.g., E. W. Nicholson, *God and His People*, has revived the argument for
covenant as relatively late.

[2]   *Presence*, p. 3. Cf. Clements, *God*, p. 1. See criticisms of Clements in Menahem
Haran, 'The Divine Presence in the Israelite Cult and the Cultic Institutions', and
of Terrien in Lawrence Frizzell, *God and His Temple*, e.g., p. 34.

[3]   Walter Brueggemann, 'Trajectories in Old Testament Literature and the Sociology of Ancient Israel', p. 162, with references to OT sociological analyses;
and cf. 'The Crisis and Promise of Presence in Israel', p. 47; 'The Epistemological
Crisis of Israel's Two Histories', p. 86. In 'Trajectories' Brueggemann applies to
these two OT traditions J. M. Robinson and H. Koester's trajectory model
(*Trajectories Through Early Christianity*); also Odil Steck, 'Theological Streams
of Tradition', pp. 183–214.

opposition of their tendencies.[4] Ollenburger's careful investigation of Zion symbolism has highlighted a consistent and pervasive concern for justice, along with a powerful and trenchant critique of royal perversions of justice. The apparent conflict between the Sinai and Jerusalem traditions should not be overstated so as to obscure their mutual claim to shared Israelite patterns of thought.[5]

There is little argument that the motif of divine presence permeates thoroughly the literary traditions of ancient Israel's several stages of existence – patriarchal tribe, amphictyony, united and divided monarchy, and dispersed, exiled and repatriated nation. And in terms of origins, there is substantial agreement that, whatever the specific relationships involved in Israel's assimilation of divine presence motifs from its ancient Near Eastern neighbours, any similarity in form has been subsumed by substantial changes in function within Israel.[6]

One natural tendency of scholarship has been to investigate divine presence along source-critical lines, arguing, for example, 'that the Elohist (E) presents a more transcendent God than the Yahwist (J), that the Priestly writer (P) stresses that transcendence more than the other two' and that apart from D, 'nowhere else in the Hebrew Bible are two characteristics of immanence and transcendence so happily combined'.[7]

G. H. Davies was somewhat pessimistic about the attempt to define presence theology by source, however.

> The material of the presence theme is so complex, and the media of the manifestation so varied, that attempts to trace various stages in the development of the doctrine have not been successful.[8]

---

[4]   Jon D. Levenson, *Sinai and Zion*, pp. 187–217; B. C. Ollenburger, *Zion, The City of the Great King*, pp. 152–5.

[5]   Ollenburger, *Zion*, pp. 59–66; see his criticism of Brueggemann, pp. 154–5. See Levenson's extended discussion of Sinai and Zion's 'manifold relationships', *Sinai*, especially pp. 209–17.

[6]   E.g., see A. B. Pritchard, *Ancient Near Eastern Texts Relating to the Old Testament*, pp. 449–50, for statements of divine presence in Egyptian and Akkadian oracles. See Thomas Mann, *Divine Presence and Guidance in Israelite Traditions*, pp. 2–4, 17, 30–105, 236–7, for references and a survey of scholarship. See Martin Buber, *Kingship of God*, pp. 99–107, for his kingly 'leader-god' behind early Yahwism; cf. F. M. Cross, *Canaanite Myth and Hebrew Epic*, pp. 94–7, 100–2, 138–41, 163–9; George Mendenhall, *The Tenth Generation*, pp. 32–5.

[7]   E. H. Maly, ' "... The Highest Heavens Cannot Contain You ... " ', pp. 24–5, 29. Cf. Clements, *God*.

[8]   'Presence of God, Cultic', *IDB* III, p. 875a.

Numerous articles and monographs are available from this century which take up some aspect of God's OT presence,[9] including *pānîm*, *kābôd*, *shem*, Shekinah, the ark, the tent of meeting and others. Analysis of theophany naturally includes assessment of the presence phenomena related to OT divine appearances.[10]

A number of scholars have focused more specifically on OT divine presence within the parameters of a particular agenda, e.g., select OT presence motifs and ANE correspondent forms; presence as encounter with the divine word; presence as the experience of God's salvation; presence as divine intervention; a dialectical reappraisal of OT and modern divine presence.[11]

A few authors have concerned themselves with the broader development of the OT theology of God's presence. R. E. Clements' *God and Temple* undertakes a comprehensive description of the evolution of presence theology in ancient Israel. He is a primary advocate of the 'conflict model', as applied to presence theology, working from the premise that the covenantal relationship of Sinai between YHWH and Israel stands in contradiction to the Jerusalem ideology of the Temple as God's dwelling-place.[12]

The most significant attempt to examine the full trajectory of ancient Israel's theology of presence is Samuel Terrien's *Elusive Presence*. Published almost concomitantly was Walter Brueggemann's 'The Crisis and Promise of Presence in Israel'. Although essentially independent in their arguments, their assessments are mutually compatible. Both pursue the issue in terms of the tension between the present and absent God – Terrien by examining in turn all the major Jewish and Christian biblical accounts of divine–human encounter for evidence of the self-concealing and self-

---

[9] Terrien, *Presence*, cannot easily be superseded as a bibliography for material prior to 1978; cf. also Brueggemann, 'Presence'; Brevard Childs, *The Book of Exodus*; more recently, Levenson, *Sinai*; J. I. Durham, *Exodus*; Ollenburger, *Zion*.

[10] See especially J. K. Kuntz, *The Self-Revelation of God*; Jörg Jeremias, *Theophanie: Die Geschichte einer alttestamentliche Gattung*.

[11] See, respectively, Mann, *Presence*; Dennis McCarthy, 'The Presence of God and the Prophetic Word'; J. A. Sanders, 'Mysterium Salutis'; Roland de Vaux, 'God's Presence and Absence in History'; E. L. Fackenheim, *God's Presence in History*, pp. 9–13.

[12] Especially pp. 79–99. See other commentary on the Sinaitic–Davidic clash in R. E. Clements, *Abraham and David*, pp. 54, 68; E. W. Nicholson, *Deuteronomy and Tradition*, p. 93; Mendenhall, *Generation*, p. 87; Brueggemann, 'Crisis', p. 86; John Bright, *A History of Israel*, p. 227. See Haran's criticism of Clements in 'Presence', pp. 251–67; also Levenson, *Sinai*, pp. 209–17.

revealing God, and Brueggemann by concentrating on divine presence and absence in the motif of 'face' in Exodus 33.12–23 and subsequently drawing connections with a number of NT texts.[13] Both also subscribe to the conflict model when juxtaposing Sinai and Jerusalem traditions, describing the resulting theological disparity in terms of ear–eye, north–south, knowing–seeing, historic–cultic dichotomies.

The beginning point for any such study must be the recognition that the issue of divine presence has important socio-anthropological implications. The enterprise of religious life stems, at least in major part, from the common individual and corporate desire for the presence of God within the human community. Religious activity (prayer, cultic ceremony, pilgrimage) is thus often regularized within the context of the recurring human motivation to be close to God. Sites of special numinous experience or theophany are therefore designated holy, structures are built to provide for residence and/or worship of the deities in proximity to the community, and cults are developed and maintained to facilitate the ongoing need to approach the divine being, and to perpetuate the pattern of encounter. This religious activity is frequently ordered and checked by reference to a body of traditions which incorporate the community's important cultic and historical texts.[14]

4.2. Divine presence and the patriarchs

In the midst of the ongoing debate over the original nature of patriarchal religion, R. W. L. Moberly has recently advanced in *The Old Testament of the Old Testament* a helpful model. Moberly has asserted that the patriarchs lived in a 'dispensation' distinct from that of Israel and Mosaic Yahwism, given the depiction of their religious ethos and practices in Genesis 12–50, and the use of the divine name in those traditions and in Exodus 3 and 6. These various traditions are in fact consistent in their depiction of Moses

---

[13] The starting-point for several studies has been the dialectic of divine accessibility and freedom; cf. Phythian-Adams, *Presence*; Brueggemann, 'Presence', pp. 680–3; J. Murphy-O'Connor, 'The Presence of God Through Christ in the Church and in the World', p. 54; Baruch Levine, 'On the Presence of God in Biblical Religion', p. 71. Most rightly recognize OT divine presence as a much more salvation-historical than metaphysical question; cf. J. C. Murray, 'The Biblical Problem: The Presence of God', p. 23, and Moberly, *Mountain*, p. 62.

[14] See Levine's helpful analogy of the human–divine relationship, 'Presence', pp. 71–2.

as the first recipient of the revelation of the name 'YHWH'. The textual evidence shows that the Yahwist was retelling the patriarchal traditions from within the context of Mosaic Yahwism, and not using a name known to the patriarchs. The patriarchal traditions are to Mosaic Yahwism as the OT is to the NT – the classical Christian appropriation of the OT as authoritative scripture through the theological exercise of typology, and the categories of promise and fulfilment, have an earlier precedent in the same appropriation of the patriarchal traditions as authoritative by the Yahwistic story-tellers and editors.

Thus, keeping in mind Moberly's thesis that Genesis 12–50 is about a religion before Israel's meeting with YHWH, we can look briefly at the general characteristics of patriarchal presence theology.[15] The narratives of Genesis 12–50 present the patriarchs as ancestral heroes whose intense moments of encounter with God are foundational to Israel's understanding of divine self-disclosure. At heart the narratives contain a collection of encounter stories, explained as divine utterances and theophanies which, with a minimum of visual features and reference to accompanying natural wonders, describe succinctly an exclusive divine–human dialogue between patriarch and God.[16] The divine promise of presence, 'I am with you', along with the concomitant narrative/human observation, 'God was/is with him/you', figures strongly in the patriarchal traditions of God's presence in theophany and divine utterance.[17] A sense of intimate communion between clan deity and clan father dominates these short instants of visitation.[18]

It is the very immediacy and personal directness of these experiences, afforded to the individual clan father, which remain clearly attested despite the later Yahwistic overlay. Although the theophanic sites are often hallowed by the patriarchs with the erection of altars, these cultic platforms are sacred places on the way, which

[15] To ask which elements in Gen. 12–50 display the unique traits of this pre-YHWH religion is a large problem. Identifying the Yahwist sections is only a rough beginning, everything else is questionable. See Claus Westermann, *Genesis 12–36: A Commentary*, pp. 107–8.

[16] Cf. Gen. 12.1–3, 7; 13.14–17; 15.1–18; 16.7–12; 17.1–22; 18.1–33; 20.6–7; 21.12–13; 22.1–2; 25.23; 26.2–5, 24; 28.12–15; 31.3, 11–13, 24; 32.1–2, 24–30; 35.1, 9–12; 46.2–4. See Kuntz's discussion of theophany, *Self-Revelation*.

[17] Cf. Gen. 21.20, 22; 26.3, 24, 28; 28.15, 20; 31.3, 5, 13; 35.3; 39.2, 3, 21, 23; 48.21; and see Chapter 5 below.

[18] Cf. T. C. Vriezen, *An Outline of Old Testament Theology*, p. 313; Terrien, *Presence*, p. 71, n.55.

do not enshrine the moment of God's presence for perpetuity.[19]
The sanctuary of the moment may include a mountain, stream, tree
or stone as part of the sacredness of the place. Divine presence is a
constant linked not with definite places[20] but with definite
persons.[21]

This corresponds well with the social conditions which the
traditions attach to the proto-Israelite clans.[22] The semi-nomadic[23]
status and social organization of the clan centred not on established
places but on personal relationships, on family and clan ties, with
protection, sustenance and direction of the clan dependent upon
proper maintenance of these intra-community bonds. Within this
context God's presence is pre-political; he is essentially peaceful.
This stands in sharp contrast to the God of the Judges, who is a
God of war and assists in the battles of his people.

The notion of cult as integrated within patriarchal family structures has little to do with the large-scale, independent cult of
established religion. Common worship of the clan god focused on
the primary relationship between clan leader and clan god. It was
the father of the household who functioned as spiritual, social and
physical leader of the clan. Abraham in particular undertook the
priestly function, imparted blessing and offered the sacrifices.
Above all, the presence of God was explicitly linked to him: he
received directly the word of God, without mediation.

The character of divine presence thus matched closely the
character of the patriarchal clan: God is the one who protects,
saves, helps, brings success and accompanies. His presence is
naturally correspondent to the clan's constant existence in insecurity: a wandering group without power or means to wage war,
subject to nature and famine. Living under constant threat explains

[19] Abraham: Shechem (Gen. 12.7), Bethel and Ai (12.8; 13.3–4), Hebron (13.18;
18.1), Salem (14.17–24), Beersheba (21.33). Isaac: Beersheba (26.25, 33). Jacob:
(32.2, 7–8), Peniel (32.30), Shechem (33.20) and Bethel (35.7; 28.10–22).

[20] See discussion of later aetiological legitimation in F. M. Cross, 'Yahweh and the
God of the Patriarchs'; and *Myth*, chap.1; Clements, *God*, pp. 12–14; Menahem
Haran, 'The Religion of the Patriarchs', pp. 30–55; Bright, *History*, pp. 99–100.

[21] The religion of the patriarchs is defined as personal even in the conflicting
hypotheses of A. Alt, 'The God of the Fathers'; and H. G. May, 'The Patriarchal
Idea of God', pp. 113–28, and 'The God of My Father', pp. 155–8, 199–200; cf.
in Clements, *God*, pp. 14–16.

[22] See the elaborations of Clement, *God*, pp. 11–16; Terrien, *Presence*, pp. 63–93.
Cf. Westermann, *Genesis 12–36*, pp. 105–13, for some of the points incorporated
here.

[23] 'Semi-nomadic' is used advisedly, cf. e.g. Gottwald, *The Tribes of Yahweh*,
pp. 448–59; Westermann, *Genesis 12–36*, pp. 74–9.

the complete absence of divine commandments, admonitions, punishments and judgements; the insecurity of patriarchal life is met by the God whose presence is integral to clan life, especially in his promises to be 'with' his people.[24]

The socio-political ramifications of semi-nomadic clan leadership disappear in early Israel, and the original relationship of clan god to clan father is dropped as the *modus operandi* for divine presence, but Israelite religion has never lost sight of the original b^erit concluded between God and Abraham in Genesis 15 and 17. Whether it can be called a 'covenant' in the Sinai sense is doubtful,[25] but Israel subsequently developed Abraham's experience of divine immediacy into the foundation of its religious identity as God's people.

4.3.   The three encounters: divine presence and Sinai

Sinai is the great symbol of Israel's social, political and religious birth, the mountain at which the slaves become free, at which Pharaoh's sort of mastery is replaced by that of YHWH,[26] at which social and economic subservience is overcome by a newly federated nationhood.[27] Most important for our considerations, Sinai functions as a primary symbol, as a paradigm, for Israel's corporate perception and sense of YHWH's presence among them, and of his will in Torah.[28]

Sinai becomes the prime pattern for all the relations of God's people – to God, within the community, and to the world. No dimension of life is left untouched – social, political, economic or

---

24 Promises of endless posterity and possessing the land do not correspond to the patriarchal period and are probably later; cf. Gen. 12.2; 13.16; 15.5; 17.4–5; 18.18; 22.17; 26.24; 28.14; 32.12; 35.11; 46.3. See Gerhard von Rad, *Old Testament Theology* I, pp. 168–73.

25 In Gen. 15.7–21 b^erit is an 'assurance' or 'promise'; Gen. 17 (P) may be an exilic address to Israel; see Claus Westermann, *The Promises to the Fathers*, pp. 159–60.

26 Note the explicit apposition of YHWH's mastery and Pharaoh's in Exod. 5.2, and the play on *'ābad* in 1.13–14 (5x); 2.23 (2x); 3.12; 4.23; 5.15 etc.

27 See Levenson, *Sinai*, p. 23; also Mendenhall's and Gottwald's readings of the Israelites as oppressed peoples in revolt against their tyrannical city-kings. Cf. Brueggemann's application in 'Trajectories'.

28 For a definition of 'symbol' which applies to these OT traditions, see Ollenburger, *Zion*, pp. 19–22. Historians are unable to say much about the historical Sinai in terms of event, location, or relation to Horeb. Cf. Martin Noth, *Exodus*, pp. 31–2; R. J. Clifford, *The Cosmic Mountain in Canaan and the Old Testament*, pp. 121–2; Levenson, *Sinai*, pp. 15–23.

religious. 'Israel could not imagine that any truth or commandment from God could have been absent from Sinai.'[29] It is no exaggeration to see Sinai as the birthplace of the people of YHWH, where he delivers their *raison d'être* as his community through encounter with his presence, agreement in covenant and reception of Torah.

The present Sinai narrative is both the literary account of that theophany and its repetition in Israel's later cultic life.[30] Thus a wide variety of special symbols and expressions of divine presence, drawn diachronically from numerous points in Israel's history and synchronically from the Mosaic and Davidic circles, meet us in the text of Exodus. Most prominent are the repeated theophanies with their accompaniment of fire and cloud (Exod. 3; 19–24; 33–4) – these are the three foundational encounters between God and his people, which contain Israel's recounting and celebration of the three most important encounter stories of divine presence.

Within the same motif the author also employs and develops the divinely uttered formula of presence ('I will be with you'; 3.12; cf. 10.10; 18.19), the revelation of the divine character and name at Moses' commissioning (Exod. 3.14; cf. 6.2–3), the guiding entities of cloud, fire and *mal'āk*, YHWH as warrior and liberating presence in his ten mighty acts and liberation from Egypt, the ark/tabernacle shrine traditions, the *kābôd* of YHWH, the challenge of the golden calf to divine presence, the divine *pānîm* and the tent of meeting. Moses' exclusive role as intercessor and mediator of YHWH's presence is emphasized. For some, Exodus thus becomes 'the book of divine presence':

> It is possible to epitomize the entire story of Exodus in the movement of the fiery manifestation of the divine presence... The book thus recounts the stages in the descent of the divine presence to take up its abode for the first time among one of the peoples of the earth.[31]

That which most sets apart divine presence at Sinai from the patriarchal accounts, however, is *holiness*. Holiness is fundamental

---

[29] Levenson, *Sinai*, p. 19.
[30] See Clements, *God*, pp. 20–7; Cross, *Myth*, pp. 163–9. For summaries of Exodus' complex tradition-history see Childs, *Exodus*, and 'Theological Responsibility', pp. 432–49; G. A. F. Knight, *Theology as Narration*, pp. x–xvi; Moberly, *Mountain*, pp. 15–43.
[31] Moshe Greenberg, *Understanding Exodus*, pp. 16–17; in Mann, *Presence*, p. 233. Also G. H. Davies, *Exodus*, pp. 18–21, 47–52; Durham, *Exodus*, p. 260; see Moberly, *Mountain*, pp. 45, 62, in reference to Exod. 32–4.

to the appearance of God at Sinai. It is central to understanding presence, election, covenant and Torah. *qdš* is never used in patriarchal religion to describe God, where sacred-profane language has yet to develop, but in Mosaic Yahwism holiness defines the nature of God and his Sinai connection to his people. From the outset (Exod. 3.5) holiness is the key ingredient to encountering God as YHWH 'with' us.

Exodus 3: The first encounter

In the composite narrative of Exodus 2.23–7.7 God responds to his people's slavery in Egypt and commissions Moses as the agent of his salvation, and in two explicit statements about his name in Exodus 3.13–15 and 6.2–3 God reveals to Moses a new way of being known: as 'YHWH'. Many of the concerns raised in the passage cannot be dealt with here, but it is worth noting this Sinai experience for (1) the nature of divine presence, (2) its foreshadowing of the initial community experience of divine presence at Sinai in Exodus 19–24, and the renewal in Exodus 32–4, and (3) its divine legitimation of Moses as the archetypal agent of God's will.[32]

The burning bush (3.2–3) does not function simply as a beacon to get Moses' attention, but is a theophanic fire, a clear symbol of divine presence (cf. 19.18; Deut. 4.11–15; Ps. 18), whose holiness has made 'holy' the ground upon which Moses has stumbled, here for the first time in Israel's story designated *hār ha'ĕlōhîm* (3.1b).[33]

Though the writer tells his story from within the perspective of Mosaic Yahwism and uses the name YHWH throughout the story (cf. 3.2, 4a, 7), God initially identifies himself to Moses as 'the God of your father(s)' (v. 6a), a clear bridge to Israel's patriarchal history; apparently Moses does not yet know God as YHWH. Moses reacts fearfully as one who has blundered unknowingly into holy presence – 'he was afraid to look at *ha'ĕlōhîm*'. The God who has attracted and compelled him to come near now demands a holy distance. With this tension, the narrative prefigures the same tug-

---

[32] Cf. Judg. 6; Jer. 1. See Martin Noth, *A History of Pentateuch Traditions*, pp. 30, 36; but note G. W. Coats, *Moses*. For studies of this theophany–call sequence see references in Zimmerli, *Ezekiel* I, pp. 97–100; Durham, *Exodus*, p. 29. I am indebted at numerous points to Moberly, *OT*, pp. 5–35.

[33] 'The mountain of God' is often taken to indicate a long-sacred site (e.g., S. R. Driver, *The Book of Exodus*, pp. 18–19), but for its new beginning here see Moberly, *OT*, pp. 8–10.

of-war between a people attracted and a people running fearfully for cover in the Sinai theophany of Exodus 19–24. Already, then, the dialectic of divine holy presence figures in the text: encountering a God whose holiness is transcendent but whose compassionate, salvific engagement seeks personal encounter.

Etymology and tradition-history have often guided interpretation of the core of the Exodus 3 theophany, the divine self-explanation of vv. 14–15.[34] More important for us are the contextual links made in the text between the divine name and divine presence, communicated in terms of God's active concern and agenda for Israel's deliverance through Moses. Here Moses' exceptional role as Israel's mediator cannot be overestimated – within the Bible only in Exodus 3.14–15; 33.19; 34.5–7, 14 does God speak about the divine name, and in each case Moses is the sole recipient of God's words.[35]

In 3.11 the sequence of objections by Moses – 'Who am I (*mî 'ānōkî*)... that I ... that I ...' is answered in 3.12 by God in the divine declaration 'I am with you' (*kî-'ehyeh 'immāk*) [36] and by his emphatic 'I have sent you forth' (*kî 'ānōkî šᵉlaḥtîkā*). This first query–response sequence is followed by a second in 3.13–15, but of a fundamentally distinctive nature. Moses now questions who God is with the voice of his people: 'What is his name?' (*mah-šᵉmô*). This is neither a question of personal inadequacy (cf. 3.11; 4.1, 10), nor merely a concern for formal identity, given that God has already been clearly identified in terms understandable to Moses and Israel in 3.6. This is a query of a singular, paradigmatic, theological-historical nature: how is Israel to know the name of God? It rises from repeated references in the narrative context of Exodus 1–3 to the pain and oppression of Israel in Egypt, and is thus a doubt-filled objection from the oppressed to a presuming Deliverer: 'If you are our God, what do you intend to do?' 'Who are you to make such promises to us?' 'What can you do?'[37]

The divine response in vv. 14–15 is thus to be understood in these terms and read in context with the previous narrative of Exodus

---

[34] For discussions and bibliographies see Cross, 'Yahweh', pp. 225–59; de Vaux, 'The Revelation of the Divine Name YHWH', pp. 48–75; W. H. Brownlee, 'The Ineffable Name of God', pp. 39–46; G. H. Parke-Taylor, *Yahweh*; Childs, *Exodus*; Durham, *Exodus*.

[35] See Moberly, *OT*, pp. 15–16.

[36] Durham's translation, 'The point is, I AM with you', emphasizes *'ehyeh* along the lines of 3:14b: 'I AM has sent me to you'; cf. *Exodus*, pp. 28, 33.

[37] Cf. Buber, *Moses*, pp. 48–55; Durham, *Exodus*, pp. 37–8.

1–3 and with the subsequent dialogue of promise, protest and proof. Moses' agency and mediation of God's revelation are specifically linked; three times in 3.13–15 the designation for God precedes *šᵉlāḥanî 'ălêkem*. The request for God's name, i.e., his specific, revealed intentions as embodied in his character and claim to credibility, elicits the divinely uttered *idem per idem* formula *'ehyeh 'ăšer 'ehyeh* of v. 14a,[38] the bold assertion of 'I am-ness', almost as a divine name, in v. 14b, and the divine name *yhwh* in v. 15.

Thus the context of Moses' commissioning is that of YHWH's saving presence and his choice to become Israel's historical Deliverer; in this sense the declaration of 3.14 becomes 'I in my saving presence shall be where I shall be', or 'I am and shall be present however I shall be present.' This YHWH is to be known by his 'I am/will be-ness', and he is about to prove his salvific presence through an array of extraordinary deeds culminating in their deliverance (cf. 3.6–7, 13, 15, 19–22).

Affirming this understanding of YHWH as 'the present God' are the repeated, divinely-uttered 'I am with' (*'ehyeh 'im*) declarations in context with the 'I am' (*'ehyeh*) declarations of Exodus 3.14.

3.12 I will be with you	*kî- 'ehyeh 'immāk*
3.14a I am that I am	*'ehyeh 'ăšer 'ehyeh*
3.14b 'I am' has sent me to you	*'ehyeh šᵉlāḥanî 'ălêkem*
4.12 I will be with your mouth	*wᵉʾānōkî 'ehyeh 'im-pîkā*
4.15 I will be with your mouth	*wᵉʾānōkî 'ehyeh 'im-pîkā*

These divine assertions of YHWH's immediate 'withness' are drawn from the early Israelite faith assertion that God 'goes with' the clan patriarch, i.e., 'with' his people. Thus the promise to accompany Moses is made continuous with his forefathers' experiences of God, but now based upon the new revelation of his divine character and name.

If Exodus 3 is a new beginning in Israel's story, with Moses' foundational encounter with God, the disclosure of his name, and the foundational YHWH-Sinai-holiness-Moses-prophecy-Israel nexus,[39] Exodus 6.2–3 is similarly paradigmatic. The opposition,

---

[38]   Cf. Exod. 4.13; 16.23; 33.19; 1 Sam. 23.13; 2 Sam. 15.20; 2 Kings 8.1; Ezek. 12.25. The *idem per idem* construction does have an intentional ambiguity about it; cf. 33.19 where the presence of God with his people is also at issue; cf. T. C. Vriezen, "*Ehje 'aser 'ehje*', pp. 498–512; Childs, *Exodus*, p. 69.

[39]   See Moberly, *OT*, p. 25.

disappointment and apparent absence and failure of God to deliver his people in Exodus 4–5 bring Moses back to YHWH with a lament (5.22–3). Exodus 6.2–3 functions as part of the divine reaffirmation – 'I am YHWH' – repeated throughout 6.2–8, and predicated upon God's recitation of reasons from the past to trust him.

Here in Exodus 3–6 begins a polarity internal to Sinai presence theology – the dialectic between YHWH's holiness, and freedom to choose his own place, manner and object of presence. YHWH chooses to commit himself as present, personal God in a binding relationship to his people, through Moses. Sinai presence is thus not surprising in its continuity with the past, but its discontinuity is also clear – God's name is YHWH, and his servant is Moses.

Exodus 19–24: the second encounter

The theophany of Exodus 19–24 constitutes the central act of God's covenant with Israel, and the most extraordinary enactment of divine presence in Israel's history.

Exodus 19.1–15: covenant and preparation. YHWH's initial address to Moses 'from the mountain' (*min-hāhār*) is a poetic summary of covenant theology (19.3b–6), couched in the careful language and phrasing of what many have taken to be the insertion of a standard covenant-renewal liturgy.[40] As the summary expression of the Sinai relationship, they echo to some degree the basic elements of ANE suzerain–vassal treaties.[41] YHWH reminds Israel in succinct summary (v. 4) of his saving presence, mighty signs and deeds which constitute YHWH's 'proofs of presence', a motif important to the Mosaic traditions,[42] as YHWH cements together the Hebrew society as his people.

In vv. 5–6 Israel is presented with the choice of becoming YHWH's covenant people: (1) YHWH's most special treasure and unique masterpiece in the whole earth, (2) his own kingdom of

---

[40] Cf. Clements, *God*, pp. 20–2; Childs, *Exodus*, pp. 366–8. Its original form probably also has a very early date; see references and arguments in Levenson, *Sinai*, p. 24; cf. also Buber, *Moses*, pp. 101–2.

[41] Cf. the seminal treatments of George Mendenhall, *Law and Covenant in Israel and the Ancient Near East*; Klaus Baltzer, *The Covenant Formulary*. The secondary literature is vast; see the summary in Dennis McCarthy, *Old Testament Covenant*.

[42] Cf. Exod. 3.19–20; 4.30–1; 7.1–12.13, 29–36; 14.5–20; 17.1–7; see Durham, *Exodus*, pp. 59–60, 192–8, 262.

priests and (3) his holy people. The affirmative response of 'all the people' (v. 8; cf. 24.3, 7) means that Israel has undertaken a ministry of God's presence to the world as a priestly kingdom of faith and servanthood, rather than through the *Realpolitik* of rulership. This requires corporate commitment to public holiness, and to a religious and social order diametrically opposed to the hierarchy of the Egyptian dynasty and Canaanite city-state.[43]

With Moses divinely authenticated as their necessary mediator (v. 9),[44] the people must prepare to meet God (19.10–15). The concern is for holiness, a cultic purity which sets aside the external acts of normal everyday life for the sake of concentration on the numinous, and a careful, temporary dedication of all to the sacred.

Exodus 19.16–25: the coming of presence. The narrator struggles for an adequate metaphor to describe the coming of YHWH's presence. Through the great, crashing storm pierces the sound of the ram's horn.[45] The people tremble fearfully, not at the horn's persistent and growing blast (19.13, 16, 19), but at its announcement that the Presence is arriving – at its signal Moses immediately leads the people forward 'to encounter (*liqra't*) God' (v. 17).[46] With the people positioned behind the designated boundaries (vv. 12, 17, 23), the phenomena which accompany the descent of YHWH's presence intensify even further (vv. 18–19). Thunder, lightning, heavy cloud, fire and thick smoke threaten to drown the human senses, driven by the ever-growing sound of the ram's horn.

The material concerning boundaries and holiness (vv. 20–5) gives pause to this dramatic scene. Levenson discerns here two contrasting movements. The first entails the intersection of God and of Israel; the second entails a barrier of holiness between God and Israel, expressed as boundaries and liturgical sanctity to protect the people. Only Moses, here the archetypal high priest, may break through the mysterious cloud. God's presence invites and repels; attracts and threatens. Thus again (cf. Exod. 3) the Mosaic traditions establish and reinforce the dialectic of the coming and

---

[43] See the discussions in Buber, *Moses*, pp. 103–4; Levenson, *Sinai*, pp. 30–1; Durham, *Exodus*, pp. 262–3.

[44] For two possible patterns behind the Mosaic office see Exod. 20.19; Deut. 5.4–5; cf. Childs, *Exodus*, pp. 350–60; Coats, *Moses*, pp. 27–36; Durham, *Exodus*, p. 264.

[45] Cf. Lev. 25.9; 2 Sam. 6.15; 1 Chron. 15.28; 2 Chron. 15.14; Ps. 47.5[6]; Isa. 27.13.

[46] Durham's translation, *Exodus*, pp. 266, 271.

mysterious Presence, at once knowable and 'other', in a tension of immanence and transcendence.[47]

The contrasting models of presence here – the invitation and preparation to meet with YHWH over against his strict instructions to remain distant and let only Moses ascend the mountain – serve to augment the implicit model of social, political and religious relationships. In its characterizations, barriers, levels of access and mysterious Presence, Sinai/Horeb is the archetypal holy place, to which correspond the patterns of the Jerusalem Temple.

Exodus 20–4: YHWH's ten words and the covenant. This is not the place for an examination of the Decalogue and its elaboration in Exodus 20–3, but its placement in the narrative enhances the theme of God's presence coming with the covenant in several ways.[48] The dominant motif of presence in Exodus 19 is echoed in the divine self-assertion in 20.2: 'I am YHWH' (*'ānōkî yhwh*).[49] As in 3.13–15 and 6.2–3, YHWH here declares to Israel his authority, who he is and the dynamic 'I am-ness' of his presence.

'You are not to have other gods in my presence' (*'al-pānâ*, v. 3): this initial command establishes the pre-eminent condition for covenant relationship with YHWH and his presence with them. The second commandment is an elaboration of the first – the prohibition against the shaping of deity images (v. 4) stands in striking contrast to the manner in which YHWH has come to Israel to deliver these words. In the midst of all the terrifying phenomena on the mountain, YHWH remains the unseen God, and he demands that no one represent divine presence in concrete form.

The making of the covenant in Exodus 24 brings to a climax the approach of YHWH's presence which began in Exodus 19, by presenting a picture of gradual ascents, from the people, to the elders, to Moses alone with God on the mountain. This again reinforces Moses' and Sinai's role as crucial archetypes of high priest and Temple. Moses is joined by the seventy elders of Israel (cf. Exod. 18.21–3; Num. 11.16–17) further up the mountain for a remarkable experience of divine presence – they 'saw' the God of

[47] See Brueggemann, 'Presence', pp. 680–3; 'Crisis', pp. 72–3, n.4. Cf. Rudolf Otto's well-known explorations of this dual aspect of 'the holy' as *mysterium tremendum et fascinans* in *The Idea of the Holy*.
[48] For Durham, *Exodus*, pp. 278–80, the Decalogue's narrative placement is primary to interpretation; cf. Childs, *Exodus*, p. 372; contra A. H. McNeile, *The Book of Exodus*, pp. lvi–lxiv; Hyatt, *Exodus*, pp. 196–7, 217.
[49] See the studies referred to in Durham, *Exodus*, pp. 283–4.

Israel[50] at his invitation and ate a meal in his presence (vv. 1–2, 9–11). What they see is not described in concrete terms but as something heavenly and glorious (cf. Isa. 6.1), viewed from the prone position of worship and limited to the rich pavement upon which his presence comes.[51] In the 'ideal end' to this narrative sequence, Moses finally climbs even higher to receive the stone law tablets, entering into the very cloud concealing the mountain.

Exodus 32–4: the third encounter – apostasy and renewal

The central theme of Exodus 32–4 is the threat which disobedience brings to the continuing existence of YHWH's people, and the centrality of his presence for the survival of their covenant.[52] Thrown into jeopardy by its monstrous sin with the golden calf (32.1–6), Israel's identity as YHWH's special covenant community is challenged by a sequence of angry utterances from Moses and YHWH (32.7–35) which climaxes in banishment by YHWH from the mountain of Presence, to an undecided fate, and the horrific declaration of his absence – YHWH will no longer go 'in your midst' ($b^e qirb^e k\bar{a}$, 33.3, 5). Moses' pleadings on his own and the people's behalf by means of the tent (33.7–11) are met by YHWH's qualified accessions and his restoration 'with' them (33.12–17). The tension of the narrative slowly unwinds with YHWH's renewed revelation of himself to Moses (33.18–34.9), the recommitment of the community as YHWH's covenant people (34.10–28) and the restoration of Moses' authority (34.29–35).

Several important highlights stand out.

(1) *Crisis*: The calf functions as more than an illegitimate symbol of Moses' representative and intermediary role, and as more than an idolatrous adoption of the common ANE bull image. The calf represents the attempt to worship YHWH himself, in terms which he has strictly forbidden.[53] The people perceive Moses' absence as

---

[50]   Note the shift from *r'h* (v. 10) to *ḥzh* (v. 11), and the history of reinterpretation and periphrasis of this language in the LXX and rabbis; see Nicholson, *God*, pp. 127–8.

[51]   This 'vision' should not be interpreted without reference to God's denial of direct sight of his *pānîm* in 33.20.

[52]   For discussions of the complex tradition-history of Exod. 32–4 see W. Beyerlin, *Origins and History of the Oldest Sinaitic Traditions*; Childs, *Exodus*, pp. 557–62, 584–6, 604–10; Moberly, *Mountain*, pp. 38–43, 116–56.

[53]   Cf. Durham, *Exodus*, pp. 421–2. Moberly, *Mountain*, pp. 46–7, finds the calf functioning in numerous ways parallel to the ark and tabernacle.

denying them access to God; the golden calf is both Moses' replacement and a representation of God's presence.

(2) *Confrontation and conflict*: Is God's withdrawal from his people threatened? Exodus 33 contains some of the OT's most careful and intricate theological analysis of the problem of divine presence. It functions as the bridge between the disobedience of Exodus 32 and the renewal of Exodus 34. The entire tenor of YHWH's relationship to Israel has changed.[54] He will not address the people directly, but says to Moses:

> 'Go! Ascend from this place, you and the people whom you have brought up from the land of Egypt.' (33.1)

The command to leave is tantamount to the primeval expulsion from the Garden (Gen. 3.14–24) or Cain's banishment from his family and the soil (Gen. 4.10–16). Israel's apostasy amounts to a rejection of YHWH's presence and covenant, and they can no longer remain at his holy mountain.[55]

But removal of divine presence from Israel is twofold. First, the people are commanded to leave Sinai/Horeb, and, secondly, YHWH can no longer go 'in their midst' (33.3, 5). The promised 'angel' (*mal'āk*) who will lead them (33.2, also 32.34) is not, there-fore, the equivalent of YHWH's presence, but at best a mode of presence distinct from and less than YHWH's personal accompani-ment and shrine presence 'in your midst' (*b^{e}qirb^{e}kā*). The logic of the narrative implies that YHWH has also repudiated his instruc-tions to build the ark and tabernacle as his symbols of presence.[56] YHWH's presence through the shrine ('Have them make me a sanctuary, so that I may dwell among them' – *w^{e}šākantî b^{e}tôkām*, 25.8; cf. 29.45–6; also Num. 14.42, 44) does not exactly correspond with his withdrawal from 'among' the people (*b^{e}qirb^{e}kā*, 33.3, 5), but the attempt to delineate 'cultic' from 'accompanying' presence is not well supported in the texts. Neither would it seem a likely dichotomy for ancient Jews.[57]

---

[54] Cf. Brueggemann, 'Crisis', pp. 48–9. Von Rad, *Theology* I, p. 288: 'from now on Israel's relationship to Jahweh is to some extent a mediated one'.

[55] So G. H. Davies, *Exodus*, pp. 237–8; Durham, *Exodus*, pp. 436–7; but cf. Moberly, *Mountain*, pp. 60–1.

[56] U. Cassuto, *A Commentary on the Book of Exodus*, p. 426, and Durham, *Exodus*, p. 437, interpret *bqrb* in terms of the accompanying tabernacle: YHWH now disallows its construction; cf. Moberly's explanation, *Mountain*, pp. 61–3.

[57] Contra, e.g., J. Reindl, *Das Angesicht Gottes im Sprachgebrauch des Alten Testaments*, pp. 224–5, who can see nothing cultic in Exod. 33.14–5; and von

The people's reaction of total grief in 33.4 and 6 seems to correspond with this interpretation: the threat is of expulsion from the mountain and the withdrawal of divine presence. In YHWH's absence there will be no covenant, ark, tabernacle, altar or cloud of glory.[58] Only the people's apparent remorse and YHWH's postponed judgement in v. 5 ('I will decide what to do with you') leave open any hope for Moses' subsequent intercession in 33.12–16.

(3) *Judgement pending*: The meeting-tent tradition (33.7–11) demonstrates the exalted position of Moses in terms of the presence motif.[59] The dominant image is provided in v. 11:

> So YHWH would speak to Moses face to face (*pānîm 'el-pānîm*), just as a man speaks to his friend.

This passage is often juxtaposed with 33.20:

> But [YHWH] said, 'You cannot see my face (*pānîm*), for a person shall not see me and live.'

The LXX and Targums apparently recognized a possible contradiction and thus translated *pānîm* with other words to avoid the difficulty, and many modern critics have argued that here two incompatible views of human access to God have been drawn from different traditions.[60] But this juxtaposition reiterates the dialectic already highlighted earlier; here in the symbol of *pānîm* is another aspect of the tension between God's immanent presence and transcendent holiness.[61]

Moberly has emphasized the position of the meeting tent 'outside the camp' (v. 7, twice) and 'far off from the camp' (v. 7) as consistent with YHWH's refusal to remain in the camp's central shrine. This meeting tent is a temporary, intermittent substitute, pending YHWH's restoration of his presence and the renewal of the covenant.

(4) *Climax and concession*: Exodus 33.12–17 is the account of Moses' urgent quest to 'know', and his insistent intercession for the restoration of God's presence 'with' (*'im*, 2x) him and the people. This unit divides into the two exchanges of vv. 12–14 and 15–17,

---

Rad, *Theology* I, pp. 234–41. See criticisms in Clements, *God*, pp. 37, 63–4, 118; cf. Moberly, *Mountain*, pp. 33–4.

[58] So Durham, *Exodus*, p. 437.   [59] See Mann, *Presence*, pp. 144–5.

[60] See the discussion and references in Moberly, *Mountain*, pp. 65–6.

[61] For discussion of *pānîm* see the bibliographies in Terrien, *Presence*, p. 159 n.78; and Brueggemann, 'Crisis'. Cf. A. R. Johnson, 'Aspects of the Use of the Term *pānîm* in the Old Testament', pp. 155–9.

each containing a request from Moses and response from YHWH, featuring the motif of knowing (*ydʿ*, 6x) and the formula 'find favour in my/your eyes' (5x).

'My presence will go (*pānâ yēlēkû*) and I will give you rest' (33.14). YHWH promises his presence but without the benefit of Moses 'knowing' or receiving any particular guarantees. *hlk* has no preposition or pronoun to indicate the position (ahead of, in the midst of)[62] or means of accompaniment, and Moses therefore continues to press for another concession, that YHWH will go 'with us' (*ʿimmānû*, v. 16).

Exodus 33.15–16 constitutes Moses' summary thesis of divine presence. For him the essence of being Israel is YHWH's presence.

> 'If your presence will not go with me, do not carry us up from here. For how shall it be known that I have found favour in your sight, I and your people? *Is it not in your going with us*, so that we are distinct, I and your people, from all other people on the face of the earth?'

Durham notes that the theological insight of the narrative at this point has universal application.

> No people, no matter how religious they are and for whatever reasons, can be a people of God without the Presence of God. Moses has posed the ultimate either/or: YHWH's decision to withdraw his presence from Israel is the decision of Israel's fate. Without YHWH's presence, in the dark and chaotic umbra of his Absence, Israel will cease to exist.[63]

YHWH concedes in 33.17. The *raison d'être* of the covenant community is rediscovered in the pluriform presence of God. He will go 'before' (*lipnê*) them as divine guide, 'with' (*ʿim*) them as the God who delivers, accompanies and empowers, and 'in their midst' (*bᵉqereb, bᵉtôk*) by means of the shrine.

(5) *Restoration and renewal*: Moses' request to see YHWH's glory (33.18, *kᵉbōdekā*)[64] and YHWH's reply with the affirmation of his presence (33.19–23) continues to echo the original sequence

---

[62] But cf. LXX: αὐτὸς προπορεύσομαί σου.   [63] *Exodus*, p. 448.

[64] Cf. Exod. 16.7; 24.16; 40.34–5; Num. 14.10. Note the apparent equation of *kābôd* (33.18, 22) and *pānîm* (33.20, 23), both in context synonymous with a full vision of YHWH himself; cf. Moberly's discussion and references, *Mountain*, pp. 76–7; Childs, *Exodus*, p. 593.

of doubts and reassurances in Exodus 3.11–4.17. As promised to Moses (33.19), God 'pronounced the name "YHWH" ... he proclaimed, "YHWH, YHWH"' (*wayyiqrā' bešēm yhwh / wayyiqrā' yhwh yhwh*, 34.5, 6), the second time a deliberate repetition in confessional form, followed by a list of five self-pronouncements describing how YHWH is YHWH. Exodus 34.6–7 functions as one of the most significant self-declarations by God in the whole OT. Subsequent Jewish tradition made much of it, as in the thirteen attributes of God.[65] The confession of divine nature in 34.6 is clearly reflected throughout the OT.[66] In the context of Israel's apostasy and YHWH's judgement, his self-description here is an appropriate recital of his compassion (cf. 32.14), long-suffering (cf. 33.12–16), slowness to anger (cf. 14.11–12) and unchanging love.

When YHWH and Israel renew their covenant relationship in 34.10–28 repeated emphasis is placed upon both the active presence of YHWH visible through his awesome work 'with' (*'im*, v. 10) his people, and upon his presence (*pānîm*, vv. 20, 23, 24) among them. The central concern of the story of Moses' glowing face is the character of YHWH's ongoing presence with Moses and the covenant community.[67] Moses has become the exclusive human channel for Israel's encounters with its God.

The tabernacle in Exodus. In the midst of the Priestly instructions in Exodus 25–31 and 35–40 are found a number of programmatic statements regarding God's presence and a sanctuary, e.g., in 25.8:

'Let them make me a sanctuary that I may dwell in their midst' *we'āšû lî miqdāš wešākantî betôkām* (cf. 29.42–6).

In Exodus 19–24 the permanent nature of God's relationship with Israel requires some permanent symbol of his presence among Israel – hence, the ark and tabernacle (Exod. 25–7; cf. Num. 5.3; 10.35–6, 2 Sam. 7.6).

Once constructed, the tabernacle is filled with YHWH's glory (*kābôd*) and the cloud of Presence accompanies Israel above the tabernacle during travels. Within the narrative purposes of Exodus,

[65] See Childs, *Exodus*, p. 598.
[66] Num. 14.18; Neh. 9.17; Pss. 86.15; 103.8; 145.8; Joel 2.13; Nahum 1.3; Jonah 4.2; cf. Exod. 20.5.
[67] See Menahem Haran, 'The Shining of Moses' Face', pp. 159–73; W. H. Propp, 'The Skin of Moses' Face – Transfigured or Disfigured?', pp. 375–86.

then, the tabernacle is continuous with Sinai; its role is, in a sense, to be a portable Sinai, providing symbolic sanctuary for the presence of YHWH. This is explicit in YHWH's command of 25.8 (cf. 29.45–6). *škn* is here distinguished from *yšb*, the usual Hebrew word for inhabiting a place, and applies to the God who dwells continually in this portable shrine, filling the place with his *kābôd*, as symbolized by the cloud.[68] In this way he fulfils his covenant pledge to be Israel's God, and takes up his abode in their midst, meets them (Exod. 25.22; 29.42–3; 30.6, 36) and goes with them (cf. Lev. 26.12–13).[69] In the reshaping of Sinaitic presence theology, YHWH's presence (*kābôd*) has been transferred from the mountain (24.16–17) to the tabernacle (40.34), so that the Sinai presence now accompanies Israel in the midst of the people.

Summary

There are several implications worth noting regarding the Exodus paradigm of presence.

(1)   The *raison d'être* for God's people arises wholly from the assumption of YHWH's will to liberate and make this people into his community, dwell among them, and promise them land. Within the Sinai narrative, presence is the *modus operandi* on the covenantal trajectory which moves God's people from slavery, through election and encounter, to full engagement and relationship with YHWH. The three encounters above provide Israel with its founding paradigms.

(2)   Fundamental to Sinai presence and the covenant between YHWH and his people is the understanding of his 'holiness', a major shift from patriarchal presence theology. Sinai brought new understandings of obedience and transgression, sin and judgement, the sacred and profane. YHWH is holy; his presence, election, covenant and Torah are holy. Israel is formed as a separate people with a distinct relationship to a holy God, the distinction lying *'in your going with us'* (Exod. 33.16).

(3)   After Exodus 32–4 the relationship is a mediated one. God's presence is experienced secondarily by his people, through Moses and the prophetic/cultic offices, the angel of presence and symbols.

---

[68] Cf. Cross, *Myth*, pp. 299, 323–4.

[69] See the various understandings of the ark in the traditions, Childs, *Exodus*, pp. 537–9; von Rad, *Theology* I, pp. 236–9; see Clements, *God*, pp. 28–35, regarding the relation of the ark and cherubim to divine presence.

The hierarchical pattern of mediation at Sinai/Horeb reflects the religious-political bounds of later Israelite cult leadership, and provides principles of social and religious organization.

(4) The Sinai narrative contains several important modes of divine presence, including (a) theophany and its accompanying phenomena, (b) divine guiding and accompanying presence 'before' the people in cloud, fire, *mal'āk* or warrior persona, (c) YHWH 'in the midst' of the people through the shrine, (d) YHWH's declared presence in the 'I am with you' formula, from the earliest traditions of Israelite religion. But these are not separate streams which can be divided between distinct theologies of manifestation (theophany) and dwelling presence (tabernacle). The Sinai narratives also communicate the paradox and complexity of YHWH's presence.

(5) YHWH's presence, as his holy mode of covenantal 'withness', is violable by his people. Presence and covenant have come by the gracious initiative of God, and can be spurned through disobedience. Chapters 32–4 of Exodus 'insist that a formulation of YHWH's presence in Israel may not be a cultic liturgical resolution which is immune to historical threat'.[70]

4.4. The Davidic/Jerusalem traditions of presence

The construct 'Royal Zion theology' arises essentially from Nathan's oracle (2 Sam. 7.8–17), 'David's' psalm (2 Sam. 23.1–7), Solomon's prayer (1 Kings 8.46–53) and YHWH's response (1 Kings 9.2–9), and several other psalms (e.g., Pss. 46, 48, 76, 89, 132).[71] At heart this theology claimed that YHWH had:

(1) chosen Jerusalem as the place for his special presence and as the chief city of his people,
(2) appointed the Davidic dynasty to rule in perpetuity from Jerusalem,
(3) established the Jerusalem Temple as central to the cult,
(4) identified for the Davidic ruler an intermediary role between him and his people, and
(5) declared Jerusalem secure against the threat of natural and supernatural forces.[72]

[70] Brueggemann, 'Crisis', p. 48.
[71] See the more detailed delineation of passages and motifs in Ollenburger, *Zion*, pp. 15–19.
[72] See J. M. Miller and J. H. Hayes, *A History of Ancient Israel and Judah*, pp. 203–4.

Chief among these is the first claim, the belief that YHWH dwells among his people in Jerusalem.

> The entire ideology of the Jerusalem temple centred in the belief that, as his chosen dwelling-place, YHWH's presence was to be found in it, and that from there he revealed his will and poured out his blessing upon his people.[73]

YHWH's Jerusalem presence is most prominent in his representation as king.[74] A number of psalms portray Jerusalem as a cosmic mountain from which YHWH himself actually reigned over all his created order, and thus protected his special city against all enemies (Pss. 46, 48, 76). Hence the special covenant relationship between YHWH and the Davidic rulers (2 Sam. 23.5; Ps. 89.19–37), complete with some references to the king as 'the son of God' (2 Sam. 7.14; Ps. 2.7). As YHWH's representative, the king mediated divine oracles and blessings and brought justice and life to the people (2 Sam. 23.2–4; Ps. 72).

Levenson has highlighted the note of conditionality that is attached to God's presence in the Temple (e.g., in 1 Kings 6.11–13; 2 Sam. 7.14–16; Ps. 89.20–38). It is the obedience of God's covenant people which evokes his presence; their disobedience renders uninhabitable and devoid his Temple. But the Hebrew scriptures also espouse the other extreme – the inviolability of Zion, as well as the Temple as a sanctuary only for the just.

One of the stable strands of presence theology linking Sinai and Jerusalem can be found in the re-enactment of the Sinai/Horeb theophany in the covenant celebration, as it was adapted and reformulated throughout the evolution of Israel's religion, as the central rallying-point for its faith and cult.[75] Furthermore, from Sinai, through the 'settlement'[76] period, and into the period of the monarchy, the ark and some form of cultic tent shrine maintained their significance as tangible symbols of the indwelling divine presence of YHWH 'among' his people.

To identify these two elements – the Sinai manifestation, and the tangible symbols of dwelling Presence – as continuing on into the Davidic stream begs questions from those scholars who see in

---

[73] Clements, *God*, p. 76.   [74] See, e.g., Ollenburger, *Zion*, pp. 23–5.

[75] Cf. examples from Deut. 33.2, 26; Judg. 5.4–5; Ps. 68.8–11 [7–10], 18 [17]; Hab. 3.3–4.

[76] A word used advisedly; see Brueggemann's discussion of Gottwald and Mendenhall in 'Trajectories'; cf. Miller and Hayes, *History*, pp. 58–60.

theophanic and cultic presence two theologies which are 'completely different'.[77] Such a distinction may be argued historically, but,
as noted above, it finds little direct support in Jewish scriptures.
The texts are no stranger to what may appear to the critic as an
inherent paradox; to assess 'temporary' divine visitation and 'permanent' divine cultic indwelling as conflicting and from different
sources undervalues what could more preferably be seen as rhetorical and theological paradox. That profound tension is captured
well in Solomon's long prayer of dedication (1 Kings 8.22–53). 'But
will God indeed dwell on earth?' he asks pointedly, safeguarding
YHWH's transcendence, even while recognizing the localization of
divine presence in the edifice through his name (cf. Deut. 4.7; Ps.
145.18).

The discontinuity between the Sinai and Jerusalem complexes of
traditions has frequently received attention in geographic terms –
Sinai survived in the north, and Zion in the south.[78] Chronological,
political and theological discontinuity have also been discussed. On
the narrative level contrasts are also apparent. The time of the
monarchy in Israel signals a new era of economic resources and
political power which provide breathing-space, not simply to
subsist as in the patriarchal era, but to evolve politically, socially
and economically as a regional power. Israel is no longer merely a
marginal, minority community preoccupied with its own survival,
but the regional focus of authority, with incumbent powers and
concerns.

The shift in the theological paradigm from Sinai to Zion corresponds with this shift in Israel's socio-political mode of existence.
Israel no longer seeks a revolution in its historical circumstances; its
liberation paradigm from the Exodus is not an appropriate pattern
for the circumstances of a nation-state. Maintenance of the *status
quo* is now paramount, for that corresponds with the maintenance
of the covenant and ruling community.

Brueggemann's statement, that the Mosaic covenant was 'radically concerned for *justice*', and the Davidic covenant 'more
concerned for *order*', is helpful here, if perhaps overly dichotomized. But the dominant perception of divine presence does move,

---

[77] Von Rad, *Theology* I, p. 237; he and others push this distinction further to
identify 'dwelling temples' and 'theophany temples' as separate structures. This
too is disputable; see Clements, *God*, p. 63 n.4.

[78] See Nicholson, *Deuteronomy*, p. 58, for bibliography on northern theology; cf.
Levenson, *Sinai*, pp. 188–90.

from YHWH as accompanying Protector and miraculous Liberator, to YHWH as majestic Presence, whose dwelling in Zion upholds his people in political, social and economic, as well as religious, terms. This does not discount the ongoing importance of the Sinai paradigm even in Jerusalem, but adds the remarkable complexities of statehood, monarchy and religious establishment to the picture. The Exodus model of Presence is now subject to the political and social realities of Jerusalem.[79]

When it was actually introduced, Solomon's Temple did not represent a radical departure from previous practice, given the already long history of the tent shrine and other cultic centres and sanctuaries.[80] And since Israel's worship already combined an emphasis on YHWH's coming in theophany with the idea of his dwelling among them, making Solomon's structure not just a 'dwelling-temple' but also the place where YHWH manifested himself, the establishment of the Temple at Jerusalem may have had stronger political and cultic, than theological, impact.[81]

The Temple was the permanent dwelling-place of YHWH, but in a mode of presence not intended to become static and fixed, given its active manifestation within the cult. Physically, YHWH's house in Jerusalem was to be a copy of his heavenly dwelling, and was not meant to tie him to an earthly dwelling or to contain a tangible representation of his image. Jerusalem's mountain thus represented the nexus of heaven and earth, where Israel could speak simultaneously of YHWH dwelling in heaven and of his presence on Mount Zion (cf. Pss. 11.4; 14.2, 7; 20.3, 7 [2, 6]; 76.3, 9 [2, 8]; 80.2, 15 [1, 14]). In numerous ways, through its symbolic features, structure and cultic practices and festivals,[82] the Jerusalem Temple explained YHWH's active presence in his created order and functioned as a spiritual and symbolic microcosm of the macrocosm; containing within itself the tension of the earthly and heavenly, the immanent and transcendent.

---

[79] The contemporary church parallels are revealing, as to who employs the Jerusalem paradigm (e.g., much recent North American and European Christianity) and who the Sinai (e.g., the Exodus orientation of numerous Latin American theologies of liberation; cf. Juan Luis Segundo, *Liberation of Theology*, pp. 110–24; J. A. Kirk, *Liberation Theology*, pp. 95–103; Ollenburger, *Zion*, p. 234; J. S. Croatto, *Exodus*).

[80] Cf. Hans-Joachim Kraus, *Worship in Israel*, pp. 134–78.

[81] For extended discussions see Clements, *God*, pp. 64–6; Terrien, *Presence*, pp. 186–9.

[82] Especially the Feast of Tabernacles, the autumn festival, which presupposes YHWH's presence as the heavenly king in the sanctuary; see Pss. 46, 48, 76, 96–7.

4.5.   Presence without the Temple

After most of four centuries under Davidic kings, the destruction of
the Temple and sacred city and the exile of the monarch proved a
watershed in Judean life. The prophets and Deuteronomists seemed
vindicated in having seen YHWH's requirement of faithfulness as
key to their survival. This was the lens through which understanding now came: YHWH had not been overthrown but had
destroyed their nation and Temple because of the people's apostasy.[83] Both the exile and the later events of 70 CE continued the
decentralization of Jewish religion, under way for years with the
growing diaspora population. Little is known of the practice of
Yahwism in exile or diaspora, except, for example, for Jews at
Elephantine in Egypt who possessed their own temple where
sacrifice was offered.

But in terms of his presence YHWH was not perceived to have
abandoned his people, and to this day the Temple has remained
critical (cf. Ezek. 11.16, 22–3; 37.26–8). As Levenson has observed:

> A central paradox of Jewish spirituality lies in the fact that
> so much of it centers upon an institution that was de-
> stroyed almost two millennia ago, the Jerusalem Temple.[84]

One explanation for this is found in the argument that intimacy
with YHWH (Israel's spiritual fulfilment) is made available in what
the tabernacle (whether tent or temple) signifies.[85] Here the goal of
the Exodus, rather than settlement in the land, becomes divine
presence in Israel's midst; the *telos* of Israel's *Heilsgeschichte*
climaxes in the tent, the vehicle of endless rendezvous with YHWH
(Exod. 29.42b–6). Levenson discusses 'the settlement tradition' and
'the Sinai tradition' (mostly P) as two climactic movements which
'define two poles not only of the Torah but of biblical spirituality in
general, and perhaps of the Jewish world view itself'.[86] Through its
worship patterns and sacrificial apparatus, ultimately established
atop Zion, the Temple (existent or not) functions as the earthly
antitype to the heavenly archetype, combining in supreme paradox
God's witness and otherness.

---

[83] Contrast another view in Jer. 44.17–18.
[84] Jon Levenson, 'The Jerusalem Temple in Devotional and Visionary Experience',
p. 32.
[85] See the parallelism between 'Temple' and 'tent' in Ps. 26.8; 27.4–5; 74.2, 7–8.
[86] 'Temple', p. 34.

Whatever the traditio-historical conundrums, the Pentateuch's concern for the tent shrine may present to the reader a dialectic between the portable shrine and the Jerusalem Temple, with a judgement on the latter, i.e., asserting an image of God as 'a delicate tabernacling presence, on the move with his people', rather than God as 'a king enthroned in his massive stone palace'.[87]

The spiritual focus given the Temple and YHWH's presence within Israel's religious vocabulary seems natural after the disappearance of its literal referent. Zion became a cosmic institution, with thematic parallels between the Temple and creation, 'rest' in the land and the Sabbath. And in the triumphant eschatological refounding of the Temple the renewal of the world is anticipated. Central to these eschatological hopes was the promise of the fulness of the divine presence on earth.[88] When the post-exilic rebuilding of the Temple brought no such miraculous return, the promise of God's presence in the midst of Israel was relegated to the eschatological realm. Strongly reflected in rabbinic literature is the doctrine that since its first rebuilding the Temple lacked, among other things, the Shekinah and the Holy Spirit.[89]

Even with the anticipation of the Temple's reconstruction, it was the synagogue which became the principal successor to the first and second Temples, for worship, community and the liturgical practice and experience of divine presence. Although sacrifice was meanwhile replaced by prayer and sacred study,[90] the Temple remained the focus of and conduit for diaspora prayers to God, with the hope of the divine presence in a perfect Temple on Zion transferred to the realm of heaven.[91]

Within this post-exilic stress on divine transcendence, the sense of God's nearness to his people gained by necessity a diversity of expression other than through Temple rites.[92] They were able to experience God's presence apart from the Temple, particularly in the synagogue, but also in their homes and communities, through

---

[87] Levenson, 'Temple', p. 33.

[88] See Hag. 1.8; 2.7; Zech. 2.10–11 [14–15]; 8.3; cf. 1.16; Mal. 3.1; *Jub.* 1.27–8; *1 Enoch* 90.29–31. Cf. Joel's reassertion, without interpretation, of God's presence in the Temple; 2.27; 3.16–17 [4.16–17]. See the fourth vision of 4 Ezra for a vision of Zion's eschatological restoration (4 Ezra 9.26–10.59); see further M. E. Stone, 'Reactions to the Destruction of the Second Temple', p. 263.

[89] See for references Clements, *God*, p. 126.   [90] Cf. Ps. 141.2.

[91] See the doctrine of a heavenly Temple and Jerusalem developed in some Jewish circles, e.g., *Asc. Isa.* 7.10; Wis. 9.8; *Apoc. Bar.* 4.2–6; *T. Levi* 3.4. Cf. *T. Dan.* 5.12–13; Gal. 4.26; Heb. 12.22; Rev. 3.12; 21.1–22.5.

[92] See Clements, *God*, pp. 130–2.

regular Sabbath worship and sacred study, in which Temple and YHWH's sovereignty have retained their significance, as cosmic symbols and archetypes.

The sectarians of Qumran did not spiritualize divine presence. They held closely to the Torah's cultic prescriptions, but rejected the authority of the high priests, transferred the symbolism of the Temple to themselves, and called their community 'a sanctuary' and 'the holy of holies' (see 1QS 5.5–7; 8.4–6; 9.3–5; 11.8; CD 3.18–4.10; 4QFlor. 1.1–7; 4QpIsa. frag. 1; 1QpHab. 12.1–4). E. P. Sanders has further noted the intensity with which community members seem to have felt that they had entered into God's presence with their initiation into the sect, and continued in God's presence forever. This sectarian consciousness of the immanence of God is the grounds for their very strict ritual purity.[93]

Jacob Neusner concludes that the primary concern of the Pharisees was that 'the Temple should be everywhere, even in the home and hearth'.[94] Such a standard called Israelites to a purity appropriate to the Temple even within their own homes. 'The extension of the Temple purity rules to the household might be seen as an expression of extreme piety. As [God's] presence is everywhere, so we should always behave as if we were in the Temple, that is, in his presence.'[95] Hence Renwick asserts that among Pharisees of the first century CE, the overarching concern was with 'finding, establishing and maintaining the presence of God in their midst'.[96] This encouraged deeper emphasis on God's heavenly nature, such as that reflected in Matthew's strong interest in 'the Kingdom of heaven' and 'heavenly Father'. Post-exilic Judaism also saw a rise in the correspondent doctrines of the Name, Word, Wisdom, Spirit, Shekinah and intermediary angelic beings, as symbolic and functional means of explaining and asserting God's proximate presence.

Despite the Temple desecration he faced, a later Psalmist's cry to God concerned a greater fear – that God himself might leave them:

> Do not move away from us, O God ...
> While your name lives among us, we shall receive mercy,
>   and the gentile will not overcome us.
> For you are our protection
>   and we will call to you, and you will hear us.
>   (*Pss. Sol.* 7.1, 6–7)

---

93 *Paul and Palestinian Judaism*, pp. 314–15.
94 *From Politics to Piety*, p. 152; cf. p. 83; see further in Renwick, *Paul*, p. 21.
95 *The Idea of Purity in Ancient Judaism*, p. 69.   96 *Paul*, p. 43.

Thus post-Temple divine transcendence did not mean divine absence from the human arena of Judaism. Israel remained convinced of God's sovereignty and presence with his people (cf. Ps. 139.7–8). Even as the Temple became a symbol of hope and loyalty, God's presence became greater than any building, and he was 'with' his people apart from any cultic edifice (Hag. 1.13). This spiritualization of God's presence also gained personal expression; his presence was as close as the humble hearts of his people who sought him.[97] There is little question that in the literature and experience of Judaism in Matthew's day, the presence of God was a commonplace issue.

Matthew's interests in God's presence as an issue for the story of Jesus are more pointed, however. As we shall see, he does exhibit his inheritance of the Mosaic paradigm of Sinai, but he also connects strongly to the 'with you' language of OT divine presence, which we shall consider next.

[97] Isa. 57.15; 66.2; see Clements, *God*, pp. 132–5.

5

'I AM WITH YOU': THE OLD TESTAMENT TRADITION OF THE SAYING

This chapter investigates that OT body of references which speaks of God's presence in terms of the saying 'I am with you' and its various forms. Matthew's connection to this saying is clear, and, though often asserted by commentators, has rarely been examined closely.

'I am with you' might appear somewhat similar to the assertion common to Greek literature of all eras that one's activities are successful 'with God' (σὺν θεῷ/θεοῖς), but the Greek expression developed without direct relation to the Hebrew formula according to Walter Grundmann.[1] Within other texts of the ANE there is little evidence of a comparable 'I am with you' religious expression.[2] H. D. Preuβ can find only two Egyptian texts, and possibly two proper names, which offer any real parallel to the language and idea of the Hebrew formula, the presence of a deity with a person, and this scarcity of occurrence stands in stark contrast to its frequency in the OT.[3] The 'with you/us' expression, then, is essentially a phenomenon of the Hebrew Bible, a frequent and powerful saying which asserts, promises or solicits divine presence. From the outset the expression evidences itself as an element of faith essentially peculiar to the people of God, strongly established in the bedrock stratum of the traditions as a fundamental component of Israelite piety.[4]

Among recent studies, those of van Unnik, Grundmann, Preuβ, Görg and Frankemölle are most notably concerned with this *Redeform*.[5] Van Unnik's 1959 study is foundational, a compilation of all

[1] 'σύν-μετά', *TDNT* VII, pp. 773–4.
[2] E.g., a search through Pritchard, *ANET*, especially pp. 3–155, 365–452, 573–86, reveals little of relevance.
[3] See Preuβ's evidence in '"... ich will mit dir sein!"', pp. 161–71.
[4] See Preuβ, "*eth*; '*im*', *TDOT* I, p. 451; Frankemölle, *Jahwebund*, pp. 73–4.
[5] Van Unnik, '*Dominus*', pp. 270–305; Grundmann, 'σύν-μετά', pp. 766–97, especially p. 775; Preuβ, 'Ich', pp. 139–73 (see p. 139 for earlier literature); Manfred

the relevant LXX occurrences organized topically. Grundmann is essentially dependent upon van Unnik, with an added overview. Preuβ incorporates van Unnik's work at several places, but favours a *traditionsgeschichtlich* trajectory for the saying. Görg often reiterates Preuβ and adds his interests in the wider context of Israel's encounter with God. More recently Frankemölle has collected the fruits of Preuβ's and Kilian's work to assert μεθ᾽ ὑμῶν as a theological *Leitidee* for Matthew.[6]

Each of these studies is both helpful and at points tendentious. Van Unnik attaches the Spirit to the saying, ending up with the overstatement that 'the man to whom this "the Lord is with you" is said becomes a pneumatic'.[7] Preuβ connects too many of the formulas to an understanding of history as God's presence in *Weg* and *Wanderung*.[8] Others have overemphasized the formula's origin in the tradition of holy wars, the cult or the Davidic covenant.[9] Frankemölle is hampered by his over-application of *Bundestheologie* to the First Gospel. My intention here is not to reinvent the wheel, but to reassess the formula saying specifically within the framework of this study.

5.1. The Hebrew text (MT)

The Jewish scriptures, in a variety of wordings and circumstances, contain at least 114 occurrences of the formula between the MT and LXX, promising or asserting that God is 'with' an individual, a group, or the nation Israel.[10] The MT shows at least 104 uses of the

---

6   Görg, '"Ich bin mit Dir"', pp. 214–40; Frankemölle, *Jahwebund*, pp. 72–9. Cf. also Trilling, *Israel*, pp. 40–3.

    Jahwebund, especially pp. 72–9; see Rudolf Kilian, *Die Verheiβung Immanuels Jes 7,14*, pp. 54–94. Frankemölle favours Preuβ's approach: 'Die Einseitigkeiten und Oberflächlichkeiten von Grundmann und v.Unnik beseitigt in einer eindringlichen Studie H. D. Preuβ' (p. 72).

7   '*Dominus*', p. 286; followed by Grundmann, 'σύν–μετά', p. 775 n. 55.

8   See 'Ich', pp. 157–8, and further comments below.

9   See Frankemölle's discussion, *Jahwebund*, pp. 73–4.

10 Gen. 21.20, 22; 26.3, 24, 28; 28.15, 20; 31.3, 5, 13; 35.3; 39.2, 3, 21, 23; 48.21; Exod. 3.12; 10.10; 18.19; Num. 14.42, 43; 23.21; Deut. 1.42; 2.7; 20.1; 31.23; (32.12); Josh. 1.5, 9, 17; 3.7; 6.27; 7.12; 14.12; 22.31; Judg. 1.19, 22; 2.18; 6.12, 13, 16; Ruth 2.4; 1 Sam. 3.19; 10.7; 16.18; 17.37; 18.12, 14, 28; 20.13; (28.16); 2 Sam. 5.10; 7.3, 9; 14.17; 1 Kings 1.37; 8.57; 11.38; 2 Kings 18.7; 1 Chron. 11.9; 17.2, 8; 22.11, 16, 18; 28.20; 2 Chron. 1.1; 13.12; 15.2, 9; 17.3; 19.11; 20.17; 25.7; 32.7, 8; 35.21; 36.23; Ezra 1.3; 1 Esdras 1.25; 2.3; Esth. 6.13; Job 29.5; Pss. 23[22].4; 46[45].7(8), 11(12); 91[90].15; Isa. 7.14; 8.8, 10; 41.10; 43.2, 5; 58.11; Jer. 1.8, 17, 19; 15.20; 20.11; 42[49].11; 46[26].28; Amos 5.14; Hag. 1.13; 2.4; Zech. 8.23; 10.5; Jdt. 5.17; 13.11; 3 Macc. 6.15.

formula, counting individually each member of any double occurrence, e.g., 'as I was with Moses, so I will be with you',[11] as well as each member of 'parallel' occurrences between Samuel–Kings and Chronicles. In the extant texts the Hebrew expression is essentially standardized, showing limited divergence.

God is always the subject of the formula, most often as *yhwh*. At least twenty-seven times God speaks with the divine 'I' of a first-person divine utterance: 'I was/am/will be with you'.[12] Otherwise God is the third person, either in human discourse (e.g., YHWH will be with you) or narration (e.g., YHWH was with him).

In about three of four instances the preposition *'im* is employed. In the remainder of cases *'et* (or its variants *'ôt* and *'it* with sufformatives)[13] is used, or rarely, the preformative *b^e-*.[14] Lexically, *'im* and *'et* are synonymous, with very little if any difference in emphasis.[15] Meaning depends on the setting and activity in context. The reader must determine, when God is 'with' someone, whether that means being 'with', 'beside', 'alongside', 'fighting for', 'by', 'near', 'in the midst of', 'among', 'in the company of', 'with the help of' or 'in association with' them.[16]

The formula is invariably personal, e.g., it makes no connection between God's presence and a locality. A full range of personal pronouns appears as the indirect object within the formula: 'I am with you/him/them'; 'YHWH is with me/you/him/us/them', as well as some proper names. In the majority of cases God is with a particular individual; fewer times he is said to be with a group or the whole people of Israel.[17]

This number includes both MT and LXX. 1 Chron. 9.20; Jer. 30.11; Ezra 34.30 are textually doubtful. Van Unnik works only with LXX references. Preuß works only with the MT, and counts singly all double references.

11. Josh. 1.5; see also Josh. 1.17; 1 Sam. 20.13; 1 Kings 1.37; 8.57.
12. Gen. 26.3, 24; 28.15; 31.3; Exod. 3.12; Deut. 1.42; 31.23; Josh. 1.5 (2x); 3.7 (2x); 7.12; Judg. 6.16 (but cf. LXX); 2 Sam. 7.9; 1 Kings 11.38; 1 Chron. 17.8; Ps. 91(90).15; Isa. 41.10; 43.2, 5; Jer. 1.8, 19; 15.20; 42(49).11; 46(26).28; Hag. 1.13; 2.4.
13. Cf. Josh. 14.12; Jer. 20.11.
14. Cf. 1 Sam. 28.16 where Samuel tells Saul: 'YHWH has departed *from* you' (MT: *mē'ā lēkā* ; LXX: ἀπὸ σοῦ).
15. So Preuß, "*eth*; *'im*', p. 449; contra BDB, p. 85.
16. Stylistic preference seems to steer the choice of preposition: patriarchal narratives – mixed; Sam.–Kings *'im* only (15x); Chronicler – *'im* only (19x); Jer., Amos and Hag. – *'et* only (9x); Zech. – *'im* only (2x).
17. See Gen. 48.21; Exod. 10.10; Num. 14.42–3; 23.21; Deut. 1.42; 2.7; 20.1; (32.12); Josh. 7.12; 22.31; Judg. 1.22; 6.13; Ruth 2.4; 1 Kings 8.57; 1 Chron. 22.18; 2 Chron. 13.12; 15.2; 19.11; 20.17; 25.7; 32.7–8; Ps. 46(45).8, 12; Isa. 8.8, 10; 41.10; 43.2, 5; 58.11; Jer. 42(49).11; 46(26).28; Amos 5.14; Hag 1.13; 2.4; Zech. 8.23;

The range of individuals who are recipients of the formula is not extensive – twenty-one central figures (never a woman) from among God's people: Abraham, Ishmael, Isaac, Jacob, Joseph, Moses, Joshua, Caleb, 'the judge', Gideon, Samuel, Saul, David, Solomon, Jeroboam, Hezekiah, Asa, Jehoshaphat, Mordecai, Job and Jeremiah, and one outsider, Neco. At times these individuals, when addressed by the presence saying, may be seen as representative 'corporate' personalities, but they also remain individuals with special and paradigmatic relationships with God.[18]

The formula is not exclusively 'in-house'. One 'outsider', Neco, pharaoh of Egypt, also has God 'with' him in precisely the same terms as apply to God's people (2 Chron. 35.21).[19] Cyrus, king of Persia, also invokes the formula when blessing the exiles returning home: 'YHWH God be with him' (2 Chron. 36.23; Ezra 1.3; cf. LXX 2 Esdras 1.25; 2.3).

In several notable cases the perfect and imperfect of *hyh* juxtapose dramatically the past and future presence of God: 'as I was with Moses, so I will be with you' (Josh. 1.5).[20]

5.2. The LXX text

The LXX text shows a tendency toward greater formalization of the Hebrew formula saying. It has several additional occurrences of the formula not found in the MT, apparently from interpretive decisions by the translators to augment the text in four cases.[21] The LXX lacks two which the MT includes, owing perhaps to dependence on different Hebrew traditions or again to interpretive translation.[22]

In terms of names the LXX uses for God, *yhwh*, *'ĕlōhîm*,*'ēl* and *ṣᵉbā'ôt* are most often translated by the appropriate κύριος, θεός or παντοκράτωρ. The nine exceptions give greater prominence to

10.5; cf. Jdt. 5.17; 13.11; 3 Macc. 6.15. Van Unnik's list (p. 302 n.52) appears incomplete, but see his comments, p. 284.

[18] Cf. Gen. 26.3, 24; 28.15; 48.21; Judg. 6.12–13; 2 Sam. 5.10 etc. This ambiguity could explain the switch in consecutive formulas in Judg. 6.12–13 between singular and plural pronouns: 'with *you* (singular) . . . with *us*'.

[19] An earlier pharaoh's utterance of the formula in Exod. 10.10 is probably sarcastic.

[20] Cf. Josh. 3.7; 1 Sam. 20.13; cf. 1 Kings 1.37; 8.57.

[21] Gen. 31.13; Esth. 6.13; Isa. 58.11; Jer. 1.17. To these may be added the five occurrences of the formula found in the additional books of the LXX: 1 Esdras 1.25; 2.3; Jdt. 5.17; 13.11; 3 Macc. 6.15.

[22] 1 Sam. 18.12; Job 29.5.

κύριος, but without any visible pattern.[23] The most striking change is the LXX's simplification of the Hebrew formula by translating *'im*, *'et* and *bᵉ-* only as μετά plus the genitive.[24] This appears as a deliberate intensification of the formulaic character of the 'with you' expression.[25]

The LXX also adds the verb, often future, to a significant number of the verbless (and probably jussive) Hebrew sayings.[26] Other times the Hebrew jussive becomes the definite Greek future; *yᵉhî* becomes ἔσται. Some ambiguous Hebrew imperfects are given the certainty of Greek futures.[27] Van Unnik finds this trend significant in so far as 'the certainty existing already in the Hebrew text is underlined and strengthened in the LXX'.[28]

5.3.   The character of presence in the saying

It would be easy to impose an anachronistic understanding on the OT 'with you' formula, given its familiar counterparts in many modern Christian liturgies.[29] The OT formula originates in divine 'I am' utterances in theophany and divine prophetic speech; these undergird the subsequent narrative observations and third-person utterances of the 'with you' saying.[30] This is characteristic of the Isaac, Jacob, Moses and Joshua stories where God's own 'I am' promise of presence provides the backbone for the added observations by others that God is or will be 'with' them.[31] YHWH's 'I am with you' is at the core of Israel's deliverance and restructuring in

---

[23]   Cf. the MT and LXX texts of Gen. 28.20; Deut. 31.23; Judg. 6.16; 2 Sam. 5.10; 1 Chron. 22.18; 2 Chron. 13.12; 36.23; Ps. 46(45).8, 12.

[24]   Num. 14.43 is the single exception among over 100 examples.

[25]   E.g., outside the 'with you' formula, LXX verbal σύν-compounds employ μετά; see Gen. 14.24; 18.23, 26; Exod. 33.16; Num. 22.35; cf. Grundmann, 'σύν-μετά', p. 768. See examples in J. B. Liddell and R. Scott, *A Greek–English Lexicon* II, pp. 1108–9 and 1690–1; cf. further in Martin Johannessohn, *Der Gebrauch der Präpositionen in der Septuaginta*, pp. 202–12.

[26]   See Gen. 26.24; 39.23; Judg. 1.22; 2 Chron. 25.7; 36.23; Pss. 23(22).4; 91(90).15; Isa. 41.10; 43.2, 5; Jer. 1.8, 19; 15.20; 42(49).11; 46(26).28; Hag. 1.13; 2.4; Zech. 8.23; although cf. 1 Chron. 22.16.

[27]   Cf. Gen. 48.21; Exod. 18.19; 1 Sam. 17.37; 20.13; 2 Sam. 14.17; 1 Chron. 22.11; 2 Chron. 19.11; 36.23; Ezra 1.3 (but note ἔστω in the parallel text of 1 Esdras 2.3); Amos 5.14.

[28]   '*Dominus*', p. 283.

[29]   See van Unnik's discussion in '*Dominus*'.

[30]   See the theophanic setting in Gen. 26.3, 24; 28.15; 31.13; Exod. 3.12; Judg. 6.12–13, 16; and prophetic speech in 2 Sam. 7.9; 1 Kings 11.38; 1 Chron. 17.8; Isa. 41.10; 43.2, 5; Jer. 1.8, 17, 19; 15.20; 42.11; 46.28; Hag. 1.13; 2.4.

[31]   See further analysis by Görg, 'Ich', pp. 222–8.

Deutero-Isaiah, is constantly reiterated as Jeremiah's empowerment
for his difficult commission, and is at the heart of the divine
rallying-cry to Judah during the Temple's reconstruction in Haggai.

Divine presence and absence

The OT formula finds both positive and negative expression. The
results are correspondingly good or devastating; e.g., if in battle
'YHWH is with us', victory is ours, but if he is not 'with' us, that
means our defeat. In several places the formula is unequivocally
negative in stating that God is not with Israel; his presence has
become absence with dire consequences.[32]

Divine 'withness' brings divine benefits; divine absence means the
loss of them or even divine judgement. When God is said to be
'with' someone the positive results are unmistakable. Success,
victory and prosperity appear, and the most concrete of results
materialize: safe travel, battles won, fame, multiplied herds, allevia-
tion of *Angst*, protection and help in distress. Conversely, for
Israel, Saul, Josiah, Job, the enemies of God's people, and others
who found themselves on the opposite side of the 'equation' of
divine presence, the results of this negative reality of divine absence
consumed them.

The formula in Israel's cult and history

The 'with you' formula occurs rarely as an element of worship or
with a connection to a liturgical setting. There are, for example, no
references in Leviticus or Ezekiel. *yhwh ṣᵉbā'ôt 'immānû* in Psalm
46.8, 12 and *'immānû 'ēl* in Isaiah 7.14; 8.8, 10 may have found
their way at some point into the Temple cult as liturgical cries or
confessions of faith.[33] As Frankemölle points out, this is too small
a literary base on which to posit wider cultic origins and connections for the formula.[34] Many of the things to which we might

---

[32] See Num. 14.42–3; Deut. 1.42; Josh. 7.12; 2 Chron. 25.7; cf. 1 Sam. 18.12; 28.16;
2 Chron. 15.2.

[33] Cf. also Ps. 23.4. See Hans Wildberger, *Jesaja 1–12*, p. 293, for *'ēl* as a well-
known formula; cf. Wilhelm Vischer, *Die Immanuel-Botschaft im Rahmen des
königlichen Zionsfestes*, p. 22, on *'im-'ēl* in 2 Sam. 23.5. Vischer calls *'immānû 'ēl*
a choral shout in the royal Zion festival liturgy. So also Mowinckel, *Psalmenstudien* II, p. 306 n.1, and *He That Cometh*, p. 111, cf. E. Hammershaimb, 'The
Immanuel Sign', pp. 124–42, especially pp. 135–6.

[34] *Jahwebund*, p. 73.

assume the OT presence formula should be attached – tent of meeting, ark, Temple, sacrifice and worship – play little visible part in the 'with you' formula's employment.

The Writings contain only seven occurrences; the prophets show nineteen uses, with fourteen of those split between Isaiah and Jeremiah. The formula, rather, is a phenomenon of the narrative and discourse materials of the historical books; it thrives in the historical sections of the Pentateuch, in Joshua and Judges, in the books of the kings and in the work of the Chronicler. Not a single formula occurs in what is generally recognized as P material.[35] This concentration emphasizes most sharply the concrete and active nature of the formula. It is not a philosophical assessment of divine ontology and omnipresence, but the promise, assertion and declaration of YHWH's distinctly personal company, activity and empowerment on behalf of his people in particular events of their individual and corporate human experience.

Divine presence and the condition of obedience

A number of texts are explicit concerning the requirement of obedience for the favour of God's presence, activity and company. For example:

> 'If you will listen to all that I command you, walk in my ways, and do what is right in my sight by keeping my statutes and my commandments, as David my servant did, *I will be with you*, and will build you an enduring house, as I built for David, and I will give Israel to you.'
>
> (1 Kings 11.38)

> The Lord was with Jehoshaphat, because he walked in the earlier ways of his father; he did not seek the Baals.
>
> (2 Chron. 17.3)

See also Joshua 7.12; 1 Kings 8.57–8; 2 Kings 18.7; 2 Chronicles 15.2; 19.11; 25.7; Psalm 91(90).15; Amos 5.14. However, this condition of Torah obedience cannot be absolute, given the examples mentioned earlier of those 'outsiders' to whom the divine presence of the formula is applied.[36]

---

[35] See Eissfeldt's delineation, *The Old Testament*, pp. 188–9, 204–6.
[36] Contra Frankemölle, *Jahwebund*, p. 77.

The formula as salutation

For some scholars the formulas in Judges 6.12 and Ruth 2.4 have the appearance of a greeting. These two texts are normally assessed as post-exilic, and Preuß speculates that the greeting form may be one of the final steps in the formula's trajectory of development.[37] But the formula in Judges 6.12 quickly exceeds the narrow format of a greeting:

> The angel of the Lord appeared to him and said to him, 'The Lord is with you, you mighty warrior.'

Gideon's incredulous reply – 'What do you mean: "YHWH is with us"?' demonstrates the concrete terms and broader arena commonly evoked by the formula's utterance. 'YHWH is with you' required a correspondingly positive reality in his people's wellbeing; he refused to accept the angel's 'with you' formula merely as a salutation.

The 'greeting' to the reapers by Boaz is suspect on similar and different grounds.

> Just then Boaz came from Bethlehem. He said to the reapers, 'The Lord be with you.' They answered, 'The Lord bless you.'   (Ruth 2.4)

If this *yhwh ʿimmākem* was a common greeting, it is simply not attested elsewhere.[38] The greeting which was commonly attested was that of 'Peace', a fact which the Syriac MS underlines by exchanging the Hebrew formula for 'Peace be with you.'[39] Ruth 2.4 is the single OT instance where the 'with you' formula might function as a greeting, but it also performs narratively as an intentional window into the quality of Boaz's character as pious and faithful, inclined to fulfil properly his levirate responsibilities.

5.4. The setting

One helpful approach to understanding better the presence formula's various applications to the events and faith of Israel is to gather the references into groups according to narrative contextual pat-

---

[37] 'Ich', p. 157, and '*'eth*; *'im*', p. 457; cf. van Unnik, '*Dominus*', pp. 272–4, 281.
[38] Contra Gustaf Dalman, *Arbeit und Sitte in Palästina*, p. 43; cf. John Gray, *Joshua, Judges and Ruth*, p. 413.
[39] See van Unnik, '*Dominus*', pp. 272–5.

terns. Van Unnik's categories do not always match the message, setting and conditions of the formula, and Preuβ seems overdependent on source analysis.

At least five categories are distinguishable (though not necessarily mutually exclusive) within the formula's narrative contexts:

(1) peace and prosperity,
(2) travel,
(3) war,
(4) liberation and deliverance, and
(5) divine commission.

Peace and prosperity

In the largest single category of references the divine presence of the 'with you' formula is seen in concrete correlation to the social, political and economic success of its recipients. With the patriarchs this could mean sustenance, enlarged herds, land, children and extra-community respect. For Israel's rulers this could mean growing fame, enthronement, political peace and the amassing of wealth.

> 'Reside in this land as an alien, and *I will be with you*, and will bless you; ... I will give all these lands ... I will make your offspring as numerous as the stars of heaven ... '
> (Gen. 26.3–4)

> And David became greater and greater, for *the Lord, the God of hosts, was with him.*   (2 Sam. 5.10)

> In those days ten men from nations of every language shall take hold of a Jew, grasping his garment and saying, 'Let us go with you, for we have heard that *God is with you.*'[40]
> (Zech 8.23)

The travels of Israel

A solid block of 'with you' sayings are employed within language of 'the way', where YHWH is present as the accompanying,

[40] See also Gen. 21.20, 22; 26.24, 28; 28.20; 31.5; 39.2–3, 21, 23; Deut. 2.7; Josh. 6.27; Judg. 6.12–13; 1 Sam. 3.19; 16.18; 18.12, 14, 28; (cf. 28.16); 2 Sam. 7.3; 1 Kings 8.57; 11.38; 2 Kings 18.7; 1 Chron. 11.9; 17.2, 8; 22.11, 16, 18; 28.20; 2 Chron. 1.1; Esth. 6.13; Job 29.5; Isa. 58.11.

protecting and guiding God. Here the formula is a concrete element in the narratives of Isaac, Moses, the Judges, and right into post-exilic *Wanderung Theologie* with reformulation in terms of 'the way' of YHWH; 'the way' of the community.[41] Here God is the accompanying divine escort, a way of talking about God's presence 'with' his people 'in the way' that has marked indelibly the language of Jewish scriptures. God is 'with' his people as shepherd, leader, protector and guarantor of safe passage.

> 'Surely the Lord your God ... knows your going through this great wilderness. These forty years *the Lord your God has been with you*; you have lacked nothing.'[42]
>
> (Deut. 2.7)

The wars of Israel

In a number of passages the 'with you' formula is explicitly localized in the tradition of holy wars.[43] God's promise to be with Israel in this context is essentially his promise of victory in battle, while his declaration of absence spells defeat.

> 'Do not go up, *for the Lord is not with you*... because you have turned back from following the Lord, *the Lord will not be with you.*' (Num. 14.42–3)

> The Lord said to [Gideon], '*But I will be with you*, and you shall strike down the Midianites, every one of them.'[44]
>
> (Judg. 6.16)

The formula's manipulation is notable in the Chronicler's claim of God's presence for Judah in the North–South wars with Israel. Also striking is the Chronicler's placement of the presence formula in the mouth of Neco, king of Egypt, Judah's opposition:

---

[41] See Preuß, 'Ich', pp. 141–5, 154–6.

[42] See also Gen. 26.3, 24; 28.20; 31.3, 13; 35.3; Exod. 3.12; Num. 14.42–3; Deut. 1.42; 20.4; 31.23; Josh. 1.9, 17; 3.7; 2 Sam. 7.9; 2 Chron. 36.23; Ezra 1.3; 1 Esdras 1.25. Preuß overemphasizes this motif as the centre of *Mitsein Jahwes*; cf. 'Ich', pp. 157, 159, 171–2.

[43] Some postulate holy wars as the original *raison d'être* for the formula of *Mitsein Jahwe*; this over-applies the evidence; see Hans-Walter Wolff, *Frieden ohne Ende*, pp. 41–3; von Rad, *Theology* II, p. 180. Cf. Frankemölle, *Jahwebund*, pp. 73–4.

[44] See also Deut. 1.42; 20.4; Josh. 14.12; Judg. 1.19, 22; 1 Sam. 17.37; 2 Chron. 13.12; 20.17; 25.7; 32.7–8.

> 'Cease opposing *God who is with me*, lest he destroy you.'
>
> (2 Chron. 35.21)

Liberation and deliverance

The saying can also carry a liberation motif, where 'I am with you' means divine rescue and help for God's people. This theme, which originates in the Exodus liberation narratives, is maintained in a special way as divine presence recurring in Israel's subsequent story of salvation history.

> He said, '*I will be with you*; and this shall be the sign for you, that it is I who sent you: when you have brought the people out of Egypt, you shall worship God upon this mountain.'
>
> (Exod. 3.12)

> '*For the Lord your God is with you*, who brought you up from the land of Egypt.'[45]
>
> (Deut. 20.1)

The 'with you' utterance is common in Jeremiah (1.8, 17, 19; 15.20; 20.11; 42[49].11; 46[26].28), and apart from 20.11 is always a divine first-person assertion of deliverance, resulting in a series of powerful testimonials of God's presence with Jeremiah, to liberate and empower him.

Divine commission

In a number of notable instances, the 'with you' formula appears as a distinct element within the commissioning of Israel's patriarchs and prophets.[46] God is personally present as divine enabler, releasing anxiety ('Do not be afraid!')[47] and providing empowerment and reassurance in the context of commissioning.

---

[45] See also Josh. 22.31; Judg. 2.18; 1 Sam. 17.37; 2 Chron. 36.23; Ezra 1.3; Ps. 90(91).15; 1 Esdras 2.3; Isa. 8.8, 10; 41.10; 43.5; 58.11; Amos 5.14; Zech. 8.23; 10.5; Jdt. 5.17; 13.11; 3 Macc. 6.15.

[46] See B. J. Hubbard, *The Matthean Redaction of a Primitive Apostolic Commissioning*, p. 67, for exploration of our presence formula or similar 'Reassurance' component in nineteen of twenty-seven examples of the Hebrew commissioning *Gattung*.

[47] Cf. Deut. 20.1; 31.23; 1 Chron. 28.20; 2 Chron. 20.17; 32.8; Isa. 41.10; 43.5; Jer. 42.11; 46.28; Hag. 2.4–5; cf. also Gen. 21.17; Deut. 31.8; 1 Sam. 4.20; and Luke 1.28–30.

But Moses said to God, 'Who am I that I should go to Pharaoh, and bring the Israelites out of Egypt?' He said, '*I will be with you ...*'
(Exod. 3.11–12)

'... take courage, all you people of the land, says the Lord; work, *for I am with you*, says the Lord of hosts, according to the promise that I made you when you came out of Egypt. My Spirit abides among you; do not fear.'
(Hag. 2.4–5)

5.5. The historical continuum of God's people

The 'with you' presence formula is primarily defined by its historical contingencies, as a narrative, after-the-fact description of God's presence and intervention in a wide variety of his people's life situations. This 'narrative-*heilsgeschichtlich*' character gives to the long string of 'I am/he is with you' occurrences a common and continuous theme, more relevant and significant than classification by text traditions or one theological *Tendenz*.

This continuity of narrative and *Heilsgeschichte* is especially evident in six explicit double formulas which build a present- or future-tense declaration of God's presence upon its occurrence in the past, e.g.:

'As I was with Moses, so I will be with you.'[48]   (Josh. 1.5)

The 'with you' formula is employed to affirm the historical continuity of YHWH's presence with his people: *'ehyeh ... ka'ăšer hāyîtî/*ὥσπερ ἤμην μετὰ Μωυσῆ ἔσομαι καὶ μετὰ σοῦ. At the heart of this continuous application of the formula is the fundamental belief in YHWH's presence with his people as the constantly recurring reason for their salvation in history.

Various OT narratives deliberately draw together the history of YHWH's people with this continuous experiential chain of divine presence. The chain is anchored in the 'with you' promises to the patriarchal families, carries through YHWH's self-declarations and 'with you' promises to Moses, links with divine 'withness' in the Exodus liberation, in YHWH's people at war and in their travels.

The chain of 'with you' promises continues with David (10x in

---

[48] See also Josh. 1.17; 3.7; 1 Sam. 20.13; 1 Kings 1.37. Cf. 'implicit' double formulas in Judg. 6.13; 1 Sam. 18.12.

Sam.–Kings, three parallels in 1 Chron.).[49] The promise formula
retains its concreteness (accompaniment, protection, deliverance)
but peace and prosperity for the nomadic clan becomes peace and
prosperity for the kingdom, in its new domestic social circumstances. The 'with you' formula is given continuity in dynastic
terms. God will be 'with' David as he was 'with' Saul, 'with'
Solomon as 'with' David, and 'with' Israel as 'with' Israel's
forefathers.[50]

Post-exilic prophecies and the Chronicles bring a stylized return
to the language and terms of 'with you' presence. Ten times in his
idealized history the Chronicler attaches the formula to battles, in
Judah's favour, where 'the war of YHWH' is elevated to high
status. Among the prophets, the formula's place in the Exodus
liberation is renewed in Deutero-Isaiah's prophetic restoration of
the nation. At the end of the Hebrew Bible the Chronicler restores
YHWH's presence 'with' Israel to the return journey of the exiles.

5.6. Implications

Despite frequent occurrence within theophany and prophetic utterance, God's presence in the 'with you' formula saying is not based
in particular divine phenomena, theophania or a-physical religious
experience. It arises out of his people's retrospective perception or
prospective anticipation of his favourable activity within their
historical reality.

The breadth of reference within the Jewish narratives points to a
wide range of exceptional experiences – cognitive, emotional,
physical and spiritual, the individual and community.[51] The
formula saying cannot be reduced to a general principle of God's
spiritual or theophanic presence with his people, but neither does it
exclude the 'withness' of the practice and symbols of God's cultic
presence.[52]

For example, the 'with you' sayings in Numbers 14.42–3 are

[49] Preuß and Frankemölle both note the tendency of Vischer and others to
overcharacterize *'im* as the key concept of the Davidic covenant, and the
Davidic era as central; see Preuß, 'Ich', p. 156; Frankemölle, *Jahwebund*, p. 74.
[50] 1 Sam. 20.13; 1 Kings 1.37; 8.57.
[51] Cf. van Unnik, *'Dominus'*, pp. 276, 284; Grundmann, 'σύν–μετά', p. 775; Preuß,
'Ich', pp. 154–5, and *"eth; 'im'*, pp. 456–8; Frankemölle, *Jahwebund*, pp. 74–5.
[52] Contra van Unnik's, Grundmann's, Preuß's, Frankemölle's and Trilling's distinctions between dynamic ('with you') and static (cultic) presence. These are too
theologically artificial for the Jewish scriptures.

linked to 14.44, where the ark and the person of Moses both define God's presence. The ʾet/ ʿim language of the formula shows affinities to other expressions where God is said to be 'among' or 'in the midst of his people' (beqereb/betôk), language also relating to God's presence through the ark/tabernacle (Exod. 33.3, 5; 34.9–10).

The 'with you' sayings therefore are not an isolated linguistic formula. They are the dominant linguistic expression on the broader spectrum of OT language of divine presence, spanning God 'with', 'among', 'in the midst of', and 'before' his people.

The 'with you' formula is YHWH's people's declaration of their faith in his will to save them – hence its primary narrative-*heilsgeschichtlich* character. The prominence of the divine 'with you' saying within the community's sacred texts of history and worship *deliberately encodes in a formulaic saying their ongoing self-perception as the people with whom God chooses to dwell and act favourably*. By observing that 'God with them' is apparent to outsiders, Jewish writers have given the formula saying the status of a definitive credo for YHWH's people.[53] Within the Jewish canon these recollections function as legitimizations of Israel's success *vis-à-vis* other nations, as explanations of Israel's demise (i.e., divine *absence*), and even as prophecies of future restoration of the people within God's favour.[54]

In summary, the OT 'with you' presence saying is a foundational element of Israelite faith and scripture, given an early terminological stereotyping. Though recast in the period of the kings into a more general formula of support, it never lost its original concrete vocabulary and application to the activities of God's people, even in prophetic oracle. The LXX translators recognized and emphasized the centrality of the Hebrew formula and further formalized its terms. When Israel's narrators, leaders and prophets proclaim again and again 'YHWH is with us', they reassert their central identity as God's people.

5.7. The formula in post-biblical Judaism

The Hebrew Bible and LXX provide the bulk of the 'with you' sayings of YHWH's presence. Only in a few extant texts from

---

[53] See Josh. 22.31; 2 Chron. 35.21; Pss. 23(22).4; 46(45).7(8), 11(12); 1 Esdras 1.25; Jdt. 13.11. Cf. Josh. 3.7; 22.31; 1 Sam. 3.19–20; 16.18; 18.28; 2 Chron. 15.9.
[54] See especially Esth. 6.13 (LXX); Zech. 8.23.

Palestinian and diaspora Judaism is the formula given further application and development.

Post-biblical Jewish writings of Semitic origin[55]

Judith employs the formula in two clear instances within its quasi-fictional narrative.[56] In 5.5–21 Achior the Ammonite tries to explain Jewish resistance to Holophernes, Nebuchadnezzar's general, and includes the declaration 'God is with them' (5.17). The formula is also a triumphant cry from the lips of Judith as she returns to the city with the head of Holophernes: 'God is with us!' (13.11). Judith, probably from the time of Judas Maccabeus, extends the OT practice of employing the presence formula within narrative contexts concerned with God's deliverance of his lowly, oppressed, weak, forlorn and helpless people (9.11).

Within its free midrashic elaboration of Genesis 1 to Exodus 12, the book of *Jubilees*[57] re-employs few of the eighteen 'with you' presence sayings found in the MT. *Jub.* 24.22 contains a straightforward citation of the formula from Genesis 26.24. God is more often spoken of as 'dwelling' with his people,[58] and covenant provides the means for God to be with his people historically (13.9) and eschatologically (*Jub.* 9.27–8).

The War Rule of the Qumran community uses the 'with you' formula in a dramatization of the final spiritual-conflict victory.

> For Adonai is holy, and *the King of glory is with us*, along with the holy beings. Warrior angels are in our muster, and He that is Mighty in War is in our throng. The army of His spirits *marches with us*.　　　　　　(1QM 12.8–9)

Great attention is paid to the necessity of ritual purity in order for the divine host to be present,[59] in line with the transfer to itself of the Temple's symbolism and presence, seeing the community as the sanctuary and 'holy of holies' (1QS 5.5–7; 8.4–10; 9.3–7 etc.).

---

[55] See these categorizations of Jewish texts by language in Emil Schürer, *The History of the Jewish People* III.1, p. v.

[56] See George Nickelsburg, *Jewish Literature Between the Bible and the Mishnah*, pp. 105–9; Schürer, *History* III.1, pp. 216–19, Eissfeldt, *OT*, pp. 586–7, for discussion and references regarding dating and the real episode lying at the origin of the Judith story.

[57] Probably second century BCE. See Schürer, *History* III.1, pp. 308–14; cf. Eissfeldt, *OT*, p. 608; Nickelsburg, *Literature*, pp. 78–9.

[58] Cf., e.g., *Jub.* 1.6, 18, 26; 18.15–16; 19.5; 25.21.

[59] See 1QM 7.3–7; cf. Schürer, *History* III.1, p. 400.

Within *Midrash Rabbah*, the formula is often reinvested with new meaning or a less direct interpretation (*vis-à-vis* YHWH). For example, in *Gen. Rab.* 28.15 the rabbis disagree over what sort of protection the 'with you' saying covers. In *Gen. Rab.* 31.5 '*immadi* is read as '*amudi*, 'my pillar, support'. In *Exod. Rab.* 3.12 comes the observation that the presence formula is 'an expression used only to one who is afraid'. Joseph's Egyptian master suspected him of witchcraft, 'until he saw the *Shekhinah* standing over him' (*Gen. Rab.* 39.3).[60]

Van Unnik notes that Targum Onkelos emphasizes divine 'help', replacing 'the Lord is with you' with 'the Memra of the Lord is to your help' (*bs' dkh*).[61]

Post-biblical Jewish writings of Greek origin

The romantic fiction of 3 Maccabees[62] employs the divine presence formula in 6.15 as essentially a reiteration of OT usage, rather than a new application of the formula to God's people in the Egyptian diaspora.

Philo turns his attention to at least sixteen of the OT texts which contain the 'with you' formula. But only seven or eight times does he appear to acknowledge the formula, and then most often within his unique paraphrastic interpretation. For example, in *Migr.* 30 Philo states in reference to Genesis 26.3 that:

> the fountain from which the good things are poured forth is the companionship of the bountiful God. He shows this to be so when to set His seal upon the flow of His kindness, He says, ἔσομαι μετὰ σοῦ.[63]

Philo defines Moses in Exodus 3.12 as a prophet seeking to know the cause of successful achievement:

> He found that it was the presence of the only God with him   (ὁ θεοῦ μονοῦ σύνοδος; *Fuga.* 140).[64]

Josephus encounters a good number of our texts in his recon-

[60] Cf. van Unnik, '*Dominus*', pp. 280, 301 nn.40–2.   [61] '*Dominus*', p. 280.
[62] See Schürer, *History* III.1, pp. 537–9; Nickelsburg, *Literature*, pp. 169, 171. Note the apparent relationship between 3 Macc. and Josephus' legends, *Cont. Ap.* 2, 5 (50–5).
[63] Cf. similarly *Som.* 1, 179 (Gen. 28.15); *Det.* 4 (Gen. 31.5); *Som.* 1, 227–8 (Gen. 31.13).
[64] Cf. also *Post.* 80 (Gen. 39.2); *Agr.* 78 (Deut. 20.1); also *Migr.* 62–3.

struction of Jewish history in *Antiquities*, but more often than not does not directly engage the 'with you' formula in these OT passages.[65] Josephus does exhibit some recognition of the theological importance of the formula, but mollifies the boldness of the 'I am with you' saying. For example, Abimelech's use of the formula when describing Isaac's success in Genesis 26.28 becomes:

> for seeing that God was with Isaac and *showered such favours upon him*, he cast him off.   (*Ant.* 1.260)

God 'being with' Jacob and Joseph is reinterpreted by Josephus as 'providence' or 'providential care' (πρόνοια; *Ant.* 2.8, 61) and in the case of Moses (Exod. 3.12) as God 'promising Himself to assist him' (*Ant.* 2.272).[66]

Josephus' tendency to soften the formula's straightforwardness is most apparent when he does not allow Egypt's Pharaoh Neco to claim the prerogative of the divine promise. Josephus' editorial note on Josiah's death explains:

> It was Destiny, I believe, that urged him on to this course in order to have a pretext for destroying him.[67]

We have one notable, yet circumspect, example of Josephus himself employing the divine presence formula in a post-biblical setting, in his version of King Herod's speech encouraging his troops about to do battle with the Arabs.[68]

> 'You have no right to say this in the first place, for those who have justice with them (μεθ᾿ ὧν), have God with them (μετ᾿ ἐκείνων), and where God is, there too are both numbers and courage.'   (*Ant.* 15.138)

Implications

When the divine 'with you' formula does appear in these post-biblical Jewish contexts it does so most frequently as an OT

[65] E.g., when commenting on Gen. 21.20, 22 (*Ant.* 1, 219); Gen. 28.15, 20 (*Ant.* 1, 280–3); Gen. 31.3, 5, 13 (*Ant.* 1, 309–11); 1 Sam. 3.19 (*Ant.* 5, 351).
[66] See more examples: *Ant.* 4.122, 128 (Deut. 1.42); *Ant.* 4.185 (Judg. 7.12); *Ant.* 5.42; 6.57 (1 Sam. 10.7); *Ant.* 6.181 (1 Sam. 17.32, 37); *Ant.* 6.196 (1 Sam. 18.14); *Ant.* 6.231 (1 Sam. 20.13); *Ant.* 7.65 (2 Sam. 5.10); *Ant.* 7.91 (2 Sam. 7.3); *Ant.* 7.338 (1 Chron. 22.11); *Ant.* 7.357 (1 Kings 1.37); *Ant.* 8.295 (2 Chron. 15.12); *Ant.* 8.394 (2 Chron. 17.3); *Ant.* 11.259 (Esth. 6.13).
[67] *Ant.* 10.76; cf. 2 Chron. 35.21; 1 Esdras 1.25.
[68] Cf. van Unnik, '*Dominus*', p. 281.

quotation or allusion, or within biblical idiom and language. Rarely is the formula given fresh application within the world and words of the authors themselves. The formula terminology is often softened.

The reticence to employ the 'with you' formula may indicate a growing circumspection regarding use of the divine name, and an evolution within the complexities surrounding portrayal of divine presence and absence.[69] Some may thus have considered the language of the formula too bold, or too clearly belonging to their biblical contexts for reapplication.

More to the point, however, is the genre of these writings. The clear narrative-*heilsgeschichtlich* context for the OT formula is not often matched in these post-biblical Jewish writings. Judith and Josephus' *Antiquities* are closest to the narrative style, and they do re-employ and newly apply the formula occasionally. The acceptable literary context for the formula is that of scriptural recounting of 'divine history'.

5.8.   The formula and Matthew

In terms of Matthew's first-century environment, this review points to the widespread currency of the 'with you' formula as a 'biblical' expression. It was not perceived as a general utterance of divine favour, but as bold scriptural shorthand employed within Israel's narrative accounts. In post-biblical Jewish literature the formula remains bound to the scriptural context and idiom of Israel's patriarchs, monarchs and prophets. Rarely do writers give the formula application to their own historical settings later than the second century BCE.

Noteworthy then is the absence in this literature of the formula's bold language being reapplied afresh to *contemporary* individuals and communities. Matthew appears responsible for the reintroduction of the formula to his audiences. His application of the formula to Jesus is a bold theological thrust, against the backdrop of the apparent reticence of these authors.

Matthew's particular concern with the boundaries of God's new people resonates strongly with the Hebrew experience of YHWH's 'withness' as integral to their community definition. The 'with you' formula presented a powerful vehicle, already foundational to

---

[69]   But there is no support here for the stereotype of an early Judaism which held to an inaccessible God; see E. P. Sanders' cautions, *Paul*, §I.10.

Israel's faith, which could be reformulated to assert the divine messianic presence of the 'God-with-us' Messiah. He adopts the formula, not only as an effective way to express his community's continuation of Israel's 'narrative-*heilsgeschichtlich*' experience of YHWH being with them, but also as a surprising new characterization of Jesus. Thus the 'YHWH is with us' of the nation Israel becomes the 'Emmanuel–God with us' of Matthew's universal ἐκκλησία, and the divine 'I am with you' of YHWH becomes the divine 'I am with you' of the risen Jesus.

The proximity of this connection is striking in another way. The last verse in Matthew's Hebrew Bible was probably Cyrus' proclamation to the returning exiles:

> 'YHWH the God of heaven has given me all the kingdoms of the earth, and he has charged me to build him a house at Jerusalem, which is in Judah. Whoever is among you of all his people, *may the Lord his God be with him.* Let him go up.'   (2 Chron. 36.23)

Here is no less than a significant mandate for Matthew's attempts at continuity and redefinition. Cyrus, an 'outsider', commissions a new chapter in the narrative-*heilsgeschichtlich* story of God's people. The boundaries of 'his people' are open for reappraisal, God's supra-ethnic sovereignty is reaffirmed, and his divine 'withness' is declared as critical to the task of rebuilding his community and place of presence.

These prove also to be the parameters for Matthew's rewriting of the story of God's presence. He continues the narrative-*heilsgeschichtlich* stream. He opens wide the question of who the people of God are. He affirms God's sovereignty. And he refocuses the *telos* of God's OT presence 'with' his people onto his story of Jesus' saving presence with the new people of God.

6

MATTHEW 1: THE BIRTH OF THE 'GOD-WITH-US' MESSIAH

The conclusions above in Chapters 2 and 3 about the rhetorical function of Matthew's presence motif resulted from applying to the text that particular set of questions which treat it as a narrative story. In Chapters 4 and 5 we looked at the presence motif via another set of questions concerning its place historically and theologically in the OT scriptures and traditions Matthew valued so highly. Having seen the importance of the patterns of presence and the divine 'with you' language of the OT we are able here to return to Matthew, to take a closer look at the evangelist's redactional artwork in Matthew 1, 18 and 28, and at the particular christology which inspired his composition. If the exercise in Chapters 2 and 3 was closer to reading and interpretation à la Krieger's 'mirror', the following conforms more to his 'window'. However, we want to employ compositional and redactional evidence here to complement our narrative reading of the Gospel; we are not reading the Gospel in order to find historical evidence for the purpose of hypothetical reconstruction.[1] The central concern of this chapter is the composition of the Matthew 1 birth story around Jesus' christological significance.

6.1. Tradition and redaction

Any investigation of Matthew's infancy narrative which turns to the secondary literature can quickly become overwhelmed by the centuries-old preponderance of interest in issues of patriarchy,

---

[1] See Culpepper, *Anatomy*, p. 5. E.g., R. Brown's separation of Matt. 1–2 into hypothetical pre-Matthean units of tradition tends toward historical reconstruction *per se*; e.g., *Birth*, pp. 104–19, 154–9; also G. M. Soares Prabhu, *The Formula Quotations in the Infancy Narrative of Matthew*, pp. 294–300; C. T. Davis, 'Tradition and Redaction in Mt 1:18–2:23', pp. 404–21.

παρθένος, and procreation sans partner.[2] Commentary on the Emmanuel naming has often come as a secondary appendage to these discussions. Such an order of emphasis, however, can be an inversion of the story's own priorities, in favour of a subsequent generation's concerns arising, e.g., out of particular cultural views of female virginity, 'purity' and human sexual nature.[3] Apart from Matthew 1–2 and Luke 1–2 the NT is virtually silent on the events of Jesus' birth (cf. Mark 1.1; 6.3; John 1.45; 7.42; Gal. 4.4; Phil. 2.5–11; Rom. 1.3).[4]

It is not difficult to highlight the differences between Matthew 1–2 and the rest of the Gospel. We have already seen from a narrative perspective the distinctness of Matthew 1–2 as the story's opening frame. As well, some of the birth stories, for all the drama and significance they add to the circumstances of Jesus' origins, appear to have little impact upon the remainder of the Gospel. Nowhere outside the initial account do we find reference to the sort of political and social ruckus which the visit of the eastern magi apparently caused in Jerusalem. The Bethlehem birth, Jesus' escape from Herod's terrible massacre, and his family's move from the south in his early childhood are never again mentioned, and are particularly absent from 13.53–8.[5] There is no reference anywhere back to the Holy Spirit's generation of this Messiah child in an extraordinary conception.

Our narrative reading of Matthew 1–2 earlier, however, revealed its rhetorical significance for the whole story, and it is possible to see Matthew's redactional hand in the key themes of the infancy narrative. In contrast to the colour of Luke's infancy narratives, Matthew's are basic sketches. Matthew 1–2 is structured to serve his many deliberate scriptural proofs of Jesus' messiahship, including the genealogy, five of the Gospel's eleven formula quotations, and numerous allusions to OT motifs.

---

[2]   See recent discussions in Margaret Davies, *Matthew*, pp. 31–5; Stock, *The Method and Message of Matthew*, pp. 26–31; Hagner, *Matthew 1–13*, pp. 13–22; Schaberg, *Illegitimacy*; R. Brown, *Birth*, pp. 517–33; Luz, *Matthew 1–7*, pp. 123–7.

[3]   Schaberg, Anderson and others are beginning to pursue some of these difficult issues.

[4]   Cf. H. von Campenhausen, *The Virgin Birth in the Theology of the Ancient Church*, pp. 17–24; V. Taylor, *The Historical Evidence for the Virgin Birth*, pp. 1–20.

[5]   Cf. 12.46–9; see discussion in Davies and Allison, *Matthew 8–18*, pp. 456–7.

As with many discussions of sources and traditions behind gospel texts, supporters can be found for each of the three basic positions on the composition of Matthew 1–2:[6] (1) Matthew wrote it freely, with minimal reference to tradition;[7] (2) Matthew synthesized a number of originally separate elements;[8] (3) Matthew adapted what was already essentially a unified story.[9]

A number of more or less commonly shared observations have shaped the discussion. It has been argued that if one extracts what is obviously Matthean, i.e., the formula quotations, the text reads more smoothly without them.[10] The genealogy appears to have a traditional basis.[11] And although there are numerous resemblances between Matthew 1.18–2.23 and the haggadic traditions and infancy legends about Moses, these do not qualify as direct antecedents to Matthew's narrative.[12]

But there is little consensus on the process and stages of formation and on what might justifiably be seen as redactional designs on meaning. Raymond Brown's well-known attempt at thorough disentanglement of tradition and redaction in Matthew 1–2 highlights two problematic implications: (1) the possibility of such an exercise losing its relevance for the meaning of the present text by undue dependence on speculative reconstruction,[13] and (2) the doubt cast over any one set of interpretive results by the disagreement of others.[14] Much of this debate seems also to project the

---

[6] See the discussions in Rudolf Bultmann, *The History of the Synoptic Tradition*, pp. 291–4; Davis, 'Tradition', pp. 414–21; A. Vögtle, *Messias und Gottessohn*; Soares Prabhu, *Quotations*, pp. 294–300; R. Brown, *Birth*, pp. 104–21; Davies and Allison, *Matthew 1–7*, pp. 190–5.

[7] See Kilpatrick, *Origins*, p. 55; Goulder, *Midrash*, pp. 228–42; Gundry, *Matthew*, pp. 13–41.

[8] See Dibelius, *From Tradition to Gospel*, pp. 128–9. Many scholars advocate that only 2.1–23 are pre-Matthean narratives, while 1.18–25 is Matthew's composition; e.g., Vögtle, *Messias*.

[9] See Strecker, *Weg*, pp. 51–5; R. Brown, *Birth*, pp. 104–19; Luz, *Matthew 1–7*, p. 102; Davies and Allison, *Matthew 1–7*, pp. 191–5.

[10] See especially Soares Prabhu, *Quotations*.

[11] The genealogy could be pre-Matthean (Strecker, *Weg*, p. 38), from an existing Jewish monarchical list of Davidids (R. Brown, *Birth*, pp. 69–70; Luz, *Matthew 1–7*, p. 108), or a Matthean adaptation of the above list and/or biblical models (Frankemölle, *Jahwebund*, p. 314; M. D. Johnson, *Genealogies*, p. 210; Davies and Allison, *Matthew 1–7*, pp. 165–7, 186–7).

[12] See Josephus, *Ant.* 2.210–16; cf. 2.205–9; *LAB* 9.10; *Ex. Rab.* 1.13 on Exod. 1.15; see further references in Luz, *Matthew 1–7*, pp. 117–18; Davies and Allison, *Matthew 1–7*, pp. 192–4.

[13] As in R. Brown, *Birth*, pp. 107–8, 154–63.

[14] E.g., Davis, 'Tradition', pp. 404–21.

post-Guggenheim presumptions of a print-based culture onto first-century texts and traditions.[15] As W. B. Tatum asserts, Matthew may have been committing to writing for the first time a cycle of *oral* infancy traditions known in his community.[16]

Despite the uniqueness of the infancy narrative, we need to recognize the rhetorical unity within Matthew 1–2 and between Matthew 1–2 and 3ff., brought to the story by the author through significant structural, thematic and literary links. The theme of the genealogy in 1.1, γένεσις Ἰησοῦ Χριστοῦ, is echoed by the appearance of the same terminology in 1.18, while the narrative of 1.18–25, with its angelic revelation, constitutes the critical explanation of how Jesus has broken the 'was the father of' pattern (ἐγέννησεν) of the genealogy in 1.16.[17] And what may appear as a large contradiction between the patriarchal and Davidic lineage in the genealogy, and the lack of human fatherhood in vv. 18–25, is resolved by Joseph's enactment of legal paternity – he obediently takes (παραλαβεῖν, παρέλαβεν, vv. 20, 24) his wife and names (καλέσεις, ἐκάλεσεν, vv. 20, 25) the child.[18] Similarities between Matthew's two accounts of Jesus' birth, the genealogical in 1.1–17 and the narrative in 1.18–25, and the two accounts of creation, the numerical in Genesis 1.1–2.3 and the narrative in Genesis 2.4–25, are also relevant.[19]

A variety of descriptions has been applied to 1.18–25, including legend, haggadic midrash, and even christological midrash.[20] A majority of scholars would now agree that the pericope comes from Matthew's hand, or that he at least reformulated it in his own terms.[21] I.e., the formula quotation is indubitably his (1.22–3), as

---

15 See Staley, *Kiss*, pp. 1–5.
16 'The Matthean Infancy Stories', p. 69. See Stanton's helpful reminder of the limitations and possibilities of redaction criticism, *Gospel*, pp. 23–53. Cf. B. H. Streeter, *The Four Gospels*, p. 266; Kilpatrick, *Origins*, p. 55; W. L. Knox, *The Sources of the Synoptic Gospels* II, p. 126.
17 So Stendahl, 'Quis', who sees 1.18–25 as the 'enlarged footnote' of the genealogy's crucial point; Stendahl's point has been built upon by many others. Cf. earlier T. Zahn, *Das Evangelium des Matthäus*, p. 77.
18 See Mishnah *B. Bat.* 8.6; cf. Luke 1.60–3.
19 W. D. Davies, *Setting*, p. 71; R. Brown, *Birth*, p. 140. Brown also notes that the two parts of Matt. 1 fit together smoothly in a fashion similar to the Adam–Noah genealogy in Gen. 5.1–32 and the Noah narrative in 6.9–9.29.
20 Respectively: Bultmann, *History*, p. 291; W. Trilling, *Die Christusverkündigung in den synoptischen Evangelien*, p. 27; R. Pesch, 'Eine alttestamentliche Ausführungsformel in Matthäus-Evangelium' 2, p. 87. See discussion in Soares Prabhu, *Quotations*, pp. 12–17.
21 On the former see Dibelius, *Tradition*, p. 128; Pesch, 'Ausführungsformel' 2,

well as the connection to the genealogy in 1.18a, and the substantial linguistic and material interconnection of the three 'dream narratives' (1.20–1, 24–5; 2.13–15, 19–23).[22] According to the canons of form criticism, the pericope also amalgamates other forms, including an angelic birth-annunciation,[23] and within the double naming an oracle of divine name-giving in vv. 22–3, borrowed from Isaiah's prophetic tradition, and couched within the form of a Matthean fulfilment-formula quotation.

Matthew 1.18–25 is tied together well by consistent style, language and organization. The evangelist's penchant for repeating key phrases is evident in 1.18–25: Joseph the dominant actor ('Ιωσήφ 5x); τίκτειν υἱόν occurs three times (vv. 21, 23, 25), παραλαβεῖν twice (vv. 20, 24), and καλοῦν τὸ ὄνομα αὐτοῦ three times (vv. 21, 23, 25), thereby linking up the constituent parts of the pericope which might otherwise be assessed as distinct in form.

The list of vocabulary in 1.18–25 amply reflects the language particular to the rest of the Gospel, even apart from the introductory formula of the fulfilment quotations. Kilpatrick identifies over forty words and phrases which occur commonly in Matthew 1–2 and the entire Gospel, and concludes 'that the section as a whole bears the stamp of the evangelist's manner'.[24] Those words in the passage which do not appear elsewhere in Matthew are in several cases made necessary by the unique requirements of the narrative (e.g., μνηστεύειν, συνέρχεσθαι, δειγματίζειν, λάθρα, μεθερμηνεύεσθαι and γινώσκειν with the meaning of sexual relations). Thus, in terms of composition, although Matthew's sources will ever remain debated, he has definitely and definitively made the material his own.

---

p. 88; Frankemölle, *Jahwebund*, p. 310; on the latter see Luz, *Matthew 1–7*, pp. 115–17.

[22] See a comparison table in Davies and Allison, *Matthew 1–7*, p. 196.

[23] Cf. Gen. 16.7–15; 17.1–3, 15–21; 21.3; Judg. 13.3–5; Luke 1.29–31. The form of the birth announcement contains angel appearance, message and naming. See the analyses and bibliographies in Bultmann, *History*, p. 292; Stendahl, 'Quis', p. 61; R. Brown, *Birth*, pp. 155–9.

[24] *Origins*, pp. 52–3. See the discussion and references in Soares Prabhu, *Quotations*, pp. 166–9. Knox, *Sources* II, p. 125, wants to temper somewhat Kilpatrick's enthusiasm, but Luz's list is as extensive, *Matthew 1–7*, p. 116. Cf. R. Brown's numbers, *Birth*, p. 105, based on Pesch, 'Ausführungsformel' 2, pp. 81–8, and E. Nellessen, *Das Kind und seine Mutter*, pp. 50–6.

Matthew 1.22–3: placement

The narrative impact of the Emmanuel quotation was established in Chapter 3, but its redactional placement in Matthew 1.22–3 also marks it as clearly important in the larger scheme of the infancy narrative, and the Gospel. Matthew's common practice is to insert his formula quotations at the end of the pericope with which they are connected. In 1.18–25 the quotation's placement in the middle deliberately retains ἐκάλεσεν τὸ ὄνομα αὐτοῦ Ἰησοῦν at the end of the episode as the narrated fulfilment of the angel's command to Joseph.

The evangelist performs an identical arrangement in Matthew 21.1–7 (cf. also Mark 11.1–7; Luke 19.28–35).[25]

Setting of the scene	1.18–19	21.1
Command	1.20–1	21.2–3
Formula quotation	1.22–3	21.4–5
Execution of the command	1.24–5	21.6–7

On the assumption that the formula quotations are a unified group with a common design and function, and that their presence in material of varied origin displays their placement by Matthew in the Gospel's final redactional stratum,[26] numerous scholars have concluded that 1.18–25 reads more smoothly and logically when freed of its latest redactional layer, the Emmanuel quotation of vv. 22–3. No longer are we faced with the apparent confusion of an angelic vision of one name and the prophetic oracle of a different one. Joseph, rather, receives the revelation and the angel's commands, wakes up, and obeys in straightforward fashion. The same assumption has also been extended to the entire infancy narrative. When stripped of its string of formula quotations, Matthew 1–2 reads with greater coherence and verve.[27]

Whether this is a key to Matthew's handling of his traditions is one matter. Such an observation does not require deconstruction of redactional layers but can lead in the other direction – understanding better the present shape of the text. Rather than being

---

[25] Pesch was the first to look carefully at this close parallel, 'Ausführungsformel' 2, pp. 79–80, and the 'formula of fulfilment': ποιέω + (ὡς or equivalent) + προσέταξεν or equivalent. See his thirty OT references in 'Ausführungsformel' 1, p. 225.

[26] Cf. Pesch, 'Ausführungsformel' 2, pp. 79–80; Soares Prabhu, *Quotations*, pp. 234–6.

[27] E.g., Soares Prabhu, *Quotations*, p. 165.

historical hiccups which interrupt the reading of an otherwise smooth narrative, the deliberately obtrusive placement of the Emmanuel quotation, and its four companions in Matthew 1–2, provide the redactor's keys to the Gospel's rhetorical design, for they signal to the reader the story's true interpretive framework.

Here is an example of where careful tradition and redaction-critical investigation can produce a conclusion –

> All else, the prediction of the birth of a son, and the assigning of a name to him, are strictly speaking super-fluous[28]

– which could derail the story's own logic, if given priority over rhetorical emphases. But the opposite is the case, for here redactional design should be used to help to confirm Matthew's predominant story considerations. The added editorial explanation μεθερμηνευόμενον in 1.23 brings into even sharper focus the quotation's anticipation that Jesus will be called 'God with us'. The heightened redactional emphasis on the Emmanuel naming turns its lack of immediate fulfilment into a Gospel-wide expectation.

6.2. Isaiah 7.14

Matthew defines Jesus' birth story as the 'fulfilment' of Isaiah's original prediction of the conception, birth and naming of the Emmanuel child. Matthew claims this fulfilment despite Isaiah's apparent lack of interest in a virgin birth, a divine child or a Messiah to be born centuries later.

Isaiah 7.14 was originally directed to King Ahaz of Judah. He was under threat during the Syro-Ephraimite war of 734 BCE, and probably unconvinced by Isaiah's counsel of neutrality and the prophet's initial attempts in 7.1–9 to assure him that the massed forces of Syria and Israel posed no threat.[29] Isaiah's sign is delivered in anger at Ahaz's obstinacy, and is a mixed prophecy: hope through the Emmanuel child and coming disaster for Judah. The identities of the mother and her child are unclear.[30] She might

---

[28] Soares Prabhu, *Quotations*, p. 239; cf. Strecker, *Weg*, p. 54.

[29] See the various discussions of Ahaz's historical situation in R. E. Clements, *Isaiah 1–39*, pp. 10–11, 78–80; Otto Kaiser, *Isaiah 1–12*, pp. 136–9, 173–5; Michael Thompson, *Situation and Theology*, pp. 30–1; Watts, *Isaiah 1–32*, pp. 96–9; Wildberger, *Jesaja*, pp. 289–90.

[30] On this question of identity, see Mowinckel, *Cometh*, pp. 112–14; R. H. Fuller, *The Foundations of New Testament Christology*, p. 24; Gerhard Delling,

be seen as personifying Zion, and Emmanuel as the collective remnant. If she is a royal consort of Ahaz she could be giving birth to a future Davidic king (e.g., Hezekiah).[31] She might be an unknown woman, or the totality of pregnant women at that moment, with Emmanuel symbolizing their corporate faith in God's deliverance. She could be Isaiah's wife; the Emmanuel child would then be the second of the prophet's three children bearing sign-names which are significant in his ministry (cf. Isa. 7.3; 8.3).

hā ʿ almâ, with the definite article, tilts the argument in favour of one particular woman known to both Isaiah and Ahaz. Isaiah, as the voice of the prophecy, is likely to play some part in the conferment of the child's name. This would support the identity as being that of a woman within the prophet's social circle, while the behaviour pattern of Isaiah 7.3 and 8.3 adds some weight to her being his wife, and Emmanuel being his child.[32]

Whatever these historical parameters, Isaiah is at minimum announcing the natural, imminent birth of a sign-child to be called 'with-us-God', a name which will embody the assurance of God's dynamic power in the midst of his people. Isaiah 7.14 in context appears to be a two-edged sign with good *and* bad news. The symbolism of the child and his name will be confirmed early in his life by peace in Judah and desolation of the northern lands, mixed with the threat of hardship for Judah.[33] The force of the prophecy in the MT lies almost entirely with the name Emmanuel, the prophet's sign to King Ahaz that God's protection will soon intervene to carry Judah past its present crisis. Isaiah 7.14–25 thus points to deliverance, but Emmanuel is not identified as the deliverer.[34]

The text's subsequent transitions into the LXX and Matthew 1.23 involve several developments.[35]

'παρθένος', *TDNT* V, pp. 831–2; Kaiser, *Isaiah*, p. 103; G. Rice, 'A Neglected Interpretation of the Immanuel Prophecy', pp. 220–7; W. Berg, 'Die Identität der "jungen Frau" in Jes 7,14.16', pp. 7–13.

[31] So held later Jewish interpreters; cf. Justin, *Dialogue*, 67.1; *Exod. Rab.* on 12.29; *Num. Rab.* on 7.48. On the child as Hezekiah see Barnabas Lindars, *New Testament Apologetic*, p. 215.

[32] Numerous difficulties remain, however: cf. Kaiser, *Isaiah*, pp. 154–5, 160.

[33] For interpretations see G. Rice, 'The Interpretation of Isaiah 7:15–17', pp. 363–9. Cf. the bad news/good news of *ʿimmānû ʾēl* in Isa. 8.8, 10.

[34] See G. B. Gray, *Isaiah*, p. 136; and cf. S. L. Edgar, 'The New Testament and Rabbinic Messianic Interpretation', pp. 47–54.

[35] See the bibliography in Boslooper, *The Virgin Birth*, p. 203, and various comments concerning LXX text form and Matthean adoption of the quotation,

MT: Behold the young woman (hā ʿalmâ) will conceive/has conceived (hārâ)
and will give birth to a son,
and she will call his name ʿimmānû ʾēl

LXX: Behold the virgin (ἡ παρθένος) will conceive (ἐν γαστρὶ ἕξει[36])
and will give birth to a son
and you will call (καλέσεις) his name Ἐμμανουήλ.

Matthew: Behold the virgin (ἡ παρθένος) will conceive (ἐν γαστρὶ ἕξει)
and will give birth to a son,
and they will call (καλέσουσιν) his name Ἐμμανουήλ [which means, 'God with us'].

The LXX translation of hā ʿalmâ by ἡ παρθένος has been widely discussed and need not concern us too directly here.[37] Even if the translators understood the term in an exact technical sense, the LXX passage requires only that someone who is now a virgin will conceive naturally.

Matthew's quotation follows the LXX. As noted in Chapter 3, καλέσουσιν instead of LXX καλέσεις demonstrates the evangelist's adaptation of the text to his rhetorical purposes, in which 'they' = 'his people' of 1.21.[38] Isaiah 7.14 was not the basis for the composition of Matthew 1.18–25, but the prophecy was added deliberately with its fulfilment formula as the redactor's final act of interpretation of his birth narrative.[39]

But why in particular did Matthew choose Isaiah 7.14 to perform his first fulfilment quotation, and as the interpretive foundation for Jesus' birth narrative? Divine utterance and the word-form of the birth-annunciation link both passages together, as well as the LXX translation of ʿimmānû ʾēl in Isaiah 8.8 (μεθ' ἡμῶν ὁ θεός) and

in Paul Christian, Jesus und seine geringsten Brüder, p. 49; Robert Gundry, The Use of the Old Testament in St Matthew's Gospel, pp. 89–91; Soares Prabhu, Quotations, pp. 229–53; R. Brown, Birth, pp. 143–53.

36 ἕξει = א A Q; λή(μ)ψεται = B L C. R. Brown, Birth, p. 145, sees the latter as the dominant reading, but the former is accepted in Ziegler's Göttingen LXX and is the reading in Rahlfs' LXX.

37 See Watts, Isaiah, p. 97; Boslooper, Birth, pp. 203–5; Box, The Virgin Birth of Jesus Christ, p. 16; Soares Prabhu, Quotations, pp. 203–31; R. Brown, Birth, pp. 148–9, 523–4.

38 Contra Strecker, Weg, p. 55, and others.

39 See H. Boers, 'Language Usage and the Production of Matthew 1:18–2:23', p. 224; and many others.

8.10 (ὅτι μεθ' ἡμῶν κύριος ὁ θεός), the OT formula for divine presence probably well known to Matthew (see above, pp. 155–6).[40] Scholars have typically highlighted linguistic and conceptual connections, such as the birth-annunciation and pregnancy of a παρθένος. Capitalizing on these elements, Matthew eschewed the MT and LXX contexts in favour of the scriptural support the text could provide for Jesus' Davidic and divine origins, and for his immediate didactic and apologetic needs. The paucity of references to Isaiah 7.14 in pre-Christian Judaism would seem to support the conclusion that the Emmanuel prophecy remained in Hebrew and LXX texts a prophetic sign of divine presence, and did not become the prophecy of a miraculous birth to a παρθένος or the expectation of a messianic figure.[41] Isaiah's Emmanuel child remained a sign *to* the House of David, and a double-edged sign at that, its content bringing peace and its royal rejection by Ahaz bringing judgement. The name and early childhood of the sign-child 'With-us-God' were a demonstration to a 'wearisome' king that the power and deliverance of the transcendent YHWH were imminently present at his people's lowest ebb.

6.3.   Matthew's use of Isaiah 7.14

Obviously then, Isaiah's prophecy does not fit snugly into Matthew's birth narrative. The messianic application of Isaiah 7.14 is particularly the province of Matthew; not only unprecedented, but an unwarranted enigma, some would argue.[42] At times Matthew's

---

[40] Twice more ʿimmānû ʾēl occurs in Isaiah, but in the rather opaque literary circumstances of the two oracles in 8.5–8 and 8.9–10 (cf. M. Thompson, *Situation*, pp. 34–5; Clements, *Isaiah*, pp. 96–7; G. B. Gray, *Isaiah*, pp. 50, 135–7; Kaiser, *Isaiah*, pp. 183–5; Wildberger, *Jesaja*, pp. 321–2). Their linguistic similarity to 7.14 is clear, given the rare use of ʾēl within the 'I am/God is with us' OT presence formula (only one other time in over 100 occurrences: Gen. 35.3; cf. Deut. 32.12). However, Isa. 8.8 and 10 are not references to a personal Emmanuel as is 7.14, but perhaps emphatic utterances: 'God is with us!' Cf. the LXX's treatment of ʿimmānû ʾēl in each case:

  7.14:   Ἐμμανουήλ
  8.8:   μεθ' ἡμῶν ὁ θεός
  8.10:   ὅτι μεθ' ἡμῶν κύριος ὁ θεός

The linguistic connection between Isa. 7.14 and 8.8, 10 is evident, but any other relationship to the particular events and the person 'Emmanuel' is unclear.

[41] Cf. Watts, *Isaiah*, p. 103; Box, *Birth*, pp. 16, 169; Gustaf Dalman, *The Words of Jesus*, p. 270; Stendahl, 'Quis', p. 62. But see 1QH 3.6ff. for the birth of a messianic figure; Tatum, 'Stories', p. 124.

[42] So Luz, *Matthäus 1–7*, p. 107; Gnilka, *Matthäusevangelium*, p. 20.

use of biblical texts can appear 'to our critical eyes, manifestly forced and artificial and unconvincing'.[43]

Matthew was one of those at the beginning of the common era who believed that the prophets had possessed a special foreknowledge about the person and mission of Jesus. Like other interpreters, Matthew shows little awareness that the prophets might actually have been delivering oracles of crucial relevance to their original audiences. Rather, Matthew sees these ancient prophets as unmatched in their exercise of the divine gift.[44] What Matthew is doing here is not odd for his times. This understanding of a continuity between the scriptures and Jesus is not one of Jesus being found acceptable in OT terms. On the contrary, the person of Jesus has finally brought OT prophecy into true light. Its obscure and sometimes cryptic message has become coherent in him.[45]

For some critics, 'fulfilment' in Matthew is therefore equivalent to a midrashic unearthing from prophecy of that hidden meaning therein which has been expressed and revealed in the Christ event.[46] It must also be remembered that Matthew does not start by attempting to prove that Jesus is the Messiah because he conforms to certain details of OT prophecy. Matthew begins with the narrative assertion that Jesus is the Messiah – he boldly heads his story in 1.1 with this interpretive 'given'. Jesus himself – his ministry, crucifixion and resurrection – has provided the revelation of truth which, as the sole hermeneutical key, unlocks the puzzles of scripture.

[43] C. F. D. Moule, *The Origin of Christology*, p. 129; see France, *Matthew*, pp. 22–7, 38–41. Stendahl comments on the history of the problem: 'from Origen onwards we can trace how Matthew's manner of quoting the OT has presented special problems to his interpreters'. Origen, Celsus, Justin, Porphyry, Eusebius, Jerome and others comment on the difficulties involved (see Stendahl, *School*, pp. 39–40).

[44] Cf. Dan. 9.1–2; 2 Esd. 12.10–39; Rom. 15.4; 1 Pet. 1.10–12; cf. also Hab. 1.5 and 1QpHab2; Hab. 2.17 and 1QpHab12.

[45] See John Barton's helpful development of these issues, *Oracles of God*, pp. 179–92.

[46] The comparison is not technically accurate, but has value, as R. T. France, 'Scripture, Tradition and History in the Infancy Narratives of Matthew', pp. 243–6, points out: 'even if Mt. 1–2 is not, formally speaking, midrash, it shares a mentality and techniques which can fairly be called "midrashic"' (p. 245). J. Barton, *Oracles*, uses the word *pesher* to describe Matthew's approach, also Moule, *Origin*, pp. 127–9. See W. D. Davies, *Setting*, pp. 208–9, and Bertil Gärtner, 'The Habakkuk Commentary (DSH) and the Gospel of Matthew', for differences between Matthew's method and the Qumran pesharim. See also France's review of typology as a Matthean methodology, *Jesus and the Old Testament*, pp. 38–43, 76–80; *Evangelist*, pp. 185–6.

Both rhetorically and historically, Matthew's interest in the child's conception is at best secondary. Isaiah 7.14 is employed because the meaning of Emmanuel 'fulfils', captures best the person and mission of Jesus as narrated in Matthew 1.1–21. Matthew's employment of the virgin birth thus manifests a more foundational reality he wants to communicate – that in his origins in the Abrahamic/Davidic line and in the creative power of the Holy Spirit, and in his coming mission of deliverance, Jesus fulfils God's preordained plan to save and be 'with' his people. Jesus' introduction as Israel's Χριστός (Matt. 1.1–21) is thus fully summed up in Isaiah's prophecy of the Emmanuel child as the potent agent of God's presence.[47]

This is further borne out in Matthew's supplied translation of Ἐμμανουήλ as μεθ' ἡμῶν ὁ θεός. Ever since the name ʿimmānû ʾēl had been simply transliterated into Ἐμμανουήλ by the LXX translators, the Greek readers of Isaiah's prophecy had lost the force of the predicted child's sign-name. Emmanuel became simply a name, without its prophetic message.

Likewise in Matthew, without the translation the significance of the name is lost for Greek audiences. Ἐμμανουήλ as a Greek name *per se* says nothing about the relationship between divine presence and Matthew's explanation of 'Jesus' being the Messiah of his people; the association between mission, name and meaning as the fulfilment of 'all this' (τοῦτο ὅλον, v. 22) is broken. With his explanation Matthew rescues from obscurity Emmanuel's significance for the non-Hebrew speakers in his audience. Any terminological correspondence between Jesus' birth and Isaiah 7.14 provides basic surface congruity; the deeper motif of fulfilment in Emmanuel is found in its translation and association with OT divine presence. Despite his dependence on LXX form, Matthew returns to the full strength of the original MT connection between YHWH's deliverance and his presence. Jesus' mission thus parallels Isaiah's original equation between deliverance and divine presence, at least in so far as in his role as God's long-planned Messiah he is best understood as the new, final and unique presence of God with his people.

Matthew's μεθερμηνευόμενον footnote also draws together the basic incongruity of the apparent bestowal of two different names to which are appended two different explanations.[48] Matthew tells

---

[47] Cf. Trilling, *Israel*, p. 41.

[48] Justin Martyr may have recognized a problem. 'It is interesting to see that Justin Martyr who quoted Isa. 7:14 on several occasions (*Dial.* 43:8, 67:1, 71:3, 84)

us that there is no tension here, rather, the occurrence of one is the fulfilment of the other. Matthew thereby declares that his explanation of 'Emmanuel' and the angel's explanation of 'Jesus' are complementary.

This translation and application of the OT divine presence formula to a child who is also himself the agent of salvation takes the promise of God's presence beyond any of its known previous applications. Because the angel's explanation of his name makes Jesus the vehicle of salvation to his people, and because Matthew's translation of Emmanuel applies to Jesus the functional, messianic character of the divine presence formula, 'God with us', Matthew has given his audience the restoration of the OT promise of divine presence in word, but has also provided the promise of presence in person. In Isaiah the Emmanuel child was only a symbol of God's deliverance which was to come by other means, namely miraculous military victory. Matthew's Emmanuel, however, is the personal agent of God's promise to save and be 'with' his people. It is not unjustifiable then to see Jesus as the embodiment of all the salvific power found in the divine biblical assertion, 'I am with you.'

This does not remove the interpreter's frustration with Matthew's use of the OT, but perhaps we are at least able to imply a motive. Within Matthew's appeal to prophecy lies the assumption that the OT and its authority as divine utterance exist independently of the narrative world of his story of Jesus, and he can thereby reinforce his truth-claims about Jesus through quotation. Israel's history as the people of God provides an external world of reference, and by quoting Isaiah 7.14 Matthew sets the stage for the rest of his story by establishing Jesus' characterization as Emmanuel, the God-with-us Messiah.

6.4. Redaction and christology

The claim is not made here that 'Emmanuel' is the most important rhetorical and/or theological motif introduced in Matthew's prologue. It is, however, certainly *one* of several primary themes in Matthew 1–2. Several decades' work on the tradition-history of Matthew 1–2 has highlighted Matthew's evident interest in four main christological themes: Jesus' (1) Davidic sonship, (2) mes-

always cites the first half about the virgin birth only. In *Apol.* 33 the full text is quoted, though not with the name IMMANUEL but with the Greek translation' (van Unnik, *'Dominus'*, p. 302 n.58).

sianic mission to his people, (3) divine sonship, and (4) identification as 'Emmanuel – God with us'. These may also be tied to the
text's layers of tradition and development.

The core message of the infancy narrative is the birth of a
messianic child of royal lineage.[49] There is little argument that one
of Matthew's primary interests in the infancy narrative is establishing a basis for Jesus' continuity with God's people Israel. 'Son
of David' is a significant means to that end, and Bornkamm and
Strecker consider it the most important title for the Jesus of the
ministry.[50] The name and title are prominent in language (1.1, 6,
17, 20) and in plot significance in the genealogy; in the angel's
address to Joseph, in the double command to take his wife and to
name her child, passing on his own Davidic lineage; and in Jesus'
subsequent entanglements with Jerusalem.

Joseph, as the most active player in the cast of Matthew 1–2, has
a critical role in establishing Jesus' Davidic connections. It is
Joseph the δίκαιος, like the righteous Joseph of scripture, who
constantly hears God in dreams and obeys faithfully, steering and
protecting his son Jesus through a series of 'Mosaic' crises.[51] The
parallel attestation of Joseph in Luke as ἐξ οἴκου Δαυίδ supports
this as a core characteristic of the earliest birth traditions. Both
infancy narratives have explicit reference to Davidic descent and a
Bethlehem birth (cf. Matt. 1.16, 20 and Luke 1.27, 32; 2.4; Matt.
2.1 and Luke 2.4–6).

It is arguable whether Matthew's use of the Davidic title is as
insufficient a penetration of Jesus' identity as Kingsbury and others
claim.[52] Too many arguments in the past have presumed: (1) that
'Matthew's christology' is an inflexible entity, with titles as static
signifiers; (2) that there can be no Gospel-wide evolution of
christology built into the story, whether a strengthening of a motif
(as seems to occur with Son of God after the infancy narrative) or a
weakening, as with Son of David; (3) that more or less exclusive

---

[49] So Nolan, *Son.*

[50] Bornkamm, *TIM*, pp. 32–3; Strecker, *Weg*, pp. 118–20.

[51] For 'righteousness' in Matthew, see Roger Mohrlang, *Matthew and Paul*,
pp. 97–100, 113–14; Benno Przybylski, *Righteousness in Matthew and His World
of Thought*, pp. 77–104. δίκαιος in Joseph should not be defined narrowly in
contrast to Matthew's wider use; contra, e.g., R. Brown, *Birth*, p. 125; Davies
and Allison, *Matthew 1–7*, p. 203. For a wider view of Torah in Palestinian
Judaism see E. P. Sanders, *Paul*, pp. 76–84, 419–28.

[52] See R. H. Fuller's criticisms, 'The Conception/Birth of Jesus as a Christological
Moment', pp. 37–52.

claims can be made regarding the predominance of a particular title or motif. Fortunately today's growing methodological pluralism has moved us beyond these fallacies.

Within Matthew's rhetoric, the Son of David–Son of God strands are never static, nor a constant volume. Son of David starts strong, but gives way to Son of God, and not as a piece of christological retrojection, but in direct relation to Matthew's narrative development of one of the story's key crises: who are the people of God? The assumption in Matthew 1 is clearly ethnic Israel, and in Matthew 28 is clearly Jesus' ἐκκλησία gathered from all nations. That Jesus comes as Son of David and is resurrected as Son of God is no surprise then, if one follows the plot. Both movements move from the particularist to the more universalist.

The motif of Jesus' mission to his people arises out of the other three main christological emphases in Matthew 1–2: Son of God, Messiah and Emmanuel. The key reference points for Jesus' Messianic persona are Jesus' designations as Χριστός (1.1, 16, 17, 18), the double naming/translations of 'Jesus' and 'Emmanuel' (1.21–5), and the magi's and Herod's perceptions of him as Βασιλεὺς τῶν Ἰουδαίων (2.2), worthy of worship (2.2, 8, 11). The narrator indicates that Herod and the Jerusalem leaders equate βασιλεύς and Χριστός:

2.2 Magi: ποῦ ἐστιν ὁ τεχθεὶς Βασιλεὺς τῶν Ἰουδαίων
2.4 Herod: ποῦ ὁ Χριστὸς γεννᾶται.

This narrative link between kingship and messiahship anticipates the same interchange of titles in the passion narrative; cf. 26.63, 68; 27.11, 17, 22, 29, 37.

Davidic sonship and messianic mission are commonly seen as original to the birth story, but the entry of divine sonship into the picture is less clear. Jesus' generation by the Holy Spirit, virginal conception and return from Egypt as ὁ υἱός μου (2.15) are most often viewed as later and mutually affirmative developments which (1) reflect the growing intensity of the community's christological convictions, and (2) offer apologetic reasoning against calumny.[53]

---

[53] E.g., Mary is nowhere called παρθένος until Matt. 1.22–3, perhaps a late addition. Natural conception is not incompatible with ἐκ πνεύματος ἁγίου; i.e., it does not deny divine sanction. The use of ἐκ with a genitive noun following γαστρὶ ἔχουσα can denote the male member responsible for the pregnancy, as in LXX Gen. 38.25 (contra Waetjen, 'Genealogy', pp. 220–5, R. Brown, *Birth*, pp. 124–5, 137; Anderson, 'Gender', p. 10). Whether συνελθεῖν (1.18) indicates sexual relations, and when it and οὐκ ἐγίνωσκεν αὐτὴν (1.25) became part of the

Some scholars have therefore reasoned that these elements in Matthew 1ff., and especially 1.23, are grounds for making 'Son of God' the primary means of understanding Jesus here.[54] But neither our narrative nor historical investigations of Emmanuel have pointed in this direction. Within the text these elements are conjoined to produce the means and evidence of divine activity at Jesus' birth, as opposed to a single focus on 'Son of God'. Each element heightens the theocentricity of Jesus' origins and mission. Hence a primary focus on something formally identified as 'Son-of-God christology' in Matthew 1–2 is problematic.

(1) First and foremost, the birth story must be read on its own terms. Kingsbury is convinced that Son of God is the essential core of Matthew's christology, and that this predication is explicitly established in Matthew 3–4, a component part of the single literary unit spanning 1.1–4.16. But we have already seen significant problems with this delineation of Matthew's structure, and reading Son of God backwards into Matthew 1–2 from Matthew 3–4 on the basis of this structure is similarly problematic.

(2) 'Son of God' is a carefully bestowed christological title in Matthew, not clearly found in the infancy narrative. The fulfilment quotation of 2.15 ('Out of Egypt I have called my son') is an ambiguous use of 'son' at best, given the primary analogy here between Jesus and Israel.[55] As a specific predication of Jesus it is not applied until the baptism (3.17: ὁ υἱός μου) and the temptations (4.3, 6: Εἰ υἱὸς εἶ τοῦ θεοῦ). Those who derive Son-of-God christology from Emmanuel blur seriously their different OT backgrounds and distinct rhetorical functions in the text.

(3) As for 'Son of God' arising from the Spirit's involvement in Jesus' conception, the role of the Spirit in Matthew 1.18–25 actually makes the 'Son of God' implication less likely. In the OT, Spirit language works more comfortably in proximity to divine presence language. It is notable how often the Spirit and the 'God is with us'

story, further complicate the question. See Schaberg's discussion, *Illegitimacy*, pp. 34–6. For calumnies about Jesus' birth and infancy in the Talmud see R. Herford, *Christianity in Talmud and Midrash*, but dating is problematic.

[54] See especially Kingsbury, *Structure*, pp. 52–3; R. Brown, *Birth*, p. 137; cf. also Seitz, 'Prologues', pp. 262–3; H. Conzelmann, 'Jesus von Nazareth und der Glaube an den Auferstandenen', p. 194; Dunn, *Christology in the Making*, pp. 49–50.

[55] Contra Kingsbury, *Structure*, p. 52. See Stendahl, 'Quis'; Fuller, 'Conception/ Birth', p. 40; Dunn, *Christology*, pp. 49–50. R. Brown speculates that the use of Emmanuel in 1.23 has prevented the explicit use of another revealed title in the birth story until 2.15; *Birth*, p. 135.

presence formula appear in close proximity in the OT text. The divine activity which accompanies God's 'with you' promise of presence and deliverance is often pneumatic in nature.[56] In light of this close connection it is not surprising to find a pneumatic explanation for Emmanuel's origin in Matthew 1.18–25.

This fourth christological motif, Emmanuel – 'God with us', is readily identified as one of the formula quotations added to the infancy narrative. But, as noted above, its redactional priority is already evident. Among the formula quotations of Matthew 1–2 it is easily the most prominent by virtue of its conspicuous placement in the middle of 1.18–25, its pointed elaboration with ὅ ἐστιν μεθερμηνευόμενον,[57] and its priority as the first fulfilment quotation of the story. But even as the fulfilment of a prophetic anticipation of Jesus' birth, in its use in Matthew the quotation itself anticipates a further fulfilment within the story: καλέσουσιν τὸ ὄνομα αὐτοῦ Ἐμμανουήλ.

The entire Gospel is to be read in light of the equation between Jesus' double naming and explanation in 1.21–3. The first explanation may reflect a popular understanding in which 'Jesus' means something like 'YHWH saves',[58] but it stands alongside the explanation for Emmanuel as no less than the Gospel's thesis statement. Along with their explanations both await the content which the Gospel-wide characterization of Jesus' person and mission will provide.

This makes the redactional capstone of Matthew's birth story, temporally and stylistically, his insertion of the Jesus/Emmanuel/God-with-us naming, quotation and interpretation. Matthew's addition makes the quotation and the explanation stand over against the events of the text with a dialogical function for the

---

[56] Cf. Num. 11.17; Deut. 34.9; Judg. 2.18; 3.10; 6.34; 11.29; 13.25; 14.6, 19; 15.14; 1 Sam. 3.19–20; 10.6–7; 16.13–14; Isa. 44.3; Hag. 1.13–14; 2.4; see van Unnik, 'Dominus', pp. 285–6.

[57] Never in the LXX; in the NT cf. in Mark 5.41; 15.22, 34; John 1.41; Acts 4.36 in the same formula. In 27.33, 46 Matthew prefers ὅ/τοῦτ' ἐστιν τὸ ὅ ἐστιν μεθερμηνευόμενον; cf. Mark 15.22, 34. See Malina, 'The Literary Structure and Form of Matt. xxviii: 16–20', p. 91, on the importance structurally of Matthew's translations.

[58] Cf. Ps. 130.8 (yᵉ hôšua = 'YHWH is help'); Judg. 13.5; Acts 4.12; see A. H. McNeile, *The Gospel According to St Matthew*, p. 8; Lagrange, *Matthieu*, p. 15; Soares Prabhu, *Quotations*, p. 239; R. Brown, *Birth*, p. 131. The etymology 'God's help' was probably known among both Hebrew and Greek-speaking Christians. Among the latter, Philo's etymology is similar: Joshua means σωτηρία κυρίου; *Mut. Nom.*, 121, on Num. 13.16.

evangelist and reader. To elaborate what Luz has noted, the inclusio of 1.23 and 28.20 creates a chiastic, reciprocal relationship: in 28.16–20 the risen one makes his *earthly* teaching the basis for the mission of discipleship and his ongoing presence, while in 1.18–25 the earthly Jesus is already presented as the *exalted* Messiah, whose divine 'withness' will become the defining characteristic of his community.[59]

Retrospective christology

One of the theses which has been argued, especially by Raymond Brown, proposes a divine Son-of-God christology which has been arrived at by a process of retrojection; a christology which, as the earliest Christians reflected upon the significance of Jesus, was seen in retrospect to apply earlier and earlier within his life.[60] Key to the 'reverse trajectory' which this thesis sets up is the assumption of Matthew's consistent employment of christological language throughout the development.

Originally, according to this scheme, Jesus was seen as Son of God in the resurrection, as in the formula of Romans 1.3–4, then in his baptism by John (cf. Matt. 3.16–17 and parallels), and finally in his conception by the Holy Spirit, without normal human parentage. For Matthew the conception of Jesus is the begetting of God's Son, and Matthew is thereby able to combat adoption christology with 'conception christology', while the fourth evangelist used pre-existence christology.[61]

While this idea of ongoing retrospection amongst early Christians is a positive attempt to explain developments historically, it assumes too readily in our case that Paul can be brought into the same line of retrojection as Matthew, and that Son of God is the operative phrase for both. It is generally agreed that the birth narratives of both Matthew and Luke contain no thought of a pre-existence christology.[62]

More to the point is whether Matthew's christological tapestry reveals as much as critics might want, in terms of history, consis-

---

[59] See Luz, *Matthew 1–7*, pp. 122–3.

[60] See R. Brown, *Birth*, pp. 29–32; 134–6. See Fuller's thorough criticism of Brown's thesis, 'Conception/Birth', pp. 37–52.

[61] Cf. Dunn, *Christology*, pp. 49–50, 56–9; R. Brown, *Birth*, p. 141.

[62] Though see Lindars, *Apologetic*, pp. 2–3; cf. R. Brown, *Birth*, pp. 142–3; Fuller, 'Conception/Birth', p. 39.

tency or focus. *In the end I would argue that Matthew's primary interests are not christological. His Gospel is written for the sake of the members of his community, to teach them, aid in their understanding of Christian life, and help them understand who they are over against the larger, dominant groups of Judaism and gentile non-believers.* That which truly resounds in Matthew's birth story is a more subtle yet powerful plethora of themes into which Jesus' Emmanuel role fits as a key explanation. Jesus' divine sonship is another of those themes, but does not play *the* central role in the infancy narrative. If there is anything retrospective about the christology of 1.23 it begins with and stems from the promise of 28.20, as part of the author's internal design of inclusio. The community which had grasped the resurrected Jesus' promise of continued presence looked back into his career and origins and, in reflecting upon his conception, found the fulfilment of Isaiah's Emmanuel – 'God-with-us' prediction.

Rather than looking for implied christology, interpretation needs to focus on those elements of the story which have narrative and redactional priority. This masthead, *that Jesus' salvation of his people will be seen as God's presence with them,* now hangs over the whole Gospel. This motif in 1.21–3 opens a major inclusio of Emmanuel presence which will close, but not end, with Jesus' final promise in 28.20, and will arise in the story at crucial points (e.g., 8.23–7; 10.41–2; 12.6; 14.22–33; 17.17; 18.20; 25.31–46; 26.29).

7

MATTHEW 18.1–20: THE PRESENCE OF JESUS AND HIS 'ΕΚΚΛΗΣΙΑ

Matthew 18.20 is unquestionably one of the pivotal texts in the Gospel which bring together explicitly divine presence and the person of Jesus.

> οὐ γάρ εἰσιν δύο ἢ τρεῖς συνηγμένοι εἰς τὸ ἐμὸν ὄνομα, ἐκεῖ εἰμι ἐν μέσῳ αὐτῶν.

Many studies of Matthew 18.20 have been dominated by questions of a historical *Sitz-im-Leben* nature, particularly in light of the saying's apparent resemblance to at least two rabbinic formulations. While evaluating the wisdom of these studies here, we will also presume the passage's participation in a whole rhetorical text, as pursued in the reading of Chapter 3. The purpose of this chapter is to investigate more closely the redactional and theological significance of Matthew 18 and the saying in 18.20, both in the Gospel and in the world of the author.

7.1. The story thus far ...

In Chapter 3 we noted a number of the plot devices which give Matthew's story its particular orientation around at least three lines of suspense and anticipation established in the narrative introduction of Matthew 1–2: (1) how Jesus will become the saviour of 'his people' and be acclaimed by them as God's Emmanuel Messiah; (2) who are to be identified as 'his people', in light of his immediate rejection by the leaders of Israel, and (3) how the conflict between Jesus and the Jewish leaders will be resolved.

From the perspective of engagement with the story's consecutive sequence, by 18.20 the narrator's control of plot and characterization has provided the implied reader with a number of other significant features which shape directly his or her perception of Matt. 18.20. Among these:

(1)   First–last/last–first criterion. In Jesus' proclamation the Kingdom of heaven turns normal human social hierarchies of authority and status on their heads when defining true greatness (cf. 5.3–12; 18.1–4).

(2)   The 'little ones' (μικροί), with the status of children, are intimately identified with the presence of Jesus in the community (18.5; cf. 25.40, 45).

(3)   Jesus' earlier transfer of authority to Peter, to 'bind and loose', is now transferred also to the members of the ἐκκλησία in general, in the context of dealing with a sinning brother (cf. 16.17–19; 18.18–19).

(4)   Jesus anticipates in 18.20 a new understanding of what it will mean for him to be in the midst of his followers, advocating a presence which moves beyond the limitations of their current dependence on his physical proximity and intervention on their behalf. He thus begins to respond to the dilemma of inability, fear and little faith among his disciples, raised previously in situations of his physical absence (8.23–7; 14.22–33; 17.14–21).

A number of historical and literary correspondences have been suggested for Matthew 18.20 and its immediate context; the help which these provide in interpreting the text is variable.[1] Matthew 18.15–20 shows full integration into the narrative of the First Gospel, thematically, compositionally and rhetorically. Verses 15–17, 18 and 19–20 have often been treated as originally separate sayings,[2] but in their present position in Matthew's story they have a coherent thematic flow.

Within extant gospel traditions Matthew 18.15–20 stands as unique. One obvious external correspondence is the quotation of Deuteronomy 19.15 in Matthew 18.16. W. D. Davies has asserted that the three-step procedure given for the correction of a brother (alone, with witnesses, and before the assembly) has a precedent of sorts in Qumran (1QS 5.25–6.1; cf. CD 9.2–3).[3]

---

[1]   See the discussions in Gnilka, *Das Matthäusevangelium* II; Davies and Allison, *Matthew 8–18*, pp. 750–91.
[2]   See W. G. Thompson, *Advice*, pp. 175–202, for references and discussion; cf. the more recent treatment of Matt. 18.15–20 by Brooks, *Matthew's Community*, pp. 100, 106–7, who similarly argues for these three separate literary units.
[3]   W. D. Davies, *Setting*, pp. 221–4; cf. Hill, *Matthew*, p. 275.

7.2   Matthew 18. The community discourse

As one of Jesus' major discourses, Matthew 18.1–35 is not an unbroken monologue, but takes its shape from his responses to two questions, posed in v. 1 by his disciples – 'Who is the greatest in the Kingdom of heaven?' – and in v. 21 by Peter, concerning repeated forgiveness of one's brother.[4] The narrator apparently assumes their location together 'in the house' or 'at home' (RSV) in Capernaum (17.24–5), again with the narrator's careful observation of their centripetal gathering – προσέρχομαι – around Jesus.

For Beare and others this formal identification of location is 'of no significance; in reality it is the risen Christ who speaks'.[5] But the rhetorical function of location has significance. That the reader should envision Jesus delivering his community discourse to his innermost circle of followers within this house setting makes for tangible, illustrative reinforcement and affective impact of his promise in 18.20. Jesus' ἐκκλησία principles of Matthew 18 are delivered by him to his inner circle of followers, in the midst of their (house) gathering.[6] Ἐκκλησία here anticipates a single localized gathering of Jesus' followers as opposed to 16.18, where Jesus' use of the term designates the universal assembly, or *qhl*, which will incorporate all followers.[7]

Jesus' discourse here anticipates a future broad-based 'community' of followers which encompasses the παιδία, μικροί, πρόβατα and ἀδελφοί, built upon his current inner circle of disciples. This future 'community', however, actually forms nowhere in Matthew's story an actual character group. The narrative carefully *anticipates* the community's existence without once providing an actual plot event of its gathering. Critics operating on the historical level often assume an easy identification between the anticipated community in the text and the historical community of the evangelist.[8] To

---

[4]   Contra R. Pesch, 'Die sogenannte Gemeindeordnung Mt 18', pp. 220, 226–7, for whom 18.15 begins (suddenly) the second half of the discourse.

[5]   *Matthew*, p. 373.

[6]   Crosby's treatment of 17.24–19.1 as a *Haustafel* is helpful at points, *House*, pp. 70–3. Matthew does not, however, support Crosby's elevation of οἶκος/οἰκία to the primary metaphor for interpreting the Gospel's ethics, theology and ecclesiology.

[7]   See Crosby's discussion of ἐκκλησία in the NT and Matthew, and its distinction from οἶκος/οἰκία, *House*, pp. 33–4.

[8]   E.g., Bornkamm, 'Bind'; G. Forkman, *The Limits to Religious Community*, p. 119; W. P. Addley, 'Matthew 18 and the Church as the Body of Christ', pp. 12–13; José Caba, 'El poder de la petición communitaria (Mt.18,19–20)', pp. 611–14.

identify Matthew 18 as 'the community discourse' must be done with the story's own temporal coordinates in view.

In Matthew 18.2–4 Jesus answers the disciples' question on Kingdom status, and uses it as prolegomenon to the issues of discipline and forgiveness in the *intra muros* relationships between the ἀδελφοί. In the parallel texts in Mark 9.34 and Luke 9.46 the issue is part of an actual dispute among the Twelve over the greatest disciple. In Matthew 18.1 the disciples put it to Jesus in the form of a general question – perhaps even a laudable question seeking a didactic answer.[9]

An object lesson proves crucial to what Jesus wants to communicate. In 18.2–4 Jesus makes the social status of the child he places 'in their midst' (ἐν μέσῳ αὐτῶν: 18.2; cf. 18.20) the measure of the disciples' own entry and rank in the Kingdom of heaven. That Jesus 'summons' (προσκαλέω) the child reinforces positively his child–disciple parallel (cf. 10.1; 15.32; 20.25). In vv. 5–6 the focus is still on the child/model disciple standing 'in their midst' but Jesus now highlights the importance of receiving 'one such child' within the fellowship. Because of his complete identification with these μικροί Jesus' own reception within the community is contingent upon the reception of the littlest members, and to reject or trip up (σκανδαλίζω) one of these μικροί is unthinkable.

The σκανδαλ- motif is maintained in vv. 7–9 as an issue of excising influences to sin from the community,[10] while proper treatment of the μικροί appears again in vv. 10–14, reinforced theocentrically by the parable of the Father's love for these little ones. Matthew 18.15–19 consists of a series of nine conditional sentences formed through the use of ἐάν and the aorist subjunctive, dealing with sequential reconciliation of the brother who sins (18.15–17) and the authority of the community's agreements (18.18–19).

Matthew 18.20 appears in the present indicative, and shifts from direct second-person address to the immediate audience to employment of the third person in the form of a general statement.[11] The thought of the Father's love for the little ones in the preceding

[9] See Held, *TIM*, pp. 236, 241.
[10] See W. G. Thompson, *Advice*, pp. 119–20. Under a 'corporate interpretation' of vv. 8–9 offenders within the community are excised from its membership; cf. Addley, 'Matthew 18', pp. 14–17; Forkman, *Limits*.
[11] See Caba's discussion, 'El poder', pp. 615–16. This could indicate separate sources (e.g., Joseph Sievers, ' "Where Two or Three ... " ', p. 178), but can also be explained stylistically.

parable is now given specific application in the interrelations of community members and the exercise of authority. Jesus' promise of presence forms the climax of a sequence of sayings uttered while a small child, one of the μικροί with whom Jesus so closely identifies himself, stands 'in their midst' as Jesus' chosen paradigm for model discipleship, and as greatest in the Kingdom.

7.3. Matthew 18.20

The language of 18.20 is consistent with both its immediate and wider context; from a redactional and comparative perspective it can be called Matthean. In Gundry's estimation the verse 'consists almost entirely of words belonging to [Matthew's] special diction'.[12] On the level of basic vocabulary the statistics tell an uncontroversial story (see table 7.1).

Table 7.1 *Matthew 18.20: vocabulary*

	Matt./Mark/Luke			employed only in Matt.'s // material	occurrences in Matt.'s *Sondergut*
οὐ	3	0	5	0	3
γάρ	123	64	97	62	15
δύο ἤ τρεῖς	2	0	0	0	2
συνάγω[13]	24	5	6	11	10
εἰς (τὸ) ὄνομα	5	0	0	3	2
ἐκεῖ	28	11	16	16	6
μέσος	7	5	14	1	4

Among the Gospels this vocabulary remains particular to Matthew's story in its application to the presence of Jesus. As José Caba has also noted, the logion is presented in Matthew in a precise adverbial-verbal parallel structure.[14] I have displayed it in figure 7.1.

$$
\left.\begin{array}{ll} \text{οὐ γαρ} & a \\ \text{εἰσιν} & b \\ \text{δύο ἤ τρεῖς συνηγμένοι} & c \end{array}\right] \!\!- \text{ εἰς τὸ ἐμὸν ὄνομα } -\!\! \left[\begin{array}{ll} a^1 & \text{ἐκεῖ} \\ b^1 & \text{εἰμι} \\ c^1 & \text{ἐν μέσῳ αὐτῶν} \end{array}\right.
$$

Figure 7.1

---

[12] *Matthew*, p. 369. Stephenson Brooks' assessment is more mixed: 'a single M saying ... probably underlies vv. 19–20' (*Matthew's Community*, p. 106)

[13] Cf. ἐπισυνάγω: 3/2/3; in parallel material Matthew has one unique occurrence (see Matt. 23.37 – twice; cf. Luke 13.34).

[14] Cf. 'El poder', p. 626.

'Two or three'

In the immediate context of v. 20 the numbers '1, 2, 3' are significant. Some see here the numeric principle of mnemotechnics.[15] This observation can be followed in two directions: first to the whole of Matthew 18, which proves to be a series of sayings connected by the words 'one' (vv. 5, 6, 10, 12, 14, 16), 'two' (vv. 8, 9, 16, 19), or 'two or three' (vv. 16, 20).[16] In any subsequent historical hearing or reading, the rhythmic utterance provides a powerful and memorable summary to the first part of the discourse (18.1–20). And this careful parallelism finds a precursor in 18.5, which is structurally, aurally and rhetorically parallel to 18.20 (see more below, pp. 196–8).

More importantly, however, these statistical and lexical preferences are also functional elements within Matthew's story. Jesus' assertion of his presence in the congregation of 18.20 follows his teaching of the threefold attempt at reconciliation of the wayward member of the ἐκκλησία in vv. 15–17, his emphatic extension (Ἀμὴν λέγω ὑμῖν)[17] in v. 18 of the authority to bind and loose (originally given to Peter, 16.19), and his parallel promise (Πάλιν [ἀμὴν] λέγω ὑμῖν) that the agreement of two ἐκκλησία members on earth will be ratified in heaven, in v. 19.

Contra some scholars, this saying in v. 19 is not merely an inserted general statement concerning prayer, corresponding to 7.7–11; 21.22 and especially John 15.7, and only connected to context by the catchwords 'heaven and earth' and 'two or three'.[18] It is, rather, closely linked to the previous and following themes of status, discipline and forgiveness within the fellowship. The 'agreement' of v. 19 corresponds to and reinforces the decision 'to bind' or 'to loose' in v. 18 – and provides the corporate application for the binding and loosing authority promised initially to Peter alone

[15] Cf. W. G. Thompson, *Advice*, pp. 194–6; Frankemölle, *Jahwebund*, pp. 27–8; B. Englezakis, '*Thomas*, Logion 30', p. 263.

[16] Frankemölle asserts that these numbers are in large part traceable to Matthean redaction, when the passage is compared with Mark 9.42–50 and Luke 17.1–3a; 15.3–7; 17.3b–4; see *Jahwebund*, p. 28 for details.

[17] This introduction (vv. 18 and 19) is commonly assessed as Matthean language; cf. 5.18–20; 10.42; 19.23–4 for parallel formulations in discourse material; Frankemölle, *Jahwebund*, p. 28.

[18] So e.g. Albright and Mann, *Matthew*, p. 221; T. W. Manson, *The Sayings of Jesus*, p. 211; Klostermann, *Matthäusevangelium*, pp. 150–1; cf. Caba, 'El poder', pp. 620–6, who posits direct redactional dependence.

in 16.19.[19] The precise nature of the authoritative power given to the community in 18.18 is not clear; it perhaps includes imposition or lifting of a ban, and authority to teach and interpret (28.19), and to forgive or retain sin.

Matthew 18.20 is linked sequentially and causally to the preceding subjunctive sequence in vv. 15–19 by its opening conjunction, γάρ. This causal connection makes Jesus' promise of presence in v. 20 the basis for the authority with which the ἐκκλησία acts and makes decisions: *because* Jesus is in their midst, 'his people' (cf. 1.21) can gain back the offending brother who listens and shun the one who does not, they can bind and loose, and they can agree and request, all with the approval of his Father in heaven. Thus the presence of Jesus becomes heaven's link with the earthly gathering. This heavenly ratification of the decisions of his gathered people reinforces Jesus' anticipated role as their mediator and implies an ongoing role for his divine filial agency.

The idea of 'two or three witnesses' constituting a quorum for proper corroboration is a principle from Deuteronomic justice (Deut. 19.15) applying to legal and quasi-legal situations, elsewhere recognized in the NT in 2 Corinthians 13.1; 1 Timothy 5.19; Hebrews 10.28. Matthew's adherence to this Deuteronomic principle extends to Jesus' trial before Caiaphas, where the ψευδομαρτυρία sought must be corroborated by two or three witnesses (Matthew 26.59–60; cf. Mark 14.55–60). The second stage of Jesus' threefold reconciliation process in Matthew 18.15–17 actually incorporates the citation from Deuteronomy, without the legal trappings.[20]

This all still takes place within the context of childlike status advocated earlier by Jesus, and the unlimited forgiveness taught in vv. 21–35. In this way the discipline of avoidance finally affixed to the offender in 18.17 does not contradict reconciliation and forgiveness but signifies the failure of the process and is a last resort. Such an excision from the community's membership also corresponds with the harsh imagery of losing hands, feet and eyes in vv. 8–10, especially when the latter are given a corporate interpretation. In vv. 15–17 the one who causes one of the μικροί to stumble in vv. 6–9 is cut off from the offended one by a barrier of separation.

---

[19] Cf. Frankemölle, *Jahwebund*, pp. 226–32; W. Trilling, *Hausordnung Gottes*, pp. 55–6; Bornkamm, 'Bind', pp. 86–8; W. G. Thompson, *Advice*, pp. 195, 200.

[20] The text of the citation is not clear. Cf. 2 Cor. 13.1. See Gundry's argument for an 'Ur-Lucianic' text, *OT*, p. 139; contrast Stendahl, *School*, pp. 138–9.

It is difficult to say how much of this picture of a quorum of corroboration between δύο μάρτυρες ἢ τρεῖς to persuade and recover the offender in 18.16 is then echoed in the quorum of δύο ἢ τρεῖς whose gathering evokes Jesus' presence in 18.20. At minimum, the rare occurrence of the phrase δύο ἢ τρεῖς provides a significant linking catchword, despite the reference to the μάρτυρες having been dropped in v. 20, and serves the numerical principle of mnemotechnics. And the concept of two or three individuals in harmony constituting a minimum authoritative voice rings true in both texts, if for entirely different ends (the presence of Jesus is certainly not 'authoritatively summoned' by the quorum in 18.20). The question of such a quorum's function is at issue three times in association with disparate activities in 18.15–20: with the 'one or two' who back up the complainant in v. 16, with the 'two' who agree and pray/request in v. 19, and with the 'two or three' who gather in Jesus' name in v. 20. The community's authority is a plural responsibility.[21] The ἐκκλησία has the power to decide which of its members belong to it and may loose (allow) or bind (ban) activities and members with the supreme authority of heaven.[22]

Thus Jesus' sayings in 18.15–20 provide for a compact series of teachings on reconciliation, discipline, community standards and the exercise of authority under the divine presence of Jesus in the local ἐκκλησία, based upon the smallest effective quorum of witnesses. It takes at least two to corroborate a testimony, at least two to agree, and at least two or three to gather. Here Jesus defines the *minyān* of his people, the requisite number of gathered followers, not simply 'for congregational worship',[23] but for formation, definition and regulation of community life in the basic social and religious unit of assembly. In Matthew 18.15–20 Jesus declares that 'two or three' must gather to constitute the functional assembly of 'his people'. [24]

---

21 Some commentators use the term 'excommunication'; cf. the comments of J. Galot, 'Qu'il soit pour toi comme le paien et la publicain'. J. Gnilka, *Matthäusevangelium* II, p. 139, uses the term in an excessively formal, ecclesiastical sense. Gundry (*Matthew*, p. 368) prefers 'ostracism' and Bonnard (*Matthieu*) 'put in quarantine'; see France, *Matthew*, p. 275.

22 See W. Trilling, *The Gospel According to St Matthew* I, p. 334. The neuter object of binding and loosing in v. 18 can refer to people; see Carson, 'Matthew', pp. 372–3.

23 So Englezakis, '*Thomas*', p. 264. The requisite number in *Sanh.* 1.6 and 1QS 6.3 is ten, based on the ten adult males from Num. 14.27.

24 Frankemölle to some extent underplays the numerical significance of the 'two or three' (*Jahwebund*, p. 34). Conversely it is notable the extent to which early Christian interpretations focused on allegorical interpretations of the 'two or three' in Matt. 18.20; see Englezakis, '*Thomas*', pp. 269–70.

Presence and authority

The initial concern of the discourse – the relative status of the disciples as members of the fellowship gathering in Jesus' name – is maintained by the narrative setting as given in 18.2: the child–disciple model placed 'in their midst'. This model is developed through careful inclusio to become the presence of Jesus 'in their midst' by v. 20 of the discourse. This inclusio of the child and Jesus 'in their midst' has immediate and wider significance, for Jesus not only equates his own reception with his followers' reception of these little ones in the immediate context (18.5) but in the story sequence his own divine and royal messiahship undergoes the same inversion to the lowest social status. He continues to predict, and ultimately experiences, his own suffering and death, thereby providing in himself the fullest model of humble discipleship for his followers. Jesus' promise of presence in v. 20 thus not only anticipates and reiterates his predictions, but his close identification with the μικροί and call for the same identity in his disciples is reflected in the inclusio of 18.2 and 20.

Becoming great in the Kingdom of heaven, i.e., becoming humble, however, does not apparently result in personal authority and power. To ask 'who is the greatest?' (18.1) is also to ask who has authority, but Jesus remains remarkably silent here on human leadership and social structures. He answers this implicit question from the disciples by reinforcing his own theocentric posture and by anticipating his future presence among them as his ongoing agency of his Father's will. Jesus' point is that Kingdom status will not derive from the elevation of one or more particular disciples but that membership in his community will require the last–first inversion which he himself will ultimately model in his predicted suffering and crucifixion. Questions of human status and authority are secondary amidst the corporate focus on himself. The authority for the disciples' activities of reconciliation and ostracism, binding and loosing, agreeing, requesting and gathering will remain heavenly in orientation, bestowed through his presence in their midst. But there is also a notable shift of authority to Jesus himself within his saying in 18.20: *he* will be the centre of the gathered ἐκκλησία, for they will gather in *his* name.

7.4. The nature of the 'gathering'

The perfect periphrastic in 18.20, εἰσιν ... συνηγμένοι, agrees with the majority of the forty instances of the construction in the NT which denote an existing condition.[25] Here the combination with the adverbial οὗ[26] ... ἐκεῖ and εἰμι produces a reference to a condition without grammatical limitation in frequency of occurrence, while the lack of any such plotted incident of the disciples gathering in Jesus' name thus far in the story creates for readers the anticipation that this mode of coming together will happen regularly and sometime soon. Correspondingly, οὗ ... ἐκεῖ sounds a further fundamental note through its generic character: the locale for these anticipated gatherings remains indeterminate.[27]

Some space has already been devoted in Chapter 3 to the particular employment of συναγ- words in Matthew's story (pp. 86–8). Apart from the lexical data which quickly demonstrate that Matthew's preference is more than stylistic,[28] examination of the occurrences of συνάγειν and συναγωγή reveals a deeper agenda, one which goes to the heart of the story's conflict between Jesus and the Jewish leaders. To follow the συνάγειν activity of the Jewish leaders in Matthew's story is to recite a number of highlights in the plot development of their antagonism to God's Emmanuel Messiah.

Synoptic comparison makes even sharper some of this Matthean characterization. In the three Gospels the double love-commandment appears in answer either to the question of the greatest commandment in the law (Matt. 22.34–40; Mark 12.28–34), or to the question of how to inherit eternal life (Luke 10.25–28). Only in Matthew 22.34 is the 'gathering' of the Pharisees noted as the prelude to this challenge of Jesus. And while the confrontations in Mark and Luke end in relative equanimity,[29] in Matthew it accelerates into another confrontation specifically between Jesus and the 'gathered' Pharisees. Whereas the plot arrangement in Matthew is the same as Mark's (great-commandment episode followed by the

---

[25] See Ernest de Witt Burton, *Syntax of the Moods and Tenses in New Testament Greek*, §84.

[26] For discussion of textual variants see W. G. Thompson, *Advice*, p. 196 n.85, and Caba, 'El poder', p. 627 n.52.

[27] Note the association elsewhere between συνάγειν and a place for gathering in Matt. 26.3, 57; cf. also Acts 4.31; 20.8 (οὗ ἦμεν συνηγμένοι); John 18.2; Rev. 16.16.

[28] See further in Frankemölle, *Jahwebund*, p. 34 n.120.

[29] In fact, at the end of their exchange in Mark, Jesus considers the scribe to be 'not far from the Kingdom of God' (Mark 12.34).

question about David's son), in Matthew the question is posed by
Jesus as a challenge to the Pharisees while they were 'gathered
together' (22.41). In Matthew's story it is after these two episodes
of confrontation between Jesus and the 'gathered' Pharisees that
'no one was able to answer him a word', or dared ask another
question (22.46). The narrator has employed συνάγειν to draw
uncompromising battle lines, and to portray Jesus as the victor on
the home territory of the religious leaders, Jerusalem and the
Temple.

In contrast, when συνάγειν has as its subject the followers of
Jesus, it is employed by Jesus in the context of activity which aligns
with the purposes and will of the Father in his Son, the Emmanuel
Messiah. Συνάγειν is used by Jesus in 18.20 to speak of his
followers coming together 'in his name' as the prerequisite for his
presence, and here the participle stands in concert with
συμφωνήσωσιν in 18.19; both imply gathering and unity.[30] In
25.35, 38 and 43 Jesus establishes the activity of συνάγειν (in this
case 'to receive strangers') as one of the universal criteria of
judgement at the coming of the Son of man. Here his language
corresponds directly with the concerns of his discourse in Matthew
18: the importance of care for the μικροί there is highlighted again
in the judgement scene of 25.31–46. Ministry to, or neglect of, the
hunger, thirst, alienation, illness and imprisonment among Jesus'
followers of ἑνὶ τούτων (τῶν ἀδελφῶν μου) τῶν ἐλαχίστων (25.40,
45) actually constitutes ministry to or neglect of Jesus himself, the
King, the Son of man, and is grounds for eternal inheritance or
punishment of those outside Jesus' gathered community.[31]

The temporal coordinate of the gathering in 18.20 in story time
is important, for it contrasts with the repeated gatherings of the
Jewish leaders. Each of their συνάγειν episodes is reported by the
narrator as a plotted incident, as a series of clandestine meetings
which surround Jesus at every turn, constituting a subversive plot
to the main story of his messianic mission. The 'gatherings'

---

[30] A. Kretzer, *Die Herrschaft der Himmel und die Söhne des Reiches*, pp. 237–8,
casts συνηγμένοι as the antithesis of the Jewish synagogue; similarly Karl Barth,
Church Dogmatics IV.2, p. 791; cf. Gnilka, *Matthäusevangelium* II, p. 140 n.27,
and many others.

[31] Cf. συνάγειν for the post-resurrection gatherings of the disciples and early
Christians in Acts 4.31; 11.26; 13.44; 14.27; 15.6, 30; 20.7, 8; cf. esp. the perfect
participle constructed with εἰμι in 4.31: ἦσαν συνηγμένοι; 20.8: ἦμεν συνηγμένοι. Luke's Gospel never uses the verb for the gathering of the disciples and
only once (22.66) for the gathering of the Jewish leaders.

implied in 18.20 are not yet plotted incidents, however. Jesus anticipates them and the reader awaits their fulfilment. In this way the plot device of anticipation has again been invoked, and the reader looks ahead to its occurrence (beyond narrative time?) as the first time (of many?) when Jesus' disciples will gather in his name and derive their Kingdom status from the peculiar authority of his presence. This also agrees with the widespread use of συνάγω elsewhere to designate the eschatological gathering of God's scattered people.[32] Matthew's Jesus has become the centre of that gathering.

Commentators have diverse opinions on the possible social or cultic characteristics of the anticipated gathering in 18.20. Jesus' presence in Matthew 18.20 is frequently compared with the Shekinah in the Temple, a possibility we will consider later (see below, pp. 192–6). Derrett, among others, has reacted sharply to attempts to contextualize the passage in a setting of worship or prayer.[33] For him the historical parallels require 18.19–20 to describe the agreement between offender and offended regarding a judicial matter;[34] Thompson, Beare, Carson and others have taken a similar tack.[35] But Derrett has overlooked the fact that Jesus has already told the complainant to take it to the community (v. 17), not to judges appointed by the disputants. Derrett also assumes that the two (or three) in vv. 19 and 20 are not the same individuals, but disputants and judges respectively – an unlikely scenario. The relationship of these historical issues to the text remains somewhat ambiguous. Matthew 18.19–20 does not preclude the situation raised by Derrett, but the passage was never so contextually narrow as he and others require.

The text itself speaks of a situation where a small cell of believers is able to act with divine authority. The tiniest possible assembly, united in prayer, gains divine ratification of their decisions because they gather in the divine presence of the Son. Englezakis thinks such activities in themselves necessitate a 'liturgical' setting. He sees in 18.20 a prayer saying, but he depends heavily on later Christian

---

[32] See a list of references in Donaldson, *Mountain*, p. 282 n.78.

[33] E.g., Dan O. Via, 'The Church as the Body of Christ in the Gospel of Matthew', p. 283, who identifies Christ's presence with the 'power of prayer'.

[34] Derrett, ' "Where Two or Three are Convened in my Name ..." ': A Sad Misunderstanding'. Derrett appears to suffer from his own case of illegitimate transfer of meaning in requiring αἰτεῖσθαι to read 'pursuing a claim'. This is not required by αἰτέω elsewhere in Matthew.

[35] Thompson, *Advice*, p. 202; Beare, *Matthew*, p. 380; Carson, 'Matthew', p. 403.

exegesis.[36] Caba categorizes the gathering of 18.20 as of a 'fundamentally religious character'[37] and interprets this in the sense of the gatherings in Acts which 'implican casisiempre un carácter religioso' (cf. Acts 11.26; 13.44; 14.27; 20.7). Caba's understanding of 'religious', however, seems overly ecclesiastical in its focus. In the end, Caba's endorsement of a three-level portrait from 18.19–20 – the intercommunication of the Earth and its affairs, the presence of Jesus as intermediary, and the Father in heaven, forming a triple-plane conception of the church which is the centre of Matthew's Gospel – runs counter to the story's own emphases.[38]

Such pictures of 'einer dreifachen Struktur' or 'un cuadro a triple nivel' are incompatible with the portrait of presence in Matthew. Jesus' agency of God's presence in the story is one of immediacy – it is the unmediated experience of the disciples and 18.20 anticipates that it will be the unmediated experience of the ἐκκλησία. Their power to bind and loose, to agree and petition effectively, and to gather, does not go through a three-stage hierarchy but is given to be employed efficaciously by them.

Frankemölle is correct that the style of the gathering is unclear;[39] certainly on historical and form-critical grounds it is not confined to a single category like prayer, eucharist, liturgy or judicial gathering. And given the temporal plot coordinates the description of this utterance as a logion of 'the Exalted Lord' also does not explain its meaning in the story.[40] Yet it is similarly futile to attempt a narrow definition of Jesus here as κύριος[41] or as the exalted Son of God.[42]

Jesus' authoritative presence in 18.20 does elaborate the assurance of v. 19 and clarifies the certainty of the community's judicial acts in vv. 15–18. 'Spiritual' and 'mystical'[43] are thus also too narrow to describe Jesus' presence here, given the dynamic quality of Jesus' saving presence throughout Matthew, and the story's

---

[36] 'Thomas', p. 266.

[37] 'El poder', p. 629: 'esa reunión sí tiere un carácter fundamentalmente religioso'.

[38] 'El poder', p. 631. Caba also cites a similar statement from Trilling, Israel, p. 99: cf. also Hausordnung, pp. 52–3; Gaechter, Das Matthäus-Evangelium, p. 603.

[39] Jahwebund, pp. 35–6.   [40] Schweizer, Matthew, p. 375.

[41] See Strecker, Weg, p. 213; Trilling, Israel, pp. 40–2; Bornkamm, 'Bind'.

[42] Kingsbury, Structure, pp. 69–70, although earlier, in Parables, p. 43, he refers frequently to Jesus speaking to the church, 'for as Jesus kyrios he resides in their midst (18:20; 28:20)' – cf. pp. 18, 34, 72, 114.

[43] See Frankemölle's references, Jahwebund, p. 36: cf. Lagrange, Matthieu, p. 356: 'mystique'.

conscious rootedness in the material and dynamic OT presence of YHWH.

The four appearances of ἐν μέσῳ in Matthew's story are always applied to the relative position of characters and provide a portrait of presence, not merely of physical proximity, but of personal encounter.[44] In each case the adverbial phrase sharpens the focus on the characters themselves by virtue of their centripetal position 'in the midst' of others: the disciples sent out as 'sheep in the midst of wolves' (10.16); Herod's daughter dancing 'in the midst of' his guests (14.6); the child placed 'in the midst of' the disciples by Jesus (18.2); and Jesus being 'in the midst of' those gathered in his name (18.20). For the content of ἐν μέσῳ in 18.20, then, we need to look back to its inclusio with 18.2, and ahead to the promise of 28.20. Jesus' presence in their midst is both enigmatic and paradoxical. The enigma comes from the open, undefined character of 18.20 and 28.20. Jesus is clearly present in all the circumstances raised in Matthew 18, but his presence also awaits its content in the anticipated future gatherings of his people. The paradox comes in the child of 18.2, the visual symbol of 'the little ones': the content of Jesus' presence is both the humility and status of the socially powerless, and the authority of heaven and earth.

The name of Jesus

The 'gathering' referred to by Jesus in 18.20 is critically qualified by εἰς τὸ ἐμὸν ὄνομα. The most obvious qualification this provides to the gathering is the prevention of misunderstanding of the bold promise in 18.19. The promise applies only if the disciples are living by Jesus' codes, in his name.[45] This orientation to 'name' also clearly sets them apart from any of the 'gathering' episodes of the Jewish leaders in Matthew's story. Each of *their* συνάγειν incidents has been *against* the name of Jesus, whereas in 18.20 the disciples will be gathering with the opposite orientation. This fundamental

---

[44] Cf. ἐν μέσῳ: Mark 2x; Luke 7x; John 2x – both textually doubtful. It could be argued that the Gospels' employment of equivalent phrases (ἀνὰ μέσον, εἰς μέσον etc.) negates any particular attention given to ἐν μέσῳ in Matthew. But two considerations remain: (1) other Gospels use ἐν μέσῳ to describe the relative positions of inanimate objects (cf. Mark 6.47; Luke 8.7; 22.55); in Matthew the phrase applies only to the close proximity of characters, i.e., personal presence. (2) In paralleled material Matthew avoids ἐν μέσῳ for inanimate objects, e.g., cf. Mark 6.47 // Matt. 14.24; Matt. 13.7 // Luke 8.7.

[45] So Margaret Davies, *Matthew*, p. 129.

contrast between the two groups ties directly into the opposing application and orientation given to συναγωγή and ἐκκλησία language in Matthew's story and highlights the ongoing conflict between Jesus and the Jewish leaders.

More important here, however, is the idea of acting 'in the name of', or invoking 'the name of', Jesus. The phrase εἰς (τὸ) ὄνομα is unknown to the other synoptic Gospels; Matthew's story uses it three times where the Markan parallel does not (Matt. 10.41–2, causally), and twice in unparalleled material (18.20; 28.19). The latter occurrences have prompted a number of commentators to speak of the phrase in terms of 'confession',[46] which may have some justification in the case of the triadic formula in 28.19. In 18.20 the phrase εἰς τὸ ὄνομα is more the *raison d'être* of those gathered than their 'confession'. Furthermore, a number of equivalent phrases are also used in Matthew's story:

τῷ (σῷ) ὀνόματι	7.22 – three times; 12.21; all in *Sondergut*
διὰ τὸ ὄνομά μου	10.22, *Sondergut*; 24.9 = Mark 13.13/ Luke 21.17
ἐπὶ τῷ ὀνόματί μου	18.5 = Mark 9.37/Luke 9.48
ἐπὶ τῷ ὀνόματί μου	24.5 = Mark 13.6/Luke 21.8
ἕνεκεν τοῦ ὀνόματός μου	19.29, editorial
ἐν ὀνόματι κυρίου	21.9 = Mark 11.9/Luke 19.38

In eleven out of fourteen instances in Matthew, disciples are acting 'in the name of' Jesus.[47] They include the true disciples who are hated (10.22), receive 'one such child' (18.5), gather together (18.20), leave everything behind (19.29), are persecuted (24.9), and are baptized (28.19) 'in the name' or 'for the sake' of Jesus. They also include false disciples – evildoers who prophesy, cast out demons and do many mighty works (7.22), and those who come as false christs (24.5) 'in the name of' Jesus. The other three instances in 10.41–2 employ εἰς ὄνομα in reference to the disciples being received during their ministry εἰς ὄνομα προφήτου ... εἰς ὄνομα δικαίου ... εἰς ὄνομα μαθητοῦ. Here too the identification between

---

[46] E.g., J. Dupont, 'Nom de Jésus', p. 535: 'Pour préciser le sens dans lequel on se réunit "au nom" de Jésus, il faudrait sans doute faire appel aux confessions de foi de la chrétienté primitive, telle que: "Jésus est le Seigneur".' See Acts 2.21; 9.14, 21; 22.16; Rom. 10.13; 1 Cor. 1.2 for the invocation of the name of Jesus; cf. W. G. Thompson, *Advice*, p. 198; Caba, 'El poder', p. 629 n.57.

[47] The citation from Ps. 118.26, repeated in Matt. 21.9 and 23.39, uses the phrase ἐν ὀνόματι κυρίου in reference to YHWH, to emphasize again Jesus' agency.

the disciples and Jesus' presence is very much at the forefront of the passage: 'He who receives you receives me' (10.40). Εἰς τὸ ὄνομα in 18.20 is thus causally understood,[48] and signifies the allegiance, or identity marker, of this particular group. Commentators have often noted that the phrase translates the Hebrew/ Aramaic lišmî and can be rendered as 'for my sake',[49] so that in a very practical sense the name of Jesus provides the divine authority which stands over the community. In each of the eleven instances listed above, the disciples, whether true or false, are actively engaged in some aspect of Jesus' messianic mission. The phrase 'in the name of' never occurs as part of a plotted event, but is always used in future-tense or subjunctive language, anticipating events which do not happen in story time, but look ahead to the disciples' mission, times of persecution, 'that day', judgement, or some other indeterminate future point beyond narrative time. The same is true of 18.20, which predicts a situation which has not arisen in the plot – the gathering of the disciples in Jesus' name.

Hence, each time the phrase or its equivalent occurs in the story, the reader is left with another anticipated, yet-unfulfilled situation to add to the list of activities which at some point will be carried out 'in his name'. From the language of these passages the reader also receives the implication that this activity 'in his name' will be undertaken in Jesus' physical absence. Thus these temporal coordinates in the story become increasingly important, in order to differentiate between plotted and anticipated events. The reader knows that the commission in Matthew 10, the gatherings in 18.20, the coming of the Kingdom (3.2; 4.17), the judgement in Matthew 24, the promise of presence in 28.20 and so on will occur.

In relation to these plot devices of prediction and anticipation, ὄνομα in 18.20 recalls the double naming in 1.21 and 23. The first was fulfilled in 1.24–5. In 18.20, however, the naming of 1.23 appears to receive another anticipatory reference.[50] Since 1.23 is a prediction not of a literal naming by Joseph, but of a corporate recognition (indefinite future plural καλέσουσιν) by the people of Jesus that he is 'God with us', in the saying in 18.20 Jesus therefore himself anticipates that corporate recognition by the members of

---

[48] Cf. Gnilka, Matthäusevangelium II, p. 140.
[49] See e.g., Hans Bietenhard, 'ὄνομα', TDNT V, pp. 274–6; Sievers, 'Where Two or Three', p. 177; cf. Frankemölle, Jahwebund, pp. 345; Grundmann, Das Evangelium nach Matthäus, p. 302.
[50] Cf. G. Braumann, 'Mit Euch, Matth. 26,29', p. 162; Caba, 'El poder', p. 630.

the ἐκκλησία. He effectively reiterates the narrator's prediction of Matthew 1.23 by looking forward to a time when the gathering of his people 'in the name of' the Emmanuel Messiah Jesus will constitute the forum for his presence. 1.23 remains unfulfilled in the plot, but 18.20 also reinforces its expectation through anticipation.

7.5.   Parallels of presence: Shekinah and Jesus

A number of parallels have also been adduced for 18.18 and 20. The best known in the latter case, long since noted by Strack–Billerbeck,[51] is the striking correspondence of 18.20 to the saying attributed to Rabbi Hananiah b.Teradyon in *M. Abot* 3.2b(3):

> If two sit together and the words between them are not of Torah, then that is a session of scorners, as it is said, *Nor hath sat in the seat of the scornful* [Ps. 1.1]. But if two sit together and the words between them are of Torah, then the *Shekhinah* is in their midst, as it is said, *Then they that feared the Lord spoke one with another; and the Lord hearkened, and heard, and a book of remembrance was written before him, for them that feared the Lord and that thought upon his name* (Mal. 3.16).

The chronological difficulties with relating this passage, compiled at least a century after Matthew, to the saying in Matthew 18.20 are well known, and Samuel Sandmel's warnings long ago against 'parallelomania' still apply.[52] At the same time, some critics have found value in pondering the comparative worlds in these two texts, and have asserted varying degrees of overlap and particular relationships of dependence.

Trilling employs this comparison with Shekinah to emphasize that Jesus' presence in 18.20 is of a static nature, giving the gathering cultic connotations, while 28.20 reflects dynamic presence.[53] Frankemölle has most strongly contested Trilling's distinction, on the basis of the LXX's undifferentiated use of ἐν μέσῳ and

---

[51] Strack–Billerbeck, *Kommentar zum Neuen Testament aus Talmud und Midrasch*, I, p. 794; cf. Samuel Lachs, *A Rabbinic Commentary on the New Testament*, p. 271.

[52] 'Parallelomania', pp. 1–13. Cf. Jacob Neusner's broader assertion of a fundamental incomprehension and discontinuity between Christianity and Judaism(s) of the first century; 'The Absoluteness of Christianity and the Uniqueness of Judaism', pp. 18–31.

[53] *Israel*, pp. 41–2.

μετά.[54] Goldberg and Sievers have also each argued for Shekinah as both Temple-oriented and independent of location.[55]

As Englezakis has noted, given the language and character of the passage, most commentators assume 18.20 to be a creation of early Christian prophecy, modelled on the *M. Abot* saying. But if Paul could speculate about being ἀπὼν τῷ σώματι παρὼν δὲ τῷ πνεύ-ματι (1 Cor. 5.3), why not Jesus? Ἐκκλησία in Matthew 18 need not be deemed evidence of later vocabulary on the basis of its subsequent institutional connotations. It is worth asking, why could Jesus himself not have postulated this future gathering of his followers 'for his name's sake'?[56] The prophetic boldness of 18.20 may represent the historical Jesus' self-perceived role as herald of God's eschatological Kingdom. Jesus' agency of divine presence in this story is Matthew's signatory formulation of the close link between the activity of Jesus and the divine purposes which both John and the synoptics hold in common.[57]

If a historical setting is to be found, it hinges on the implied antithesis of 18.20. In the story ἐκκλησία provides a powerful counterpoint to the reverse, antagonistic orientation of συναγωγαῖς αὐτῶν, and this could apply in the historical community/ies from which the story emanates. Divine authority and heavenly presence are in Matthew 18.20 the symbols of the community of Jesus' followers. The special claim of Matthew's author to represent God's people is an assertion over against those who have been gathering *against* his Lord. In the story and in the historical world referenced by it these opponents could be traditional Jewish leaders who have for generations claimed as their exclusive right the corporate ratification of YHWH's presence, now being claimed by Jesus' followers in such texts as Matthew's.

However, the juxtaposition between ἐκκλησία and συναγωγή, if referenced historically through Matthew, is not as simple as Christian versus Jewish gatherings. Here Saldarini's insistence that Matthew's community is a Jesus-centred gathering inside of Judaism runs into Stanton's insistence that Matthew's concern is

[54] *Jahwebund*, pp. 30–2; cf. Strecker, *Weg*, p. 213.
[55] Sievers, 'Where Two or Three', p. 178; A. M. Goldberg, *Untersuchungen über die Vorstellung von der Schekhinah in der frühen rabbinischen Literatur*, pp. 388, 453–4.
[56] So Englezakis, '*Thomas*', pp. 263–4; cf. Joachim Jeremias, *New Testament Theology*, §17.
[57] So Christopher Rowland, *Christian Origins*, pp. 174–5; cf. Matt. 10.40–2; Luke 10.16; John 5.23; 7.16; 12.44–5; 13.20; 14.9; 15.23.

for a group of Jewish-Christian communities broken away from their parent body. No specific Jewish gathering in first-century CE literature is called ἐκκλησία, even though LXX interchanges the term with συναγωγή.[58] So the ἐκκλησία founded by Jesus in Matthew 16.18 is a distinct use of the term.

Given the ongoing questions about and possibility of 18.20's authenticity, can its long-asserted correspondence with *M. Abot 3.2b* still remain illustrative, at least in terms of interpretive background? Much of this discussion has centred on the question of the origins of the rabbinic concept of Shekinah and its relation to Matthew 18.20, a question remaining essentially unsolved.[59] The noun never once occurs in the Hebrew Bible or the Dead Sea Scrolls. The verb *škn*, 'to dwell, rest or abide', occurs frequently in the OT along with its derivatives, in reference to God and his sanctuary,[60] and in numerous places the verb through rabbinic use and interpretation of the texts became substantive in form.[61] But rabbinic references to the actual term *šᵉkînâ* cannot reliably be dated early enough to provide temporal correspondence with Matthew, including the oft-cited occurrences in the *Aleinu* prayer, the Eighteen Benedictions and Targum Onkelos.[62]

On the other hand, 2 Maccabees 14.35 may provide a Greek correspondence from outside rabbinic literature, with its reference to a prayer of the Jerusalem priests for the purity of the 'Temple of your indwelling' (ναὸν τῆς σῆς σκηνώσεως); the closest semantic and formal Hebrew parallel for σκηνώσις is *šᵉkînâ*. Such Greek references to the Temple as the 'house of God's dwelling' may lie behind the development of the term Shekinah, possibly before 70 CE.[63]

More important, however, is Sievers' observation that Shekinah in rabbinic literature became synonymous with divine presence in

---

58 So Stanton, 'Revisiting', pp. 16–17; see Meeks, *The First Urban Christians*, pp. 79–81.

59 See the attempts by L. Bouyer, 'La Schékinah, Dieu avec nous'; Terrien, *Presence*, pp. 404, 409, 420, to address the issue.

60 E.g., Exod. 25.8, 9; 29.45; Num. 5.3; Ps. 74.2; see Sievers, 'Where Two or Three', p. 171; Terrien, *Presence*.

61 E.g. Num. 35.34 'in the midst of which I dwell' – *škn* is subsequently understood by *Sifre. Num.* to indicate *šᵉkînâ*; cf. Frankemölle, *Jahwebund*, p. 34.

62 Cf. Targum Onkelos: Gen. 9.27 'And he shall cause his Shekinah to dwell in the tabernacle of Shem'; Exod. 25.8 'And I will cause my Shekinah to dwell among them'; Exod. 29.45 'And I will cause my Shekinah to dwell among the Israelites'.

63 Cf. Goldberg, *Untersuchungen*, pp. 439–42; Sievers, 'Where Two or Three', p. 172.

all modes, not confined to the Temple sanctuary. That *Mekhilta de Rabbi Ishmael* interprets Exodus 20.24 as both God's presence restricted to the Temple and God's presence with one, two or three holding court, or ten in the synagogue, underlines the distinction and tension between different views of divine presence,[64] and at least 'weakens Goldberg's thesis that there was no connection between the ideas of the *Shekhinah* in the Temple and in the community'.[65] Other differences arise: whereas other traditions[66] focus on preoccupation with Torah as the main prerequisite for the presence of the Shekinah with one or two persons,[67] the Mekhilta highlights only fear of the Lord and remembrance of his name. These various traditions seem to be struggling more with the problem of God's absence and presence than with the place to pronounce his name.

The concept and terminology of 'Shekinah' may not be clearly traceable to the first century CE, but the striking correspondence between Matthew 18.20 and the saying of Hananiah b.Teradyon points at minimum to two distinct religious circles, Jewish and Christian, dealing with similar questions about divine presence in terms of their own community identity and experience. As Englezakis points out, concern about God's presence with the believer in any case predates the Christian *monaxoi*, predates Matthew 18.20, and is a broader query within Judaism, Christianity and Islam.[68] In the later rabbinic formulation the focus of gathering is 'words of Torah', and in Matthew 'my name'; in the former the presence bestowed is 'Shekinah', in Matthew it is the intimate experience of Jesus' divine authority. Evidence for the source of Matthew 18.20 is too scanty, the origin of the Shekinah concept is too clouded, and the contexts of the two sayings too distinct to point to any specific historical–literary relationship.[69] We cannot assert that Matthew

---

[64] See 1 Kings 8.12–13.27; Goldberg, *Untersuchungen*, pp. 471–530.

[65] Sievers, 'Where Two or Three', p. 173; see Goldberg, *Untersuchungen*, p. 500.

[66] E.g., the Mishnah's only two occurrences of Shekinah in *M. Abot* 3.2b.

[67] See examples in Sievers, 'Where Two or Three', pp. 173–4.

[68] *'Thomas'*, p. 265.

[69] W. D. Davies, *Setting*, p. 225: 'a christified bit of rabbinism', goes too far; so also Bultmann, *History*, pp. 147–8, 149, 150–1; Michel, 'The Conclusion of Matthew's Gospel', p. 40 n.7, and many others. Bornkamm, 'Bind', p. 88, suggests that 'the Christian logion was formulated antithetically in relation to the Jewish conception of the Shekinah', and G. Barth, *TIM*, p. 127, talks about the replacement of Torah in 18.20 with ὄνομα, and in place of Shekinah, Jesus. Christian, *Brüder*, p. 46, also sees too easily an identification between the Shekinah and the presence of God in Jesus throughout Matthew, depending on Strack–Billerbeck to assume that 'Die Vorstellung von der Schechina reicht sicher in das 1.Jh.n.Chr.' (p.328

18.20 was composed as the antithesis to the claims of the Shekinah saying, or that Matthew wanted to replace the presence of Torah with Jesus, or to equate Jesus with Shekinah – such a relationship is supported neither rhetorically nor historically. But the lack of evidence for a link between *these* two particular historical, religious circles does not obviate either the rhetorical antithesis within the story or possible reference to the very real historical antithesis between the two religious worlds of Matthew's communities and their counterparts in Judaism.[70] The main thrust of supersession in 18.20 is thus not against Shekinah *per se*, but against the συνάγειν activity of those referenced in the story as the Jewish leaders – Matthew's Jesus is at minimum claiming for his community the authority of heaven which these opponents had assumed was theirs.

It becomes possible at this point in Matthew's story to talk about Jesus asserting for himself functions of YHWH. It is important for Matthew to establish lines of continuity in his story between Israel and the ἐκκλησία, between YHWH's presence and Jesus. But at numerous points these lines of continuity are becoming lines of transformation. Jesus himself now manifests YHWH's divine presence (whether or not thought of in terms of Shekinah) to the smallest possible gathering of his own people, given the condition of his name as their focus, i.e., their gathering in alignment with his filial agency of God's messianic will and presence.

7.6.   Modes of presence: Jesus and 'the little ones'

One illustrative correspondence to Matthew 18.20 arises from within Matthew's story, with 18.5 (see table 7.2).

Here the parallelism of the *a* and *a¹* elements in each verse is noteworthy. In 18.5 the δέξηται–δέχεται parallel evokes an identification between the direct objects of both verbs; ἓν παιδίον τοιοῦτο is parallel to ἐμὲ and hence the stated equivalence between receiving/welcoming Jesus and receiving/welcoming 'one of these

---

n.100) According to Morton Smith's categories we are dealing with a 'parallel with a fixed difference', *Tannaitic Parallels to the Gospels*, p. 152 (cf. Sievers, 'Where Two or Three', p. 176).

But cf. Frankemölle, *Jahwebund*, p. 30: 'Mt 18:20a findet in Aboth III 2 kein Vorbild', and pp. 29–30 for a list of stylistic and material differences; also Bonnard, *Matthieu*, p. 446. Van Unnik, '*Dominus*', p. 288: the content of the two sayings is as different as it is similar.

[70] See Pesch, 'Gemeindeordnung', p. 228: 'Die Christen lösen sich von dem Synagogen verband und glauben an die geistige Gegenwart ihres Herrn in ihrer Mitte.'

Table 7.2 *Parallelism in Matthew 18.5 and 18.20*

Matt. 18.5		Matt. 18.20	
a	ὃς ἐὰν δέξηται ἓν παιδίον τοιοῦτο	*a*	οὗ γάρ εἰσιν δύο ἢ τρεῖς συνηγμένοι
b	ἐπὶ τῷ ὀνόματί μου	*b*	εἰς τὸ ἐμὸν ὄνομα
*a*¹	ἐμὲ δέχεται	*a*¹	ἐκεῖ εἰμι ἐν μέσῳ αὐτῶν

children'. Element *b* – ἐπὶ τῷ ὀνόματί μου – provides the core of the parallelism and the identification between Jesus and the child.

Likewise, in 18.20 a verbal parallel exists in the *a* and *a*¹ elements between εἰσιν and εἰμι. This is strengthened further by the parallel locatives οὗ and ἐκεῖ to provide for the correspondence between the real presence of the two or three gathered in element *a* and Jesus' presence in their midst in element *a*¹. Based on the parallel structure, the tangible nature of the gathering in element *a* extends equally to the presence described in element *a*¹; Jesus' presence in their midst is perceived as no less real than the actual gathering of the ἐκκλησία members. Again, element *b* – εἰς τὸ ἐμὸν ὄνομα – provides the same core for the parallelism as in 18.5, and here fuses the two presences within the one experience of gathering.

The tradition in 18.5 of a parallelism between receiving the disciples and receiving Jesus is known by several Gospels, but employed most emphatically in Matthew's story.

Matt. 10.40	ὁ δεχόμενος ὑμᾶς ἐμὲ δέχεται ...
Matt. 18.5	ὃς ἐὰν δέξηται ἓν παιδίον τοιοῦτο ... ἐμὲ δέχεται
Matt. 25.40	ἐφ' ὅσον ἐποιήσατε ἑνὶ τούτων ... ἐμοὶ ἐποιήσατε
Luke 10.16	ὁ ἀθετῶν ὑμᾶς ἐμὲ ἀθετεῖ
John 13.20	ὁ λαμβάνων ἄν τινα πέμψω ἐμὲ λαμβάνει

This principle in Matthew's story, of repeatedly identifying the welcome and treatment of the disciples and little children as tantamount to welcoming and caring for their Messiah, Jesus, evokes for some a scenario where the opposite is the case and needs powerful challenging and correction. Certainly within the rhetorical world of the story Jesus makes no secret of the basic antagonism to be faced by his followers (e.g., 5.10–12, 44; 10.16–23; 23.34–5). This is a condition which thus may also apply in some fashion historically, in the post-Easter world referenced by the story. To welcome one of the μικροί is to receive Jesus; to reject one of the μικροί is to reject Jesus. Even here in the positive parallelism of 18.5 and 20 the story's fundamental ideological opposition between Jesus and the Jewish leaders emerges. Alignment with or against the μικροί means alignment with or against Jesus, and Jesus has again passed on (as with the keys of the Kingdom) a measure of his own agency of the Father to his disciples – they are now agents of him. Their presence is in some measure his presence, through this commissioned agency.

This rhetorical equivalence between Jesus and the little ones/children/disciples sets up a paradigm for the network of relationships inside and outside the ἐκκλησία. In these relationships the presence of Jesus becomes a powerful motivating and guiding force religiously and socially. For the members of the ἐκκλησία, this functional identification of Jesus' presence with themselves and the marginalized brings both a greater internal cohesion and a clearer external hedge to those opposed to them and their Messiah. Divine presence here provides parameters, authority and focus for the members' activities, as well as a yardstick for their entrance into the ἐκκλησία, while 25.31–46 adds important eschatological weight to the criteria for final acceptance among or rejection from the people of God. On the strength of this parallelism the ἐκκλησία can challenge those gathered against it with an authoritative identity – reception/rejection of Jesus' followers invokes no less than divine sanction/condemnation, based on Jesus' ongoing post-Easter agency of divine presence with his followers.

That Matthew's story brings together the parallelism of 18.5 with the parallelism of 18.20 thus fortifies Jesus' presence as the functional element of equivalence in both verses.

Summary

To return to our original question, what does Jesus' presence in 18.20 mean in the story? How will Jesus be 'in their midst'? The image is first and foremost an anticipation of something unknown, unexperienced and somewhat undefined. But in Matthew 18.1–20 it is predicated upon Jesus' complete identification with his marginalized followers: 'Whoever receives one such child in my name receives me' (18.5; cf. 10.40; 25.40, 45) – Jesus' agency of divine presence is intimately bound up with the humility of the μικροί, their place as first in the Kingdom and with his Father, and their treatment by others.

In Matthew 18.1–20 Jesus' presence is promised as the future experience of his heavenly authority among his gathered followers, in their efforts to reconcile, discipline, bind and loose, and agree and pray together. That Jesus is 'in the midst' of those gathered in his name brings divine ratification to the daily functions, religious and social boundaries, and standards and mores of the ἐκκλησία. Implied within this dynamic promise *for* the ἐκκλησία is the counter-claim *against* the particular συναγωγή gatherings of his opponents; orientation around Jesus' name means heaven's ratification of the former and its activities, while orientation against Jesus means heaven's judgement and divine absence for the latter.

Thus this presence of Jesus 'in their midst' is not just the regulation of disputatious church members, or a good feeling, or a practised cultic expression, or religious acknowledgement of a corporate desire. It is real empowerment when God's little people gather in Jesus' name. It is the social and religious experience of his gathered people being filled with divine authority, focus and cohesion for the ordinary and extraordinary events in the life of their community.

Matthew 18.1–20 therefore offers fundamental principles for community definition; 'his people', those whom Jesus has come to save and who will call him 'Emmanuel', are those who will gather in his name in 18.20. Οὐ γάρ εἰσιν ... συνηγμένοι ..., ἐκεῖ εἰμι is not an open-ended declaration of 'pan-christology' which guarantees Jesus' presence, blessing and authority whenever and wherever a couple of ἐκκλησία members meet.[71] His divine presence and authority will go hand in hand with gathering 'in his name', in the context of pressing questions of community life and group self-definition *vis-à-vis* outside social and religious forces.

Ultimately, however, the story also maintains its own rhetorical sense of ambiguity as to the precise character of Jesus' presence. The promise he utters in 18.20 is upon the premise of his own predictions of his future death, resurrection and physical absence from his followers – these events remain as yet unrealized and undefined in the plot. Furthermore, his promise anticipates that future period – πάσας τὰς ἡμέρας ἕως τῆς συντελείας τοῦ αἰῶνος (28.20) and points to the ἐκκλησία's ongoing experience of Emma-

---

[71] E.g., Frankemölle borders on making 18.20 too universal (*Jahwebund*, p. 230): Jesus is always present with his community where and when they are found together – because he is their Lord and helper. Cf. also Philip Cunningham, *Jesus and the Evangelists*, p. 194.

nuel's presence then, not as an objective description in terms of vision, word or spirit, but in terms of the members' corporate apprehension of his personal power and authority.

Finally, the precise function of the present Jesus is not delimited in Matthew 18.1–20. The story is rhetorically deliberate in neither narrowing the function of Jesus' presence to the single issue of community discipline, nor leaving it broadly open as an unqualified guarantee of divine accommodation and approval. Jesus' statement here 'denies importance to the presence of an institution, the size of the community, the sanctity of the place, the blessing of an official functionary, or visible success in the world',[72] and instead focuses on the importance of the members' harmony in binding, loosing, petitioning and gathering in Emmanuel's presence. Once again Matthew's story works within the broad stream of YHWH's *Mitsein* among his people Israel, but sees Jesus as both the radical transformation and personal embodiment of that divine function.

[72] Schweizer, *Matthew*, p. 375.

8

MATTHEW 28.16–20: THE PRESENCE OF THE RISEN JESUS

The final words of the First Gospel are a promise uttered by the risen Jesus to 'the Eleven':

καὶ ἰδοὺ ἐγὼ μεθ᾽ ὑμῶν εἰμι πάσας τὰς ἡμέρας
ἕως τῆς συντελείας τοῦ αἰῶνος.

They conclude Matthew's account in 28.16–20 of Jesus' post-Easter appearance to his disciples on a Galilean mountain. This carefully crafted climax brings together several major strands of the story, including: mountain as a locus of christological significance; the manner and meaning of the risen Jesus' appearance; the disciples' obedience, worship and doubt; Jesus' claim to reception of divine authority; making disciples as a universal commission; baptism in the triadic name as ritual initiation into the community; the centrality of Jesus' ἐντολαί for the community; and the promise of his risen, continuous presence with his commissioned disciples.

Thus it is claimed that the last pericope of Matthew contains *in nuce* the essence of the Gospel; it provides the 'abstract' for Matthew's 'dissertation', but more, it is, in rhetorical and theological terms, both a digest and *telos* of the work.[1] Michel's assertion that the conclusion 'is the key to the understanding of the whole book' has some merit.[2]

The consensus on the importance of Matthew's final pericope does not extend to its interpretation. The literature devoted to 28.16–20 is both plentiful and diverse. This may be because

> der Schlüsseltext des ganzen Buches ist zugleich auch der
> Text, in dem sich wie in keinem anderen die Probleme des

---

[1]   The importance of Matthew's conclusion was particularly noted by Lohmeyer in 1945 in 'Mir ist' and by Michel in 1950 in 'Abschluß' (ET 'Conclusion'), p. 21, and has been incorporated by the majority of Matthean scholars to date in their treatments of the passage.
[2]   'Conclusion', p. 35.

> ganzen Buches wie in einem brennpunkt sammeln[3]
>
> (the key text of the whole book is at the same time also the text in which as nowhere else the problems of the whole book are gathered in a focal point).

My intention here is not to revisit extensively the available secondary commentary on the text of Matthew 28.16–20, but to investigate it specifically as part of Matthew's redactional strategy around his presence motif. We have already seen some of the rhetorical strategy of Matthew's conclusion above in Chapter 3. In Jesus' final appearance and words we find a resolution of the story crisis concerning the identity and boundaries of 'his people', and we witness the complete alignment of the reader with the narrator, Jesus and the Eleven in temporal and ideological terms. Yet this final alignment does not force narrative closure; the open temporal and dialogical framework given to Jesus' promised presence connects the story to its post-narrative world, so that the story's structures, point of view and unresolved tensions guide the readers to seek completion of the story within their own experiences. Jesus' promised presence not only concludes the Gospel's narrative frame, with the divine utterance of Jesus' post-resurrection authority, but given the nexus of all these elements in 28.16–20 it also provides the bridge between God and his people in the post-narrative world of the commission. The question here is to what degree these distinct rhetorical strategies are also reflected in Matthew's composition and redaction of the Gospel's climax.

8.1.   The text: language, style and composition

We possess no direct extra-Matthean parallels to Matthew 28.16–20. Matthew may have reshaped Mark's allusion to Jesus' promise to see his disciples in Galilee.[4] Some also speculate that Matthew 28.9–20 depends on a lost Markan ending originally attached to Mark 16.8.[5] For others Matthew 28.16–20 is one of several extant stories about the risen Jesus appearing to his disciples, showing affinities to that group which has the commis-

[3]   Lange, *Das Erscheinen des Auferstandenen im Evangelium nach Matthäus*, p. 19.
[4]   See full discussion in Pheme Perkins, *Resurrection*, pp. 131–7.
[5]   E.g., Allen, *Matthew*, pp. 590–1; Gundry, *Matthew*, pp. 590–1. But cf. Klostermann, *Matthäus*, p. 228; Lange, *Erscheinen*, pp. 172–4; Hubbard, *The Matthean Redaction of a Primitive Apostolic Commissioning*, pp. 101–4, 137–49.

sioning *Gattung* at its heart (cf. Luke 24.44–9; Acts 1.4–8; John 20.19–23), but being characteristically singular. Tradition-criticism has frequently assessed Jesus' words in vv. 18b–20 as three separable sayings, v. 18b; 19–20a; 20b.[6] Although numerous sources have been posited, and possible allusions in the text to earlier prototypes in LXX Daniel 7.13–14, prophetic commissionings and Mosaic typology, the historical core and traditional pattern of the account have been all but erased and reformulated for Matthew's purposes. Kingsbury's detailed analysis of vocabulary and style concludes that Matthew himself probably composed the passage.[7]

Matthew 28.16–20 divides naturally between narrative preamble (vv. 16–18a) and Jesus' discourse (vv. 18b–20).

8.2. The narrative framework: Matthew 28.16–18a

Οἱ δὲ ἕνδεκα μαθηταὶ ἐπορεύθησαν εἰς τὴν Γαλιλαίαν εἰς τὸ ὄρος οὗ ἐτάξατο αὐτοῖς ὁ Ἰησοῦς, καὶ ἰδόντες αὐτὸν προσεκύνησαν, οἱ δὲ ἐδίστασαν. καὶ προσελθὼν ὁ Ἰησοῦς ἐλάλησεν αὐτοῖς λέγων ...

The characters and setting (v. 16)

The precise reference to the remaining core of Jesus' followers as 'the Eleven' (οἱ δὲ ἕνδεκα) is probably Matthew's own designation.[8] This follows his tendency to identify the disciples as οἱ δώδεκα [μαθηταὶ/ἀπόστολοι][9] and is the corollary of his detailed narration of Judas' death in 27.3–10 (*Sondergut*).[10]

Matthew has a particular interest in Jesus' post-resurrection return to Galilee. Εἰς τὴν Γαλιλαίαν occurs four times between 26.32 and 28.16. Matthew 26.32 and 28.7 are paralleled in Mark 14.28 and 16.7. Twice more the phrase is repeated in Matthew by Jesus (28.10) and the narrator (28.16). The return of the disciples

---

[6] So, e.g., G. Barth, *TIM*, pp. 131–3; Bornkamm, 'Lord', pp. 205–8; F. Hahn, *Mission in the New Testament*, p. 64; Joachim Jeremias, *Jesus' Promise to the Nations*, p. 39; Trilling, *Israel*, pp. 21–45; Malina, 'Structure', p. 87.

[7] 'Composition'.

[8] There is evidence for 'the Eleven' being a traditional designation, but not in any material parallel to Matthew. See Luke 24.9, 33; Acts 1.26; 2.14; cf. 1.13–14; also Mark 16.14. See the post-resurrection 'Twelve' in John 20.24–5; 1 Cor. 15.5.

[9] Cf. Matt. 10.1, 2, 5; 11.1; 20.17; 26.14, 20, 47.

[10] See Meier, 'Two Disputed Questions in Matt. 28:16–20', p. 408; Kingsbury, 'Composition and Christology of Matthew 28:16–20', p. 575; Jane Schaberg, *The Father, Son and the Holy Spirit*, p. 43; against Hubbard, *Commissioning*, p. 113.

εἰς τὴν Γαλιλαίαν is thus traditional, but its emphasis in Matthew 28 is editorial. The deliberate repetition recaptures Galilee thematically as a place of rhetorical and theological significance in Matthew's Gospel. Earlier we saw that Jesus' geographic movements in Matthew highlight the opposition to him from Israel's leadership (e.g., 4.12). This return 'to Galilee' draws the reader from the conclusion of the Gospel back to its beginning and the story of Jesus' origins (2.22), with a strong element of literary inclusio.[11]

Arguments appear more commonly for than against a tradition behind Matthew 28's commissioning mountain.[12] Mountain-tops are popular elsewhere for theophany-type settings, and some elements in οὗ ἐτάξατο αὐτοῖς ὁ Ἰησοῦς appear non-Matthean.[13] But many parallels cited are demonstrably independent or actually stem from accounts such as 28.16–20. Matthew is fond of τὸ ὄρος as a site of christological importance, as is visible in strong redactional evidence for this setting in 5.1, 8.1 and 15.29. Out of sixteen occurrences of ὄρος Matthew has at least six mountains with particular christological significance: 4.8; 5.1; 8.1; 15.29; 17.1, 9; 24.3; 28.16. The addition of the mountain setting to Jesus' rhetorically and theologically significant return εἰς τὴν Γαλιλαίαν thus appears to be Matthew's editorial development.

The final mountain has a coordinating and climactic role by which it summarizes and epitomizes the rhetorical and christological characteristics of Matthew's previous peak experiences.[14] Strong elements of Sinai and Moses typology can be granted here in the case of readers informed by Jewish tradition. For example, οὗ ἐτάξατο recalls the meeting arrangements for Sinai in Exodus 3.12; 19.11, and ἐντέλλομαι in Matthew 28.19 echoes frequent Deuteronomy LXX usage.[15] But as Donaldson has argued, moun-

---

[11] See the discussion above, p. 66. Lange, *Erscheinen*, pp. 358–91, also develops Matthew's Galilee symbolism; contra Trilling, *Israel*, pp. 131–4.

[12] See discussion and references in Donaldson, *Mountain*, pp. 138–40, 171–4.

[13] See 'parallel' gnostic traditions listed by J. M. Robinson, 'On the *Gattung* of Mark (and John)', pp. 29–31; and Pheme Perkins, *The Gnostic Dialogue*, pp. 31, 42.

[14] Cf. W. Schmauch, *Orte der Offenbarung und der Offenbarungsort im Neuen Testament*, pp. 71–2; Lange, *Erscheinen*, pp. 393–440; Donaldson, *Mountain*, pp. 5–12, 174–88.

[15] K. Smyth, 'Matthew 28', finds the 'rendezvous motif' characteristic of OT theophanies (Exod. 19.10–17; 24.1, 12; 33–4; Num. 12.4–9). W. D. Davies' pessimism, *Setting*, pp. 83–6, is not always heeded. See the Sinai links variously discussed by Lohmeyer, 'Mir', pp. 24–5, 44; Hubbard, *Commissioning*, pp. 92–4; Perrin, *Resurrection*, pp. 51–2; Allison, *Moses*, pp. 262–6.

tains in the writings of Matthew's day are typically eschatological and refer to Zion, with YHWH or the messianic king enthroned there. For the appropriate reader the significance cannot be missed. Instead of the law on Zion, Jesus' teachings are now made Torah for his new people on the mountain in Galilee. Instead of YHWH's presence on Zion (*Jub.* 1.17) it is Jesus who promises divine presence with the disciples from the mountain in Galilee.[16]

Jesus' appearance and the disciples' reaction (vv. 17–18a)

Προσκυνέω is an important word for Matthew (13x; Mark 2x; Luke 2x). He often adds this specific term to the Markan account to describe the attitude of those approaching Jesus. Matthew is the only evangelist to use the term in the appearance accounts, and he does so twice.[17] Διστάζω appears only twice in the NT, both times in Matthew, and both times associated with προσκυνέω (cf. 14.31–3).

Lively discussion has arisen over the translation of οἱ δὲ ἐδίσ-τασαν.[18] Οἱ δέ is construed to refer to a variety of different subjects: i.e., 'they worshipped him, but ...'

(1) '*some who were present* [in excess of the Eleven] doubted'[19]
(2) '*some* [of the Eleven] doubted'[20]
(3) 'they *all doubted as well*'.[21]

The first interpretation holds little weight any longer. As to the

---

[16] Donaldson, *Mountain*, p. 180: 'wherever Mosaic typology appears elsewhere in the Gospel, it is transcended by and absorbed into some higher christological pattern'.

[17] Luke 24.52 is textually doubtful; see Bruce Metzger, *A Textual Commentary on the Greek New Testament*, p. 190.

[18] See the specific treatments of this subject by Beda Rigaux, *Dieu l'a ressuscité*, pp. 254–6; C. H. Giblin, 'A Note on Doubt and Reassurance in Matthew 28:16–20', pp. 68–75, for much of the following material.

[19] E.g., Allen, *Matthew*, p. 305; Plummer, *Matthew*, p. 427; McNeile, *Matthew*, p. 484; Klostermann, *Matthäus*, p. 230. Cf. R. D. Culver, 'What is the Church's Commission?', pp. 105–6.

[20] Many commentators, e.g., Schniewind, *Matthäus*, p. 275; Stendahl, 'Matthew', p. 798; Floyd Filson, *Matthew*, p. 305; Frans Neirynck, 'Les femmes au tombeau', p. 180 n.1; cf. also K. L. McKay, 'The Use of *hoi de* in Matthew 28.17d', pp. 71–2; R. W. van der Horst, 'Once More', pp. 27–30.

[21] E.g., Bonnard, *Matthieu*, p. 418; I. P. Ellis, 'But Some Doubted', pp. 574–7; Grundmann, *Matthäus*, pp. 572, 576; Giblin, 'Doubt', pp. 68–71.

doubters, readers cannot avoid completely the Eleven as the subject, even if a wider audience is not ruled out.[22]

The majority opt for the second reading. Among them some protest that v. 17a and b taken together seem to force an almost impossible contrast: worshipping and doubting. But this apparent contradiction is best seen in light of Matthew's wider rhetorical interests. The narrator employs προσκυνέω, with Jesus as the object, in a range of pre- and post-resurrection settings. He also paints the disciples in non-idealistic hues; they are often followers of meagre but developing faith. And in 14.31–3 διστάζω appears with προσκυνέω, in Matthew's version of the water-walking story. His juxtaposition there of doubt and worship is comparable to the juxtaposition in 28.17. Both describe the wavering doubt and worship of unidealized followers, consistent with his frequent characterization of them as ὀλιγόπιστος (see 6.30; 8.16; 14.30; 16.8; 17.20). 'Doubt' is not therefore unbelief, but 'little faith'.[23]

The doubt of the disciples has quite different meanings in other Easter texts. In Luke 24.41 Jesus eats food to overcome the disciples' doubts and to prove he is not a ghost; he provides resurrection proof through sight and touch. Similarly, in John 20.24–5 doubting Thomas touches Jesus' wounds. In Mark 16.14 the risen Jesus appears to unbelieving disciples who doubted the message about his resurrection. In Matthew, however, their doubt is not overcome by sight and touch, but is addressed (although not explicitly removed) by Jesus' declaration as well as his 'approach' (v. 18). Προσέρχομαι is his own term (Matt. 52x; Mark 5x; Luke 10x; NT 87x). This is only the second time Matthew has used it for an action of Jesus; his editorial use of the word in 17.7 has a similar context. There Jesus 'approaches' the terror-stricken disciples after his transfiguration, likewise a specific movement of reassurance and utterances to quell their uncertainty.[24] Jesus' approach in 28.18 is

---

[22] See also Giblin, 'Doubt', p. 68, on the attempt to reinterpret the verbal aspect of the phrase (e.g., 'sie, die da früher gezweifelt hatten', in Klostermann, *Matthäus*, on Lagrange); cf. Lohmeyer, *Matthäus*, p. 415.

[23] 'Their doubt should not be construed as positive disbelief or refusal to worship', Giblin, 'Doubt', p. 71; contra Klostermann, *Matthäus*, pp. 230–2; cf. also John Calvin, *A Harmony of the Gospels* III, p. 249; Karl Barth; 'An Exegetical Study of Matthew 28:16–20', pp. 59–61.

[24] In Matt. 17.6–7 Jesus' reassurance involves the further gesture of physical contact (ἅπτομαι, also 14.31); cf. Hubbard, *Commissioning*, pp. 77–8, where the texts of 17.6–7 and 28.16–20 are compared in parallel columns.

therefore an extremely unusual shift in action for his protagonist, supported rhetorically and redactionally.

Yet it remains striking that the last thing said of the disciples in Matthew's story is that they doubted Jesus. No motives for doubt are articulated; we might presume the apparent insufficiency of Jesus' ὅραμα in v. 17a. In this respect their response may simply be mixed. The disciples worshipped, with some uncertainty and hesitation about the reality of the resurrection. To require of their worship that it arise from purest belief and unsullied adoration would for Matthew falsely dichotomize faith and doubt and demand of the disciples a response beyond their characterization within the First Gospel (cf., e.g., 8.23–7; 14.22–33; 16.13–28; 17.6–7, 17–20).

The third reading above, 'they all doubted as well', therefore makes most sense. Matthew 27.22b–3 provides another context in which oἱ δέ implies 'all' of the original subject.[25] If Matthew had wanted to differentiate the subjects of vv. 16a and 17a (oἱ δὲ ἕνδεκα ... προσεκύνησαν) from v. 17b (oἱ δὲ ἐδίστασαν) he would have given the reader more specific direction, as elsewhere in his story (cf. 8.21; 16.14; 21.9; 25.3–4, 29). What is at issue is that doubt exists at all within this inner circle of worshipping followers to whom the risen Jesus has appeared – the debate whether 'some' or 'all doubted' is secondary. When Jesus' commission is given αὐτοῖς (v. 18) this can only mean 'the Eleven'. Consequently, oἱ δὲ ἐδίστασαν in v. 17b, standing as it does between the Eleven who worship and the same Eleven who receive the commission, refers at least to the doubting Eleven.

In connection with the immediate context, ἰδόντες is the direct fulfilment of the reiterated promise in 28.7c, 10d that the disciples would 'see' Jesus in Galilee. The event, however, is notably anticlimactic in comparison with its build-up. Matthew's text is remarkably silent about the nature and details of Jesus' appearance, and consequently ambiguous.[26] It is difficult, then, to establish the

---

[25] Matt. 26.67 is one debatable exception where oἱ δέ translates 'and some', but the synonymous verbs and more carefully defined context make clear the difference in subjects; see the discussion by P. Benoit, 'Les outrages à Jésus prophète', pp. 91–110, especially pp. 91–3.

[26] Cf. the more specific details in Luke 24.16, 31–42; John 20.14–20, 27; 21.4, 12; also Markan appendix 16.12. As K. Barth, 'Study', p. 57, has noted, it is the story of Jesus and the women (28.8–10) which actually establishes Jesus' identity as the crucified one who has risen. See Dunn's discussion of the resurrection appearances in *Jesus and the Spirit*, chap. 5.

origin and setting of Jesus' appearance and sayings in 28.16–20. Suggestions have ranged from proleptic or actual parousia[27] to a heavenly vision of the ascended Jesus, who in resurrection transcended death by translation to heaven, perhaps in the manner of Enoch and Elijah.[28] On the other hand vv. 16–17 could be a primitive appearance tradition joined by Matthew to the utterances in vv. 18–20 which originated earlier as prophetic 'I'-sayings in the community.[29]

Matthew's account, however, does not allow a definitive judgement between a heavenly vision and an earthly appearance.[30] As for the origin of Jesus' words, Matthew's text again resists easy ascription. The text's features and emphases evidence a skilful blend of tradition, prophecy and editorial composition. The dominant theme of commissioning and reassurance does rest well with the commissioning traditions of the risen Jesus. The emphatic first-person voice in his pronouncement of authority, gentile mission and divine presence, and the polemical edge of the utterance, correspond well with the profile of Christian prophecy.[31]

The fact that Matthew does not elaborate ἰδόντες in v. 17 cannot be supplemented or prejudged by tradition. Matthew's deliberate emphasis in 28.7 and 10 on 'going and seeing' has already been noted. The simple description ἰδόντες in v. 17 is equally deliberate, for it is consistent with the disciples' typical mixed response of worship and doubt. It ultimately focuses the pericope on Jesus' declaration, mission mandate and promised presence, which take them beyond a momentary 'seeing' to the sustained experience of his risen presence 'with' them.

Matthew 28.20b thus becomes a clear commentary on ἰδόντες in v. 17, for the story implies a risen Jesus who, in relation to his disciples, is in transition from earthly master to heavenly Lord. The missing epiphanic characteristics which leave ἰδόντες blank are redactionally replaced by the more important non-visual features of

---

[27] E.g., J. A. T. Robinson, *Jesus*, pp. 131, 136.

[28] Cf. Schweizer, *Matthew*, p. 528; Meier, 'Two', p. 411; Schaberg, *Father*, p. 89.

[29] So, e.g., F. W. Beare, 'Sayings of the Risen Jesus in the Synoptic Tradition', pp. 164–5; Fuller, *The Formation of the Resurrection Narratives*, p. 90; A. Sand, *Das Gesetz und die Propheten*, p. 168; M. E. Boring, *Sayings of the Risen Jesus*, pp. 204–6.

[30] See Dunn, *Jesus*, pp. 116, 124, on 'Christophanies' and 'Christepiphanies', with reference to J. Lindblom, *Geschichte und Offenbarungen*.

[31] See Boring, *Sayings*, pp. 204–6.

divine authority and presence.[32] In his utterance of vv. 18–20 Jesus provides the final redefinition of how the disciples should 'see', consistent with his training of them during the storm, crowd-feedings, water-walking, healing attempts and Passover meal. They are sent to Galilee to 'see' Jesus (28.7, 10) in accordance with tradition, but in Matthew the inadequacy of sight is met by the greater ὅραμα of Jesus' revealed authority, commission and divine presence.

Matthew is also aware that his reader's ἐκκλησία would be helped little by an appearance account where disciples' doubts are dispelled by the sight and touch of the risen Jesus, when their own doubts cannot be answered in a similar fashion, but only through his prophetic promise of presence.[33] Matthew has chosen the format of Jesus' final encounter with his followers to give his own particular answer to the problem of believing without seeing.[34] Klostermann is right to see the admission of doubt as an historical reminiscence, 'daβ der Glaube an die Auferstehung nicht sofort Allgemeingut gewesen war'[35] ('that belief in the resurrection did not immediately become general opinion').

8.3. Jesus' declaration: Matthew 28.18b

Ἐδόθη μοι πᾶσα ἐξουσία ἐν οὐρανῷ καὶ ἐπὶ [τῆς] γῆς.

The Father has given Jesus supreme and universal authority. The use of ἐξουσία in Matthew is not frequent (10x; Mark 10x; Luke 16x), but its placement makes for significant characterization of Jesus. To take one prominent example, in Mark 1.21–2 those attending the synagogue in Capernaum are astonished at the ἐξουσία of Jesus as he taught there one Sabbath. But the Matthean parallel in 7.29 gives ἐξουσία a radically broader application. The public astonishment at the ἐξουσία of Jesus' teaching is used to summarize the whole of the Sermon (Matt. 5–7) and to emphasize

---

[32] For Matthew the risen Jesus apparently remains unchanged in appearance. The reaction of the guards and two Marys (28.1–8: terror, fainting, fear, great joy) to the appearance and message of YHWH's angel is more striking than the women's reaction to the risen Jesus himself (28.9: prostrate worship). Cf. the epiphanic features in the transfiguration account, 17.1–8.

[33] For similar problems in third-century traditions see Strack–Billerbeck II, p. 586; in Michel, 'Conclusion', pp. 32–3.

[34] See Matt. 8.5–13; 12.38–42; 16.1–4; cf. Mark 15.32; John 4.48; 6.30; 20.8; 20.29.

[35] *Matthäus*, p. 231.

Jesus' authority as the new interpreter of the law, and as the teacher of true Torah, Kingdom principles and the divine will.

Apart from Mark 1.27 (Matthew does not have the pericope), Matthew parallels in his own contexts each of Mark's uses of ἐξουσία which describes Jesus' deeds and words, and he has the term in 9.8 where Mark 2.12 does not. In Matthew ἐξουσία refers to several aspects of Jesus' authority:

7.29	teaching (Mark 1.22)
9.6	forgiving sins (Mark 2.10)
9.8	forgiving sins (editorial)
8.9	healing and exorcism (Luke 7.8)
10.1	healing and exorcism authority given to disciples (Mark 6.7)
21.23–7	(4x) teaching, healing, receiving children's praise and overturning tables in the Temple (Mark 11.28–33).[36]

In the *Sondergut* of 28.18 πᾶσα and ἐν οὐρανῷ καὶ ἐπὶ [τῆς] γῆς specifically define the risen Jesus' ἐξουσία in cosmic terms. In Matthew Jesus refuses the Tempter's offer of πάσας τὰς βασιλείας τοῦ κόσμου καὶ τὴν δόξαν αὐτῶν (4.8; cf. Luke 4.5–6) in exchange for worship (προσκυνέω), in direct contrast to his exaltation in 28.18 through his subservience to the Father.[37]

The anarthrous πᾶς occurs enough here to be considered a Matthean idiom.[38] More importantly, πᾶς appears four times within 28.18b–20, where it unifies Jesus' sayings within a stylistic and thematic whole, giving the Gospel's conclusion unqualified theological weight and rhetorical power:

πᾶσα ἐξουσία ...
πάντα τὰ ἔθνη ...
πάντα ὅσα ἐνετειλάμην ...
πάσας τὰς ἡμέρας ...

---

[36] See Lange's discussion, *Erscheinen*, pp. 24–96; including the five ἐξουσία passages in Mark and Q material which Matthew has omitted or altered (pp. 91–6); cf. Hübner, *Das Gesetz in der synoptischen Tradition*, pp. 196–207; Mohrlang, *Matthew*, pp. 72–4.

[37] Cf. 'all things' (πάντα) from the 'Father, Lord of heaven and earth' in Matt. 11.27; also cf. ἐξουσία in John 17.2; 1 Cor. 15.24; Eph. 1.21; Col. 1.16–20; 2.10; 1 Pet. 3.22; Rev. 2.26–7; 13.2; also Phil. 2.9–10.

[38] So Kingsbury, 'Composition', p. 576; see Matt. 3.15; 5.11; 23.27–35; 24.22 (= Mark 13.20); cf. 2.3. See Gundry's lists for πᾶς; *Matthew*, pp. 595, 647.

The adjective πᾶς marks the pericope not just as his own literary composition but as his special concluding manifesto.[39]

Ἐν οὐρανῷ καὶ ἐπὶ [τῆς] γῆς is similarly well represented in Matthew, for heaven and earth are placed in conjunction or opposition in Matthew thirteen times (Mark 2x; Luke 5x) in a variety of forms, and only three have synoptic parallels.[40]

For Matthew there is something new in Jesus' reception of πᾶσα ἐξουσία of v. 18, beyond the πάντα of 11.27. Matthew's earthly Jesus teaches, heals, exorcizes and forgives sins with authority, but the Jesus who speaks here is risen, stands atop the story's final mountain, and the authority he now claims is as universal as 'heaven and earth'. He has unprecedented ability to command a world-wide mission (and thus to close the unfinished business of Matt. 10), and because of this authority is able to promise his own constant presence in divine terms.[41] What qualifies ἐξουσία in 28.18 as new is thus both its rhetorical flourish as part of the Gospel's climax and terminology – the 'heaven and earth' description, the universal parameters of the four 'all' phrases, and the redactional employment of Jesus' first-person narrative closure to the story.

Though concerned with the exaltation of Jesus, the passage remains highly theocentric. This is the first meeting of Jesus with his disciples since his arrest and crucifixion, and from the events subsequent we can assume that the divine passive of resurrection (ἠγέρθη in 28.6, 7)[42] implies the same divine agent as ἐδόθη in 28.18b, i.e., resurrection in Matthew has meant both Jesus being raised from the dead and the bestowal of his unlimited authority.[43] There is, therefore, 'eine universale Ausweitung' of Jesus' ἐξουσία here.[44]

The picture of exaltation in 28.18b–20 is delivered directly and

---

[39] Cf. especially G. Barth, *TIM*, pp. 71–3; also Lange, *Erscheinen*, pp. 150–2, 328–9; Kingsbury, 'Composition', p. 579.

[40] See the discussions in Kilpatrick, *Origins*, p. 49; Trilling, *Israel*, pp. 24–5; Lange, *Erscheinen*, p. 147; Hubbard, *Commissioning*, pp. 82–3; Kingsbury, 'Composition', p. 576.

[41] Contra Strecker, *Weg*; Bornkamm, 'Lord', p. 208, who minimize the difference between the authority of Matthew's earthly and risen Jesus; similarly Lange, *Erscheinen*, pp. 45, 177; Donald Verseput, 'The Role and Meaning of the "Son of God" Title in Matthew's Gospel', p. 540; see Meier, 'Two', p. 413.

[42] Cf. Matt. 11.5; 14.2; 16.21; 17.23; 26.32; 27.52, 64.

[43] See Joachim Jeremias, *Theology*, p. 310; W. D. Davies, *Setting*, p. 360; Meier, 'Two', p. 412.

[44] Trilling, *Israel*, pp. 22, 24.

simply. Matthew may have found inspiration from the enthronement model of LXX Daniel 7.13–14 but Matthew places it within a non-apocalyptic context, removes any mythological descriptions, sets it into first-person parlance, and redefines ἐξουσία in accordance with his own emphases on teaching, discipleship, ἐντολαί and divine presence.[45] Furthermore, the disciples' new mission, as well as Jesus' presence, comes before the end of time.

8.4.   Jesus' mandate: Matthew 28.19–20a

As the consequence and on the basis of (οὖν, v. 19a) his possession of universal authority Jesus charges his followers with a mission, to 'make disciples', explained in the participial imperatives of 'baptizing' and 'teaching' – πορευθέντες οὖν μαθητεύσατε πάντα τὰ ἔθνη.

This command proper shows every indication of Matthean language, style and composition. The nominative participle πορευθέντες is a common Matthean insertion[46] and in good Matthean style recalls its previous use, ἐπορεύθησαν in v. 16.[47] This use of the circumstantial participle attending an imperative is a stylistic and often editorial feature elsewhere in Matthew.[48] Of the four NT occurrences of μαθητεύω three are in Matthew, and the two in 13.52 and 27.57 are demonstrably redactional. Matthew 28.19 and Acts 14.21 are the only active uses of the verb in the NT, with Matthew 13.52 and 27.57 as deponent.[49]

'All the nations' unlocks the Gospel's mission finally to the whole world, in a theme which began as early as the magi. Ἔθνος (14x; Mark 5x; Luke 11x) shows at least seven editorial insertions in Matthew, while πάντα τὰ ἔθνη (4x; Mark 2x; Luke 2x) shows one

---

[45]   See discussion of the Daniel link in Vögtle, 'Das christologische und ekklesiologische Anliegen von Mt 28:18–20', pp. 267–8; Lange, *Erscheinen*, pp. 175–8, 212, 350; J. P. Meier, 'Salvation-History in Matthew', pp. 203–15; *Law and History in Matthew's Gospel*; 'Two', pp. 413–16; Donaldson, *Mountain*, pp. 176–7, 181.

[46]   Eight times in paralleled material; see Gundry, *Matthew*, p. 595. For πορεύομαι see v. 16.

[47]   Similarly, Matt. 10.6, 7; 21.2, 6; see also 2.8, 9; 11.4, 7; 28.7, 11; with other verbs in 2.9–10; 2.12–13; 8.25–6; 9.6–7; 9.15, 18; 12.39, 46; 14.15, 23; 17.4–5; see Kingsbury, 'Composition', p. 576; Schaberg, *Father*, p. 43.

[48]   See especially 9.13; 10.7; cf. also 2.8; 11.4; 17.27; 28.7.

[49]   See Bl.-Debr. §148, 3. Cf. μαθητὰς ποιεῖ in John 4.1 which seems closer to the Hebrew ʿāśâ talmîdîm; see Lange, *Erscheinen*, p. 308. Μαθητεύω does not occur in the LXX, Josephus or Philo.

synoptic parallel (24.14 = Mark 13.10), one redactional use by Matthew (24.9) and two uses in his *Sondergut* (25.32 and 28.19).

The question of whether πάντα τὰ ἔθνη means 'Gentiles' (exclusive of Israel) or 'nations' (inclusive of Israel) has caused considerable debate, and touches on an issue central to the Gospel. Hare and Harrington, Walker and Lange have opted for the former, along with the rejection and replacement of Israel within *Heilsgeschichte*.[50] However, even though the emphasis in 28.19 is undeniably on the new element of gentile mission, explicit reference to the rejection of Israel would be required to posit the end of the mission commanded in Matthew 10. Jesus' transfer of the Kingdom from one ἔθνος to another in 21.43 is uttered to his primary audience in the Temple, the chief priests and elders. Furthermore, in Matthew 21.43 the ἔθνος must include Jews and Gentiles; similarly with 'all nations' in 24.9, 14; 25.32. But as noted above the tension over Matthew's own seemingly contradictory stance on mission to the Jews and Gentiles is not completely resolved in 28.19.[51] It is important here also that 'all nations' may have an ambiguity which plays well with different readers.

Kingsbury's and Schaberg's analysis indicates that the triadic ὄνομα baptismal formula of 28.19b is essentially Matthean, according to its language and literary style.[52] Its formulaic nature and unprecedented juxtaposition of Father, Son and Holy Spirit have provoked serious questions, however, about its place in Matthew. C. K. Barrett points out that even if the three-member formula were an early interpolation, so early that not a single extant MS contains the short formula, we are still left with the same problem: explaining the early appearance of the triadic baptismal formula almost contemporary to Matthew.[53]

The development of the formula is closely bounded temporally on the one side by the initial single-member baptismal formulas well represented in Luke and Paul and on the other by the almost contemporary parallel in *Didache* 7.1–3.[54] Jane Schaberg argues

---

[50] See Douglas Hare and Daniel Harrington, '"Make Disciples of All the Gentiles"', pp. 359–69; Walker, *Heilsgeschichte*, pp. 111–12; Lange, *Erscheinen*, pp. 300–5. Cf. here also K. W. Clark, 'The Gentile Bias in Matthew'.

[51] See further Tagawa's short survey of the issue, 'People and Community in the Gospel of Matthew', pp. 155–8.

[52] See Kingsbury, 'Composition', pp. 577–8; Schaberg, *Father*, p. 44.

[53] *Spirit*, p. 103.

[54] See baptism ἐν/ἐπί/εἰς τῷ/τὸ ὄνομα(τι) τοῦ 'Ιησοῦ in Acts 2.38; 8.16; 10.48; 19.5; cf. Rom. 6.3; 1 Cor. 1.13, 15; 6.11; 10.1–4. Bultmann, *History*, p. 151,

that the Matthew 28.19 formula is undeniably unique among triadic NT texts.[55] The formula's novelty may also indicate its employment in a particular geographic setting.

Schaberg, Lange and Hubbard are among those who have recently investigated these questions at length. Any attempt to synthesize their labours makes it clear that the origins, authenticity and development of the formula are not easily available. At best we can speculate that Matthew 28.19b is a second-generation development of single-member christological baptismal traditions and of more elementary triadic texts which circulated commonly. From our reading of the Gospel here, however, Matthew appears to have developed and/or incorporated the formula in its current form without fully integrating it theologically into his story.

The importance of this discussion here is that, despite the triadic formula, 'Spirit' does not define the divine presence in 28.20b, which remains the promise of *Jesus'* presence. Matthew's acceptance, adaptation and/or composition of the three-member baptismal formula functions to refine the identity of the ἐκκλησία in the face of other proximate religious groups, particularly those which used baptism. The First Gospel is the ἐκκλησία-oriented Gospel. Here μαθητεύσατε ... βαπτίζοντες ... διδάσκοντες functions as the membership guide for the ἐκκλησία. Baptism, as the rite of initiation into the fellowship, brings the initiate into the inner circle under the authority and name of the Father, Son and Holy Spirit. Within Matthew the addition of 'Father' to the simple christological formula for baptism in the name of Jesus is strikingly consistent with the patrocentricity of the First Gospel, and reflects Matthew's explicit concern to establish in his Gospel the identity of the true Israel in continuity with the language and symbols of Judaism. The inclusion of 'Holy Spirit' may be a fulfilment of John's prediction about Jesus' baptism in 3.11.

The pre-eminence of teaching and law in the First Gospel comes to a head in the third element of the mission mandate: διδάσκοντες αὐτοὺς τηρεῖν πάντα ὅσα ἐνετειλάμην ὑμῖν. The Eleven are not only to initiate the new disciples into the ἐκκλησία through baptism but to teach obedience to the tradition of Jesus' commands. Teaching, though not prominent statistically in the occur-

postulates the simple christological ὄνομα as the original tradition behind Matthew's text. See Hahn's argument, *Mission*, p. 67, for the appearance of the triadic baptismal formula as early as the latter half of the first century.

[55] See her reasons in *Father*, pp. 10–15; with references to other triadic NT texts.

rences of διδάσκω (14x; Mark 17x; Luke 17x), is the distinctive activity of Matthew's Jesus. Matthew appears to eliminate eleven of Mark's seventeen uses of διδάσκω, in favour of those which correspond to his own understanding of teaching as Jesus' primary activity and narrative characterization. In 4.23; 5.2; 11.1; 21.23 Matthew adds διδάσκω in several editorially critical passages, each time portraying Jesus as the teacher, in 'their' synagogues, on the mountain, in 'their' cities and in the Temple. The parallel διδάσκω statements in 5.19 (possibly in anticipation of 28.20a) elaborate the crucial importance for Jesus that his followers teach and practise the law.

The careful way in which Matthew proceeds with his use of διδάσκω makes its occurrence in 28.15 (ἐδιδάχθησαν, *Sondergut*) surprising, but the subject of the verb provides the explanation. The high priests and the elders 'teach' the soldiers in 28.11–15 to deceive and lie for money, in direct contrast to Jesus' teaching throughout the Gospel and his instructions in 28.20. Lange may be correct in that 'hier nimmt die Darstellung des Matthäus die Art eines Pamphlets an' ('here Matthew's portrayal takes on the style of a lampoon'),[56] but Matthew's inclusion seems deliberately ironic in light of the contrast struck with Jesus' mandate to teach only a few sentences later. The type of teaching going on in 28.15 certainly upholds the narrator's Gospel-wide characterization of the Jewish leaders as thoroughly antagonistic to God's will.

In 28.20 teaching becomes the disciples' responsibility for the first time, a key role in building the ἐκκλησία, and an inevitable corollary, along with baptism, of the command to make disciples. Teaching, as well as its content, τηρεῖν πάντα ὅσα ἐνετειλάμην ὑμῖν, is described in Matthean terms, using his style and vocabulary. Πάντα ὅσα ἐνετειλάμην ὑμῖν is an example of Matthew borrowing an OT idiom, this one found especially in LXX Deuteronomy.[57] Every use of τηρέω in the First Gospel is an editorial insertion or occurs in *Sondergut*,[58] and in 23.3 Matthew also uses τηρέω with πάντα ὅσα. Πάντα ὅσα in Matthew (7x; Mark 3x; Luke 2x) has only one synoptic parallel.[59]

---

[56] *Erscheinen*, p. 318.
[57] See, e.g., LXX Exod. 7.2; Deut. 1.3, 41; 4.2; 12.11; 13.11; 30.8; Josh. 1.7; Jer. 1.7; see further in Trilling, *Israel*, p. 37.
[58] Matt. 6x; Mark 1x; Luke 0x. Matt. 19.17 (cf. Mark 10.18; Luke 18.19); 23.3 (cf. Mark 12.37–40); 27.36 (cf. Mark 15.25); 27.54 (cf. Mark 15.39); 28.4, 20.
[59] 21.22 = Mark 11.24. The four in *Sondergut* are probably editorial (13.44, 46;

Of his four occurrences of ἐντέλλομαι (Mark 2x; Luke 1x), Matthew employs two to characterize Jesus' instructions to his disciples, once when descending the mountain of transfiguration (17.9) and here on the final mountain of commissioning. This unique use of ἐντέλλομαι in the synoptics categorically redefines Jesus' sayings as fundamental religious truth, as ἐντολαί.[60] Early on, Matthew's Jesus, in the midst of teaching his own commands, paused to establish the importance of the role of teacher (5.17–20) and here the reader is left in no doubt as to the divine and binding essence of Jesus' ἐντολαί.

The subjects of the four uses of ἐντέλλομαι in Matthew provide an illuminating pattern of the transition of the authority to give commands, from God in 4.6 (cf. 15.4), to Moses in 19.7, to Jesus in 17.9 and 28.20. This deepens the significance of the OT idiom in 28.20 by highlighting the authoritative nature of Jesus' 'law' in Matthew as superseding that of Moses, penetrating as never before to the heart of true Torah. This is especially apparent in 19.7–9 with the contrast between Moses' divine command and that of Jesus which supersedes it: Μωϋσῆς ἐνετείλατο ... λέγω δὲ ὑμῖν.

8.5. Jesus' promise: Matthew 28.20b

Within Matthew law and presence are bound together. Nowhere is this more evident than in 28.20, where Jesus' law and presence have become community and Gospel. As Frank Gorman has noted, this is solidly based in the Hebrew understanding that in Torah, God's people find wholeness, community and God's presence (Deut. 32.15–20, 46–7; Ps. 19).[61] YHWH's 'Gospel' for his people Israel was their very definition by his presence (Exod. 33.14–16, see above, pp. 126–9). Matthew appears to have revisited quite deliberately the Sinai paradigm here, where the giving of the law, the formation of community and the presence of YHWH came together.

That tabernacle-building instructions appear immediately along-

---

18.25; 23.3) and 7.12 (cf. Luke 6.31) certainly is; see further in Lange, *Erscheinen*, p. 316.

[60] Cf. Matt. 5.19; 15.3; 19.17; 22.36, 38, 40. For discussion of whether Jesus ever gives a formal system of commandments; see Wayne Meeks, *The Moral World of the First Christians*, p. 140; R. S. McConnell, *Law and Prophecy in Matthew's Gospel*, p. 99; Joachim Rohde, *Rediscovering the Teaching of the Evangelists*, p. 63.

[61] See 'When Law Becomes Gospel' for this discussion.

side the terrifying presence of God on Sinai is no accident. Theophanic presence requires sacred space for God's people to remain his. In Matthew law is also life and sacred space is found in gathering around the risen Jesus. Jesus' law is not simply a behavioural guide, but its enactment brings into being and maintains community, into the midst of which Jesus' presence can come (cf. Matt. 5.3–10, 19; 7.15–20, 24; 12.33; 18.4, 15–35; 19.16–22; 22.34–40). Through obedience to Jesus the new community realizes the meaning of its existence and experiences the transforming presence of Jesus in its midst.

Jesus' final words are thus rooted rhetorically and redactionally in the context provided by 28.16–20.

καὶ ἰδοὺ ἐγὼ μεθ' ὑμῶν εἰμι πάσας τὰς ἡμέρας
ἕως τῆς συντελείας τοῦ αἰῶνος.

Ἰδοὺ ἐγώ is redactional in Matthew 10.16; 11.10; 23.34, reflecting the fact that Matthew uses ἐγώ more often than the other synoptic writers, as well as his particular tendency to add ἐγώ to first-person sayings for reasons of both style and emphasis.[62] Most first-person sayings by Jesus in the First Gospel are uttered within his self-conscious identity and role as authoritative teacher, often declaring 'I say to you'.

The particular phrase πάσας τὰς ἡμέρας is a hapax legomenon in the NT. At the same time, however, the repetitious use of πᾶς has already been identified as a prominent editorial feature of this pericope, while ἡμέρα (45x; Mark 27x; Luke 83x) is often the subject of Matthew's editorial insertions. Matthew most often uses ἡμέρα in reference to a temporal era, or sometimes to refer to that eschatological 'day' at the end.[63] Matthew's dependence upon Deuteronomic language in v. 19 above appears also to continue with πάσας τὰς ἡμέρας, found precisely in this form in LXX Deuteronomy 4.40 and 5.29. In LXX Deuteronomy 4.40 Moses tells the people:

'Keep his statutes and his commandments, ὅσας ἐγὼ ἐντέλλομαί σοι σήμερον for your own well-being and that

---

62 ἐγώ: Matt. 29x; Mark 16x; Luke 22x (John 132x). At least thirteen occurrences of ἐγώ in Matthew come from his own hand, including the phrase which appears six times verbatim in 5.22–44: ἐγὼ δὲ λέγω ὑμῖν. Three others are in Sondergut. Twelve times in Matthew ἐγώ has a clear synoptic parallel.
63 Matthew parallels all but five of Mark's uses of ἡμέρα, employs seventeen of his own, and uses ἡμέρα nine times in Sondergut.

of your descendants after you, so that you may long remain in the land that the Lord your God is giving you πάσας τὰς ἡμέρας.'

Matthew uses and consistently inserts ἕως into his sources.[64] Συντελείας τοῦ αἰῶνος is found only six times in the NT, five of them in Matthew, hence here widely accepted as his own composition (cf. Matt. 18.39, 40, 49; 24.3). Except for 24.3, each instance of the phrase is spoken by Jesus. As it stands in the First Gospel, then, the promise of presence in v. 20b reflects in detail the work of Matthew.[65] If he was dependent upon some primitive Christian tradition the present text has subsumed any evidence of pre-Matthean wording. Furthermore, we have no comparable statement applied to Jesus elsewhere in the relevant gospel materials which might evidence a primitive tradition.

The more obvious point, however, is that any lines of dependence run directly to the antecedent symbols and language of Judaism, especially to the OT 'with you' promise formula of divine presence. Matthew has reinterpreted the divine promise in unique christological fashion, by taking the well-known first-person utterance of YHWH and placing it in the mouth of Jesus. Of the 114 MT and LXX occurrences of the promise formula in its various first- and third-person forms, several LXX variations are very close to Matthew 28.20b.

ἐγώ εἰμι μεθ' ὑμῶν (Hag. 1.13)
μεθ' ὑμῶν ἐγώ εἰμι (Jer. 49[42].11; Hag. 2.4)
μετὰ σοῦ ἐγώ εἰμι (Jer. 1.8, 17, 19)
καὶ ἰδοὺ ἐγὼ μετὰ σοῦ (Gen. 28.15)
καὶ ἰδοὺ ἐγὼ μεθ' ὑμῶν εἰμι (Matt. 28.20)

None, however, provides Matthew with his particular word order. He gives special emphasis to the emphatic 'I' and the prepositional phrase 'with you'. The LXX examples have ἐγώ εἰμι in subject–verb conjunction, apart from the verbless formula in Genesis 28.15.

That 28.20b (and, substantially, 28.16–20) is Matthew's own redactional formulation only strengthens the observations in Chapter 3 regarding its rhetorical, structural and thematic impor-

---

[64]   Matt. 38x; Mark 15x; Luke 28x; see Kilpatrick, *Origins*, p. 49; Gundry, *Matthew*, p. 597, lists at least thirteen insertions by Matthew into common tradition.
[65]   Contra Meier, 'Two', pp. 414–15.

tance as the culmination of the Gospel and of the motif of divine presence as developed from Jesus' infancy. The full rhetorical, thematic and theological weight of Matthew's deliberate structural inclusio between 1.23 and 28.20 becomes apparent. That Matthew begins his story of the Messiah Jesus as the infant with the anticipated title 'Emmanuel – God with us', who at the end becomes that divine Emmanuel persona in his promise to remain with his followers always, is Matthew's way of purposefully framing and developing his Gospel around the Emmanuel Messiah.

Matthew's choice of a mountain-top is therefore doubly significant, not only for the Sinai images it evokes in relation to law and community, but for the implicit clash with Zion. For the reader, who has seen Jesus abandon Zion and withdraw his presence from the holy city, the promise of 28.20 to his new people is the return of divine presence. Here rhetorical and referential significance of the new people come together. The narrative turn to the nation producing the fruits of the Kingdom has been a slow, but deliberate, plot evolution. Since Matthew 2 the narrator has been preparing the reader for Jerusalem's rejection. Hence the mountain of Matthew 28.16–20 is more than just a *topos*. The communities behind Matthew's Gospel, the ἐκκλησίαι who see themselves gathered around him on that mountain, are not looking to a rebuilding of the temple or a gathering of the nations to Zion (Isa. 25.6; 56.7). For Matthew's first-century communities who know of Jerusalem's destruction, and feel daily the tension of their marginalization from Judaism, Jesus becomes the focus now and eschatologically of the gathered nations and God's presence.

9

JESUS' PRESENCE AND MATTHEW'S CHRISTOLOGY

Who then is Matthew's God-with-us Messiah? Does the first evangelist tie together the various rhetorical and redactional strands we have examined into something which can be called an Emmanuel christology? How do Matthew's new ideas around God's presence help us to understand his story's continuity and discontinuity with Judaism? Several issues require comment for us to answer these questions.

I could start and end by answering the second question with a simple 'yes'. In a traditional sense we have probably marshalled enough evidence and gospel references to posit the existence of an 'Emmanuel christology' in Matthew. *Matthew does have a clear interest in identifying Jesus as God with us and in developing the significance of his Emmanuel characterization at key points throughout the story. Emmanuel applied to Jesus is more than a static proper name but is part of Matthew's christology which makes possible his soteriology.* For Matthew Jesus' significance as God with us impacts his birth, mission, risen character and post-resurrection communities. If we look through the normal categories for NT christology Matthew's Emmanuel is consistent with his other elements of conception christology but reveals no open connection to incarnational or pre-existence christology.[1]

Matthew never openly asserts that Jesus is divine. Although I have used the term 'divine presence' continuously in connection with Jesus, it does not require that Jesus is God. But did Matthew's Emmanuel motif breach Jewish orthodoxy about God? It is possible within the Gospel's socio-religious context that the tradition of Jesus' naming as 'Emmanuel – God with us' and his Yahwistic 'I am with you' declaration were provocative. Such provocation would also have intensified if any later communities perceived his

---

[1] See a recent employment of these categories in Raymond Brown, *Introduction to New Testament Christology*, pp. 129–41.

identification in 18.20 with Shekinah. We cannot do more than speculate about the reception of Matthew's development of the Emmanuel Messiah in his 'parting of the ways' context. It is probably not excessive to claim, however, that this christological development functioned as a clear parameter between Matthew's communities and his Jewish counterparts. Although his language does not seem to carry ontological implications, through Emmanuel Matthew is at least claiming a basic functional or representative equivalence between Jesus and God.

I have already noted some discomfort with the accepted idea of 'Matthew's christology'. Matthew does not have a christology *per se* in the traditional theological sense. His rich and diverse christological themes and motifs will not fit under a single banner or title, though many commentators have attempted this. One reason for this is that Matthew did not write as a theologian and hence his Gospel is not a christology. An obvious statement perhaps, but the interpreter of Matthew needs to heed carefully the primary shape and interests provided by the text, in comparison with other NT writings.

We need Leander Keck's reminder that the historical reconstruction of early Christian christology should not be confused with NT christology. In his address to the SNTS in 1985, Keck asserted that pursuit of a historically reconstructed Jesus and preoccupation with the history of titles makes NT christologies unintelligible.[2] Not only does NT christology via title-dominated study reflect an inadequate view of language and stumble over the plurality of titles in the text, it bypasses christology itself in favour of words as concepts and etymologies as christologies. For Keck renewal of NT christology requires pursuit of central questions like 'what is the overall construal of Jesus' identity and significance in the text? What is the structure of this christology and to what extent are the logical correlates expressed? What degree of coherence and completeness does this christology have?' (p. 372).

I am encouraged by Keck's 'whole-text' approach to christology, an approach I have tried to make focal in this study, at least with a narrative approach to the motif of presence. Keck's assumption that diverse christologies interacted with each other almost from the start of the Christian era is an important principle to apply even within the different christologies of Matthew's text alone. This does

---

[2] 'Toward the Renewal of New Testament Christology'.

not negate the pursuit of a text's social context in order to comprehend its christology, but it does mean that enquiry into the origins of Christ's pre-existence, for example, needs to look more for the significance of such an articulation where it is found than for the details of who first articulated it and where it fits on a historical trajectory. Hence the correlation between Matthew's God-with-us christology and the social identity and situation of those in Matthew who held to it is of more value than historical reconstruction of its development.

We can say about Matthew's presence motif that it was not already prominent in the sources on which he drew, unlike most of his major christological emphases which he adapts or develops from Mark and Q. The christological focus given to divine presence in Matthew 1.23; 8.23–7; 12.6; 14.22–33; 17.17; 18.20; 25.31–46; 26.29; 28.20 arises in great measure from Matthew's own redactional focus and rhetorical skill. Matthew's redactional changes and *Sondergut* are not more important than the traditions he incorporates, but his characterization of Jesus as the God-with-us Messiah is uniquely his own. And in light of current enquiries into the social world behind Matthew, we can say that his Emmanuel christology, if he has such, has been shaped by two primary forces: (1) the 'parting of the ways' – his communities' recent and ongoing experiences of leaving the fold of Judaism – and (2) his use and transformation of OT divine presence themes and language. Both of these forces are clearly linked to Matthew's continuity and discontinuity with Judaism. It is for both rhetorical and socio-historical reasons that Matthew has drawn deeply from and sought to supersede his literary and religious heritage in order to describe this Jesus as 'God with us'.

Studies of Christian origins these days retain a high level of interest in the 'parting of the ways' with Judaism. Numerous Matthean scholars are thus also preoccupied with discerning accurately behind the First Gospel the stage of relationship between Matthew's communities and their parent body of Judaism, on the *intra muros–extra muros* spectrum.[3] Whether the desired accuracy is possible is doubtful. I have already agreed with Stanton that the evangelist's situation is probably much more pluralistic than recently assumed, i.e., his people of concern include a number of affiliated Christian communities linked over a geographic area.

---

[3]   See, e.g., the debate between Saldarini (*Community*) and Stanton ('Revisiting').

But we need also to push away from the idea that the Gospel reflects its social situation as temporally static. Like any text, and probably more than most, Matthew captures not one single moment of its communities' socio-historical context, but several, perhaps even conflicting, moments. This pluralism in Matthew's reflected social context would arise both for geographic reasons (Matthew's communities are at different stages of their debate with Judaism throughout the Gospel's region of influence) and for temporal reasons (Matthew contains traditions from both before and after different communities split from Judaism and relationships with local Jewish synagogues evolved). What this means for the 'parting of the ways' discussion is that Matthew may reflect both *intra muros* and *extra muros* moments. I agree with those who see evidence of a recent *extra muros* situation behind Matthew, especially given its heightened polemic against the Jewish leaders, their synagogues and their claims of divine presence, but elements of the text (e.g., 10.5–6; 17.24–7; 23.2–3) still allow some room for *intra muros* arguments like those of Saldarini and his predecessors.[4] This is due in part, I would argue (although the area requires further investigation), to the text's reflection of plural socio-religious settings.

So if Matthew has an Emmanuel christology it has arisen first from socio-religious accident, not from theological reflection. In other words, the first evangelist did not set out to write any particular christology, whether Son of God, Son of David or Emmanuel in title. Given his literary skills, he would have been much clearer and more consistent if that was his agenda. His focus on these aspects of Jesus' person probably developed not to meet a theological need but to address a socio-religious dilemma. Matthew's author set out to write his life and Gospel of the Messiah Jesus as meaningful and relevant to the dominant social and religious forces acting every day on the communities with which he was linked. His Jesus makes sense of those social and religious forces by defining and legitimizing the identity his audiences claim as the new people of God.

Much of Matthew's material is already determined by the communities' received traditions from Mark and Q. But the way in

---

[4] See Stanton's recent reappraisal of the four views of Matthew's relationship between synagogue and church, *Gospel*, pp. 113–45. Stanton is the most articulate defender of a recent, painful parting of Matthew's (mixed) communities from Judaism.

which Matthew accepts, redacts, adds to or crafts his entire message allows him to counter those forces which threaten and challenge these communities. For example, his Son-of-David 'christology' may actually respond to Jewish claims that the earthly Jesus' royal credentials were lacking. His glorious coming of the Son of man and King in final judgement may respond to the very real need among the 'little ones' and 'the least' (10.42; 18.6, 10, 14; 25.31–46) in his communities for the hope of final vindication of their current opposition and rejection (5.10–12; 10.14–23, 32–9). In the same way Matthew's Emmanuel 'christology' is both rhetorical and social in origin: it underpins his narrative characterization of Jesus in a story that gains literary independence from its social setting, but which probably also counteracts directly a series of Jewish claims about the nature, location and practice of divine presence. However, this Jesus–God-with-us characterization in Matthew is not an isolated strand which can be historically extracted from the whole. For this reason we have assessed it within Matthew's entire corpus.

9.1.   The Temple, worship and Jesus' presence

We have looked at many of the christological interactions of the presence motif with the wide range of characterizations of Jesus in Matthew. Some questions remain about the interaction of Jesus as Emmanuel with the Temple, and its relationship to worship in Matthew. The Temple figured importantly several times in our reading above. It provided the critical reference point for Jesus' astounding proclamation implying that he was 'greater than the Temple' (12.6). He alludes to the city's burning in the wedding-feast parable (22.7). He symbolically destroyed the Temple's sacrificial worship system, then declared the 'house' of Jerusalem 'desolate', withdrew from the Temple and predicted its total destruction (23.38–24.2). The exclusiveness of Temple ideology and the holy city's claim to divine presence are overturned by Jesus' actions and warnings. Jesus' threat to destroy and promise to rebuild the Temple dominate his opponents' accusations against him at his trial (Matt. 26.61). These all appear connected with Jesus' expectations of eschatological restoration, although, as E. P. Sanders argues, we can never be certain how well Jesus was understood by his contemporaries.[5]

---

[5]   The trial accusation is a deeply embedded tradition. Cf. Mark 14.58; John 2.18–22; cf. Mark 13.2. E. P. Sanders considers Jesus' activity in the Temple as

In other traditions early Christians took up God's OT promise to be with his people and applied it to his dwelling by means of the Holy Spirit in the church, the body of Christ (1 Cor. 3.16; 6.19; cf. Rev. 21.22). But Matthew has bypassed the emphasis on the Spirit's indwelling in favour of identifying the person and ἐκκλησία of Jesus in Sinaitic terms as the only adequate shrine for God on earth among his people. To Matthew Jesus and his followers are the true Temple. In him and in their gathering around him they capture the immanence side of the divine transcendence–immanence spectrum with which Israel wrestled so long.

Matthew's use of προσκυνέω supports well this argument for the relocation of worship and God's presence from the Temple and its adherents to Jesus and his followers. Compared to other Gospels, προσκυνέω is an unusually important activity in Matthew (13x; Mark 2x; Luke 2x; John 8x). Even more striking, of the thirteen times Matthew uses προσκυνέω Jesus is its genuine object ten times, as opposed to only a single such occurrence in each of the other Gospels. Matthew also applies the term to describe those approaching Jesus both before and after the resurrection, right from the infancy narrative through to the final commissioning.

Matthew also often employs this specific term when the Markan parallel does not.[6] Matthew is the only evangelist to use the term in the appearance accounts, and he does so twice.[7] As already noted, διστάζω appears only twice in the NT, both times in Matthew, and both times associated with προσκυνέω (see 14.31–3; 28.17).

The use of προσκυνέω elsewhere in the NT reinforces its special importance for Matthew. Outside of Matthew Jesus is worshipped (προσκυνέω) only by the Gerasene demoniac (Mark 5.6; absent from Matthew's story in 8.29), in mockery by the soldiers (Mark 15.19; omitted in Matt. 27.30; cf. γονυπετέω in Matt. 27.29), by a man with restored sight (John 9.38) and by God's angels (Heb. 1.6).[8] It is notable that Jesus is not once the object of προσκυνέω in

---

'the surest starting point' for his investigation; see his discussion, *Jesus*, pp. 61–90.

6   E.g., Matt. 8.2; cf. Mark 1.40: γονυπετῶν (see textual problems)
    Matt. 9.18; cf. Mark 5.22: πίπτει πρὸς τοὺς πόδας αὐτοῦ
    Matt. 14.33; cf. Mark 6.51: καὶ λίαν [ἐκ περισσοῦ] ἐν ἑαυτοῖς ἐξίσταντο
    Matt. 15.25; cf. Mark 7.25: ἐλθοῦσα προσέπεσεν πρὸς τοὺς πόδας αὐτου
    Matt. 20.20; cf. Mark 10.35: προσπορεύονται

7   The term in Luke 24.52 is textually doubtful; see Metzger, *Commentary*, p. 190.

8   Note also the comparable gesture of kneeling before Jesus (γονυπετέω) in Matt. 17.14; 27.29; Mark 1.40; 10.17; as well as those who 'fall in front of him' or 'at his feet': Mark 5.22; Luke 5.12; 8.41; 17.16; John 11.32; cf. 18.6.

the twenty-four occurrences in Revelation, while worship of God alone is emphasized in 19.10 and 22.8–9.

The occurrences of προσκυνέω in Matthew are as follows:

2.2	the magi:	ἤλθομεν προσκυνῆσαι αὐτῷ
2.8	Herod:	κἀγὼ ἐλθὼν προσκυνήσω αὐτῷ
2.11	the magi:	καὶ πεσόντες προσεκύνησαν
4.9	the Tempter:	Ταῦτά σοι πάντα δώσω ἐὰν πεσὼν προσκυνήσῃς μοι
4.10	Jesus:	Κύριον τὸν θεόν σου προσκυνήσεις καὶ αὐτῷ μόνῳ λατρεύσεις
8.2	a leper:	προσελθὼν προσεκύνει αὐτῷ
9.18	a ruler:	ἐλθὼν προσεκύνει αὐτῷ
14.33	disciples:	προσεκύνησαν
15.25	Canaanite woman:	ἡ ἐλθοῦσα προσεκύνει αὐτῷ
18.26	king and servant:	πεσὼν οὖν ὁ δοῦλος προσεκύνει αὐτῷ
20.20	mother of James and John:	ἡ μήτηρ ... προσκυνοῦσα καὶ αἰτοῦσά τι
28.9	two Marys:	ἐκράτησαν αὐτοῦ τοὺς πόδας καὶ προσεκύνησαν αὐτῷ
28.17	the Eleven:	καὶ ἰδόντες αὐτὸν προσεκύνησαν, οἱ δὲ ἐδίστασαν.

Heinrich Greeven declares that in the NT the object of προσκυνέω is always understood to have divine status.[9] This is a bold assertion, if applied to Matthew, where it would mean that at least ten times Jesus is worshipped as divine, perhaps even as God. Realistically, however, our (any) text is more fluid and polyvalent. We cannot assume that any narrator, including Matthew's, is able to use a verb ten times in the same text with a completely univalent meaning. Each use in Matthew is contextually different, with at least eight different worshippers or groups of worshippers offering obeisance to Jesus for different reasons. Beginning with the magi, he builds an index of προσκύνησις which starts with their perception of him as the divine child-king and elevates in the end to worship of the risen Jesus, the Emmanuel Messiah.

All this takes place within a story where Jesus emphatically affirms that worship is to be offered only to God (Matt. 4.9–10). How then do we reconcile Jesus' citation of Deuteronomy 6.13 to the Tempter with his open reception of προσκύνησις throughout the Gospel?[10] The citation makes it obvious that Jesus' equality with God is not at issue. Even beyond Jesus' encounter with the Tempter, nowhere in Matthew's portrayal are Jesus and God

[9] 'προσκυνέω', *TDNT* VI, p. 763.
[10] Although LXX Deut. 6.13 does not use προσκυνέω; cf. Luke 4.7–8; Acts 10.26; Rev. 19.10; 22.9.

simply identified.[11] Jesus' self-perception throughout the Gospel is clearly within the hierarchical relationship of the Son to his Father (even within the triadic baptismal formula in 28.19; see Chapter 3 for more on Matthew's theocentricity). For Matthew, YHWH is the only true God, and worship of Jesus his Son, the Emmanuel Messiah, is a christological window to his divine agency of his Father's will. Worship of Jesus in Matthew does not conflict with worship of God, but is his followers' way of recognizing Jesus' divine sonship and God's presence among them in Jesus, i.e., some kind of perceptual equivalence between them.

The various characters in Matthew who worship Jesus provide some context. When the magi worship Jesus as king of the Jews they do not simply bend their knees, but fall on their faces; a noteworthy action because of the tendency in Judaism to think of prostration as proper only in the worship of God.[12] The same can be said of the mother's prostration in 20.20, given her question of status in Jesus' Kingdom. In 8.2; 9.18 and 15.25 the attitude of the supplicants' worship is filled with faith in Jesus' divine powers as healer. In 14.33; 28.9 and 17 the disciples (men and women) recognize Jesus as God's Son, as the very presence of God with them in the extraordinary evidence of the moment. Here Peter, James and John's experience on the transfiguration mountain must be added – they 'fell on their faces and were filled with awe' (17.6). So Jesus is consistently the object of προσκύνησις and δῶρον as king, divine healer, Son of God and 'the Son' of the Father, but he is not God. Both Jesus and the narrator remain theocentric to the end. Both Jesus and his followers exist to do the will of the Father.

With C. F. D. Moule we can say that προσκυνέω often provides genuine glimpses into Jesus' 'numinous' presence during his earthly ministry, which have been intensified by Matthew in his story.[13] For Jesus' followers in the narrative these moments are part of the growth in their understanding and perceptions of him as 'God with us'; they demonstrate again his divine, centripetal force gathering his true followers into his inner circle. Within προσκυνέω the reader has gained another narrative index to Jesus' divine presence, and to a range of genuine and proper responses to God's Messiah.

---

[11] Gundry (*Matthew*, p. 594) and others come too easily to an equation between Jesus and God in our texts. France, *Evangelist*, pp. 308–11, is more balanced here. See R. Brown's assessment of NT evidence on this question, *Introduction*, pp. 171–95.

[12] Cf. Davies and Allison, *Matthew 1–7*, p. 248.   [13] *Origin*, p. 176.

Those who truly worship Jesus in Matthew are the most important characters to his ministry – Jesus' disciples, followers and the marginalized. Those who truly worship Jesus in Matthew become a microcosm of the coming Kingdom – men, women, lepers, Gentiles, the marginalized – these provide the shape of 'his people'.

9.2.   Wisdom and the presence of Jesus

If worship of Jesus is another window in Matthew to his portrait as God with us, proponents of wisdom christology in Matthew might also want to make the same claim. Lately the effort has been made to demonstrate that wisdom speculation was a central feature of the christology of both Q and Matthew.[14] The general thesis runs as follows: (1) in Jewish wisdom literature from Proverbs to Sirach and the Wisdom of Solomon, Wisdom is portrayed as a semi-personified mediator, God's agent in creation. She came from God and made her home among his people, to be the channel of God's guidance and his blessings. Wisdom is personified as a speaker of oracles, and as sending her envoys, who are rejected by each generation. (2) Jesus and John in Q are the last great envoys of Wisdom, and, as with their predecessors, are persecuted and killed; hence doom will fall on 'this generation'. (3) Matthew has, in particular, altered Q so as to identify Jesus with Wisdom. For example, in Matthew 23.34 Jesus declares: 'Therefore *I* send you prophets, wise men and scribes.' Then Jesus laments Jerusalem 'killing the prophets and stoning those who are *sent* to you' (23.37).

The important Matthean passages in question are few: Matthew 11.19, 25–30; 23.34–9.[15] Sophia–Jesus identification in Matthew is not without its detractors.[16] But for our purposes the sparseness of its evidence – in only two Q texts – highlights the difficulty of pulling together all of Matthew's christological concerns. On one level Wisdom and divine presence could be tied to the same arena of discussion, wrestling with Jesus' expression of God's immanence and transcendence among his people. Matthew may be using Emmanuel and Sophia to demonstrate parallel instances of his

[14] Proponents include Felix Christ, *Jesus Sophia*; R. G. Hamerton-Kelly, *Pre-Existence, Wisdom and the Son of Man*; M. J. Suggs, *Wisdom, Christology and Law in Matthew's Gospel*; J. M. Robinson, '"Logoi Sophon?"', and 'Jesus as Sophos and Sophia'; Robinson and Koester, *Trajectories*; Burnett, *Testament*.

[15] Cf. also four other secondary passages: Luke 2.40–52; Matt. 2.12; 6.2; 12.38–42 and pars., studied by Christ, *Jesus*, pp. 61–2.

[16] See M. D. Johnson, 'Reflections', for a thorough critique.

adoption and transformation of traditions from Judaism of God's way of being and acting among his new people.

However, comprehending Matthew's wisdom christology, i.e., Jesus as Sophia, is a much steeper challenge to his audiences than the *de facto* presentation of Jesus as Emmanuel – God with us. For Jesus to be understood as Sophia incarnate requires readers/hearers who are familiar with Matthew's sources. In terms of a narrative reading, then, wisdom christology has little if any foothold within the rhetoric of the story. But for readers with the appropriate background understanding, Jesus Sophia is a minor, collaborative image in support of Matthew's Emmanuel Messiah.

9.3. Spirit and presence

Instead of pursuing its full christological implications, a number of commentators have equated Matthew's presence motif with other evangelists' focus on the Holy Spirit.[17] But this amounts to illegitimate transference to Matthew of the ideas of Luke, John and Paul, who talk about divine support, authority and power in the church in terms of the Spirit (Luke 24.29; Acts 1.4–5; 2.1–21; John 20.19–23; 1 Cor. 15.45 etc.).

Matthew, however, is particularly careful with his Spirit language, apparently avoiding the suggestion that the Holy Spirit is the Spirit of Jesus, as in Mark 2.8; 3.30; 8.12.[18] But Matthew clearly supports straightforward references to πνεῦμα as the Spirit of God in OT terms, a divine agent of blessing, approval and inspiration working on behalf of his people. Even Jesus' supernatural conception by the Spirit does not step beyond the bounds of πνεῦμα as the creative power of God, as commonly understood within popular Jewish writings and Hellenistic Judaism.[19]

Therefore to see Jesus' final promise in Matthew 28.20 as the same assurance given in Luke 24.49; Acts 1.4–5; 2.1–4; John 20.19–25; 1 Corinthians 15.45; etc., with only a difference in terminology, requires that Matthew actively reject a 'pneumatology' or Spirit terminology which he may not even have had access to. This is insufficient rationale for the strength and breadth

---

[17] See Luz, 'Disciples', p. 112; Crosby, *House*, *passim*; Hubbard, *Commissioning*, pp. 121–3, and Ziesler, 'Presence', pp. 90–5.

[18] Cf. Matt. 9.4; Matt. 12.31–2, 38–9; 16.1–4.

[19] Cf. Schweizer, 'πνεῦμα', *TDNT* VI, pp. 396–404; Barrett, *Spirit*, pp. 102–3, 114–17.

of Matthew's presence motif. For Matthew it is paramount that Jesus is with his people in the way that YHWH was with Israel. His personal and community experience, his data, his understanding of Jesus and scripture, drive him that way. For Matthew Spirit language is secondary to his community's primary experience of the present, risen Jesus. The rhetorical and redactional structuring of Matthew's conclusion is bent on one thing – the emphatic continuity of the risen Jesus with the earthly Jesus. For this reason Matthew speaks of *Jesus'* continuing presence with his people, rather than speaking of the Spirit. The serious difference from the other NT writers is the profound depth to which Matthew has plumbed God's personal presence as liberator in the OT as the foundation for describing his same experience of Jesus the Messiah.

9.4.   The poor, the little ones and Jesus' presence

> If you wish to be perfect, go, sell your possessions, and give the money to the poor, and you will have treasure in heaven; then come, follow me.   (Matt. 19.21)

To be with Jesus, in his inner circle, is costly. In Matthew 19.16–30 Jesus does not criticize the rich young man's obedience to the law, but Jesus' final challenge to obtain wholeness, full obedience and commitment to the cause includes the socio-economic dimension. The young man's rejection of the call to discipleship is then contrasted with the disciples, who Peter says have 'left everything' in their commitment to Jesus (19.27). The question here is whether God with us in Matthew's christology encompasses the poor and socially marginalized in a special way, as is frequently claimed by commentators.[20]

Thomas Schmidt claims that hostility to wealth is a fundamental religious tenet leading to eternal life across all synoptic Gospels, and is independent of the socio-economic circumstances behind the text.[21] What Matthew emphasizes, in his disciples' practice of δικαιοσύνη, is justice which is both social and economic (cf. Matt. 3.15; 5.6, 10, 20; 6.1, 33; 11.5; 19.21; 21.32).

In Weberian terms, charismatic leaders and their followers, in order to carry out their mission, must relinquish normal ties,

---

[20]   See, e.g., Crosby, *House*, for the thesis that justice in the form of reordered relationships and resources is a central image in Matthew.
[21]   *Hostility to Wealth in the Synoptic Gospels*, pp. 118, 161–4.

vocations and family duties.[22] Those in Matthew's story who were victims of their leaders' and prophets' *anomie*, or the normlessness of their marginalization and poverty, found a special identity with Jesus' charisma. Among the Gospels, only Matthew uses ἀνομία, most often in relationship with the charismatic activity of true and false prophets.[23] I would thus assert that Jesus' charisma in Matthew is one clear manifestation of his divine presence as the Emmanuel Messiah. The identification of marginalized people with Jesus, and his identification in turn of his presence with their needs, performs a reciprocal equivalence. The public phenomenon of Jesus' magnetism in Matthew, whereby he draws people to himself with a clear centripetal force and creates his inner circle of followers, is the charismatic nature of his presence. This connection transcends Jesus' earthly ministry to become a defining characteristic of his ἐκκλησία, and of the final judgement.

In Matthew, οἱ πτωχοί are characterized as subjects integral to Jesus' central mission (11.2–6). His disciples' sacrifice on behalf of the poor brings heavenly reward, and is critical to entry to the Kingdom (19.21–6). The poor in Matthew are part of that group of marginalized people which includes οἱ μικροί and οἱ ἐλάχιστοι, an underclass which also brings in the πρόβατα, παιδία, τεκνά, Gentiles, women and diseased untouchables. With these Jesus delights to identify himself and he promises to them the favour of divine blessing and Kingdom priority.

Jesus' collective call to form God's people involved at heart a number of challenges to existing socio-political values and codes, including table fellowship,[24] Torah interpretation and Temple hierarchy,[25] Sabbath requirements,[26] and a new people and social order for the Kingdom.[27] Jesus' charge to seek God's βασιλείαν and his δικαιοσύνην (6.33) is paradigmatic of conversion in

---

22 See Weber, *Economy and Society*, pp. 111–58, and *The Sociology of Religion*, pp. 46ff.; and see Stephen Barton's recent comprehensive look at the priority of the Kingdom of God over family and household responsibilities, *Discipleship and Family Ties in Mark and Matthew*.

23 Matt. 7.23; 13.41; 23.28; 24.12; cf. 5.12; 10.41; 13.17; 23.34, 37.

24 See 8.11–12; 9.10–12; 11.19; 22.1–14; and Norman Perrin, *Rediscovering the Teaching of Jesus*, pp. 102–8.

25 See 5.17–20, 21–48; 21.12–17; and Marcus Borg, *Conflict, Holiness and Politics in the Teachings of Jesus*, p. 62.

26 See 12.1–8, 9–14.

27 See 11.25–30; 18.1–35; 19.19–30; 25.31–46; cf. 6.10; 7.21; 12.44, 50; 13.55; 18.14; 21.31; 23.37–9, and see Crosby's approach to these challenges, *House*, pp. 198–203.

Matthew, a process of seeking and finding represented in the
Kingdom parables of Matthew 13 and in Jesus' challenge to the
rich young man and his words on riches (19.21–30). Following
Jesus thus means the reordering of one's relationships and resources on behalf of the poor, and thereby seeking after God's
Kingdom and justice, a journey made nearly impossible by prosperity (19.23–4; 6.21, 24). *Entering* this Kingdom is a major
concern in Matthew; it appears in Jesus' sayings and in each of his
five main discourses,[28] and in the narrative.[29] Ultimately, entrance
to the Kingdom will require meeting the Son of man's standards
for justice as described in 25.31–46. Here Matthew's identification
of Jesus with the marginalized, and the eschatological consequences
of practising Kingdom ethics, are most vivid. The δίκαιοι will be
separated from the others, not on the basis of any apparent
allegiance, but, as David Catchpole notes, 'on the basis of whether
they have or have not done anything to alleviate human need'. The
poor and needy are the heart of the discourse – 'the essential
demand is defined as διακονία', service which 'shows itself as
δέχεσθαι and the satisfying of physical needs'. 'Such service is
performed for all in need and without restriction', and here
'eschatological blessing is promised to the person who takes the
role of the servant'.[30]

But if Jesus' identification with the poor and marginalized is
integral to his Emmanuel christology, Matthew 25.31–46 appears
to be a stumbling-block. In our narrative reading above (see
pp. 95–6) it became clear that Matthew is concerned here with the
judgement of *the world* on the basis of its treatment of the hungry,
naked, ill, imprisoned and foreigners *among the disciples*. Schuyler
Brown and Graham Stanton may be right that the tension between
this list of the poor and 'my brothers, the least' points to an earlier
(perhaps Jesus' own) universalist parable of judgement and exhor-
tation to serve all the poor.

So why has the first evangelist employed the apocalyptic genre to
declare the eschatological importance of Jesus' identification with
Matthew's communities? Clearer community boundaries? Consola-
tion? Group solidarity? Probably all of the above. In the final
discourse of Matthew 24–5 the new people of God are being driven
towards their final commission to all nations (24.14) while being

[28] Cf. 5.20; 7.13–14, 21; 8.12; 11.12; 13.41–3; 18.3, 8, 19; 19.23; 21.31; 23.13.
[29] Cf. 5.19; 8.11; 11.11.
[30] Catchpole, 'The Poor on Earth and the Son of Man in Heaven', p. 389.

warned of torture, hatred and death by all nations, in the context of
economic, social and political chaos, and community splits
(24.6–12). In this context, 25.31–46 provides final vindication and
comfort. It sums up with eschatological gravity Jesus' messianic,
God-with-us identification with and empowerment of his people
(1.21–3; 8.24–7; 10.40–2; 18.20; 26.29–40; 28.20). In 25.31–46 Jesus'
'little ones', 'the least' of Matthew's beleaguered communities, find
solace in their complete vindication by their Emmanuel Messiah as
the ruling, eschatological king judging all nations. Matthew thus
elevates this particularist interpretation of the final judgement for
the sake of his communities struggling over against the larger forces
of Judaism and the gentile world.

This does, of course, raise the issue of *Wirkungsgeschichte*, in
Luz's terminology, i.e., almost 2000 years of disparate, sometimes
contradictory interpretations of Matthew 25.31–46. Does Matthew's own apparent interpretation for his social context apply and
override? (1) Despite any of our assertions as to the interpretation
of 25.31–46, it remains a thoroughly disputed and difficult passage,
especially if an earlier eschatological discourse by Jesus is posited.
(2) Over the years the discourse has required interpretation in
socio-political settings radically different from Matthew's own. The
social status and political power of many Christian communities
today stand diametrically distant from that early social marginalization of Christians. Hence the hermeneutical dilemma of
25.31–46. The particularist interpretation may have arisen from
Matthew's participation in the parting of the ways between Christianity and its parent, but the universalist interpretation is clearly
more applicable and relevant to many Christians today. This
pericope is definitely ripe ground for our reading pursuits, as they
entwine with considerations of canon. More study is required to
understand the move from Matthew's world to ours.

10

CONCLUSION

> O Lord, you have searched me and known me . . .
> Where can I go from your spirit?
>   Or where can I flee from your presence?
> If I ascend to heaven, you are there;
>   If I make my bed in Sheol, you are there.
>
> (Ps. 139.1, 7–8)

Many years ago the Hebrew psalmist was overwhelmingly convinced of the presence of God. The human quest after divine presence has taken dramatically different turns in different eras. Today many post-Christian societies more often ask 'Does God exist?' or 'Who is God?' than assume divine presence. Almost two millennia ago the first evangelist provided a strong voice in a moment of significant transition between religious eras. His is a story of social and religious continuity and discontinuity between two sets of communities, for both of which the presence of God was an essential defining characteristic.

In the current moment of biblical criticism, the means of assessing a concern such as the presence motif within the ancient text of Matthew have multiplied to the point, some claim, of disparity. The choice in this study to employ both narrative and redaction criticism has not been for the sake of a new eclecticism, but is an attempt to respond authentically to some of the structural, historical and theological dimensions which the text exhibits. We have sought to read Matthew as both a mirror and a window – as a unified and dynamic story that invites readers to inhabit imaginatively its narrative world and seeks to structure their responses, and as a text with a historical author and context.

The story

In applying narrative criticism to the presence motif in Matthew's story we have seen the rhetorical importance of the Matthew 1–2 prologue: here the narrator establishes the setting, ideological point of view and primary conflicts of the story. God's past presence with his people provides the foundation for a new era of divine presence in Jesus' birth. The genealogy and narrative make clear Matthew's inheritance of Israel and its paradigms.

God's presence in the person and mission of his Messiah finds emphatic explanation in an important double naming. 'Jesus' and 'Emmanuel' are linked, for as Messiah, Jesus will save 'his people', who will call him Emmanuel – God with us. Matthew's Gospel from this point on is a gradual unfolding of the content of these ascriptions and their characterizations of the Messiah. The crises of Jerusalem and the magi in Matthew 2 initiate the story's elemental conflicts. Within this environment Jesus must work out the substance of his mission: who are the people of God? How will he as the Emmanuel Messiah save them? How will the deadly antipathy between Jesus and his opponents be resolved?

Jesus' adult preparation in Matthew 3.1–4.11 further reinforces these themes: Jesus' coming as a special advent of God's presence, the story's acceptance–rejection motif and Matthew's theocentric focus. Jesus' Galilean ministry takes shape with two concentric circles of disciples and crowds drawn by his centripetal presence. Jesus calls apart those of his inner circle, teaches them, demonstrates his ministry and gives them a mission like his own. The story tension created by this mission's apparent lack of fulfilment implies the disciples' need for more faith and a better grasp of Jesus' empowering presence. Jesus begins to explain the equivalence of his presence and his followers (10.41–2; cf. 18.5; 25.31–46).

Ironically, the Jewish leaders see intuitively the divine significance and threat of his presence, and by Matthew 11–12 their opposition becomes public. Jesus proclaims his supersession of the Temple (12.6). Despite moments of clarity and developing perception (e.g., 13.51–2; 16.5–12, 13–20; 17.13), in a number of incidents – storms and water-walking (8.24–7; 14.22–32); feeding stories (14.13–21; 15.32–9); Peter's rebuke (16.21–3); the disciples' healing attempt (17.14–21); the Supper and Garden abandonment (26.29–56) – the disciples demonstrate their continued dependence upon Jesus' *physical* proximity and intervention for empowerment and faith.

By the critical juncture of 16.13 Jesus anticipates his suffering and death, and the building of his own ἐκκλησία. His presence 'in their midst' (18.20) becomes the focal point for the future gatherings of his followers. Matthew 18 advances several crucial principles of membership in his ἐκκλησία. The narrative polarization grows between the gatherings of ἐκκλησία μου and συναγωγαί αὐτῶν.

In Matthew 19.1 Jesus reverses his lifelong flight from Jerusalem and looks ahead to his suffering. His entry to the city reawakens the royal Davidic expectations of the Jerusalem crowd. His presence in the Temple provokes an escalating series of conflicts with his opponents which culminates in his condemnation of the Jewish leaders, rejection of Jerusalem, physical and symbolic withdrawal of divine presence from the Temple and Jerusalem, and prediction of the Temple's destruction. The story has come back full circle to Matthew 2 with judgement pronounced on the leaders of God's people, who even then rejected God's agent of divine presence among them. In the table fellowship of Matthew 26, Jesus being 'with' the disciples (μετά, 9x) gains definition beyond the physical – he models the key symbols for their ongoing faith in and celebration of his presence in the post-resurrection ἐκκλησία.

The narrative close (27.51–28.20) provides a careful summary of themes and thorough evocation of the story's beginnings. The Jewish leaders remain consistent to the end, blindly opposed to God's presence and power among them. In the critical finale of 28.16–20, the risen Jesus gathers his followers to the Galilee mountain-top. The disciples are obedient, restored and worshipful, and yet doubtful of his risen presence. The risen Jesus reassures them with his authority, issues a world-wide commission, and declares his divine presence in the first-person voice of YHWH.

This final rhetorical structuring brings the narrator, Jesus, the disciples and the implied reader into temporal and ideological alignment. The commission is thus a beginning and an ending; Jesus' command and presence is applicable to both disciples and readers. The fundamental conflicts and characterizations of the story carry over into the post-narrative world, but the disciples can now minister as Jesus' emissaries in the divine authority of his risen presence. The finale's open-ended dialogue, temporal unboundedness and unfulfilled commissioning connect the story to the readers' own contexts, so that Jesus' ongoing teaching and ministry, and the texts' structures, point of view and unresolved tensions, call for their completion of the story within their own contexts.

The setting in Judaism

Ancient Israel and early Judaism grappled not so much with the existence of God as with the special places and conditions for human encounter with divine immanence. For the people of the Jewish scriptures YHWH's presence was not simply a by-product of the covenant, but a gift which preceded it, and hence the very reason for their existence. YHWH's presence was the foundational blessing for his people to discover. His dwelling among them had to be faithfully maintained; nothing could take place for his people apart from it.

Israel's central quest to establish and maintain the presence of God was formed out of its various stages of experience, and was expressed in diverse paradigms, under which lie a fundamental unity. The patriarchal stories of clan god and clan father provided a foundation for understanding divine call and accompanying 'withness'. Sinai supplied Israel's primary pattern of presence, forever after told, retold and celebrated in the cult. All of Israel's life somehow originated at the mountain of God. YHWH's Sinai presence brought Moses, election, Torah, covenant and the tent shrine. YHWH's presence became their origin, survival, identity and *raison d'être* (Exod. 33.16; Ezek. 37.28).

Jerusalem and the kings forced a paradigm shift, to accommodate new socio-political realities. Sinai and Jerusalem presence had a fundamental continuity, for God's call, covenant and dwelling among his people remained central convictions. But new concerns arose, and different (and sometimes competing) rationales for God's presence with Israel developed around Jerusalem and the Temple. Prophets like Jeremiah and Micah fought strongly the view of Jerusalem as God's guarantee of divine security and blessing, and the Deuteronomists recast YHWH's personal abode to be the dwelling of his name in the Temple.

With the upheaval of the Temple's loss, the exile and reconstruction, divine presence remained central to the Israel of both Palestine and the diaspora, but was reinterpreted. Ezekiel and the Priestly composers spoke of YHWH's 'glory' as the mode of his presence. Tension arose between the conviction and promise of YHWH's dwelling amidst his people, and their immediate experience of his absence. The tension grew into an increased wrestling over the interplay of divine immanence and transcendence, with impact for Jewish understandings of history, theology and eschatological hope. Various texts witness development of other means of expressing divine immanence, e.g., Shekinah and Sophia, while maintaining holy divine transcendence. Periphrastic language for divine encounter and holy presence increased, along with mediating powers, and growth in eschatological longings, in the midst of diverse growth in Judaisms.

The 'I am with you/God is with us' saying stands as a remarkably consistent formulaic expression of divine presence in the Jewish scriptures. Its dominant appearance within narrative-*heilsgeschichtlich* contexts agrees with its application of concrete 'help' vocabulary to personal situations of individual leaders and to Israel's corporate community, and occasionally to 'outsiders'. The formula functions as an important description, promise or anticipation of God's saving immanence, retrospectively and immediately, 'with' his people.

The author

Matthew inherited directly this central and evolving quest after divine presence in Judaism, and its central paradigms. In particular he found in Jesus a new paradigm for the central symbols of Sinai, and that Jesus made sense of divine presence in his bold personification of the divine 'I am with you' utterance. Given Matthew's inheritance of these traditions, his commentators have always pondered his Jesus, mountains and sermons for their reflections of Moses, Sinai and Torah. But Matthew's clearest legacy came from Israel's core emphasis on YHWH as their 'I am with you' liberator, and the completely pervasive nature of the Exodus tradition in Israel, which emphasized God's active role in history. And the Emmanuel Messiah Jesus took on this role in the history of God's people in Matthew. His presence as his people's divine liberator, mountain-top teacher and κύριος stands in continuity with the Exodus paradigm and the language of the 'with you' formula.

Likewise, the importance of divine presence in Matthew 1–2 climaxes with inclusio in 28.16–20, as the key legitimizing factor for, and manifestation of, Jesus' risen authority. Where in Exodus 33 'the issue of Yahweh's presence is enmeshed in the issue of Moses' vocation',[1] in Matthew God's presence *is* the issue of Jesus' vocation. Matthew reflects a new struggle, and he reorients the

---

[1]   Brueggemann, 'Crisis', p. 65.

Jewish questioning after the where and how of God's presence and absence, to focus upon the risen Jesus and his followers. In answer to his readers' quest for divine presence Matthew replies with the risen Emmanuel Messiah, who brings divine authority and presence into the midst of his people, who are now to be gathered from all nations.

That which appears as a clear rhetorical motif within the narrative story, and as a dominant *heilsgeschichtlich* motif in the Jewish literature around Matthew, is consistent with the editorial priorities of the evangelist. Matthew's key presence passages (1.23; 8.23–7; 10.41–2; 12.6; 14.22–33; 17.17; 18.20; 25.31–46; 26.29; 28.20) are part of his own considered reflections and christological assessments of Jesus, supported and woven throughout the Gospel.

For example, Jesus' identification as Emmanuel – God with us is one of four main theological themes in Matthew 1–2, intertwined with Davidic sonship, divine sonship and his messianic mission to 'his people'. And in his translation of Emmanuel as 'God with us', Matthew has deliberately reintroduced the Hebrew meaning of the name, lost to Greek speakers, and explicitly made Jesus' messiahship the new expression of YHWH's OT presence.

Jesus' rhetorical inversion of first–last Kingdom criteria in Matthew 18, where normal human social hierarchies are turned on their head, is also supported as a wider redactional theme. How will Jesus be present 'in their midst'? – as a child, one of the μικροί; when his followers gather to reconcile, bind and loose, agree and pray together in his name. These gatherings, however, are also in the future, undefined and rhetorically open, in Jesus' radical fulfilment of the YHWH *Mitsein* paradigm.

Jesus' final promise of presence is wholly Matthean redactionally and theologically, the most dramatic and pregnant 'I am' saying of the synoptics. It connects the risen Jesus to the building of his future ἐκκλησία, by means of his bold embodiment of the first-person utterance of YHWH: 'I am with you', now extended 'always, to the end of the age'.

In character, 28.16–20 is a paradigmatic, somewhat 'suprahistorical' text, embodying less emotion and less interest in historical details and phenomena than the narration of Jesus' death and the women at the tomb. The passage is open-ended – there is no farewell, Jesus does not leave and he specifically promises to remain. This passage is to address all time – the present and future of his entire ἐκκλησία. The narrative and post-narrative worlds are linked by his presence: the readers, Jesus, the characters and the narrator meet. Thus 28.16–20 functions as the transition point in the continuum between the earthly and risen Jesus. These two horizons of Matthew have been apparent at various points within the story, but here they are enlarged (πᾶς, 4x). Authority is a major element in linking the two sides of the continuum (11.25–7; 28.18), as is worship of Jesus. The cosmic proportions of Jesus' authority (v.18b) enable him to command a world-wide mission, to mandate his earthly teaching as required learning for all new followers, and to speak with the voice of YHWH of his own divine presence.

Some implications

The story's centripetal focus on Jesus is central to Matthew's characterization of him as God's presence. In Matthew his people gather (συνάγω) around Jesus himself, not on a mountain, or in the Temple. Within his Gospel-wide conflict with the religious leaders of Israel, Jesus replaces Zion as the centre, for both Jews and Gentiles, of eschatological fulfilment. This is the reality of the centripetal force of Jesus' presence throughout and following the story. That which draws the magi at the beginning only foresees the gathering of πάντα τὰ ἔθνη anticipated at the end. In a manner distinct from the other Gospels, Jesus in Matthew has replaced Jerusalem and the Temple as the focus of God's presence and salvation. Jesus' threats of Temple destruction and promise of rebuilding do have in mind the long-awaited Jewish promise of Zion's restoration, but will be answered according to Matthew through the fulfilled commission, with the gathering of the ἐκκλησία not to Zion, but to Jesus, who is himself the 'God-with-us' locus.

To use later Christian language, the presence motif in Matthew can also be seen as the 'grace' pole of the grace–works spectrum. Matthew has been accused of being the 'Gospel of works', with its emphasis on *miṣwôt,* parallel to the traditions of the Sinai covenant, using the eschatological hammer to coerce obedience, thereby threatening to make Jesus and his teaching out to be a mechanism for the dispensation of rewards and punishments. But Jesus' presence becomes the note of grace, the transcendent God's gift of immanence in his Emmanuel Messiah, which corresponds to both the restoration of YHWH's presence in Exodus 33 and the mysterious tension of his Zion dwelling. Matthew is not necessarily thereby dichotomized into the spiritual experience of divine presence and ἐντολαί – grace and works – but affirms both simultaneously and interdependently. Hence Matthew maintains and enlarges Israel's two-sided biblical relationship between God and his people, upholding 'both activity and passivity as proper postures for both partners'.[2] Each of presence, obedience and the ἐκκλησία presupposes the others. That precedent paradox which lies at the heart of Jewish spirituality has been carried through by Matthew into the new age inaugurated by the Emmanuel Messiah amidst his ἐκκλησία, even as Jesus newly expresses the immanence of the transcendent YHWH.

Matthew's presence motif involves a narrative and theological movement from theocentricity in Matthew 1–2 to christocentricity in 28.16–20; from numerous manifestations of divine immanence with the people of God as the Emmanuel Messiah as introduced in Matthew 1–2 to the risen Jesus as the christological focus of divine presence in the final commissioning; from the narrator's '*God* with us' to Jesus' '*I* am with you'. This movement entails the dramatic transfer of ἐξουσία to Jesus, practised throughout his healing and teaching ministry, highlighted in 11.27 and fully bestowed in 28.18. This ἐξουσία is the symbol and reality of Jesus' abiding power among his disciples. The risen Jesus' authoritative presence is the basis for all exercise of human authority in the ἐκκλησία. The challenge to Jesus' followers in Matthew 28.16–20 is to move beyond their struggles with ὀλιγοπιστία, deepen their faith, and find empowerment in the divine ἐξουσία of Jesus' presence. The doubt of the earthly disciples follows them to the final scene, so that Jesus' reassuring presence and ἐξουσία stand for all readers as the recurring invitation to abandon their doubt, move beyond their need for Jesus' earthly persona, and worship and live in his abiding, risen presence.

Matthew's inheritance of the Sinai presence paradigm again comes to mind, as well as the doubtful response of recipients in many Hebrew commissioning stories. Moses' request to see YHWH's glory (Exod. 33.18) and YHWH's reply with the affirmation of his presence continue to echo the original sequence of doubt and reassurance in Exodus 3–4. The Moses of Exodus 33.18 reflects the popular desire for majestic phenomena, a secure vision, a cultic

[2] So Levenson, 'Temple', pp. 50–1, in application to Israel's Temple worship.

guarantee of divine presence, somewhat like the disciples in Matthew 28.17, while the divine reflections of Exodus 33.19–23 and Matthew 28.18b–20 function as the proper correctives of these misconceptions. Presence in both Exodus and Matthew is assured through the personal divine word of promise, in anticipation of future experience of presence, and not as religious certitude.

Where does this leave Matthew's reader? Since Matthew 1 the reader has received from the narrator a knowledge of Jesus which is *superior* to that of the disciples in the story; he/she alone is able to judge what it truly means to follow Jesus. In being the only one to receive the full impact of the Gospel's narrative rhetoric, the implied reader is 'with' Jesus more than any of his followers in the story. Thus it is through obedient disciples and readers that the tensions of the Gospel are to be carried forward and resolved – 'his people' are formed as readers respond in obedience at the end of the story. The story's rhetorical agenda is successful, and Jesus' future promises of presence with his ἐκκλησία come to fulfilment, in the midst of readers-become-followers gathered in his name.

In Matthew 28.16–20 the reader is challenged to obey Jesus' teaching and follow him as the model for discipleship. Jesus' commission in 28.19–20 looks retrospectively over his entire teaching ministry (πάντα ὅσα ἐνετειλάμην) and thus achieves literary closure for the Gospel. And because the inclusio formed between 1.23 and 28.20 causes convergence of the narrator's (1.23) and Jesus' declarations of divine presence (28.20), the implied reader is made a recipient of his final promise.

To borrow Matthew's own language, each reader is to become a final redactor or γραμματεύς, be 'discipled for the Kingdom of heaven', and take up the challenge to 'bring from their treasure' both the 'old' (Matthew's story) and the 'new' (their contemporary situation), and continue interpreting and writing the story of Jesus for their post-narrative world (13.52). The reader is called to concrete application, to the πρᾶξις (16.27) of adopting Matthew's and Jesus' system of values, joining horizons and interpreting the way of Jesus; in other words, the active hermeneutical exercise which is 'inseparable from the wider social relations between writers and readers'.[3] In story form, Matthew calls the reader to follow his model of discipleship, reshaped to fit the new situation of the generation after Jesus.

---

[3]   Eagleton, *Theory*, pp. 205–6.

This explains the implicit invitation and deliberate open-ended structure of Matthew's climax, very different from Mark's lack of closure and resolution. Jesus' earthly presence has set the parameters for his disciples but is only a preliminary model for post-resurrection experiences. Key passages in Matthew place the presence motif in primary relation not to the activities of the earthly disciples in the story, but to their anticipated ministry in the post-narrative world: 'Emmanuel' as the future declaration by 'his people' (1.23); the lessons of Jesus' divine empowerment and presence in the storms, water-walkings and feedings; the prospective ἐκκλησία principles concerning the μικροί, discipline, forgiveness, prayer and gathering (Matt. 18); the coming Supper celebrations of his salvation and presence (26.18–20); the eschatological drinking of the cup in the Kingdom (26.29); the commands to baptize, teach and make disciples (28.19–20). In all of these, the image of Jesus 'with them', 'in their midst', is an anticipation of a post-Easter, authoritative divine presence yet to be thoroughly understood and defined, and only initially experienced in Jesus' final appearance.

Along with Matthew's character as a story anticipating completion beyond itself, does Matthew also end on a note of rhetorical subversion with its ambiguous language about presence? Are the readers' expectations subverted? After all, what is presence at the end of Matthew? – not the authoritative magnificent activities of the anointed Messiah king, the divine Son of God, but the promises of empowerment and of Jesus' divine 'withness' to a group of doubting disciples who will face persecution and troubles; not convincing theophanic phenomena, but identification with the μικροί. Jesus' resurrection is powerful, but the irony is strong: God manifests his divine authority and presence not in Jerusalem, but in Galilee; not on a throne, but in an upside-down kingdom; not in the capital city with political and military strength, but on a wilderness mountain with teaching and healing; not in divine appearances, but through future 'gatherings' of followers; not in power and wealth, but in poverty and humility; in alliance not with the power-brokers, but with 'the little ones'; not with the thousands, but with 'two or three'; not in the Temple, but in his risen Son. The son of Abraham, son of David, Emmanuel Lord Messiah in the end naturally looks a little questionable to his closest followers, despite his claim to 'all authority in heaven and earth'.

At the end of the story the Jerusalem leaders remain in power, in control of Israel, and apparently able to convince the people of their version of Jesus' story (28.11–15). The end of Matthew is thus the continuation of the struggle, more than the triumphant end to the story. The base of God's salvation has shifted dramatically since Matthew 1, when perhaps a more 'traditional' episode in Israel's story of salvation was expected by the reader. Despite elements of continuity (the law – as redefined by Jesus – and scriptures; God's presence, and his will to deliver his people), the elements of discontinuity stand in sharp relief (geography, ethnicity and the redefinition of God's people; Jesus' identification as God's presence and salvation; the new gathering (ἐκκλησία) versus the old (συναγωγή); the role of women; etc.).

But herein also lies the story's true inversion of the socio-religious *status quo*: Jesus, with all authority in heaven and earth, is most present with the little ones, his new people. His centripetal presence goes on pulling the marginalized to the centre of the Kingdom, calling them to his radical form of justice, humility and spirituality.[4] The intimate identification of his presence with the little ones jolts his audience from any self-contentment, with a new awareness of his presence in the unexpected. Such a christology and ethic still holds a profound challenge for us, our churches and institutions.

[4]   Stephen Barton, *The Spirituality of the Gospels*: the sense of God's presence is the starting-point for spirituality in Matthew. He ties together spiritual formation in Matthew with the dominant elements of the presence motif, and finds that spirituality in the First Gospel is something learned by being with Jesus in total commitment to discipleship and the ἐκκλησία.

BIBLIOGRAPHY

Abrams, M. H. *A Glossary of Literary Terms*. 4th edition. London: Holt, Rinehart and Winston, 1981.

Achtemeier, Paul J. *Mark*. Proclamation Commentaries, 2nd edition. Philadelphia: Fortress, 1986.

Adam, A. K. M. 'Matthew's Readers, Ideology, and Power'. In SBLSP 1994. Atlanta: Scholars Press, 1994, pp. 435–49.

Addley, W. P. 'Matthew 18 and the Church as the Body of Christ'. *Biblical Theology* 26 (1976), pp. 12–18.

Albright, W. F., and Mann, C. S. *Matthew*. AB. Garden City, New York: Doubleday, 1971.

Allen, W. C. *Matthew*. ICC. Edinburgh: T. and T. Clark, 1907.

Allison, Dale. *The New Moses: A Matthean Typology*. Minneapolis: Fortress, 1993.

'The Structure of the Sermon on the Mount'. *JBL* 106 (1987), pp. 423–45.

Alt, A. 'The God of the Fathers'. 1929. ET in his *Essays on Old Testament History and Religion*. Oxford: Blackwell, 1966, pp. 3–100.

Alter, Robert and Kermode, Frank. *The Literary Guide to the Bible*. Cambridge, Mass.: Belknap, 1987.

Anderson, Janice Capel. 'Double and Triple Stories, the Implied Reader, and Redundancy in Matthew'. *Semeia* 31 (1985), pp. 71–89.

'Matthew: Gender and Reading'. *Semeia* 28 (1983), pp. 3–27.

'Over and Over and Over Again: Studies in Matthean Repetition'. Ph.D. Dissertation, University of Chicago, 1985. Published as *Matthew's Narrative Web: Over, and Over, and Over Again*. JSNTSS 91. Sheffield: JSOT Press, 1994.

Aune, David. *The New Testament in its Literary Environment*. Minneapolis: Fortress, 1987.

'The Problem of the Genre of the Gospels: A Critique of C. H. Talbert's *What is a Gospel?*'. In *Gospel Perspectives: Studies of History and Tradition in the Four Gospels*, Volume II, eds. R. T. France and David Wenham. Sheffield: JSOT Press, 1981, pp. 9–60.

Bacon, B. W. 'The "Five Books" of Moses against the Jews'. *The Expositor* 15 (1918), pp. 56–66.

Studies in Matthew. London: Constable, 1930.

Baird, J. A. *Audience Criticism and the Historical Jesus*. Philadelphia: Westminster, 1969.

Bal, Mieke. 'The Laughing Mice, or: On Focalization'. *Poetics Today* 2 (1981), pp. 202–10.

Balch, David, ed. *Social History of the Matthean Community: Cross-Disciplinary Approaches.* Minneapolis: Fortress, 1991.

Baltzer, Klaus. *The Covenant Formulary.* 1964. ET Philadelphia: Fortress, 1971.

Barclay, William. *The Letter to the Hebrews.* Philadelphia: Westminster, 1955.

Barr, James. 'Reading the Bible as Literature'. *BJRL* 56 (1973), pp. 10–33.

Barrett, C. K. *The Holy Spirit and the Gospel Tradition.* 2nd edition. London: SPCK, 1966.

Barth, Gerhard. 'Matthew's Understanding of the Law'. In *Tradition and Interpretation in Matthew*, eds. G. Bornkamm, G. Barth and H. J. Held. 2nd edition. ET London: SCM Press, 1982, pp. 58–163.

Barth, Karl. *Church Dogmatics* (ET of *Kirchliche Dogmatik*). 13 volumes. Edinburgh: T. and T. Clark, 1936–69.

'An Exegetical Study of Matthew 28:16–20'. ET of *Auslegung von Matthäus 28,16–20.* Basle: Basler Missionsbuchhandlung G.M.b.h., 1945. In *The Theology of Christian Mission*, ed. G. H. Anderson. 1961, pp. 55–71.

Barton, John. *Oracles of God: Perceptions of Ancient Prophecy in Israel After the Exile.* London: Darton, Longman and Todd, 1986.

Reading the Old Testament: Method in Biblical Study. London: Darton, Longman and Todd, 1984.

Barton, Stephen. *Discipleship and Family Ties in Mark and Matthew.* SNTSMS 80. Cambridge: Cambridge University Press, 1994.

The Spirituality of the Gospels. London: SPCK, 1992.

Bauer, David. *The Structure of Matthew's Gospel: A Study in Literary Design.* JSNTSS 31; BLS 15. Sheffield: JSOT Press, 1988.

Bauer, W. *A Greek–English Lexicon of the New Testament and Other Early Christian Literature.* Trans. and adapted from W. Bauer's *Griechisch–Deutsches Worterbuch* by W. F. Arndt and F. W. Gingrich. 2nd edition, revised F. W. Gingrich and F. W. Danker. Chicago: University of Chicago Press, 1979.

Beare, F. W. *The Earliest Records of Jesus.* New York, Nashville: Abingdon Press, 1962.

The Gospel According to Matthew: A Commentary. Oxford: Blackwell, 1981.

'Sayings of the Risen Jesus in the Synoptic Tradition'. In *Christian History and Interpretation: Studies Presented to John Knox*, eds. W. R. Farmer, C. F. D. Moule, R. R. Niebuhr. Cambridge: Cambridge University Press, 1967.

Bengel, J. A. *Gnomon of the New Testament.* 2 volumes, 1742. ET Edinburgh: T. and T. Clark, 1857.

Benoit, P. *L'évangile selon saint Matthieu.* Paris, 1961.

'Les Outrages à Jésus prophète (Mc xiv.65 par)'. In *Neotestamentica et Patristica*, O. Cullmann Festschrift. NovTSup 6. Leiden: E. J. Brill, 1962, pp. 91–110.

Berg, W. 'Die Identität der "jungen Frau" in Jes 7,14.16'. *BN* 13 (1980), pp. 7–13.

Best, Ernest. *Following Jesus.* JSNTSS 4. Sheffield: JSOT Press, 1981.

Betz, H. D. 'The Sermon on the Mount: Its Literary Genre and Function'. *JR* 59 (1979), pp. 285–97.

Beyerlin, W. *Origins and History of the Oldest Sinaitic Traditions.* Oxford: Blackwell, 1965.

Bietenhard, Hans. 'ὄνομα'. *TDNT* V, ed. G. Friedrich. ET Grand Rapids: Eerdmans, 1967, pp. 242–81.

Boers, H. 'Language Usage and the Production of Matthew 1:18–2:23'. In *Orientation by Disorientation*, ed. R. A. Spencer, pp. 217–33.

Boismard, M.-E. *Synopse des quatre évangiles* II. Paris: Les Editions du Cerf, 1972.

Bonnard, P. 'Composition et signification historique de Matthieu XXVIII'. In *De Jésus aux évangiles*, ed. I. de la Potterie, pp. 130–40.

L'évangile selon saint Matthieu. CNT 1, 2nd edition. Neuchâtel: Delachaux et Niestlé, 1970.

Booth, Wayne C. *Critical Understanding.* Chicago: University of Chicago Press, 1979.

'Distance and Point of View: An Essay in Clarification'. *Essays in Criticism* 11 (1961), pp. 60–79.

The Rhetoric of Fiction. 2nd edition. Chicago: University of Chicago, 1983.

A Rhetoric of Irony. Chicago: University of Chicago Press, 1974.

Borg, Marcus J. *Conflict, Holiness and Politics in the Teachings of Jesus.* SBEC 5. New York and Toronto: Edwin Mellen, 1984.

Boring, M. E. *Sayings of the Risen Jesus: Christian Prophecy in the Synoptic Tradition.* SNTSMS 46. Cambridge: Cambridge University Press, 1982.

Bornkamm, Günther. 'The Authority to "Bind" and "Loose" in the Church in Matthew's Gospel: The Problem of Sources in Matthew's Gospel'. In *The Interpretation of Matthew*, ed. G. Stanton, pp. 85–97.

'End-Expectation and Church in Matthew'. In *Tradition and Interpretation in Matthew*, eds. G. Bornkamm, G. Barth and H. J. Held. 2nd edition. ET London: SCM Press, 1982, pp. 15–51.

'The Risen Lord and the Earthly Jesus: Matthew 28:16–20'. In *The Future of Our Religious Past*, ed. J. M. Robinson. London: SCM Press, 1971, pp. 203–29. Also in *TIM*, pp. 301–27.

'The Stilling of the Storm in Matthew'. In *Tradition and Interpretation in Matthew*, eds. G. Bornkamm, G. Barth and H. J. Held. 2nd edition. ET London: SCM Press, 1982, pp. 52–7.

Barth, Gerhard, and Held, Heinz Joachim, eds. *Tradition and Interpretation in Matthew.* 2nd edition. London: SCM Press, 1982.

Boslooper, Thomas. *The Virgin Birth.* London: SCM, 1962.

Bouyer, L. 'La Schékinah, Dieu avec nous'. *BVC* 20 (1957/8), pp. 19ff.

Box, G. H. *The Virgin Birth of Jesus Christ.* London: Sir Isaac Pitman and Sons, 1916.

Braumann, G. 'Mit euch, Matth. 26,29'. *TZ* 21 (1965), pp. 161–9.

Bright, John. *A History of Israel.* 3rd edition. Philadelphia: Westminster, 1981.

Brooks, Stephenson. *Matthew's Community: The Evidence of His Special Sayings Material.* JSNTSS 16. Sheffield: JSOT Press, 1987.

Brown, Francis, Driver, S. R., and Briggs, C. A. *A Hebrew and English Lexicon of the Old Testament With an Appendix Containing the Biblical Aramaic.* Oxford: Clarendon Press, 1907.

Brown, Raymond E. *The Birth of the Messiah: A Commentary on the Infancy Narratives in Matthew and Luke.* New York: Doubleday, 1977.

An Introduction to New Testament Christology. New York: Paulist, 1994.

Jesus, God and Man. New York: Macmillan and Co., 1967.

Brown, Schuyler. 'Biblical Philology, Linguistics and the Problem of Method'. *Heythrop Journal* 20 (1979), pp. 295–8.

'Faith, the Poor and the Gentiles: A Traditional-Historical Reflection on Matthew 25:31–46'. *TJT* 6 (1990), pp. 171–81.

'The Matthean Community and the Gentile Mission'. *NovT* 22 (1980), pp. 193–221.

'The Mission to Israel in Matthew's Central Section'. *ZNW* 69 (1978), pp. 73–90.

'Reader Response: Demythologizing the Text'. *NTS* 34 (1988), pp. 232–7.

Brownlee, W. H. 'The Ineffable Name of God'. *BASOR* 226 (1977), pp. 39–46.

Brueggemann, Walter. 'The Crisis and Promise of Presence in Israel'. *HBT* 1 (1979), pp. 47–86.

'The Epistemological Crisis of Israel's Two Histories (Jer 9:22–23)'. In *Israelite Wisdom: Theological and Literary Essays in Honor of Samuel Terrien*, eds. John G. Gammie, Walter A. Brueggemann, W. Lee Humphreys, James M. Ward. Missoula, Mont.: Scholars Press, 1978, pp. 85–105.

'Presence of God, Cultic'. *IDBSup.* Nashville and New York: Abingdon, 1976, pp. 680–3.

'Trajectories in Old Testament Literature and the Sociology of Ancient Israel'. *JBL* 98 (1979), pp. 161–85.

Bruner, F. Dale. *Matthew: A Commentary.* Volume I: *The Christbook. Matthew 1–12.* Waco, Texas: Word Books, 1987. Volume II: *The Churchbook: Matthew 13–28.* Dallas and London: Word Publishing, 1990.

Buber, Martin. *Kingship of God.* 3rd edition. ET London: George Allen and Unwin, 1967.

Moses. Oxford and London: East and West Library, 1946.

Bultmann, Rudolph. *The History of the Synoptic Tradition.* 2nd edition. ET Oxford: Basil Blackwell, 1968.

Burnett, Fred. 'Characterization and Reader Construction of Characters in the Gospels'. *Semeia* 63 (1993), pp. 1–28.

'Exposing the Anti-Jewish Ideology of Matthew's Implied Reader: The Characterization of God as Father'. *Semeia* 59 (1992), pp. 155–91.

The Testament of Jesus-Sophia: A Redaction-Critical Study of the Eschatological Discourse in Matthew. Washington: University Press of America, 1981.

'The Undecidability of the Proper Name "Jesus" in Matthew'. *Semeia* 54 (1991), pp. 123–44.

Burridge, R. A. *What are the Gospels? A Comparison with Graeco-Roman Biography*. Cambridge: Cambridge University Press, 1992.

Burton, Ernest de Witt. *Syntax of the Moods and Tenses in New Testament Greek*. Chicago: University of Chicago Press, 1900.

Caba, José. 'El poder de la petición communitaria (Mt.18,19–20)'. *Gregorianum* 54 (1973), pp. 609–54.

Calvin, John. *A Harmony of the Gospels*. 3 volumes. In *Calvin's New Testament Commentaries*, eds. David W. Torrance and Thomas F. Torrance. Edinburgh: The Saint Andrew Press, 1972.

Campenhausen, H. von. *The Virgin Birth in the Theology of the Ancient Church*. ET, London: SCM Press, 1964.

Carson, D. A. 'Christological Ambiguities in Matthew'. In *Christ the Lord: Studies in Christology Presented to Donald Guthrie*, ed. H. H. Rowden. Leicester: Inter-Varsity Press, 1982, pp. 97–114.

God with Us: Themes from Matthew. Ventura: Regal Books, 1985.

'Matthew'. In *The Expositor's Bible Commentary* VIII, ed. F. E. Gaebelein. Grand Rapids: Zondervan, 1984, pp. 1–599.

Cassuto, U. *A Commentary on the Book of Exodus*. 1951. ET Jerusalem: Magnes Press, 1967.

Catchpole, David. 'The Poor on Earth and the Son of Man in Heaven: A Re-Appraisal of Matthew XXV:31–46'. *BJRL* 61 (1979), pp. 355–97.

Charlesworth, James H., ed. *The Old Testament Pseudepigrapha*. 2 volumes. London: Darton, Longman and Todd, 1983, 1985.

Chatman, Seymour. *Story and Discourse: Narrative Structure in Fiction and Film*. Ithaca, New York: Cornell University Press, 1978.

Childs, Brevard. *The Book of Exodus*. OTL. Philadelphia: Westminster, 1974.

'Theological Responsibility'. *Int* 18 (1964), pp. 432–49.

Christ, Felix. *Jesus Sophia: Die Sophia-Christologie bei den Synoptikern*. ATANT 57. Zürich: Zwingli Verlag, 1970.

Christian, Paul. *Jesus und seine geringsten Brüder*. Erfurter Theologische Schriften 12. Leipzig: St Benno-Verlag, 1974.

Clark, K. W. 'The Gentile Bias in Matthew'. *JBL* 66 (1947), pp. 165–72.

Clements, R. E. *Abraham and David: Genesis 15 and its Meaning for Israelite Tradition*. SBT II/5. London: SCM Press, 1967.

Exodus. Cambridge: Cambridge University Press, 1972.

God and Temple. Oxford: Blackwell, 1965.

Isaiah 1–39. NCB. London: Marshall, Morgan and Scott, 1980.

Clifford, R. J. *The Cosmic Mountain in Canaan and the Old Testament*. Harvard Semitic Monograph Series 4. Cambridge, Mass.: Harvard University Press, 1972.

Coats, G. W. 'The King's Loyal Opposition: Obedience and Revolution in the Moses Traditions'. In *Canon and Authority in the Old Testament*, eds. G. W. Coats and B. O. Long. Philadelphia: Fortress, 1977, pp. 91–109.

Moses: Heroic Man, Man of God. JSOTSS 57. Sheffield, JSOT Press, 1988.

Combrink, H. J. B. 'The Changing Scene of Biblical Interpretation'. In *A South African Perspective on the New Testament: Essays by South African New Testament Scholars presented to Bruce Manning Metzger during his Visit to South Africa in 1985*, eds. J. H. Petzer and P. J. Hartin. Leiden: E. J. Brill, 1986, pp. 9–17.

'The Macrostructure of the Gospel of Matthew'. *Neot* 16 (1982), pp. 1–20.

'Reference and Rhetoric in the Gospel of Matthew'. Paper given at the SNTS Annual Conference, Cambridge, 1988.

'The Structure of the Gospel of Matthew as Narrative'. *TynBul* 34 (1983), pp. 61–90.

Conzelmann, H. 'Jesus von Nazareth und der Glaube an den Auferstandenen'. In *Der historische Jesus und der kerygmatische Christus*, eds. H. Ristow and K. Matthiae. Berlin: Evangelische Verlagsanstalt, 1960.

Croatto, J. Severino. *Exodus: A Hermeneutics of Freedom*. ET Maryknoll, New York: Orbis Books, 1981.

Crosby, Michael H. *House of Disciples: Church, Economics and Justice in Matthew*. Maryknoll, New York: Orbis Books, 1988.

Cross, F. M. *Canaanite Myth and Hebrew Epic: Essays in the History of the Religion of Israel*. Cambridge, Mass.: Harvard University Press, 1973.

'Yahweh and the God of the Patriarchs'. *HTR* 55 (1962), pp. 225–59.

Crossan, D. 'A Form for Absence: The Markan Creation of Gospel'. *Semeia* 12 (1978), pp. 41–55.

Culley, Robert. 'Introduction'. *Semeia* 62 (1993), pp. vii–xiii.

Culpepper, R. Alan. *Anatomy of the Fourth Gospel: A Study in Literary Design*. FFNT. Philadelphia: Fortress, 1983.

'Story and History in the Gospels'. *RevExp* 81 (1984), pp. 467–78.

Culver, R. D. 'What is the Church's Commission? Some Exegetical Issues in Matthew 28:16–20'. *BETS* 10 (1967), pp. 115–26.

Cunningham, P. A. *Jesus and the Evangelists: The Ministry of Jesus in the Synoptic Gospels*. New York: Paulist Press, 1988.

Dalman, Gustaf. *Aramäisch-neuhebräisches Handwörterbuch*. 2nd edition. Frankfurt: Kauffmann, 1922.

Arbeit und Sitte in Palästina. Volume III, 2nd edition. Hildesheim: Georg Olms, 1964.

The Words of Jesus. ET Edinburgh: T. and T. Clark, 1902.

Daube, D. *The New Testament and Rabbinic Judaism*. London: Athlone, 1956.

Davies, G. H. *Exodus: Introduction and Commentary*. Torch Bible Commentaries. London: SCM Press, 1967.

'Presence of God'. *IDB* 3. Nashville and New York: Abingdon, 1962, pp. 874–5.

Davies, Margaret. *Matthew*. Sheffield: JSOT Press, 1993.

Davies, W. D. *The Gospel and the Land: Early Christianity and Jewish Territorial Doctrine*. Berkeley: University of California Press, 1974.

The Setting of the Sermon on the Mount. Cambridge: Cambridge University Press, 1964.

and Allison, Dale. *A Critical and Exegetical Commentary on The Gospel*

According to Saint Matthew. Volume I: *Matthew 1–7*. Volume II: *Matthew 8–18*. ICC. Edinburgh: T. and T. Clark, 1988, 1991.

Davis, C. T. 'Tradition and Redaction in Mt 1:18–2:23'. *JBL* 90 (1971), pp. 404–21.

Delling, Gerhard. 'παρθένος'. *TDNT* V, ed. G. Friedrich. ET Grand Rapids: Eerdmans, 1967, pp. 826–37.

Derrett, J. D. M. ' "Where Two or Three are Convened in My Name ...": A Sad Misunderstanding'. *ExpT* 91 (3, 1979), pp. 83–6.

Detweiler, Robert. 'After the New Criticism: Contemporary Methods of Literary Interpretation'. In *Orientation by Disorientation*, ed. R. A. Spencer, pp. 3–23.

Dibelius, Martin. *Die Formgeschichte des Evangeliums*. 4th edition. Tübingen: J. C. B. Mohr, 1961. ET *From Tradition to Gospel*. London: Ivor Nicholson and Watson, 1934.

Di Marco, A. 'Der Chiasmus in der Bibel, 3.Teil'. *LB* 38 (1976), pp. 37–58.

Dodd, C. H. *New Testament Studies*. Manchester University Press, 1953.

'The "Primitive Catechism" and other Sayings of Jesus'. In his *More New Testament Studies*. Manchester: Manchester University Press, 1968, pp. 11–29.

Donaldson, Terence L. *Jesus on the Mountain: A Study in Matthean Theology*. JSNTSS 8. Sheffield: JSOT Press, 1985.

Downing, F. G. 'Contemporary Analogies to the Gospels and Acts'. In *Synoptic Studies: The Ampleforth Conferences of 1982 and 1983*, ed. C. M. Tuckett. JSNTSS 7. Sheffield: JSOT Press, 1984, pp. 51–66.

Drazin, Israel. *Targum Onkelos to Exodus: An English Translation of the Text With Analysis and Commentary*. Hoboken: Ktav, 1990.

Driver, S. R. *The Book of Exodus*. Cambridge: Cambridge University Press, 1911.

Duke, Paul D. *Irony in the Fourth Gospel*. Atlanta: John Knox, 1985.

Dunn, J. D. G. *Christology in the Making: A New Testament Inquiry into the Origins of the Doctrine of the Incarnation*. Philadelphia: Westminster, 1980.

Jesus and the Spirit: A Study of the Religious and Charismatic Experiences of Jesus and the First Christians as Reflected in the New Testament. Philadelphia: Westminster, 1975.

Unity and Diversity in the New Testament: An Inquiry into the Character of Earliest Christianity. Philadelphia: Westminster, 1977.

Dupont, J. 'Nom de Jésus'. *DBSup* 6 (1960), p. 535.

Durham, J. I. *Exodus*. Word Biblical Commentaries 3. Waco, Texas: Word, 1987.

Eagleton, Terry. *Criticism and Ideology*. London: New Left Books, 1976.

Literary Theory: An Introduction. London: Blackwell, 1983.

Edgar, S. L. 'The New Testament and Rabbinic Messianic Interpretation'. *NTS* 5 (1958), pp. 47–54.

Edwards, R. A. *Matthew's Story of Jesus*. Philadelphia: Fortress Press, 1985.

'Reading Matthew: The Gospel as Narrative'. *Listening* 24 (1989), pp. 251–61.

'Uncertain Faith: Matthew's Portrayal of the Disciples'. In *Discipleship in the New Testament*, ed. Fernando Segovia. Philadelphia: Fortress, 1985, pp. 47–61.

Eissfeldt, Otto. *The Old Testament: An Introduction*. ET Oxford: Blackwell, 1965.

Ellis, E. E. 'Gospel Criticism: A Perspective on the State of the Art'. In *Das Evangelium und die Evangelien*, ed. P. Stuhlmacher, pp. 27–54.

Paul's Use of the Old Testament. 1957. Reprinted, Grand Rapids: Baker, 1981.

Ellis, I. P. 'But Some Doubted'. *NTS* 14 (1967/8), pp. 574–80.

Ellis, P. F. *Matthew: His Mind and His Message*. Collegeville: Liturgical Press, 1974.

Englezakis, B. '*Thomas*, Logion 30'. *NTS* 25 (1979), pp. 262–72.

Fackenheim, E. L. *God's Presence in History: Jewish Affirmations and Philosophical Reflections*. New York: New York University Press, 1970.

Fenton, J. C. 'Inclusio and Chiasmus in Matthew'. *SE* 1, ed. F. L. Cross (TU 73. Berlin: Akademie Verlag, 1959), pp. 174–9.

'Matthew and the Divinity of Jesus (Matthew 1:20–23)'. In *Studia Biblica 1978* 2, ed. E. A. Livingstone. Sheffield: JSOT Press, 1980.

Saint Matthew. Harmondsworth: Penguin, 1963.

Filson, Floyd V. *The Gospel According to St Matthew*. BNTC. London: Adam and Charles Black, 1960.

Finan, Barbara. 'Panentheism and Interpersonal Presence: A Trinitarian Perspective'. *Listening* 24 (1989), pp. 73–84.

Finkel, Asher, and Frizzell, Lawrence, eds. *Standing Before God: Studies on Prayer in Scriptures and Tradition with Essays: In Honor of John M. Oesterreicher*. New York: KTAV, 1981.

Forkman, G. *The Limits of Religious Community*. Lund: Coniectanea Biblica, 1972.

Forster, E. M. *Aspects of the Novel*. New York: Harcourt Brace, 1927.

Fowler, Robert. *Loaves and Fishes: The Function of the Feeding Stories in the Gospel of Mark*. SBLDS 54. Chico, Calif.: Scholars Press, 1981.

'Who is "The Reader" of Mark's Gospel?' In *SBLSP 1983*. Atlanta: Scholars Press, 1983, pp. 31–53.

France, R. T. *The Gospel According to Matthew: An Introduction and Commentary*. Leicester: Inter-Varsity Press, 1985.

Jesus and the Old Testament. London: Tyndale Press, 1971.

Matthew: Evangelist and Teacher. Grand Rapids: Zondervan, 1989.

'Scripture, Tradition and History in the Infancy Narratives of Matthew'. In *Gospel Perspectives* II, eds. R. T. France and D. Wenham. Sheffield: JSOT Press, 1981, pp. 239–66.

'The Worship of Jesus: A Neglected Factor in Christological Debate?' In *Christ the Lord: Studies in Christology Presented to Donald Guthrie*, ed. H. H. Rowden. Leicester: Inter-Varsity Press, 1982, pp. 17–36.

Frankemölle, Hubert. *Jahwebund und Kirche Christi: Studien zur Form- und Traditionsgeschichte des Evangeliums nach Matthäus*. NTAbh new series 10. Münster: Aschendorff, 1974.

Freedman, H. and Simon, M., eds. *Midrash Rabbah*. 10 volumes. London: Soncino Press, 1939.

Freyne, Sean. *Galilee, Jesus and the Gospels: Literary Approaches and Historical Investigations.* Philadelphia: Fortress Press, 1988.

Frizzell, Lawrence, ed. *God and His Temple – Reflections on Professor Terrien's 'The Elusive Presence: Toward a New Biblical Theology'.* Institute of Judaeo-Christian Studies. S. Orange, N.J.: Seton Hall University, 1980.

Frye, Northrop. 'Literary Criticism'. In *The Aims and Methods of Scholarship in Modern Languages and Literature,* ed. J. Thorpe. New York, 1963, pp. 57–69.

Frye, Roland. 'A Literary Perspective for the Criticism of the Gospels'. In *Jesus and Man's Hope* II, eds. D. G. Miller and D. Hadidian. Pittsburgh: Pittsburgh Theological Seminary, 1971, pp. 193–221.

Fuller, R. H. 'The Conception/Birth of Jesus as a Christological Moment'. *JSNT* 1 (1978), pp. 37–52.

The Formation of the Resurrection Narratives. New York, Macmillan, 1971.

The Foundations of New Testament Christology. New York: Scribners, 1965.

'The Virgin Birth: Historical Fact or Kerygmatic Truth?' *BR* 1 (1956), pp. 1–8.

Gadamer, Hans-Georg. *Truth and Method.* ET London: Sheed and Ward, 1975.

Gaechter, P. *Die literarische Kunst im Matthäusevangelium.* SBS 7. Stuttgart: Verlag Katholisches Bibelwerk, 1965.

Das Matthäus-Evangelium. Innsbruck: Tyrolia Verlag, 1963.

Garland, D. E. *The Intention of Matthew 23.* NovTSup 52. Leiden: E. J. Brill, 1979.

Gärtner, Bertil. 'The Habakkuk Commentary (DSH) and the Gospel of Matthew'. *ST* 8 (1955), pp. 1–24.

The Temple and the Community in Qumran and the New Testament. SNTSMS 1. Cambridge: Cambridge University Press, 1965.

Gaston, Lloyd. *No Stone on Another: Studies in the Significance of the Fall of Jerusalem in the Synoptic Gospels.* NovTSup 23. Leiden: Brill, 1970.

Genette, Gerard. *Narrative Discourse: An Essay in Method.* ET Oxford: Blackwell, 1980.

Gerhardsson, Birger. *The Mighty Acts of Jesus According to Matthew.* ScrMin 1978/79: 5. ET Lund: C. W. K. Gleerup, 1979.

The Testing of God's Son. CBNT 2.1. Lund: C. W. K. Gleerup, 1966.

Gibbs, J. M. 'Mark 1.1–15, Matthew 1.1–4.16, Luke 1.1–4.30, John 1.1–51: The Gospel Prologues and their Function'. *SE* 6, ed. E. A. Livingstone (TU 112. Berlin: Akademie Verlag, 1973), pp. 154–88.

Giblin, C. H. 'A Note on Doubt and Reassurance in Matthew 28:16–20'. *CBQ* 37 (1975), pp. 68–75.

Gnilka, J. *Das Matthäusevangelium.* HTKNT I/1, 2. Freiburg: Herder, 1986, 1988.

Goldberg, A. M. *Untersuchungen über die Vorstellung von der Schekhinah in der frühen rabbinischen Literatur.* SJ 5. Berlin, 1969.

Goldin, J. *The Living Talmud: The Wisdom of the Fathers.* New York: New American Library, 1957.

Görg, Manfred. '"Ich bin mit Dir": Gewicht und Anspruch einer Redeform im Alten Testament'. *TGl* 70 (1980), pp. 214–40.

Gorman, Frank. 'When Law Becomes Gospel: Matthew's Transformed Torah'. *Listening* 24 (1989), pp. 227–40.

Gottwald, Norman K. *The Tribes of Yahweh: A Sociology of the Religion of Liberated Israel, 1250–1050 BCE.* London: SCM Press, 1979.

Goulder, Michael D. *Midrash and Lection in Matthew.* London: SPCK, 1974.

Gray, G. B. *Isaiah.* ICC. Edinburgh: T. and T. Clark, 1912.

Gray, John. *Joshua, Judges and Ruth.* NCB. London: Marshall, Morgan and Scott, 1986.

Gray, Sherman W. *The Least of My Brothers. Matthew 25:31–46: A History of Interpretation.* SBLDS 114. Atlanta: Scholars Press, 1989.

Green, H. B. 'The Command to Baptize and Other Interpolations'. *SE* 4 (TU 102. Berlin: Akademie Verlag, 1968), pp. 60–3.

  The Gospel According to Matthew. NClB. Oxford: Oxford University Press, 1975.

  'The Structure of St Matthew's Gospel'. *SE* 4 (TU 102. Berlin: Akademie Verlag, 1968), pp. 47–59.

Greenberg, Moshe. *Understanding Exodus.* Melbon Research Center Series 2/1: *The Heritage of Biblical Israel.* New York: Behrman House, 1969.

Greeven, Heinrich. 'προσκυνέω'. *TDNT* VI, ed. G. Friedrich. ET Grand Rapids: Eerdmans, 1968, pp. 758–66.

Grundmann, Walter. *Das Evangelium nach Matthäus.* THKNT, 2nd edition. Berlin: Evangelische Verlagsanstalt, 1981.

  'σύν–μετά'. *TDNT* VII, ed. G. Friedrich. ET Grand Rapids: Eerdmans, 1971, pp. 766–97.

Guelich, Robert A. 'The Gospel Genre'. In *Das Evangelium und die Evangelien*, ed. Peter Stuhlmacher, pp. 183–219.

  The Sermon on the Mount: A Foundation for Understanding. Waco, Texas: Word Books, 1982.

Gundry, Robert. *Matthew: A Commentary on his Literary and Theological Art.* Grand Rapids: Eerdmans, 1982.

  'Recent Investigations into the Literary Genre "Gospel"'. In *New Dimensions in New Testament Study*, eds. R. N. Longenecker and M. C. Tenney. Grand Rapids: Zondervan, 1974, pp. 97–114.

  The Use of the Old Testament in St Matthew's Gospel with Special Reference to the Messianic Hope. NovTSup 18. Leiden: E. J. Brill, 1967.

Hagner, Donald. *Matthew 1–13.* Word Bible Commentary 33A. Dallas: Word, 1993.

Hahn, F. *Mission in the New Testament.* 1963. ET London: SCM Press, 1965.

Hamerton-Kelly, R. G. *Pre-Existence, Wisdom and the Son of Man.* SNTSMS 21. Cambridge: Cambridge University Press, 1973.

Hammershaimb, E. 'The Immanuel Sign: Some Aspects of Old Testament Prophecy from Isaiah to Malachi'. *ST* 3 (1951), pp. 124–42.

Haran, Menahem. 'The Divine Presence in the Israelite Cult and the Cultic Institutions'. *Bib* 50 (1969), pp. 251–67.

'The Nature of the "*'ohel mo'edh*" in Pentateuchal Sources'. *JSS* 5 (1960), pp. 50–65.

'The Religion of the Patriarchs: An Attempt at a Synthesis'. *ASTI* 4 (1965), pp. 30–55.

'The Shining of Moses' Face: A Case Study in Biblical and Ancient Near Eastern Iconography'. In *In the Shelter of Elyon*, Festschrift G. W. Ahlström, eds. W. Boyd Barrick and John R. Spencer. JSOTSS 31. Sheffield: JSOT Press, 1984, pp. 159–73.

Hare, D. R. A. *Matthew*. Louisville: John Knox, 1993.

The Theme of the Jewish Persecution of Christians in the Gospel According to St Matthew. SNTSMS 6. Cambridge: Cambridge University Press, 1967.

and Harrington, Daniel J. '"Make Disciples of All the Gentiles" (Matthew 28:19)'. *CBQ* 37 (1975), pp. 359–69.

Harrington, Daniel. *The Gospel of Matthew*. Sacra Pagina 1. Collegeville: Liturgical Press, 1991.

Hartman, L. 'Scriptural Exegesis in the Gospel of St Matthew and the Problem of Communication'. In *L'évangile selon Matthieu*, ed. M. Didier, pp. 131–52.

Hawkins, J. C. *Horae synopticae*. Revised edition. Oxford: Clarendon, 1909.

Held, H. J. 'Matthew as Interpreter of the Miracle Stories'. In *Tradition and Interpretation in Matthew*, eds. G. Bornkamm, G. Barth and H. J. Held. 2nd edition. ET London: SCM Press, 1982, pp. 165–299.

Hengel, Martin. *Judaism and Hellenism: Studies in their Encounter in Palestine during the Early Hellenistic Period*. 2 volumes. ET Philadelphia: Fortress, 1974.

Herford, R. Travers. *Christianity in Talmud and Midrash*. New Jersey: Williams and Norgate, 1966.

Hill, David. 'The Figure of Jesus in Matthew's Gospel: A Response to Professor Kingsbury's Literary-Critical Probe'. *JSNT* 21 (1984), pp. 37–52.

The Gospel of Matthew. NCB. London: Marshall, Morgan and Scott, 1972.

Greek Words and Hebrew Meanings: Studies in the Semantics of Soteriological Terms. SNTSMS 5. Cambridge: Cambridge University Press, 1967.

Hirsch, E. D. Jr. *Validity in Interpretation*. New Haven, Conn.: Yale University Press, 1967.

Holmes, W. H. G. *The Presence of God: A Study in Divine Immanence and Transcendence*. London: SPCK, 1923.

Holtzmann, H. J. *Die Synoptiker*. HKNT I.1. Tübingen: J. C. B. Mohr, 1901.

Horst, R. W. van der. 'Once More: The Translation of οἱ δέ in Matthew 28.17'. *JSNT* 27 (1986), pp. 27–30.

Howell, David. *Matthew's Inclusive Story: A Study in the Narrative Rhetoric of the First Gospel*. JSNTSS 42. Sheffield: JSOT Press, 1990.

Hubbard, B. J. *The Matthean Redaction of a Primitive Apostolic Commis-*

sioning: An Exegesis of Matthew 28:16–20. SBLDS 19. Missoula, Mont.: Scholars Press, 1974.

Hübner, H. Das Gesetz in der synoptischen Tradition. Witten: Luther-Verlag, 1973.

Hummel, R. Die Auseinandersetzung zwischen Kirche und Judentum im Matthäusevangelium. BET 33. Munich: Chr. Kaiser Verlag, 1963.

Hurtado, Larry. One God, One Lord: Early Christian Devotion and Ancient Jewish Monotheism. London: SCM Press, 1988.

Hyatt, J. P. Commentary on Exodus. NCB. London: Oliphants, 1971.

Iser, Wolfgang. The Act of Reading: A Theory of Aesthetic Response. Baltimore: Johns Hopkins University Press, 1978.

The Implied Reader: Patterns in Communication in Prose Fiction from Bunyan to Beckett. Baltimore: Johns Hopkins University Press, 1974.

Jeremias, Joachim. Jerusalem in the Time of Jesus. ET Philadelphia: Fortress, 1969.

Jesus' Promise to the Nations. ET London: SCM Press, 1958.

New Testament Theology. ET New York: Charles Scribner's Sons, 1971.

Jeremias, Jörg. Theophanie: Die Geschichte einer alttestamentliche Gattung. WMANT 10. Neukirchen-Vluyn: Neukirchener Verlag, 1965.

Johannessohn, Martin. Der Gebrauch der Präpositionen in der Septuaginta. Göttingen: Gesellschaft der Wissenschaften, 1925.

Johnson, A. R. 'Aspects of the Use of the Term pānîm in the Old Testament'. In Festschrift Otto Eissfeldt zum 60 Geburtstage, ed. J. Fück. Halle: Niemeyer, 1947, pp. 155–9.

Johnson, L. T. 'On Finding the Lukan Community: A Cautious Cautionary Essay'. In SBLSP 1979 1, ed. Paul Achtemeier. Missoula: Scholars Press, 1979, pp. 87–100.

Johnson, M. D. The Purpose of the Biblical Genealogies. SNTSMS 8. 2nd edition. Cambridge: Cambridge University Press, 1988.

'Reflections on a Wisdom Approach to Matthew's Christology'. CBQ 36 (1974), pp. 44–64.

Kaiser, Otto. Isaiah 1–12. 2nd edition. ET John Bowden. London: SCM Press, 1983.

Kea, Perry. 'Writing a bios: Matthew's Genre Choices and Rhetorical Situation'. In SBLSP 1994. Atlanta: Scholars Press, 1994.

Keck, Leander. 'Ethics in the Gospel According to Matthew'. Iliff Review 40 (1984), pp. 39–56.

'Toward the Renewal of New Testament Christology'. NTS 32 (1986), pp. 362–77.

'Will the Historical-Critical Method Survive? Some Observations'. In Orientation by Disorientation, ed. R. A. Spencer, pp. 115–27.

Kee, Howard. 'Messiah and the People of God'. In Understanding the Word, ed. J. C. Butler. Sheffield: JSOT Press, 1985, pp. 341–58.

Kermode, Frank. The Genesis of Secrecy: On the Interpretation of Narrative. Cambridge, Mass.: Harvard University Press, 1979.

Kieffer, René. 'Was heißt das, einen Text zu kommentieren?' BZ 20 (1976), pp. 212–16.

Kilian, Rudolf. Die Verheißung Immanuels Jes 7,14. SBS 35. Stuttgart: Verlag Katholisches Bibelwerk, 1968.

Kilpatrick, G. D. *The Origins of the Gospel According to St Matthew.* Oxford: Clarendon, 1946.

Kingsbury, J. D. *The Christology of Mark's Gospel.* Philadelphia: Fortress, 1983.

'Composition and Christology of Matthew 28:16–20'. *JBL* 93 (1974), pp. 573–84.

'The Developing Conflict between Jesus and the Jewish Leaders in Matthew's Gospel: A Literary-Critical Study'. *CBQ* 49 (1987), pp. 57–73.

'The Figure of Jesus in Matthew's Story: A Literary-Critical Probe'. *JSNT* 21 (1984), pp. 3–36.

'The Figure of Jesus in Matthew's Story: A Rejoinder to David Hill'. *JSNT* 25 (1985), pp. 61–81.

Jesus Christ in Matthew, Mark and Luke. Philadelphia: Fortress, 1981.

'The "Jesus of History" and the "Christ of Faith" in Relation to Matthew's View of Time – Reaction to a New Approach'. *CTM* 37 (1966), pp. 502–8.

Matthew. 2nd edition, Proclamation Commentaries. Philadelphia: Fortress, 1986.

Matthew as Story. 2nd edition. Philadelphia: Fortress, 1988.

Matthew: Structure, Christology, Kingdom. Philadelphia: Fortress, 1975; London: SPCK, 1976.

'Observations on the "Miracle Chapters" of Matthew 8–9'. *CBQ* 40 (1978), pp. 559–73.

The Parables of Jesus in Matthew 13. London: SPCK, 1969.

'Reflections on "The Reader" of Matthew's Gospel'. *NTS* 34 (1988), pp. 442–60.

'The Title "Son of David" in Matthew's Gospel'. *JBL* 95 (1976), pp. 591–602.

'The Verb *akolouthein* ("to follow") as an Index to Matthew's View of His Community'. *JBL* 97 (1978), pp. 56–73.

Kirk, J. A. *Liberation Theology: An Evangelical View from the Third World.* Atlanta: John Knox, 1979.

Klostermann, E. *Das Matthäusevangelium.* 2nd edition. Tübingen: J. C. B. Mohr, 1927.

Knight, G. A. F. *Theology as Narration: A Commentary on the Book of Exodus.* Edinburgh: Handsel Press, 1976.

Knox, W. L. *The Sources of the Synoptic Gospels.* 2 volumes. Ed. H. Chadwick. Cambridge: Cambridge University Press, 1953, 1957.

Kraus, Hans-Joachim. *Worship in Israel: A Cultic History of the Old Testament.* 1962. ET Oxford: Blackwell, 1966.

Krentz, Edgar. 'The Extent of Matthew's Prologue: Toward the Structure of the First Gospel'. *JBL* 83 (1964), pp. 409–14.

The Historical-Critical Method. Guides to Biblical Scholarship: OT Series. Philadelphia: Fortress, 1975.

Kretzer, A. *Die Herrschaft der Himmel und die Söhne des Reiches: Eine redaktionsgeschichtliche Untersuchung zum Basileiabegriff und Basileiaverständnis im Matthäusevangelium.* SBM 10. Stuttgart: Verlag Katholisches Bibelwerk, 1971.

Krieger, Murray. *A Window to Criticism: Shakespeare's Sonnets and Modern Poetics*. Princeton: Princeton University Press, 1964.

Kümmel, W. G. *Introduction to the New Testament*. Revised edition. ET Nashville: Abingdon, 1975.

Kuntz, J. K. *The Self-Revelation of God*. Philadelphia: Westminster Press, 1967.

Lachs, Samuel. *A Rabbinic Commentary on the New Testament: The Gospels of Matthew, Mark and Luke*. Hoboken, N.J.: KTAV, 1987.

Lagrange, M.-J. *Evangile selon saint Matthieu*. 7th edition. EBib. Paris: Librairie Lecoffre, 1948.

Lange, J. *Das Erscheinen des Auferstandenen im Evangelium nach Matthäus: Eine traditions- und redaktionsgeschichtliche Untersuchung zu Mt. 28,16–20*. FB 11. Würzburg: Echter-Verlag, 1973.

Lanser, Susan S. *The Narrative Act: Point of View in Prose Fiction*. Princeton: Princeton University Press, 1981.

Lategan, Bernard. 'Current Issues in the Hermeneutical Debate'. *Neot* 18 (1984), pp. 1–17.

'Reference: Reception, Redescription, and Reality'. In *Text and Reality*, Bernard Lategan and W. Vorster, pp. 67–93.

'Structural Relations in Matthew 11–12'. *Neot* 11 (1977), pp. 115–29.

and Vorster, Willem. *Text and Reality: Aspects of Reference in Biblical Texts*. SBL Semeia Studies. Philadelphia: Fortress, 1985.

Lemcio, Eugene. *The Past of Jesus in the Gospels*. SNTSMS 68. Cambridge: Cambridge University Press, 1991.

Léon-Dufour, X. 'L'annonce à Joseph'. In *Etudes d'évangile*. Paris, 1965, pp. 65–81.

'The Synoptic Gospels'. In *Introduction to the New Testament*, eds. A. Robert and A. Feuillet. New York: Declée, 1965, pp. 140–321.

Levenson, Jon. 'The Jerusalem Temple in Devotional and Visionary Experience'. In *Jewish Spirituality: From the Bible Through the Middle Ages*, ed. Arthur Green. New York: Crossroad Publishing Company, 1985, pp. 32–61.

Sinai and Zion: An Entry into the Jewish Bible. Minneapolis: Winston Press, 1985.

Levine, Baruch. 'On the Presence of God in Biblical Religion'. In *Religions in Antiquity: Essays in Memory of E. R. Goodenough*. Leiden: E. J. Brill, 1968, pp. 71–87.

Liddell, J. B., and Scott, R. *A Greek–English Lexicon*. New edition, 2 volumes. Oxford: Clarendon, 1940.

Lindars, Barnabas. *New Testament Apologetic: The Doctrinal Significance of the Old Testament Quotations*. London: SCM Press, 1961.

Lindblom, J. *Geschichte und Offenbarungen*. Lund: C. W. K. Gleerup, 1968.

Lohmeyer, E. *Das Evangelium Matthäus*. KEKNT, 2nd edition. Göttingen: Vandenhoeck und Ruprecht, 1958.

'"Mir ist gegeben alle Gewalt": Eine Exegese von Mt. 28,16–20'. In *In memoriam Ernst Lohmeyer*, ed. W. Schmauch. Stuttgart: Evangelisches Verlagswerk, 1951, pp. 22–49.

Lohr, C. H. 'Oral Techniques in the Gospel of Matthew'. *CBQ* 23 (1961), pp. 403–35.

Luz, Ulrich. 'The Disciples in the Gospel according to Matthew'. In *The Interpretation of Matthew*, ed. G. Stanton, pp. 98–128.

Das Evangelium nach Matthäus, Pt. 1, *Mt 1–7*. Pt. 2, *Mt 8–17*. EKKNT I/1 & 2. Neukirchen-Vluyn: Neukirchener & Benziger, 1985, 1990. ET: *Matthew 1–7: A Commentary*. Trans. W. C. Linss. Minneapolis: Augsburg, 1989.

Matthew in History: Interpretation, Influence, and Effects. Minneapolis: Fortress, 1994.

and Peter Lampe. 'Diskussionsüberblick'. In *Das Evangelium und die Evangelien*, ed. Peter Stuhlmacher, pp. 413–31.

Magness, J. L. *Sense and Absence: Structure and Suspension in the Ending of Mark's Gospel*. SBL Semeia Studies. Atlanta: Scholars Press, 1986.

Mailloux, Steven. *Interpretive Conventions: The Reader in the Study of American Fiction*. London: Cornell University Press, 1982.

Malbon, Elizabeth Struthers. 'Disciples/Crowds/Whoever: Markan Characters and Readers'. *NovT* 28 (1986), pp. 104–30.

Malina, Bruce. 'The Literary Structure and Form of Matt. xxviii:16–20'. *NTS* 17 (1970), pp. 87–103.

and Neyrey, Jerome. *Calling Jesus Names: The Social Value of Labels in Matthew*. Sonoma, Calif.: Polebridge, 1988.

Maly, E. H. '"... The Highest Heavens Cannot Contain You ..." (2 Kgs 8,27): Immanence and Transcendence in the Deuteronomist'. In *Standing Before God*, eds. Asher Finkel and Lawrence Frizzell, pp. 23–30.

Mann, Thomas. *Divine Presence and Guidance in Israelite Traditions: The Typology of Exaltation*. Baltimore and London: Johns Hopkins University Press, 1977.

Manson, T. W. *The Sayings of Jesus*. London: SCM Press, 1937.

Marxsen, W. *The Resurrection of Jesus of Nazareth*. ET London: SCM Press, 1970.

Matera, Frank. 'The Ethics of the Kingdom in the Gospel of Matthew'. *Listening* 24 (1989), pp. 241–50.

'The Plot of Matthew's Gospel'. *CBQ* 49 (1987), pp. 233–53.

'The Prologue as the Interpretive Key to Mark's Gospel'. *JSNT* 34 (1988), pp. 3–20.

May, H. G. 'The God of My Father: A Study of Patriarchal Religion'. *JBR* 9 (1941), pp. 155–200.

'The Patriarchal Idea of God'. *JBL* 60 (1941), pp. 113–28.

McCarthy, Dennis. *Old Testament Covenant*. Richmond: John Knox, 1972.

'The Presence of God and the Prophetic Word'. *Concilium: Scripture* 10, No.5 (Dec. 1969), pp. 12–18.

McConnell, R. S. *Law and Prophecy in Matthew's Gospel*. TD 2. Basle: Reinhardt, 1969.

McKay, K. L. 'The Use of *hoi de* in Matthew 28.17d'. *JSNT* 24 (1985), pp. 71–2.

McKnight, Edgar. *The Bible and the Reader: An Introduction to Literary Criticism*. Philadelphia: Fortress, 1985.

Postmodern Use of the Bible: The Emergence of Reader-Oriented Criticism. Nashville: Abingdon, 1988.

McNeile, A. H. *The Book of Exodus*. London: Methuen, 1908.
　The Gospel According to St Matthew. London: Macmillan and Co., 1915.
　'*Tote* in St. Matthew'. *JTS* 12 (1911), pp. 127–8.
Meeks, W. *The First Urban Christians*. New Haven: Yale, 1983.
　The Moral World of the First Christians. London: SPCK, 1987.
Meier, J. P. 'John the Baptist in Matthew's Gospel'. *JBL* 99 (1980),
　pp. 383–405.
　*Law and History in Matthew's Gospel: A Redactional Study of Mt.
　5:17–48*. AnBib 71. Rome: Biblical Institute Press, 1976.
　'Salvation-History in Matthew: In Search of a Starting Point'. *CBQ* 37
　(1975), pp. 203–15.
　'Two Disputed Questions in Matt. 28:16–20'. *JBL* 96 (1977), pp. 407–24.
　The Vision of Matthew: Christ, Church and Morality in the First Gospel.
　New York: Paulist Press, 1979.
Mendenhall, George. *Law and Covenant in Israel and the Ancient Near
　East*. Pittsburgh: The Biblical Colloquium, 1955.
　The Tenth Generation: The Origins of Biblical Tradition. Baltimore and
　London: Johns Hopkins University Press, 1973.
Metzger, Bruce. 'The Formulas Introducing Quotations of Scripture in the
　New Testament and the Mishnah'. *JBL* 70 (1951), pp. 297–307.
　A Textual Commentary on the Greek New Testament. London, New
　York: United Bible Societies, 1971.
Meyer, B. F. *The Aims of Jesus*. London: SCM Press, 1979.
Meye Thompson, M. 'The Structure of Matthew'. *Studia Biblica et
　Theologica* 12 (1982), pp. 195–238.
Michel, Otto. 'The Conclusion of Matthew's Gospel: A Contribution to
　the History of the Easter Message'. In *The Interpretation of Matthew*,
　ed. G. Stanton, pp. 30–41.
Miller, J. M. and Hayes, J. H. *A History of Ancient Israel and Judah*.
　London: SCM Press, 1986.
Minear, Paul. 'The Disciples and the Crowds in the Gospel of Matthew'.
　ATR Supplementary Series 3 (1974), pp. 28–44.
　Matthew: The Teacher's Gospel. London: Darton, Longman and Todd,
　1984.
Moberly, R. W. L. *At the Mountain of God: Story and Theology in Exodus
　32–34*. JSOTSS 22. Sheffield: JSOT Press, 1983.
　The Old Testament of the Old Testament. Philadelphia: Fortress Press,
　1992.
Mohrlang, Roger. *Matthew and Paul: A Comparison of Ethical Perspec-
　tives*. SNTSMS 48. Cambridge: Cambridge University Press, 1984.
Moore, Stephen. 'Doing Gospel Criticism As/With a Reader'. *BTB* 19
　(1989), pp. 85–93.
　Literary Criticism and the Gospels: The Theoretical Challenge. New
　Haven, Conn.: Yale University Press, 1989.
　*Poststructuralism and the New Testament: Derrida and Foucault at the
　Foot of the Cross*. Minneapolis: Fortress/Augsburg, 1994.
Morgan, Robert, with Barton, John. *Biblical Interpretation*. OBS. Oxford:
　Oxford University Press, 1988.
Morris, Leon. 'The Gospels and the Jewish Lectionaries'. In *Gospel*

Perspectives 3: *Studies in Midrash and Historiography*, eds. R. T. France and David Wenham. Sheffield: JSOT Press, 1983, pp. 129–56.

Moule, C. F. D. 'Fulfilment Words in the New Testament: Use and Abuse'. *NTS* 14 (1967/8), pp. 293–320.

An Idiom Book of New Testament Greek. 2nd edition. Cambridge: Cambridge University Press, 1959.

The Origin of Christology. Cambridge: Cambridge University Press, 1977.

Moulton, W. F., and Geden, A. S. *A Concordance to the Greek Testament.* 3rd edition. Edinburgh: T. and T. Clark, 1926.

Mowinckel, S. *He That Cometh.* ET Nashville and New York: Abingdon, 1954.

Psalmenstudien. 6 volumes in 2. Amsterdam: P. Schippers, 1961.

Murphy-O'Connor, J. 'The Presence of God Through Christ in the Church and in the World'. *Concilium: Scripture* 10, No.5 (Dec. 1969), pp. 54–60.

Murray, J. C. 'The Biblical Problem: The Presence of God'. In *The Problem of God: Yesterday and Today.* New Haven, Conn.: Yale University Press, 1964, pp. 5–30.

Neirynck, Frans. ''ΑΠΟ ΤΟΤΕ 'ΗΡΞΑΤΟ and the Structure of Matthew'. *ETL* 64.1 (1988), pp. 21–59.

'Les femmes au tombeau: étude de la rédaction Matthéenne'. *NTS* 15 (1968/9), pp. 168–90.

'Le rédaction matthéenne et la structure du premier évangile'. In *De Jésus aux évangiles*, ed. I. de la Potterie, pp. 41–73.

Nellessen, E. *Das Kind und seine Mutter.* SBS 39. Stuttgart: Verlag Katholisches Bibelwerk, 1969.

Neusner, Jacob. 'The Absoluteness of Christianity and the Uniqueness of Judaism: Why Salvation is Not of the Jews'. *Int* 43 (1989), pp. 18–31.

From Politics to Piety: The Emergence of Pharisaic Judaism. Englewood Cliffs, N.J.: Prentice-Hall, 1973.

The Idea of Purity in Ancient Judaism. Leiden: E. J. Brill, 1973.

Method and Meaning in Ancient Judaism, Second Series. Chico, Calif.: Scholars Press, 1981.

Nicholson, E. W. *Deuteronomy and Tradition.* Oxford, 1967.

God and His People: Covenant and Theology in the Old Testament. Oxford: Clarendon, 1986.

Nickelsburg, George. *Jewish Literature Between the Bible and the Mishnah: A Historical and Literary Introduction.* London: SCM Press, 1981.

Nolan, B. M. *The Royal Son of God: The Christology of Matthew 1–2 in the Setting of the Gospel.* Göttingen: Vandenhoeck und Ruprecht, 1979.

Noth, Martin. *Exodus: A Commentary.* OTL. ET London: SCM Press, 1962.

A History of Pentateuchal Traditions. 1948. ET Englewood Cliffs, N.J.: Prentice-Hall, 1972.

Ollenburger, B. C. *Zion, The City of the Great King: A Theological Symbol of the Jerusalem Cult.* JSOTSS 41. Sheffield: JSOT Press, 1987.

Otto, Rudolf. *The Idea of the Holy.* New York: Oxford University Press, 1923.

Overman, Andrew. *Matthew's Gospel and Formative Judaism: The Social World of the Matthean Community*. Minneapolis: Fortress, 1990.

Parke-Taylor, G. H. *Yahweh: The Divine Name in the Bible*. Waterloo, Ontario: Wilfred Laurier University Press, 1975.

Patte, Daniel. *The Gospel According to Matthew: A Structural Commentary on Matthew's Faith*. Philadelphia: Fortress, 1987.

What is Structural Exegesis? Guides to Biblical Scholarship. Philadelphia: Fortress, 1976.

Perkins, Pheme. 'Christology and Mission: Matthew 28:16–20'. *Listening* 24 (1989), pp. 302–9.

The Gnostic Dialogue. New York and Toronto: Paulist Press, 1980.

Resurrection. Garden City: Doubleday, 1984.

Perrin, Norman. 'The Evangelist as Author: Reflections on Method in the Study and Interpretation of the Synoptic Gospels and Acts'. *BR* 17 (1972), pp. 5–18.

'The Interpretation of the Gospel of Mark'. *Int* 30 (1976), pp. 115–24.

Rediscovering the Teaching of Jesus. NTL. London: SCM Press, 1967.

The Resurrection Narratives. London: SCM Press, 1977.

Pesch, R. 'Eine alttestamentliche Ausführungsformel in Matthäus-Evangelium' Part 1: *BZ* 10 (1966), pp. 220–45; Part 2: *BZ* 11 (1967), pp. 79–95.

Matthäus der Seelsorger. SBS 2. Stuttgart: Verlag Katholisches Bibelwerk, 1966.

'Die sogenannte Gemeindeordnung Mt 18'. *BZ* 7 (1963), pp. 220–35.

ed. *Zur Theologie der Kindheitsgeschichten: Der heutige Stand der Exegese*. Schriftenreihe der kath. Akademie Freiburg. Munich: Zink, 1981.

Petersen, Norman. *Literary Criticism for New Testament Critics*. Philadelphia: Fortress, 1978.

'Literary Criticism in Biblical Studies'. In *Orientation by Disorientation*, ed. R. A. Spencer, pp. 25–52.

'Point of View in Mark's Narrative'. *Semeia* 12 (1978), pp. 97–121.

'The Reader in the Gospel'. *Neot* 18 (1984), pp. 38–51.

Rediscovering Paul: Philemon and the Sociology of Paul's Narrative World. Philadelphia: Fortress, 1985.

Phythian-Adams, W. J. *The People and the Presence: A Study of the At-One-Ment*. Oxford University Press, 1942.

Plummer, Alfred. *An Exegetical Commentary on the Gospel According to St Matthew*. 1915. Reprinted, Grand Rapids: Baker Book House, 1982.

Poland, Lynn. *Literary Criticism and Biblical Hermeneutics: A Critique of Formalist Approaches*. Chico, Calif.: Scholars Press, 1985.

Polzin, Robert. 'Literary and Historical Criticism of the Bible: A Crisis in Scholarship'. In *Orientation by Disorientation*, ed. R. A. Spencer, pp. 99–114.

Powell, Mark. 'The Plot and Subplots of Matthew's Gospel'. *NTS* 38 (1992), pp. 187–204.

What is Narrative Criticism?. Minneapolis: Fortress, 1990.

Preuß, H. D. ' "... ich will mit dir sein!" ' *ZAW* 80 (1968), pp. 139–73.

"*eth*; '*im*'. *TDOT* I, eds. G. J. Botterweck and Helmer Ringgren. Grand Rapids: Eerdmans, 1974, pp. 449–63.

Pritchard, A. B., ed. *Ancient Near Eastern Texts Relating to the Old Testament.* 3rd edition with supplement. Princeton: Princeton University Press, 1969.

Propp, W. H. 'The Skin of Moses' Face – Transfigured or Disfigured?'. *CBQ* 49 (1987), pp. 375–86.

Przybylski, Benno. *Righteousness in Matthew and his World of Thought.* SNTSMS 41. Cambridge: Cambridge University Press, 1980.

'The Role of Mt. 3:13–4:11 in the Structure and Theology of the Gospel of Matthew'. *BTB* 4 (1974), pp. 222–35.

Rad, Gerhard von. *Old Testament Theology.* 2 volumes. ET New York: Harper, 1962, 1965.

Rahlfs, A. *Septuaginta.* 2 volumes in one. Stuttgart: Deutsche Bibelgesellschaft, 1935, 1979.

Rahner, Karl. 'The Presence of the Lord in the Christian Community at Worship'. In *Theological Investigations* X, trans. David Bourke. New York: Seabury, 1973, pp. 71–83.

Reindl, J. *Das Angesicht Gottes im Sprachgebrauch des Alten Testaments.* Erfurter Theologische Studien 25. Leipzig: St Benno-Verlag, 1970.

Renwick, David. *Paul, the Temple, and the Presence of God.* Brown Judaic Studies 224. Atlanta: Scholars Press, 1991.

Rhoads, David. 'Narrative Criticism and the Gospel of Mark'. *JAAR* 50 (1982), pp. 411–34.

and Michie, Donald. *Mark as Story: An Introduction to the Narrative of a Gospel.* Philadelphia: Fortress, 1982.

Rice, G. 'The Interpretation of Isaiah 7:15–17'. *JBL* 96 (1977), pp. 363–9.

'A Neglected Interpretation of the Immanuel Prophecy'. *ZAW* 90 (1978), pp. 220–7.

Rigaux, Beda. *Dieu l'a ressuscité: exégèse et théologie biblique.* Gembloux: Duculot, 1973.

The Testimony of St Matthew. ET Chicago: Franciscan Herald Press, 1968.

Robinson, J. A. T. *Jesus and His Coming.* London: SCM Press, 1957.

Redating the New Testament. London, 1976.

Robinson, J. M. 'Jesus as Sophos and Sophia: Wisdom Traditions and the Gospels'. In *Aspects of Wisdom in Judaism and Early Christianity*, ed. R. L. Wilken. Notre Dame: University of Notre Dame Press, 1975, pp. 1–16.

' "Logoi Sophon?": On the Gattung of Q'. In *Trajectories through Early Christianity*, eds. James Robinson and Helmut Koester. Philadelphia: Fortress, 1971, pp. 71–113.

'On the *Gattung* of Mark (and John)'. In *Jesus and Man's Hope* I, ed. D. G. Buttrick. Pittsburgh: Pittsburgh Theological Seminary, 1970, pp. 99–129. Reprinted in his *The Problem of History in Mark and other Marcan Studies.* Philadelphia: Fortress, 1982, pp. 11–39.

and Koester, H. *Trajectories Through Early Christianity.* Philadelphia: Fortress, 1971.

Robinson, T. H. *The Gospel of Matthew.* London: Hodder and Stoughton, 1928.

Rohde, Joachim. *Rediscovering the Teaching of the Evangelists*. NTL. ET London: SCM Press, 1968.

Rowland, Christopher. *Christian Origins*. London: SPCK, 1985.

The Open Heaven: A Study of Apocalyptic in Judaism and Early Christianity. London: SPCK, 1982.

Sabourin, Leopold. *The Gospel According to Matthew*. Bandra, Bombay, India: St Paul Publications, 1982.

Saldarini, Anthony. *Matthew's Christian-Jewish Community*. Chicago: University of Chicago, 1994.

Sand, A. *Das Gesetz und die Propheten: Untersuchungen zur Theologie des Evangeliums nach Matthäus*. BU 11. Regensburg: Pustet, 1974.

Sanders, E. P. *Jesus and Judaism*. London: SCM Press, 1985.

Paul and Palestinian Judaism: A Comparison of Patterns of Religion. London: SCM Press, 1977.

and Davies, Margaret. *Studying the Synoptic Gospels*. London: SCM Press; Philadelphia: Trinity Press International, 1989.

Sanders, J. A. 'Mysterium Salutis'. In *Ecumenical Institute for Advanced Theological Studies: Year Book 1972–73*. Jerusalem: Tantur, 1973, pp. 105–27.

Sandmel, Samuel. 'Parallelomania'. *JBL* 81 (1962), pp. 1–13.

Schaberg, Jane. *The Father, Son and the Holy Spirit: The Triadic Phrase in Matthew 28:19b*. SBLDS 61. Chico, Calif.: Scholars Press, 1982.

The Illegitimacy of Jesus: A Feminist Theological Interpretation of the Infancy Narrative. San Francisco: Harper and Row, 1987.

Schenk, Wolfgang. 'Das Präsens Historicum als makrosyntaktischen Gliederrungssignal im Matthäusevangelium'. *NTS* 22 (1976), pp. 464–75.

Die Sprache des Matthäus. Göttingen, 1987.

Schieber, H. 'Konzentrik im Matthäusschluss. Ein form- und gattungskritischer Versuch zu Matthäus 28,16–20'. *Kairos* 19 (1977), pp. 286–307.

Schlatter, A. *Der Evangelist Matthäus*. 3rd edition. Stuttgart, 1948.

Schmauch, W. *Orte der Offenbarung und der Offenbarungsort im Neuen Testament*. Göttingen: Vandenhoeck und Ruprecht, 1956.

Schmid, J. *Das Evangelium nach Matthäus*. Regensburger NT I. Regensburg: Pustet, 1965.

Schmidt, Thomas. *Hostility to Wealth in the Synoptic Gospels*. JSNTSS 15. Sheffield: JSOT Press, 1987.

Schneider, Johannes. 'προσέρχομαι'. *TDNT* II. Grand Rapids: Eerdmans, 1964, pp. 683–4.

Schniewind, J. *Das Evangelium nach Matthäus*. NTD, 11th edition. Göttingen: Vandenhoeck und Ruprecht, 1968.

Scholes, Robert and Kellogg, Robert. *The Nature of Narrative*. London: Oxford University Press, 1966.

Schürer, Emil. *The History of the Jewish People in the Age of Jesus Christ (175BC–AD 135)*. ET of *Geschichte des judischen Volkes im Zeitalter Jesu Christi*, 1901–9. 3 volumes. Rev. and ed. Geza Vermes and Fergus Millar, Edinburgh: T. and T. Clark, 1973–87.

Schweizer, Eduard. *The Good News According to Matthew*. ET Atlanta: John Knox, 1975.

'Die Kirche des Matthäus'. In his *Matthäus und seine Gemeinde*, pp. 138–70. ET 'Matthew's Church'. In *The Interpretation of Matthew*, ed. G. Stanton, pp. 129–55.

Matthäus und seine Gemeinde. SBS 71. Stuttgart: Verlag Katholisches Bibelwerk, 1974.

'The "Matthean Church"'. *NTS* 20 (1974), pp. 215ff.

'Matthew's View of the Church in his 18th Chapter'. *AusBR* 21 (1973), pp. 7–14.

'Observance of the Law and Charismatic Activity in Matthew'. *NTS* 16 (1969/70), pp. 213–30.

'πνεῦμα: The New Testament'. *TDNT* VI. ET Grand Rapids: Eerdmans, pp. 396–455.

Segundo, Juan Luis. *Liberation of Theology*. ET Maryknoll, New York: Orbis Books, 1976.

Seitz, O. J. F. 'Gospel Prologues: A Common Pattern?' *JBL* 83 (1964), pp. 262–3.

Selden, Raman. *A Reader's Guide to Contemporary Literary Theory*. Brighton: The Harvester Press, 1985.

Senior, D. P. 'The Ministry of Continuity: Matthew's Gospel and the Interpretation of History'. *Bible Today* 82 (1976), pp. 670–6.

The Passion Narrative According to Matthew: A Redactional Study. BETL 29. Leuven: Leuven University, 1975.

Shuler, Philip. *A Genre for the Gospels: The Biographical Character of Matthew*. Philadelphia: Fortress, 1982.

Sievers, Joseph. '"Where Two or Three ...": The Rabbinic Concept of *Shekhinah* and Matthew 18,20'. In *Standing Before God*, eds. Asher Finkel and Lawrence Frizzell, pp. 171–82.

Smith, Morton. *Tannaitic Parallels to the Gospels*. JBL manuscript series 6. Philadelphia: 1951.

Smyth, K. 'Matthew 28: Resurrection as Theophany'. *ITQ* 42 (1975), pp. 259–71.

Soares Prabhu, G. M. *The Formula Quotations in the Infancy Narrative of Matthew: An Inquiry into the Tradition History of Matthew 1–2*. AnBib 63. Rome: Biblical Institute Press, 1976.

'Jesus in the Gospel of Matthew'. *Biblebhashyam* 1 (1975), pp. 37–54.

Spencer, R. A., ed. *Orientation by Disorientation: Studies in Literary Criticism and Biblical Criticism Presented in Honor of William A. Beardslee*. PTMS 35. Pittsburgh: Pickwick, 1980.

Staley, Jeffrey. *The Print's First Kiss: A Rhetorical Investigation of the Implied Reader in the Fourth Gospel*. SBLDS 82. Atlanta: Scholars Press, 1988.

Stanton, Graham. 'The Communities of Matthew'. *Int* 46 (1992), pp. 379–91.

A Gospel for a New People: Studies in Matthew. Edinburgh: T. and T. Clark, 1992.

'The Gospel of Matthew and Judaism'. *BJRL* 66 (1984), pp. 264–84.

'The Gospel Traditions and Early Christological Reflection'. In *Christ, Faith and History*, eds. S. W. Sykes and J. P. Clayton. Cambridge: Cambridge University Press, 1972, pp. 191–204.

Jesus of Nazareth in New Testament Preaching. SNTSMS 27. Cambridge: Cambridge University Press, 1974.

'Matthew: ΒΙΒΛΟΣ, ΕΥΑΓΓΕΛΙΟΝ, or ΒΙΟΣ?'. In ed. I. van Seg-
broeck, et al., *The Four Gospels 1992* (FS F. Neirynck) II.2. Leuven:
University Press and Peeters, 1992, pp. 1188–201.
'On the Christology of Q'. In *Christ and the Spirit in the New Testament*.
Festschrift C. F. D. Moule, eds. B. Lindars and S. S. Smalley. Cambridge: Cambridge University Press, 1973, pp. 25–40.
'The Origin and Purpose of Matthew's Gospel: Matthean Scholarship
from 1945–1980'. *Aufstieg und Niedergang der Römischen Welt* II.25.3,
eds. H. Temporini and W. Haase. Berlin: De Gruyter, 1983,
pp. 1889–951.
'The Origin and Purpose of Matthew's Sermon on the Mount'. In
Tradition and Interpretation in the New Testament, E. E. Ellis Fest-
schrift, ed. G. F. Hawthorne. Grand Rapids: Eerdmans, 1987,
pp. 181–92.
'Revisiting Matthew's Communities'. In SBLSP 1994. Atlanta: Scholars
Press, 1994, pp. 9–23.
'Salvation Proclaimed: Matthew 11:28–30'. *ExpT* 94 (1982), pp. 3–9.
ed. *The Interpretation of Matthew*. Issues in Religion and Theology 3.
London: SPCK, 1983.
Steck, Odil. 'Theological Streams of Tradition'. In *Tradition and Theology
in the Old Testament*, ed. Douglas A. Knight. Philadelphia: Fortress,
1977, pp. 183–214.
Stendahl, Krister. 'Matthew'. In *Peake's Commentary on the Bible*, eds.
M. Black and H. Rowley. London: Thomas Nelson and Sons, 1962,
pp. 769–98.
'Quis et Unde? An Analysis of Matthew 1–2'. In *The Interpretation of
Matthew*, ed. G. Stanton, pp. 56–66.
The School of St Matthew and its Use of the Old Testament. Revised
edition. Philadelphia: Fortress, 1968.
Sternberg, Meir. *Expositional Modes and Temporal Ordering in Fiction*.
London: Johns Hopkins University Press, 1978.
Stock, Augustine. *The Method and Message of Matthew*. Collegeville:
Liturgical Press, 1994.
Stone, M. E. 'Reactions to the Destruction of the Second Temple:
Theology, Perception and Conversion'. *JSJ* 12 (1981), pp. 195–204.
Strack, H. L., and Billerbeck, P. *Kommentar zum Neuen Testament aus
Talmud und Midrasch*. Volumes I–III. Munich: C. H. Beck'sche
Verlagsbuchhandlung, 1956.
Strecker, G. 'The Concept of History in Matthew'. *JAAR* 35 (1967),
pp. 219–30.
Der Weg der Gerechtigkeit: Untersuchung zur Theologie des Matthäus.
FRLANT 82. Göttingen: Vandenhoeck und Ruprecht, 1962.
Streeter, B. H. *The Four Gospels*. London: Macmillan and Co., 1924.
Stuhlmacher, Peter, ed. *Das Evangelium und die Evangelien*. WUNT 28.
Tübingen: J. C. B. Mohr, 1983.
Styler, G. M. 'Stages in Christology in the Synoptic Gospels'. *NTS* 10
(1963/4), pp. 398–409.
Suggs, M. J. *Wisdom, Christology and Law in Matthew's Gospel*. Cam-
bridge, Mass.: Harvard University Press, 1970.

Suleiman, Susan. 'Ideological Dissent from Works of Fiction: Toward a Rhetoric of the *Roman à thèse*'. *Neophilologus* 60 (1976), pp. 162–77.

'Varieties of Audience-Oriented Criticism'. In *The Reader in the Text*, eds. S. R. Suleiman and I. Crosman. Princeton: University Press, 1980, pp. 1–45.

Tagawa, Kenzo. 'People and Community in the Gospel of Matthew'. *NTS* (1969/70), pp. 149–62.

Talbert, Charles. *What is a Gospel? The Genre of the Canonical Gospels.* Philadelphia: Fortress, 1977.

Tannehill, Robert. 'The Disciples in Mark: The Function of a Narrative Role'. *JR* 57 (1977), pp. 386–405.

'Gospel of Mark and Narrative Christology'. *Semeia* 16 (1979), pp. 57–95.

The Narrative Unity of Luke–Acts: A Literary Interpretation. Volume I: *The Gospel According to Luke.* Volume II: *The Acts of the Apostles.* Philadelphia: Fortress, 1986, 1990.

The Sword of His Mouth. Semeia Supplements. Philadelphia: Fortress Press, 1975.

Tatum, W. Barnes. 'The Matthean Infancy Stories: Their Form, Structure and Relation to the Theology of the Evangelist'. Ph.D. dissertation, Duke University, 1966.

'The Origin of Jesus Messiah (Mt 1:1, 18a): Matthew's Use of the Infancy Traditions'. *JBL* 96 (1977), pp. 523–35.

Taylor, V. *The Historical Evidence for the Virgin Birth.* Oxford: Clarendon, 1920.

Terrien, Samuel. *The Elusive Presence: Toward a New Biblical Theology.* Religious Perspectives 26. San Francisco: Harper and Row, 1978.

Theissen, Gerd. *Miracle Stories of the Early Christian Tradition.* Trans. F. McDonagh. Edinburgh: T. and T. Clark, 1983.

Thiselton, Anthony. 'The New Hermeneutic'. In *New Testament Interpretation: Essays on Principles and Methods*, ed. I. Howard Marshall. Grand Rapids: Eerdmans, 1977, pp. 308–33.

'Reader-Response Hermeneutics, Action Models, and the Parables of Jesus'. In *The Responsibility of Hermeneutics*, eds. Roger Lundin, Anthony C. Thiselton and Clarence Walhout. Grand Rapids: Eerdmans, 1985, pp. 79–113.

The Two Horizons: New Testament Hermeneutics and Philosophical Description. Grand Rapids: Eerdmans, 1970.

Thompson, Michael. *Situation and Theology: Old Testament Interpretation of the Syro-Ephraimite War.* Prophets and Historians Series 1. Sheffield: Almond Press, 1982.

Thompson, W. G. 'An Historical Perspective in the Gospel of Matthew'. *JBL* 93 (1974), pp. 243–62.

Matthew's Advice to a Divided Community: Matthew 17:22–18:35. AnBib 44. Rome: Biblical Institute Press, 1970.

Tompkins, Jane. 'Introduction to Reader-Response Criticism'. In *Reader-Reader Criticism: From Formalism to Post-Structuralism*, ed. Jane P. Tompkins. London: Johns Hopkins University Press, 1980, pp. ix–xxvi.

Trilling, W. *Die Christusverkündigung in den synoptischen Evangelien.* Munich: Kösel, 1969.

The Gospel According to St Matthew. NTSR, 2 volumes. ET London: Sheed and Ward, 1969.

Hausordnung Gottes. Düsseldorf, 1960.

Das wahre Israel: Studien zur Theologie des Matthäusevangeliums. 3rd edition, SANT 10. Munich: Kösel-Verlag, 1964.

Tuckett, Christopher. *Reading the New Testament: Methods of Interpretation.* London: SPCK, 1987.

Upkong, Justin. 'The Immanuel Christology of Matthew 25:31–46 in African Context'. In ed. John Pobee, *Exploring Afro-Christology.* Frankfurt: Peter Lang, 1992, pp. 55–64.

Uspensky, Boris. *A Poetics of Composition: The Structure of the Artistic Text and Typology of a Compositional Form.* ET Berkeley, Los Angeles and London: University of California Press, 1973.

Van Aarde, A. G. 'God Met Ons: Dié Teologiese Perspektief van die Matteusevangelie'. D.D. dissertation, University of Pretoria, South Africa, 1982.

'Plot as Mediated through Point of View: Matthew 22:1–14: A Case Study'. In *A South African Perspective on the New Testament: Essays by South African New Testament Scholars presented to Bruce Manning Metzger during his Visit to South Africa in 1985,* eds. Petzer and Hartin. Leiden: E. J. Brill, 1986, pp. 62–75.

van Tilborg, Sjef. *The Jewish Leaders in Matthew.* Leiden: E. J. Brill, 1972.

van Unnik, W. C. '*Dominus Vobiscum*: The Background of a Liturgical Formula'. In *New Testament Essays: Studies in Memory of T. W. Manson,* ed. A. J. B. Higgins. Manchester: Manchester University Press, 1959, pp. 270–305.

'L'usage de σῴζειν "sauver" et ses dérivés dans les évangiles synoptiques'. In *La formation des évangiles: problème synoptique et Formgeschichte.* n.p. 1957.

de Vaux, Roland. 'Arche d'alliance et tente de réunion'. In *A la rencontre de Dieu,* Mémorial A. Gelin. Le Puy, 1961, pp. 55–70. ET: 'Ark of the Covenant and Tent of Reunion'. In his *The Bible and the Ancient Near East.* Garden City: Doubleday, 1971, pp. 136–51.

'God's Presence and Absence in History: The Old Testament View'. *Concilium: Scripture* 10, No.5 (Dec. 1969), pp. 5–11.

'The Revelation of the Divine Name YHWH'. In *Proclamation and Presence: OT Essays in Honour of Gwynne Henton Davies,* eds. John I. Durham and J. Roy Porter. London: SCM Press, 1970, pp. 48–75.

Verseput, Donald. 'The Role and Meaning of the "Son of God" Title in Matthew's Gospel'. *NTS* 33 (1987), pp. 532–56.

Via, Dan O. 'The Church as the Body of Christ in the Gospel of Matthew'. *SJT* 11 (1958), pp. 271–86.

'Structure, Christology, and Ethics in Matthew'. In *Orientation by Disorientation,* ed. R. A. Spencer, pp. 199–217.

Vischer, Wilhelm. *Die Immanuel-Botschaft im Rahmen des königlichen Zionsfestes.* Theologische Studien 45. Zürich: Evangelischer Verlag, 1955.

Vögtle, A. 'Das christologische und ekklesiologische Anliegen von Mt 28.18–20'. *SE* 2, ed. F. L. Cross (TU 87. Berlin: Akademie Verlag, 1964), pp. 266–94.

Messias und Gottessohn: Herkunft und Sinn der Matthäischen Geburts- und Kindheitsgeschichte. Theologische Perspektiven. Düsseldorf: Patmos, 1971.

Vorster, W. S. 'The Historical Paradigm – Its Possibilities and Limitations'. *Neot* 18 (1984), pp. 104–23.

'Mark: Collector, Redactor, Author, Narrator?' *JTSA* 31 (1980), pp. 46–61.

'Meaning and Reference: The Parables of Jesus in Mark 4'. In *Text and Reality*, B. C. Lategan and W. Vorster, pp. 27–65.

Vriezen, T. C. *An Outline of Old Testament Theology*. 2nd edition. Oxford: Blackwell, 1970.

'*Ehje 'aser 'ehje*'. In *Festschrift Alfred Bertholet*, ed. W. Baumgartner, O. Eissfeldt, K. Elliger and L. Post. Tübingen: J. C. B. Mohr, 1950, pp. 498–512.

Waetjen, Herman. 'The Genealogy as the Key to the Gospel According to Matthew'. *JBL* 95 (1976), pp. 220–5.

The Origin and Destiny of Humanness: An Interpretation of the Gospel According to Matthew. Corte Madera, Calif.: Omega, 1976.

Walker, Rolf. *Die Heilsgeschichte im ersten Evangelium*. FRLANT 91. Göttingen: Vandenhoeck und Ruprecht, 1967.

Watson, Francis. Review of R. Morgan, *Interpretation. Theology* 92 (1989), pp. 298–9.

Watts, John. *Isaiah 1–32*. Word Bible Commentary XXIV. Waco, Texas: Word Books, 1985.

Weaver, Dorothy Jean. 'The Missionary Discourse in the Gospel of Matthew: A Literary Critical Analysis'. Ph.D. dissertation, Union Theological Seminary in Virginia, 1987. Published as *Matthew's Missionary Discourse: A Literary Critical Analysis*. JSNTSS 38. Sheffield: JSOT Press, 1990.

Weber, Max. *Economy and Society: An Outline of Interpretive Sociology*. Volume II. Eds. Günther Roth and Claus Wittich. ET Berkeley: University of California Press, 1978.

The Sociology of Religion. ET Boston: Beacon, 1963.

Weeden, T. J. *Mark: Traditions in Conflict*. Philadelphia: Fortress, 1971.

Weiss, B. *Das Matthäus-Evangelium*. 9th edition. Kritisch-exegetischer Kommentar I/1. Göttingen: Vandenhoeck und Ruprecht, 1898.

Westermann, Claus. *Genesis 1–11/Genesis 12–36/Genesis 37–50: A Commentary*, 1974. 3 volumes. ET Minneapolis: Augsburg, 1984, 1985, 1986.

The Promises to the Fathers: Studies on the Patriarchal Narratives. ET Philadelphia: Fortress, 1980.

Wilckens, Ulrich. 'σοφία'. *TDNT* VII. ET Grand Rapids: Eerdmans, 1971, pp. 465–528.

Wildberger, Hans. *Jesaja 1–12*. BKAT 10/1. Neukirchen-Vluyn: Neukirchener Verlag, 1972.

Wimsatt, William, and Beardsley, Monroe. *The Verbal Icon*. Lexington, Ky.: University of Kentucky Press, 1954.

Wink, Walter. *The Bible in Human Transformation: Toward a New Paradigm for Biblical Study*. Philadelphia: Fortress, 1973.

Wittig, Susan. 'A Theory of Polyvalent Reading'. In SBLSP 1975 2, pp. 169–84. Missoula, Mont.: Scholars Press, 1975.

Wolff, Hans Walter. *Frieden ohne Ende: Eine Auslegung von Jes 7,1–17 und 9,1–6*. Neukirchen-Vluyn: Neukirchener Verlag, 1962.

Zahn, T. *Das Evangelium des Matthäus*. Kommentar zum Neuen Testament I. Leipzig: Deichert, 1903.

Ziesler, J. A. 'Matthew and the Presence of Jesus'. *Epworth Review* 11 (1984), Part 1: pp. 55–63; Part 2: pp. 90–7.

Zimmerli, Walther. *Ezekiel*. 1969. ET Hermeneia Commentary, 2 volumes. Philadelphia: Fortress Press, 1979, 1983.

'I Am Yahweh'. In his *I am Yahweh*. Atlanta: John Knox, 1982, pp. 1–28.

INDEX OF PASSAGES

Old Testament

Genesis

1.1–2.3	160	18.26	142
1.13–14	116	20.6–7	114
2.4–25	160	21.3	161
2.23	116	21.12–13	114
3.12	116	21.17	148
3.14–24	125	21.20, 22	114, 139, 146, 154
4.10–16	125	21.33	115
4.23	116	22.1–2	114
5.1–32	160	22.17	116
5.15	116	25.23	114
6.9–9.29	160	26.2–5	114
9.27	194	26.3	114, 139, 140, 141, 142, 147, 153
12–50	113–14	26.3–4	146
12.1–3	114	26.24	114, 116, 139, 140, 141, 142, 146, 147, 152
12.2	116	26.25	115
12.7	114, 115	26.28	139, 146, 154
12.8	115	26.33	115
13.3–4	115	28.10–22	115
13.14–17	114	28.12–15	114
13.16	116	28.14	116
13.18	115	28.15	114, 139, 140, 141, 142, 153, 154, 218
14.17–24	115	28.20	114, 139, 142, 146, 147, 154
14.24	142	31.3	114, 139, 140, 147, 154
15	116	31.5	114, 139, 146, 153, 154
15.1–18	114	31.11–13	114
15.5	116	31.13	114, 139, 141, 142, 147, 153, 154
15.7–21	116	31.24	114
16.7–12	114	32.1–2	114
16.7–15	161	32.2, 7–8	115
17	116	32.12	116
17.1–3	161	32.24–30	114
17.1–22	114	32.30	115
17.4–5	116	33.20	115
17.15–21	161	35.1	114
18.1	115	35.3	114, 139, 147, 166
18.1–33	114	35.7	115
18.18	116	35.9–12	114
18.23	142	35.11	116
		38.25	171

39.2	114, 139, 153	14.11–12	128
39.2–3	146	16.7	127
39.3	114, 139	16.23	120
39.21	114, 139, 146	17.1–7	121
39.23	114, 139, 142, 146	18.19	117, 139, 142
46.2–4	114	18.21–3	123
46.3	116	19	123
48.21	114, 139, 140, 141, 142	19–24	117, 118, 119, 121, 128
		19.1–15	121
Exodus		19.3–6	121
1–3	119–20	19.4	121
1.15	159	19.5–6	121
2.23–7.7	118	19.8	122
3	113, 117–20, 122	19.9	122
3–4	241	19.10–15	71, 122
3–6	121	19.10–17	204
3.1	118	19.11	204
3.2	118	19.12	122
3.2–3	118	19.13	122
3.4	118	19.16	122
3.5	118	19.16–25	122
3.6	118, 119	19.17	122
3.6–7	120	19.18	118
3.7	118	19.18–19	122
3.11	119	19.19	122
3.11–12	149	19.20–5	122
3.11–4.17	149	19.23	122
3.12	117, 119, 120, 139, 140, 142, 147,	20–3	123
	148, 153, 154, 204	20–4	123
3.13	120	20.2, 3, 4	123
3.13–15	118–20, 123	20.5	128
3.14	117, 119–20	20.19	122
3.14–15	119	20.24	195
3.15	120	24	123
3.19–20	121	24.1	204
3.19–22	120	24.1–2	124
4–5	121	24.3, 7	122
4.1	119	24.9–11, 10, 11	124
4.10	119	24.12	204
4.12	120	24.16	127
4.13	120	24.16–17	129
4.15	120	25–7	128
4.19–20	62	25–31	128
4.30–1	121	25.8	125, 128–9, 194
5.2	116	25.9	194
5.22–3	121	25.22	129
6	113	29.42–3	129
6.2–3	117, 118, 120–21, 123	29.42–6	128, 134
6.2–8	121	29.45	194
7.1–12.13	121	29.45–6	125, 129
7.2	215	30.6	129
10.10	117, 139, 140, 141	30.36	129
12.29–36	121	32	125
14.5–20	121	32–4	117–18, 124, 129, 130

32.1–6	124	*Numbers*	
32.7–35	124	5.3	128, 194
32.14	128	10.35–6	128
32.34	125	11.16–17	123
33	125, 238, 240	11.17	173
33–4	117, 204	12.4–9	204
33.1	125	13.16	173
33.2	125	14.10	127
33.3	124, 125, 151	14.18	128
33.4	126	14.27	183
33.5	124, 125, 126, 151	14.42	125, 139
33.6	126	14.42–3	140, 143, 147, 150
33.7	126	14.43	139, 142
33.7–11	124, 125	14.44	125, 151
33.11	126	23.21	139, 140
33.12–14	126	35.34	194
33.12–16	126, 128		
33.12–17	124, 126	*Deuteronomy*	
33.12–23	113	1.3, 41	215
33.14	127	1.42	139, 140, 143, 147, 154
33.14–15	125	2.7	139, 140, 146, 147
33.14–16	216	4.2	215
33.15–16	127	4.7	132
33.15–17	126	4.11–15	118
33.16	127, 129, 142, 237	4.40	217
33.17	127	5.4–5	122
33.18	127, 241	5.29	217
33.18–34.9	124	6.13	226
33.19	119, 120, 128	12.11	215
33.19–23	127	13.11	215
33.20	126, 127	19.15	177, 182
33.22	127	20.1	139, 140, 148, 153
33.23	127	20.4	147
34	125	30.8	215
34.5	128	31.23	139, 140, 142, 147, 148
34.5–7	119	32.15–20	216
34.6	128	32.46–7	216
34.6–7	128	33.2	131
34.9–10	151	33.26	131
34.10	128	34.9	173
34.10–28	124, 128		
34.14	119	*Joshua*	
34.20, 23, 24	128	1.5	139, 140, 141, 149
34.29–35	124	1.7	215
35–40	128	1.9	139, 147
40.34	129	1.17	139, 140, 147, 149
40.34–5	127	3.7	139, 140, 141, 147, 149, 151
40.35	2	6.27	139, 146
		7.12	139, 140, 143, 144
Leviticus		14.12	139, 140, 147
26.12–13	129	22.31	139, 140, 148, 151
25.9	122		
		Judges	
		1.19	139, 147

1.22	139, 140, 142, 147
2.18	139, 148, 173
3.10	173
5.4–5	131
6	118
6.12	139, 145
6.12–13	141, 142, 146
6.13	139, 140, 149
6.16	139, 140, 142, 147
6.34	173
7.12	154
11.29	173
13.3–5	161
13.5	173
13.25	173
14.6, 19	173
15.14	173

Ruth

2.4	139, 140, 145

1 Samuel

3.19	139, 146, 154
3.19–20	151, 173
4.20	148
10.6–7	173
10.7	139, 154
16.13–14	173
16.18	139, 146, 151
17.32	154
17.37	139, 142, 147, 148, 159
18.12	139, 141, 143, 146, 149
18.14	139, 146, 154
18.28	139, 146, 151
20.13	139, 140, 141, 142, 149, 150, 154
23.13	120
28.16	140, 143, 146

2 Samuel

5.10	139, 141, 142, 146, 154
6.15	122
7.3	139, 146, 154
7.6	128
7.8–17	130
7.9	139, 140, 142, 147
7.14	131
7.14–16	131
14.17	139, 142
15.20	120
23.1–7	130
23.2–4	131
23.5	131, 143

1 Kings

1.37	139, 140, 141, 149, 150, 154
6.11–13	131
8.12–13.27	195
8.22–53	132
8.46–53	130
8.57	139, 140, 141, 146, 150
8.57–8	144
9.2–9	130
11.38	139, 140, 142, 144, 146

2 Kings

8.1	120
18.7	139, 144, 146

1 Chronicles

9.20	140
11.9	139, 146
15.28	122
17.2	139, 146
17.8	139, 140, 142, 146
22.11	139, 142, 146, 154
22.16	139, 142, 146
22.18	139, 140, 142, 146
28.20	139, 146, 148

2 Chronicles

1.1	139, 146
13.12	139, 140, 142, 147
15.2	139, 140, 143, 144, 154
15.9	139, 151
15.14	122
17.3	139, 144, 154
19.11	139, 140, 142, 144
20.17	139, 140, 147, 148
25.7	139, 140, 142, 143, 144, 147
32.7	139
32.7–8	140, 147
32.8	139, 148
35.21	139, 141, 148, 151, 154
36.23	139, 141, 142, 147, 148, 156

Ezra

1.3	139, 141, 142, 147, 148
34.30	140

Nehemiah

9.17	128

Esther

6.13	139, 141, 146, 151, 154

Job

29.5	139, 141, 146

Psalms
1.1 192
2.7 131
11.4 133
14.2 133
14.7 133
18 118
19 216
20.3 133
20.7 133
23.4 139, 142, 143, 151
26.8 134
27.4–5 134
46 130–1, 133
46.7 139, 151
46.8 140, 142, 143
46.11 139, 151
46.12 140, 142, 143
47.5 122
48 130, 133
68.8–11 131
68.18 131
72 131
74.2 134, 194
74.7–8 134
76 130–1, 133
76.3, 9 133
80.2, 15 133
86.15 128
89 130
89.19–37 131
89.20–38 131
90.15 148
91.15 139, 140, 142, 144
96–7 133
103.8 128
118.26 190
130.8 173
132 130
139.1 234
139.7–8 157, 234
141.2 135
145.8 128
145.18 132

Isaiah
6.1 124
7.1–9 163
7.3 164
7.14 105, 139, 143, 163–9
7.14–25 164
8.3 164
8.5–8 166
8.8 139, 140, 143, 148, 164–6

8.9–10 166
8.10 139, 140, 143, 148, 164–6
25.6 219
27.13 122
40.3 63
41.10 139, 140, 142, 148
43.2 139, 140, 142
43.5 139, 140, 142, 148
44.3 173
56.7 219
57.15 137
58.11 139, 140, 141, 146, 148
66.2 137

Jeremiah
1 118
1.7 215
1.8 139, 140, 142, 148, 218
1.17 139, 141, 142, 148, 218
1.19 139, 140, 142, 148, 218
15.20 139, 140, 142, 148
20.11 139, 140, 148
30.11 140
42.11 139, 140, 142, 148
44.17–18 134
46.28 139, 140, 142, 148
49.11 218

Ezekiel
11.16 134
11.22–3 134
12.25 120
37.26–8 134
37.28 237

Daniel
7.13–14 203, 212
9.1–2 167

Joel
2.13 128
2.27 135
3.16–17 135

Amos
5.14 139, 140, 142, 144, 148

Jonah
4.2 128

Nahum
1.3 128

Habakkuk
1.5 167

2.17	167
3.3–4	131

Haggai

1.8	135
1.13	137, 139, 140, 142, 218
1.13–14	173
2.4	139, 140, 142, 173, 218
2.4–5	148, 149
2.7	135

Zechariah

1.16	135
2.10–11	135
8.3	135
8.23	139, 140, 142, 146, 148, 151
10.5	139, 141, 148

Malachi

3.1	135
3.16	192

New Testament

Matthew

1	61, 79, 96, 101, 157, 171, 242, 244
1–2	50–64, 78, 79, 80, 101, 157–75, 176, 235, 238, 239, 241
1–9	60
1.1	36, 46, 52–5, 80, 89, 104, 160, 167, 170–1
1.1–2	101
1.1–17	42, 52, 54, 61, 160
1.1–21	168
1.1–23	56
1.1–4.16	155, 172
1.1–4.22	51
1.2	104
1.5–20	101
1.6	90, 170
1.11	54
1.12	54
1.16	55, 160, 170–1
1.17	36, 54, 55, 104, 170–1
1.18	36, 55, 160, 171
1.18–19	162
1.18–25	55, 59, 101, 159–64, 172–4
1.18–2.23	54, 101, 159
1.19	58
1.19–20	39
1.20	53, 55, 100, 101, 160–1, 170
1.20–1	161–2
1.21	45, 46, 56–9, 61, 66, 72, 81–2, 96, 161, 164, 182, 191
1.21–3	36, 57–8, 61–2, 74, 75, 81, 87, 107, 173, 175, 233
1.21–5	171
1.22	33, 45, 168
1.22–3	37, 43, 54–6, 160–2, 171
1.23	3, 17–21, 46, 57, 59, 84, 94, 101, 105, 108, 161–4, 172, 174–5, 191–2, 219, 222, 239, 242. 243
1.24	53, 160–1
1.24–5	55, 58, 161–2, 191
1.24–2.23	101
1.25	57, 160–1, 171
2	52, 58–61, 78, 92, 93–4, 99, 105, 219, 235, 236
2.1	90, 101, 170
2.1–2	60, 104
2.1–10	40
2.1–12	84
2.1–23	75, 159
2.2	40, 59–60, 90, 101, 102, 171, 226
2.3	39, 46, 60, 64, 90, 99, 210
2.3–4	38
2.3–18	60
2.3–23	101
2.4	86, 171
2.5–6	43, 54
2.7–8	60
2.8	40, 101, 171, 212, 226
2.9	60, 90, 101, 212
2.9–10	212
2.10	39, 60, 101
2.11	40, 60, 101, 171, 226
2.12	39, 40, 100, 228
2.12–13	212
2.13	40, 46, 53, 100, 101
2.13–14	39
2.13–15	65, 161
2.15	43, 45, 54, 60, 64–5, 77, 171, 172
2.16	39, 46, 60
2.16–18	40
2.17	45
2.17–18	43, 54
2.19	53, 100, 101
2.19–21	62
2.19–23	62, 161
2.20	46, 101
2.22	39, 101, 204
2.22–3	66
2.23	42, 43, 45, 52, 54
3	52, 64, 93
3–4	172
3.1	42, 52, 63
3.1–12	40, 67
3.1–4.11	51, 63–6, 235

3.2	63, 67, 85, 98, 191	5–9	71
3.3	43, 46, 63	5.1	40, 69, 103, 204
3.4	42, 66	5.1–2	69
3.5–7	65	5.2	45, 215
3.7	64, 66, 67	5.3–10	217
3.7–10	38, 64	5.3–12	81, 177
3.7–12	44, 70	5.5	89
3.8	47, 67, 92	5.6, 10	230
3.8–10	64	5.10–12	72, 197, 224
3.9	64, 104	5.11	210
3.10	66, 67	5.12	231
3.10–12	63	5.17	45
3.11	63, 73, 214	5.17–20	47, 71, 216, 231
3.11–12	63	5.18	44
3.12	64, 67, 86–7	5.18–20	181
3.13	37, 65, 66	5.19	95, 215, 216, 217, 232
3.14	63	5.20	44, 70, 92, 230, 232
3.15	45, 63–4, 210, 230	5.21–2	71
3.16	37, 64–5	5.21–48	231
3.16–17	40, 65, 83, 174	5.22	44, 46
3.17	64–5, 77, 78, 98, 172	5.22–4	95
4.1	37, 46, 65	5.22–44	217
4.1–11	39, 41, 65, 81	5.26	44
4.2	37	5.27–8	71
4.3	40, 46, 77–8, 172	5.28	44
4.6	77–8, 83, 172, 216	5.31–2	71
4.8	103, 204, 210	5.32	44
4.9	226	5.33–4	71
4.9–10	226	5.34	44
4.10	47, 83, 226	5.35	89, 90
4.11	40	5.38–9	71
4.12	51, 76, 98, 204	5.39	44
4.12–16	66	5.43–4	71
4.12–22	51, 82	5.44	44, 197
4.12–25	51	5.47	95
4.12–18.35	66	5.48	47
4.13	66	6.1	230
4.14	45	6.1–18	92
4.14–16	43, 66	6.2	44, 86, 228
4.15–16	104	6.5	44, 86
4.17	45, 51, 66, 67, 70–1, 73, 74, 82, 85, 98, 191	6.10	231
		6.16	44
4.17–16.20	51	6.21	232
4.18	46, 81	6.24	46, 47, 232
4.18–22	67, 94	6.25, 29	44
4.19	71	6.30	77, 80, 206
4.20, 22	40, 71	6.33	47, 230, 231
4.23	35, 42, 45, 67, 71, 86, 215	7.3–5	95
4.23–4	94	7.7–11	181
4.23–5	66	7.12	216
4.24	40, 45	7.13–14	232
4.25	35, 40, 68, 69	7.15–20	217
4.25–6	94	7.16–20	64, 67
5–7	51, 67, 81, 103, 209	7.19	67

7.21	47, 231, 232	9.18	40, 212, 225, 226, 227
7.22	190	9.19	40
7.23	231	9.20	40
7.24	217	9.20–1	35, 39
7.24–7	71	9.21–2	45
7.28	45, 69, 71	9.22	37
7.28–9	39, 69	9.26	40
7.29	38, 45, 68, 69, 209–10	9.27	40, 45, 89
8–9	71	9.28	40
8.1	40, 69, 71, 103, 204	9.31	40
8.1–2	35	9.32–3	35
8.2	40, 45, 225, 226, 227	9.32	40
8.3	45	9.33	39
8.5	40	9.33–6	68
8.5–13	35, 79, 209	9.35	45, 71, 86
8.7	45	9.35–6	35
8.8	45	9.35–11.1	71, 72
8.9	210	9.36	37, 68, 79, 89
8.10	37, 40, 44	10	73, 78, 84, 92, 105–6, 191, 211, 213
8.10–12	64, 71	10.1	179, 203, 210
8.11	44, 104, 232	10.2	203
8.11–12	231	10.2–4	46
8.12	95, 232	10.4	72, 98
8.13	40, 41, 45	10.5	92, 203
8.16	40, 45, 206	10.5–6	68, 72, 79, 106, 223
8.17	43, 45	10.5–42	72
8.18	69	10.6	68, 72, 212
8.19	40	10.7	85, 98, 212
8.21	67, 207	10.14–23	224
8.22	40	10.16	189, 217
8.23	40	10.16–23	73, 197
8.23–7	72, 77, 175, 177, 207, 222, 239	10.17	67, 86
8.24–7	233, 235	10.18	90, 104
8.25	40, 45, 77	10.18–20	73
8.25–6	212	10.21	74
8.26	77, 80	10.22	190
8.27	38, 72, 78	10.23	79, 106
8.29	78, 225	10.25	46
8.33	40	10.32–9	224
9	73	10.35–9	67
9.2	35, 37, 40, 45	10.38	40, 82
9.3	38	10.38–9	98
9.3–18	94	10.40	191, 197–8
9.4	37, 46, 229	10.40–2	193, 233
9.5	45	10.41	231
9.6	45, 210	10.41–2	175, 190, 235, 239
9.6–7	212	10.42	85, 95, 181, 224
9.8	39, 45, 69, 210	11	74
9.9	40, 67	11–12	73–5, 235
9.10–12	231	11.1	45, 72, 203, 215
9.12	35	11.2	40, 41, 76, 80, 98
9.13	212	11.2–6	73, 231
9.14	40	11.4	212
9.15	212	11.5	45, 211, 230

11.6	81	13.1–33	76
11.7	69, 212	13.2	86–7
11.8	90	13.10	40
11.10	217	13.10–17	69
11.10–11	63	13.14–15	43
11.11	95, 232	13.15	45
11.12	232	13.16	81
11.16–19	73, 84	13.16–17	76
11.19	228, 231	13.17	231
11.20	45, 73, 74, 82	13.20	102
11.20–4	73, 95	13.24–30	78
11.25–6	75, 81	13.30	67, 86–7
11.25–7	85, 240	13.31–2	84
11.25–30	75–6, 81, 93, 104, 228, 231	13.34	46
11.27	75, 78, 210, 211, 241	13.35	43, 45
11.28	75	13.36	40
11.28–30	75	13.36–43	95
11.29	89	13.36–52	76
12	74	13.41	231
12.1	38	13.41–3	232
12.1–8	231	13.42	67
12.6	75–6, 91, 93, 106, 175, 222, 224, 235, 239	13.44	102, 215
		13.46	215
12.8	76	13.47	87
12.9	86	13.50	67
12.9–14	86–7, 231	13.51	76
12.10	38	13.51–2	235
12.14	40, 41, 46, 76, 82	13.52	212, 242
12.15	37, 40, 45	13.53	45
12.17	45	13.53–8	158
12.17–21	43	13.54	39, 45, 86
12.18	104	13.55	231
12.21	104, 190	13.57	39
12.22	40, 45	13.58	46
12.23	39, 68, 69, 89	14.1	41
12.25	37	14.1–2	76
12.30	76, 86–7	14.1–12	40, 83
12.31–2	229	14.1–13	98
12.33	217	14.2	211
12.33–5	64, 67	14.3–12	42
12.34	64, 67	14.5	68, 69, 76
12.38–9	229	14.5–6	39
12.38–42	209, 228	14.6	189
12.38–45	84	14.9	39, 90
12.39	38, 212	14.13	40, 76
12.40	82	14.13–21	79, 235
12.41–2	76, 95	14.14	37, 45, 68, 89
12.44	231	14.15	40, 79, 212
12.46	69, 212	14.16, 17	79
12.46–50	103, 158	14.17–19	79
12.47	74	14.19–20	79
12.49–50	95	14.22–33	72, 77, 86, 175, 177, 207, 222, 235, 239
12.50	47, 75, 231		
13	76, 85, 232	14.23	39, 41, 212

14.24	41	16.19	85, 181–2
14.26	37	16.20	81
14.26–8	80	16.21	45, 73, 74, 80, 82, 89, 98, 211
14.28	41, 83	16.21–2	80
14.28–31	81	16.21–3	235
14.30	38, 45, 77, 206	16.21–28.20	51
14.31	37, 77, 80, 104, 206	16.22	83
14.31–3	205–6	16.23	47, 83
14.33	40, 77–8, 80, 98, 104, 225, 226, 227	16.24	40
		16.24–5	100
14.34	77	16.27	242
14.35	40	17.1	102, 204
14.35–6	78	17.1–8	41, 209
15	92	17.4–5	212
15.1–9	78	17.5	64, 83, 98
15.1	40, 78	17.6	38, 227
15.3	38, 216	17.6–7	40, 206–7
15.3–9	47	17.7	104, 206
15.4	83, 216	17.9	83, 98, 102, 204, 216
15.12	40, 78	17.9–13	83
15.12–15	80	17.12	76, 82, 83, 98
15.14	38, 78	17.13	37, 46, 83, 235
15.21–8	35	17.14	40, 69, 225
15.21	78	17.14–21	80, 84, 86, 177, 235
15.22	45, 89	17.15	45
15.23	40, 79	17.17	19, 84, 175, 222, 239
15.24	68, 79	17.17–20	207
15.25	40, 225, 226, 227	17.18	45
15.28	40, 45	17.19	40
15.29	103, 204	17.20	80, 84, 206
15.30	40, 45, 69	17.21–2	98
15.30–2	39	17.22	89
15.31	69	17.22–3	82, 85
15.32	68, 79, 89, 179	17.23	38, 211
15.32–9	79, 235	17.24	89
15.33, 34–6, 36–7	79	17.24–5	178
16	81, 85	17.24–7	223
16.1	38, 40, 46	17.24–19.1	178
16.1–4	209, 229	17.25	37, 90
16.4	82, 84	17.27	212
16.5–12	79, 235	18	85–8, 157, 176, 193, 236, 239, 243
16.8	37, 80, 206	18.1	40, 178–9, 184
16.12	38, 46, 80, 83	18.1–4	177
16.13	236	18.1–14	90
16.13–16	80	18.1–20	198–200
16.13–20	82, 235	18.1–35	85, 178, 231
16.13–28	207	18.2	86, 179, 184, 189
16.14	69, 207	18.2–4	85, 179
16.16	36, 80, 83, 98	18.3	232
16.17	37, 81–2	18.4	217
16.17–19	177	18.5	177, 181, 184, 190, 196–8, 235
16.17–20	81	18.5–6	179
16.18	81, 88, 178, 194	18.5–9	92
16.18–19	81	18.5–20	85

18.6	85, 95, 181, 182, 224,	19.28	40
18.6–9	182	19.29	190
18.7–9	85, 179	20.17	89, 203
18.8	181, 232	20.17–19	89
18.9	181	20.18–19	82, 98
18.10	85, 95, 181, 224	20.20	40, 225, 226, 227
18.10–14	179	20.22–3	89
18.11	45	20.24	38
18.12	181	20.25	179
18.12–13	85	20.26–8	92
18.14	85, 95, 181, 224, 231	20.28	60, 82, 89
18.15	95, 178	20.29	40, 89
18.15–17	103, 177, 179, 181–2	20.29–31	68
18.15–18	188	20.30	45
18.15–19	179, 182	20.30–1	89
18.15–20	85, 177, 183	20.31	45, 89
18.15–35	217	20.34	37, 40, 89
18.16	177, 181, 183	21.1	89, 98, 162
18.17	182	21.1–7	162
18.18	177, 181–3, 192	21.1–10	62
18.18–19	177, 179	21.1–22	89
18.19	181, 186, 188–9, 232	21.2–3	162
18.19–20	88, 177, 180, 187–8	21.2–6	90
18.20	3, 19, 21, 86–8, 94, 103, 105,	21.4	45
	106, 107, 175, 176–200, 221–2,	21.4–5	43, 162
	233, 236, 239	21.5	89
18.21	40, 80, 95, 103, 178	21.6–7	40, 162
18.21–35	182	21.8–11	68
18.25	216	21.9	40, 93, 190, 207
18.26	226	21.10–11	40
18.35	95, 103	21.10	39, 89, 90
18.39, 40, 49	218	21.11	69, 90
19	92	21.12	89
19.1	45, 88–9, 236	21.12–13	90
19.2	40, 68–9	21.12–17	231
19.3	38, 40, 41, 46	21.14	40, 45
19.7	83, 216	21.15	38
19.7–9	216	21.17	89
19.8	38	21.18	37, 89
19.13	40	21.18–22	91
19.16	40	21.20	38
19.16–22	217	21.22	181, 215
19.16–30	230	21.23	40, 45, 89, 215
19.17	215	21.23–7	45, 210
19.19–30	231	21.25	41
19.21	40, 230	21.25–6	40
19.21–6	231	21.26	69, 76
19.21–30	232	21.31	230, 231, 232
19.22	39	21.31–2	91
19.23	232	21.32	230
19.23–4	181, 232	21.34	98
19.25	38	21.35–9	91
19.25–7	80	21.43	91, 95, 104, 213
19.27	40, 67, 230	21.45	38

21.46	38–9, 46, 76	24	93–4, 191
22.1–14	91, 231	24–5	94, 232
22.6–7	99	24.1	40, 62, 89, 94
22.7	90–1, 93, 224	24.2	90
22.10	86–7	24.3	40, 89, 94, 103, 204, 218
22.11, 13	90	24.4–14	93
22.15	40, 41, 91	24.5–25.46	93
22.16	45	24.6–12	233
22.18	37, 46	24.9	95, 190, 213
22.19	40	24.12	231
22.22	38	24.14	95, 104, 213, 232
22.23	46, 69	24.15	42, 43, 46, 94
22.23–8	44	24.15–31	94
22.32	104	24.22	210
22.33	39, 68	24.30	95
22.34	86, 185	24.34	84
22.34–5	38	25	95
22.34–40	185, 217	25.3–4	207
22.35	46	25.21, 23	102
22.36, 38, 40	216	25.29	207
22.41	86, 186	25.31–46	95–6, 175, 186, 198, 222,
22.46	38, 45, 91, 94, 186		224, 231–3, 235, 239
23	47, 92	25.32	86–7, 95, 96, 104, 213
23.1	68, 94	25.34	90
23.2	70	25.35, 38, 43	86–7, 186
23.2–3	223	25.40	90, 103, 177, 186, 197–8
23.2–7	68, 78	25.45	177, 186, 198
23.2–12	92	26	96–9, 236
23.2–36	38	26–8	99
23.3	215, 216	26.1	45
23.6	86	26.2	82, 98
23.8	95, 103	26.3	41, 86, 185
23.13	92, 232	26.3–5, 7	40
23.13–15	68, 78	26.8	38
23.14, 15	92	26.10	37
23.16	68, 78, 92	26.14	41, 203
23.17, 19, 23	92	26.14–16	40
23.24	68, 78, 92	26.16	45, 46, 74, 99
23.25	92	26.17	40
23.26	68, 78, 92	26.18	97, 99
23.27	92	26.18–20	243
23.27–35	210	26.20	97, 203
23.28	231	26.20–5	98
23.29	92	26.25	46
23.29–36	84	26.28	60, 96, 100
23.33	64, 67, 92	26.29	19, 21, 93, 97, 175, 222, 239,
23.34	86–7, 92, 217, 228, 231		243
23.34–5	92, 197	26.29–40	233
23.34–9	228	26.29–56	235
23.37	180, 228, 231	26.31–2	103
23.37–9	92, 231	26.32	203, 211
23.38	90, 93–4	26.36	97
23.38–24.2	106, 224	26.37–44	37
23.39	93, 190	26.38	97

26.39	39	27.29	90, 102, 171, 225
26.39–44	41, 47	27.30	225
26.40	97	27.33	46, 173
26.42, 44	39	27.36	215
26.45	82	27.37	60, 90, 102, 171
26.45–6	98	27.40	45, 99
26.47	68–9, 203	27.42	45, 90
26.48	41, 46	27.46	46, 173
26.49, 50	40	27.51	52, 101
26.51	97	27.51–3	40
26.52–4	99	27.51–4	100
26.54	45	27.51–28.20	51, 52, 100–8, 236
26.55	45, 68	27.52	211
26.56	18, 42, 45, 97	27.52–3	42
26.57	86, 98, 185	27.53	42, 43
26.57–75	41	27.54	33, 39, 101, 215
26.58	40	27.55	40, 101
26.59	46	27.55–6	100
26.59–60	38, 182	27.55–28.10	101
26.61	224	27.57	212
26.61–2	99	27.57–8	40
26.63	80, 171	27.61	100
26.64	45, 93, 98	27.62	86
26.67	207	27.62–5	40
26.68	99, 171	27.62–6	101
26.69	97	27.63–6	41
26.69–75	40	27.64	100, 211
26.71	97	28	157, 171, 204
26.75	38	28.1–8	40, 209
27	90, 99	28.1–11	100
27.1	99	28.2	53, 101
27.1–2	41	28.2–7	101
27.3	46	28.4	215
27.3–5	41	28.5–7	103
27.3–10	40, 203	28.6	211
27.6	46	28.7	101, 103, 203, 207–9, 211, 212
27.8	42, 43, 46	28.8	39, 101, 102
27.9–10	43	28.8–10	207
27.10	100	28.9	40, 101, 104, 209, 226, 227
27.11	90, 102, 171	28.9–10	101
27.14	39, 100	28.9–20	202
27.15	46	28.10	95, 101, 103, 203, 207, 208
27.15–16	46	28.11	101, 102, 212
27.17	80, 86, 100, 171	28.11–15	40, 41, 101, 102, 107, 215,
27.18	37, 39, 100		244
27.19	58, 100	28.12	86
27.20	41, 46, 69, 100	28.15	42, 43, 46, 102, 215
27.22	80	28.16	101, 103, 203, 204, 207, 212
27.22–3	207	28.16–17	208
27.23	100	28.16–18	203–9
27.24	39, 100	28.16–20	3, 44, 61, 101, 103, 107, 174,
27.25	61, 99, 100		201–19, 236, 238–42
27.27	86	28.17	38, 40, 101, 104, 106, 207–8,
27.27–31	41		225, 226, 227, 242

28.17–18   205–9
28.17–20   101
28.18   40, 45, 104, 105, 203, 206–7, 208–12, 240, 241
28.18–20   18, 73, 104, 106–7, 202, 208, 209, 242
28.19   18, 58, 95, 101, 106, 182, 190, 204, 212–14, 227
28.19–20   203, 212–19, 242, 243
28.20   3, 17–21, 47, 83–4, 96, 101, 103, 106, 108, 174–5, 188–9, 191–2, 199, 202, 208, 214–19, 222, 229, 233, 239, 242

Mark
1.1   158
1.21–2   209
1.22   210
1.24   33
1.27   210
1.40   225
2.8   229
2.10   210
2.12   210
3.11   33
3.30   229
5.6   225
5.7   33
5.22   225
5.41   173
6.3   158
6.7   210
6.47   189
6.51   225
7.25   225
8.12   229
9.34   179
9.37   190
9.42–50   181
10.17   225
10.18   215
10.35   225
11.1–7   162
11.9   190
11.24   215
11.28–33   210
12.28–34   185
12.34   185
12.37–40   215
13.2   224
13.6   190
13.10   213
13.13   190
13.14   33, 94

13.20   210
14.28   203
14.51–2   29
14.55–60   182
14.58   224
15.19   225
15.22   173
15.25   215
15.32   209
15.34   33, 173
15.39   215
16.7   203
16.8   29, 202
16.12   207
16.14   203, 206

Luke
1–2   158
1.1–4   31, 33
1.27   170
1.28–30   148
1.29–31   161
1.32   170
1.35   2
1.60–3   160
2.4   170
2.4–6   170
2.40–52   228
4.5–6   210
4.7–8   226
5.12   225
6.31   216
7.8   210
8.7   189
8.41   225
9.46   179
9.48   190
10.16   193, 197
10.25–8   185
13.3   180
15.3–7   181
16.16   74
17.1–3   181
17.3–4   181
17.16   225
18.19   215
19.28–35   162
19.38   190
21.8   190
21.17   190
22.55   189
22.66   186
24.9   203
24.16   207

24.29	229
24.31–42	207
24.33	203
24.41	206
24.44–9	203
24.49	229
24.51	2
24.52	205, 225

John

1.14, 16	41
1.41	173
1.45	158
2.18–22	224
2.21	33
3.11	41
4.1	212
4.48	209
5.23	193
6.30	209
7.16	193
7.42	158
9.38	225
11.32	225
12.44–5	193
13.20	193, 197
14.9	193
15.7	181
15.23	193
17.2	210
18.2	185
18.6	225
20.8	209
20.14–20	207
20.19–23	203, 229
20.24–5	203, 206
20.27	207
20.29	209
21.4, 12	207
21.24	41

Acts

1.2	2
1.4–5	229
1.4–8	203
1.9–11	2
1.13–14	203
1.26	203
2.1–4	229
2.1–21	229
2.14	203
2.21	190
2.38	213
2.42ff.	2

4.12	173
4.31	185, 186
4.36	173
7.49–50	2
8.16	213
9.14, 21	190
10.26	226
10.48	213
11.26	186, 188
13.44	186, 188
14.21	212
14.27	186, 188
15.6, 30	186
19.5	213
20.7	186, 188
20.8	185, 186
22.16	190

Romans

1.3	158
1.3–4	174
5.1–2	2
6.3	213
8.38f.	2
10.13	190
12.1	2
15.4	167

1 Corinthians

1.2	190
1.13, 15	213
3.16	2, 225
6.11	213
6.19	2, 225
7.26, 36	2
10.1–4	213
15.5	203
15.24	210
15.45	229

2 Corinthians

2.14–3.18	2
6.16	2
13.1	182

Galatians

4.4	158
4.26	135

Ephesians

1.21	210

Philippians

2.5–11	158

2.9–10	210	Josephus	
Colossians		*Cont.Ap.*	
1.16–20	210	2	153
2.10	210	5.50–5	153
1 Timothy		*Antiquities*	
5.19	182	1.219	154
		1.260	154
Hebrews		1.280–3	154
1.6	225	1.309–11	154
4.14–16	3	2.8	154
6.19–20	3	2.61	154
9.24	3	2.205–9	159
10.19–22	3	2.210–16	159
10.28	182	2.272	154
12.22	135	4.122	154
		4.128	154
1 Peter		4.185	154
1.10–12	167	5.42	154
2.9ff.	3	5.351	154
3.22	210	6.57	154
		6.181	154
Revelation		6.196	154
1.5–6	3	6.231	154
2.26–7	210	7.65	154
3.12	135	7.91	154
13.2	210	7.338	154
16.16	185	7.357	154
19.10	226	8.295	154
21.1–22.5	135	8.394	154
21.2–3	3	10.76	154
21.22	3, 225	11.259	154
22.8–9	226	15.138	154
22.9	226		
		Jubilees	
Early Jewish writings		1.6	152
		1.17	205
2 Apoc.Bar.		1.18	152
4.2–6	135	1.26	152
		1.27–8	135
1 Enoch		9.27–8	152
90.29–31	135	18.15–16	152
		19.5	152
1 Esdras		24.22	152
1.25	139, 141, 147, 151, 154	25.21	152
2.3	139, 141, 142, 148		
		Judith	
2 Esdras		5.5–21	152
1.25	141	5.17	139, 141, 148, 152
2.3	141	9.11	152
12.10–39	167	13.11	139, 141, 148, 151, 152
4 Ezra		*2 Maccabees*	
9.26–10.59	135	14.35	194

3 Maccabees
6.15   139, 140, 141, 148, 153

Midrash
Genesis Rabbah
28.15   153
31.5   153
39.3   153

Exodus Rabbah
1.13   159
3.12   153
12.29   164

Numbers Rabbah
7.48   164

Mishnah
Sanhedrin
1.6   183

Philo
Agr.
78   153

Det.
4   153

Fuga.
140   153

LAB
9.10   159

Migr.
30   153
62–3   153

Mut. Nom.
121   173

Post.
80   153

Som.
1.179   153
1.227–8   153

Psalms of Solomon
7.1, 6–7   136

Qumran Literature
CD
3.18–4.10   136
9.2–3   177

1   *QM*
7.3–7   152
12.8–9   152

1QpHab
2   167
12   167
12.1–4   136

1QS
5.5–7   136, 152
5.25–6.1   177
6.3   183
8.4–6   136
8.4–10   152
9.3–5   136
9.3–7   152
11.8   136

4QFlor
1.1–7   136

Testament of Levi
3.4   135

Testament of Daniel
5.12–13   135

Wisdom
9.8   135

Early Christian writings

Asc.Isa.
7.10   135

Didache
7.1–3   213

Justin Martyr
Apology
33   169

Dialogue
43.8   168
67.1   164, 168
71.3, 84   168

AUTHOR INDEX

Achtemeier, P. J. 29
Adam, A. K. M. 46
Addley, W. P. 178–9
Albright, W. F., and Mann, C. S. 65,
    181
Allen, W. C. 17, 65, 202, 205
Allison, D. 7, 62, 70, 204
Alt, A. 115
Anderson, J. C. 10, 32–9, 43, 45–7, 53,
    55, 63, 67, 76, 79, 82, 100, 103, 107,
    158, 170
Aune, D. 8, 9

Bacon, B. W. 6, 8, 17
Baird, J. A. 68
Bal, M. 31
Baltzer, K. 121
Barclay, W. 3
Barr, J. 12
Barrett, C. K. 213, 229
Barth, G. 18, 19, 195, 203, 211
Barth, K. 186, 206–7
Barton, J. 12, 26, 167
Barton, S. 231, 244
Bauer, D. 7, 10, 18, 20, 21–2, 26, 34,
    51–2, 60, 74
Beare, F. W. 70, 178, 187, 208
Benoit, P. 93, 207
Berg, W. 164
Best, E. 2
Betz, H. D. 70
Beyerlin, W. 124
Bietenhard, H. 191
Boers, H. 165
Boismard, M.- E. 6
Bonnard, P. 7, 57, 93, 183, 196, 205
Booth, W. 30–4, 46
Borg, M. 231
Boring, M. E. 208
Bornkamm, G. 8, 18, 43–4, 72, 94, 170,
    178, 182, 188, 195, 203, 211

Boslooper, T. 164–5
Bouyer, L. 194
Box, G. H. 166
Braumann, G. 191
Bright, J. 112, 115
Brooks, S. 177, 180
Brown, R. 50, 53, 55, 99, 100, 157–61,
    165, 170–4, 220, 227
Brown, S. 11, 12, 72, 95, 232
Brownlee, W. H. 119
Brueggemann, W. 110–13, 116, 123,
    125–6, 130–2
Bruner, F. D. 56
Buber, M. 111, 119–20, 122
Bultmann, R. 17, 159–61, 195, 213
Burnett, F. 57–8, 94, 228
Burton, E. W. 184

Caba, J. 178–81, 185, 188, 190–1
Calvin, J. 206
Campenhausen, H. von 158
Carson, D. 43, 56–7, 183, 187
Cassuto, U. 125
Catchpole, D. 232
Chatman, S. 8, 29–34, 36, 40, 42, 45
Childs, B. 112, 117, 119–24, 127–9
Christ, F. 228
Christian, P. 195
Clark, K. W. 213
Clements, R. E. 2–3, 110–12, 115, 117,
    121, 126, 129, 131–3, 135, 137, 163, 166
Clifford, R. J. 116
Coats, G. W. 118, 122
Combrink, H. J. B. 7–10, 14, 101
Conzelmann, H. 172
Croatto, J. S. 133
Crosby, M. 4, 54, 178, 229–31
Cross, F. M. 111, 115, 117, 119, 129
Crossan, D. 2
Culpepper, R. A. 9, 15, 16, 32–6, 40, 47,
    99, 157

288

Culver, R. D. 205
Cunningham, P. A. 199

Dalman, G. 145, 166
Davies, G. H. 111, 117, 125
Davies, M. 6, 158, 189
Davies, W. D. 8, 66, 160, 167, 177, 195, 204, 211
Davies, W. D., and Allison, D. 5–7, 9, 19, 34, 45, 51–2, 61, 65–6, 69, 101, 158–9, 161, 170, 177, 227
Davis, C. T. 157, 159
Delling, G. 163
Derrett, J. D. M. 187
Detweiler, R. 29
Di Marco, A. 7
Dibelius, M. 159–60
Dodd, C. H. 19
Donaldson, T. L. 65, 69–70, 79, 83, 103, 187, 204–5, 212
Downing, F. G. 8
Driver, S. R. 118
Duke, P. D. 99
Dunn, J. D. G. 172, 174, 207–8
Dupont, J. 190
Durham, J. I. 112, 117–19, 121–7

Eagleton, T. 12, 14, 29, 46, 242
Edgar, S. L. 164
Edwards, R. A. 10, 33, 51, 55, 62, 69, 74, 75, 79, 92, 102, 104
Eissfeldt, O. 144, 152
Ellis, E. E. 5
Ellis, I. P. 205
Englezakis, B. 187, 193, 195, 181, 183, 193

Fackenheim, E. L. 112
Fenton, J. C. 18, 57, 60
Filson, F. V. 205
Forkman, G. 178–9
Forster, E. M. 28, 35
Fowler, R. 4, 32
France, R. T. 6–7, 19, 65, 84, 90, 167, 183, 227
Frankemölle, H. 8, 19, 21–2, 25–6, 43, 58, 61, 74, 101, 138–9, 143–4, 147, 150, 159, 161, 181–3, 185, 188, 191–2, 194, 196, 199
Freyne, S. 66
Frizzell, L. 110
Frye, N. 10, 29
Fuller, R. H. 163, 170, 172, 174, 208

Gadamer, H.-G. 4, 5, 14

Gaechter, P. 101, 188
Galot, J. 183
Garland, D. E. 92, 94
Gärtner, B. 167
Gaston, L. 90
Genette, G. 34
Gerhardsson, B. 65
Gibbs, J. M. 50
Giblin, C. H. 205–6
Gnilka, J. 166–7, 183, 186, 191
Goldberg, A. M. 193–5
Görg, M. 138–9, 142
Gorman, F. 216
Gottwald, N. 115–16, 131
Goulder, M. 8, 159
Gray, G. B. 164, 166
Gray, J. 145
Green, H. B. 7, 60
Greenberg, M. 117
Greeven, H. 226
Grundmann, W. 138–9, 142, 150, 191, 205
Guelich, R. A. 8, 10, 69
Gundry, R. 7, 8, 20, 56, 65, 67, 159, 165, 180, 182–3, 202, 210, 212, 218, 227

Hagner, D. 158
Hahn, F. 203, 214
Hamerton-Kelly, R. G. 228
Hammershaimb, E. 143
Haran, M. 110, 112, 115, 128
Hare, D. 94, 213
Hartman, L. 45
Hawkins, J. C. 43
Held, H. J. 20, 71, 179
Herford, R. 172
Hill, D. 20, 52, 63, 65, 93, 117
Hirsch, E. D. 11
Holmes, W. H. G. 1
Holtzmann, H. J. 17
Horst, R. 205
Howell, D. 8, 10–12, 16, 18, 26, 29, 33–4, 36, 42, 44–5, 47, 49, 50, 56, 58, 63, 67–8, 74, 76, 89, 91, 97, 108
Hubbard, B. J. 148, 202–4, 206, 211, 214, 229
Hübner, H. 210
Hummel, R. 25
Hyatt, J. P. 123

Iser, W. 32, 49

Jeremias, Joachim 203, 211

Jeremias, Jörg 112
Johannessohn, M. 142
Johnson, A. R. 126
Johnson, M. D. 53, 104, 159, 228
Johnson, L. T. 68

Kaiser, O. 163–4, 166
Kea, P. 9
Keck, L. 16, 221
Kee, H. 65
Kermode, F. 29
Kieffer, R. 10
Kilian, R. 139
Kilpatrick, G. D. 8, 18, 159–61, 211
Kingsbury, J. D. 7, 8, 10, 15, 20, 22, 26,
   29, 33–7, 40, 45, 47, 51–2, 63, 65, 71,
   73–4, 84, 94, 97, 99, 170, 172, 188,
   203, 210–13, 218
Kirk, A. 133
Klostermann, E. 17–18, 65, 181, 202,
   205–6, 209
Knight, G. A. F. 117
Knox, W. L. 160–1
Koester, H. 110
Kraus, H. -J. 133
Krentz, E. 51
Kretzer, A. 186
Krieger, M. 12, 13, 16, 157
Kümmel, W. G. 8
Kuntz, J. K. 112, 114

Lachs, S. 192
Lagrange, M. -J. 65, 173, 188
Lange, J. 202, 204, 210–16
Lanser, S. 34, 36
Lategan, B. 11, 12, 33, 74
Lemcio, E. 43–4
Léon-Dufour, X. 18
Levenson, J. 110–12, 116–17, 121–2,
   131–2, 134–5
Levine, B. 113
Liddell, J. B., and Scott, R. 142
Lindars, B. 164, 174
Lindblom, J. 208
Lohmeyer, E. 18, 51, 67, 201, 204, 206
Lohr, C. 99–101
Luz, U. 5–6, 10, 12, 19, 25, 42, 45, 51–2,
   61–2, 65, 67, 69, 74, 158–9, 161, 166,
   174, 229, 233
Luz, U., and Lampe, P. 42

Magness, L. 73, 108
Mailloux, S. 32
Malbon, E. S. 68

Malina, B. 173, 203
Malina, B., and Neyrey, J. 45
Maly, E. H. 111
Mann, T. 111–12, 117, 126
Manson, T. W. 181
Marxsen, W. 19–20
Matera, F. 7, 50–1, 108
May, H. G. 115
McCarthy, D. 112, 121
McConnell, R. S. 216
McKay, K. L. 205
McKnight, E. 32
McNeile, A. H. 17, 74, 123, 173, 205
Meeks, W. 194, 216
Meier, J. P. 52, 67, 203, 208, 211–12, 218
Mendenhall, G. 111–12, 116, 121, 131
Metzger, B. 205, 225
Meyer, B. F. 90
Michel, O. 18, 195, 201, 209
Miller, J. M., and Hayes, J. H. 130, 131
Minear, P. 35, 68
Moberly, R. W. L. 10, 113–14, 117–20,
   124–7
Mohrlang, R. 170, 210
Moore, S. 5, 9, 14–15, 28–9, 31–2, 34–5,
   50
Morgan, R. 4, 5, 14, 28
Morris, L. 8
Moule, C. F. D. 167, 227
Mowinckel, S. 143, 163
Murphy-O'Connor, J. 113
Murray, J. C. 113

Neirynck, F. 7, 51–2, 205
Nellessen, E. 161
Neusner, J. 136, 192
Nicholson, E. W. 110, 112, 124, 132
Nickelsburg, G. 152–3
Nolan, B. M. 52, 99, 170
Noth, M. 116–17

Ollenburger, B. C. 110–12, 116, 130–1,
   133
Otto, R. 123

Parke-Taylor, G. H. 119
Patte, D. 14, 65, 99
Perkins, P. 202, 204
Perrin, N. 3, 29, 204, 231
Pesch, R. 160–2, 178, 196
Petersen, N. 8, 12, 14–16, 29, 31, 35–6,
   47, 94, 103
Phythian-Adams, W. J. 1
Plummer, A. 17, 205

Poland, L. 9
Polzin, R. 4, 11, 14, 16
Powell, M. 9
Preuß, H. D. 138–40, 145–7, 150
Pritchard, A. B. 111, 138
Propp, W. H. 128
Przybylski, B. 83, 170

Rad, G. von 116, 125–6, 129, 132, 147
Rahlfs, A. 165
Reindl, J. 125
Renwick, D. 2, 136
Rhoads, D., and Michie, D. 29, 30, 35–6
Rice, G. 163
Rigaux, B. 205
Robinson, J. A. T. 6, 19, 208
Robinson, J. M. 110, 204, 228
Robinson, J. M., and Koester, H. 228
Robinson, T. H. 17
Rohde, J. 216
Rowland, C. 193

Saldarini, A. 68, 193, 222–3
Sand, A. 208
Sanders, E. P. 90, 136, 155, 170, 224
Sanders, E. P., and Davies, M. 6
Sanders, J. A. 112
Schaberg, J. 53, 55, 158, 172, 203, 208, 212–14
Schenk, W. 43, 95
Schieber, H. 101
Schlatter, A. 17, 55
Schmauch, W. 204
Schmidt, T. 230
Schneider, J. 40
Schniewind, J. 70, 205
Scholes, R., and Kellogg, R. 30, 35
Schürer, E. 152–3
Schweizer, E. 19, 50, 65, 70, 188, 200, 208, 229
Segundo, J. L. 133
Seitz, O. J. F. 172
Selden, R. 29
Senior, D. P. 7, 99
Shuler, P. 9, 60
Sievers, J. 179, 191, 193–6
Smith, M. 196
Smyth, K. 204
Soares Prabhu, G. M. 157, 159–63, 165, 173
Staley, J. 14, 29, 31, 160
Stanton, G. 5, 7–9, 18, 22, 35, 68, 76, 91, 160, 193–4, 222–3, 232
Steck, O. 110

Stendahl, K. 8, 55, 160–1, 166–7, 172, 182
Sternberg, M. 40, 50, 67
Stock, A. 158
Stone, M. E. 135
Strack, H. L., and Billerbeck, P. 192, 195, 209
Strecker, G. 9, 25, 159, 163, 165, 170, 188, 193, 211
Streeter, B. H. 160
Styler, G. M. 20
Suggs, M. J. 228
Suleiman, S. 32

Tagawa, K. 213
Talbert, C. 9
Tannehill, R. 29, 31, 74
Tatum, W. 163, 166
Taylor, V. 158
Terrien, S. 1–3, 19, 110, 112, 114–15, 126, 133, 194
Theissen, G. 67, 74
Thiselton, A. 4, 8, 12, 14, 16
Thompson, M. 163
Thompson, M. M. 52, 101, 166
Thompson, W. G. 82, 177, 179, 181, 185, 187, 190
Tompkins, J. 32
Trilling, W. 18, 61, 91, 139, 150, 160, 168, 182–3, 188, 192, 203–4, 211, 215
Tuckett, C. 7

Uspensky, B. 33–6, 39–40, 43, 45

van Aarde, A. G. 10, 12, 21–6, 35, 37
van Tilborg, S. 38, 69
van Unnik, W. C. 17–9, 138–42, 145–6, 150, 153–4, 169, 173, 196
Vaux, R. de 112, 119
Verseput, D. 211
Via, D. 52, 187
Vischer, W. 143, 150
Vögtle, A. 159, 212
Vorster, W. S. 16
Vriezen, T. C. 114, 120

Waetjen, H. 55, 171
Walker, R. 9, 38, 213
Watson, F. 4
Watts, J. 163, 165–6
Weaver, D. J. 34, 36, 40, 44, 45, 47, 70, 73, 98, 106, 108
Weber, M. 230–1
Weeden, T. J. 2

Westermann, C. 114–16
Wildberger, H. 143, 163, 166
Wimsatt, W., and Beardsley, M. 11
Wink, W. 5, 16
Wittig, S. 70

Wolff, H. W. 147

Zahn, T. 160
Ziesler, J. A. 2–3, 19, 43, 229
Zimmerli, W. 118